I0824146

# DARK HORSE

# DARK HORSE

## HARNESSING HIDDEN POTENTIAL IN WAR AND LIFE

AMATANGELO "AJ" PASCIUTI

WITH NEIL McGINNESS

HarperCollins Leadership

An Imprint of HarperCollins

Darkhorse


Published by HarperCollins Leadership, an imprint of HarperCollins Focus LLC, 501 Nelson Place, Nashville, TN 37214, USA.



ISBN 978-1-4002-5622-8 (ePub)
ISBN 978-1-4002-5497-2 (HC)



HarperCollins Publishers, Macken House, 39/40 Mayor Street Upper, Dublin 1, D01 C9W8, Ireland (https://www.harpercollins.com)

Library of Congress Control Number: 2025940097

Art Direction: Ron Huizinga
Cover design: Micah Kandros
Interior Design: Neuwirth & Associates, Inc.

Printed in the United States of America
26 27 28 29 30 LBC 5 4 3 2 1

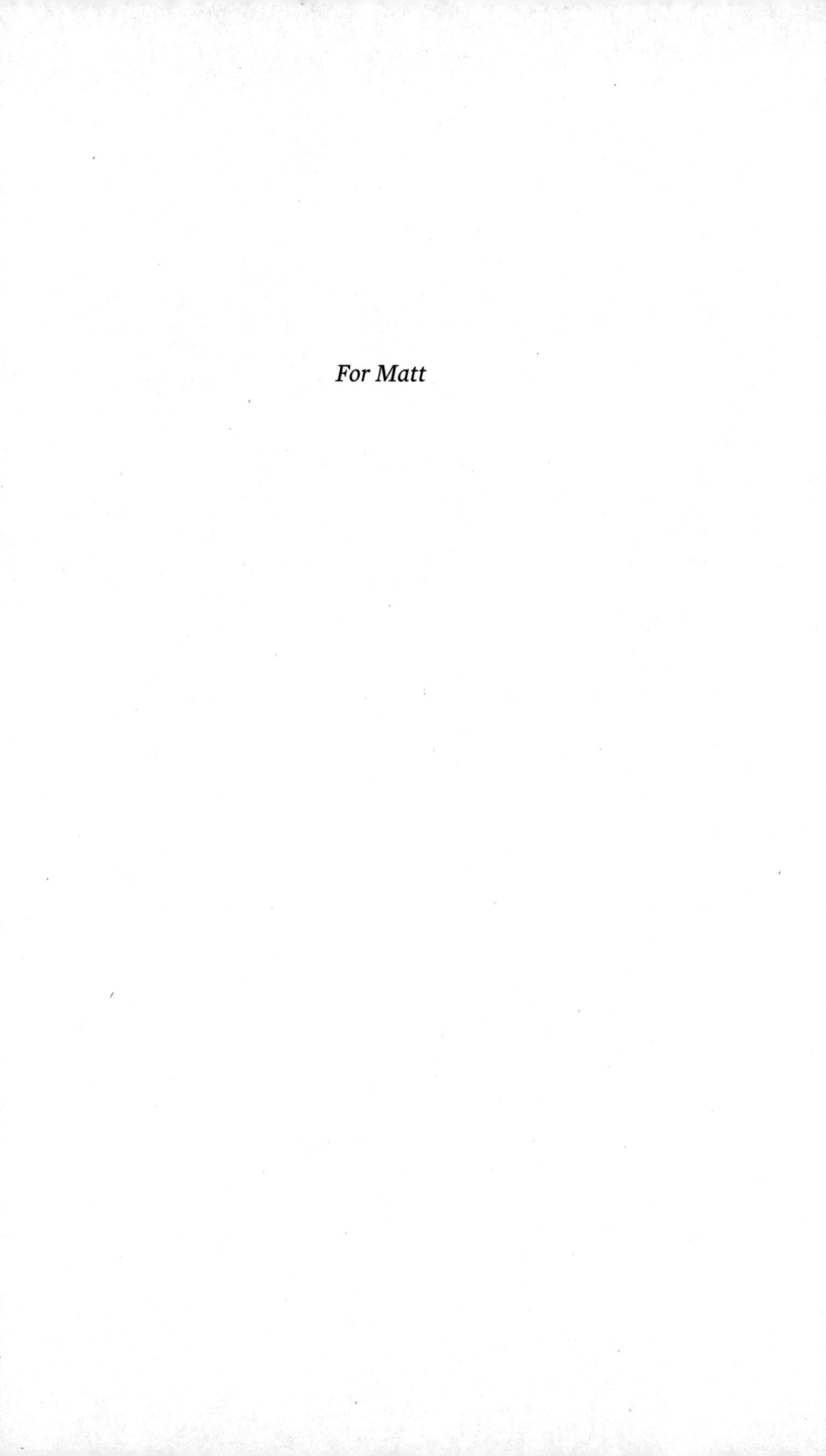

*For Matt*

**Darkhorse**
/därk ˈhôrs/

*noun*
noun: **darkhorse**

1. a competitor about whom little is known but who unexpectedly succeeds.
(*New American Oxford Dictionary*)

In US military usage, the term "darkhorse" refers to an individual or unit that is underestimated but achieves unexpected success. The darkhorse can turn the tide in war.

The 3rd Battalion, 5th Marines, "3/5" is known as Darkhorse Battalion.

Author Amatangelo "AJ" Pasciuti served with 3/5 and was a Darkhorse Sniper.

## CONTENTS

Look at a man the way he is,
and he only becomes worse.
Look at a man as he could be,
and he becomes what he should be.

—Goethe

## Chronological Record: AJ Pasciuti (2002–2023)

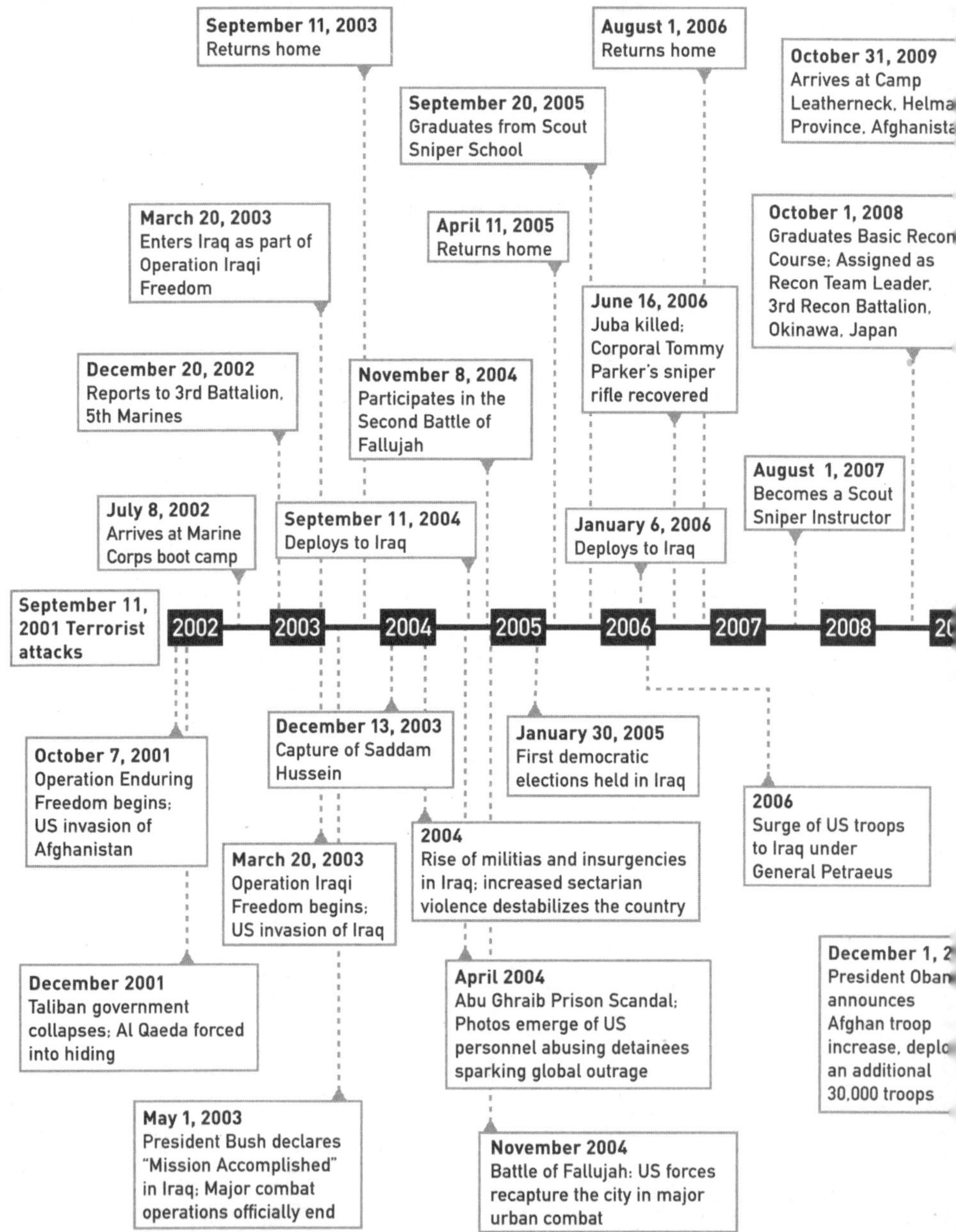


## Timeline of Major US Milestones in the War on Terror (2001–20

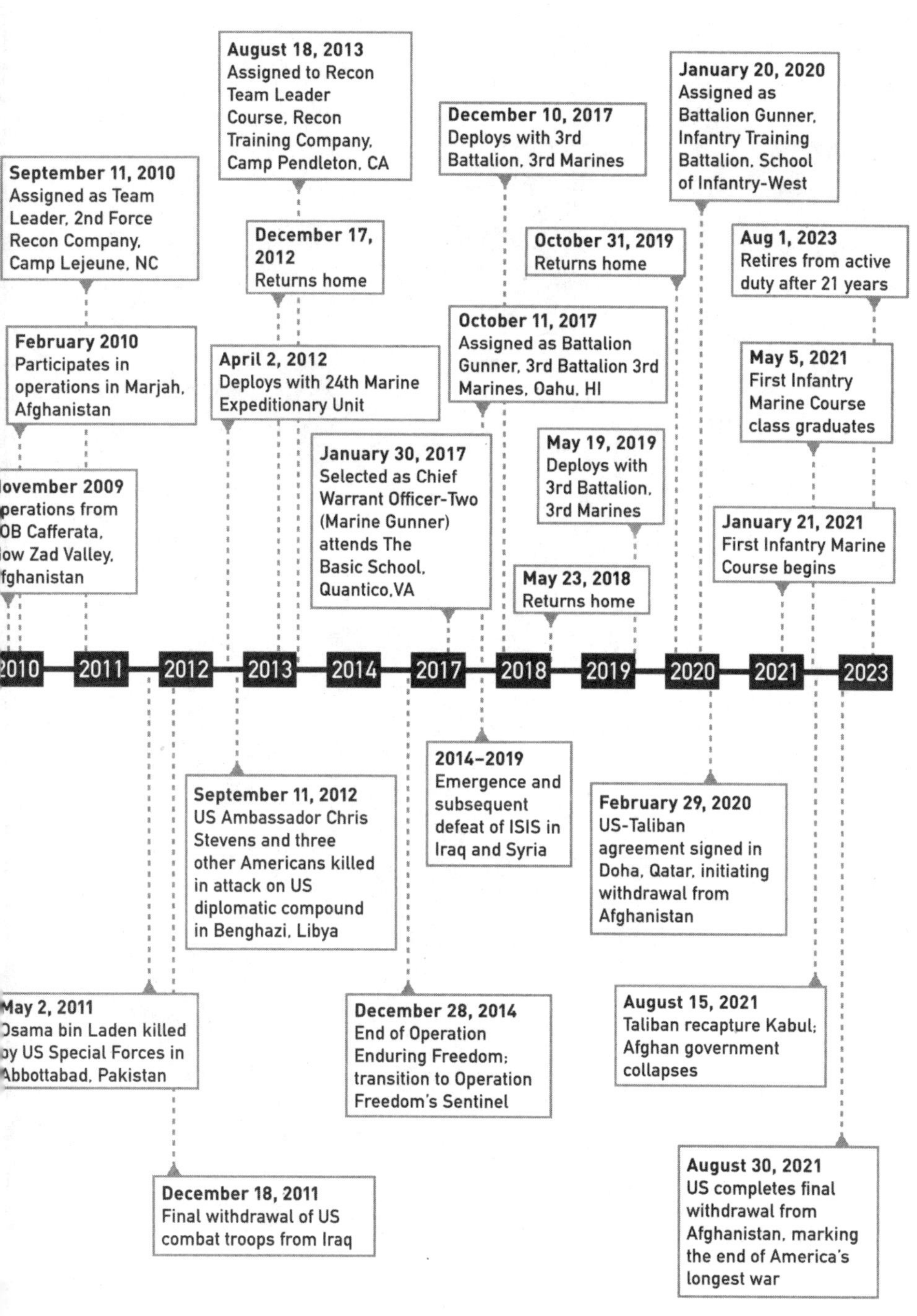

September 11, 2010
Assigned as Team Leader, 2nd Force Recon Company, Camp Lejeune, NC
February 2010
Participates in operations in Marjah, Afghanistan
ovember 2009
perations from OB Cafferata, ow Zad Valley, fghanistan
August 18, 2013
Assigned to Recon Team Leader Course, Recon Training Company, Camp Pendleton, CA
December 17, 2012
Returns home
April 2, 2012
Deploys with 24th Marine Expeditionary Unit
January 30, 2017
Selected as Chief Warrant Officer-Two (Marine Gunner) attends The Basic School, Quantico,VA
December 10, 2017
Deploys with 3rd Battalion, 3rd Marines
October 11, 2017
Assigned as Battalion Gunner, 3rd Battalion 3rd Marines, Oahu, HI
October 31, 2019
Returns home
May 19, 2019
Deploys with 3rd Battalion, 3rd Marines
May 23, 2018
Returns home
January 20, 2020
Assigned as Battalion Gunner, Infantry Training Battalion, School of Infantry-West
Aug 1, 2023
Retires from active duty after 21 years
May 5, 2021
First Infantry Marine Course class graduates
January 21, 2021
First Infantry Marine Course begins
2010
2011
2012
2013
2014
2017
2018
2019
2020
2021
2023
September 11, 2012
US Ambassador Chris Stevens and three other Americans killed in attack on US diplomatic compound in Benghazi, Libya
May 2, 2011
Osama bin Laden killed by US Special Forces in Abbottabad, Pakistan
December 18, 2011
Final withdrawal of US combat troops from Iraq
2014–2019
Emergence and subsequent defeat of ISIS in Iraq and Syria
December 28, 2014
End of Operation Enduring Freedom; transition to Operation Freedom's Sentinel
February 29, 2020
US-Taliban agreement signed in Doha, Qatar, initiating withdrawal from Afghanistan
August 15, 2021
Taliban recapture Kabul; Afghan government collapses
August 30, 2021
US completes final withdrawal from Afghanistan, marking the end of America's longest war

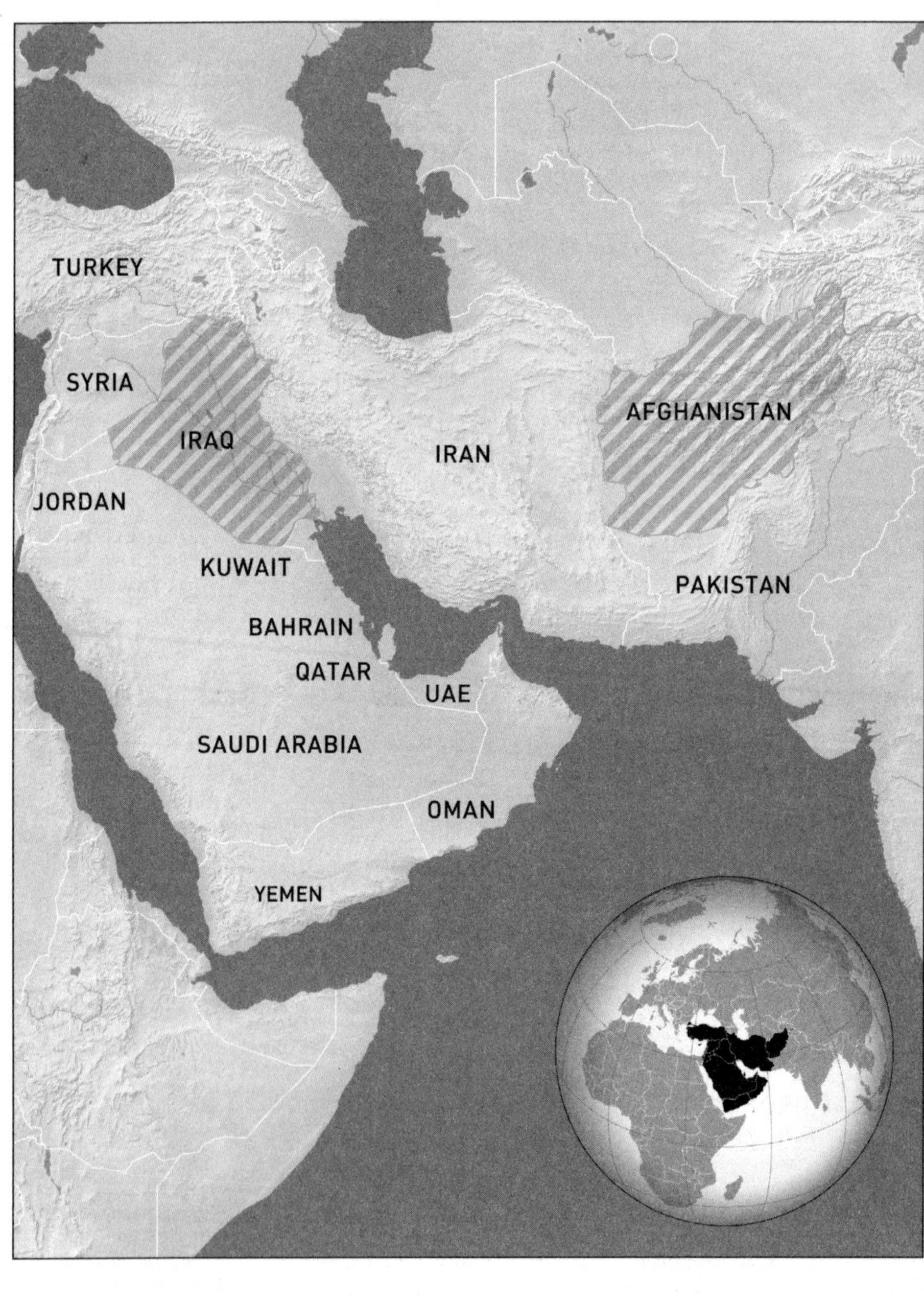
TURKEY
SYRIA
IRAQ
IRAN
AFGHANISTAN
JORDAN
KUWAIT
PAKISTAN
BAHRAIN
QATAR
UAE
SAUDI ARABIA
OMAN
YEMEN

# PROLOGUE

"Listen up, Marines!" The Chief Instructor at Scout Sniper School Camp Pendleton cleared his throat. "Go ahead," he ordered, nodding to an instructor in the back of the classroom. "Press play." The projector screen flickered to life, as the audio boomed from two small speakers. Horses galloping into battle tangled with the guttural tones of an Islamic war hymn that swelled and gave way to a soft, rising call to prayer.

My stomach twisted as the audio echoed off the curved metal walls of the old Quonset hut. The screen showed a grainy image of what appeared to be Marines at a checkpoint washed in dust and heat. Four guards stood around a Humvee, scanning traffic. The camera rocked and shook; the operator was moving clumsily while panning across the scene.

I had seen these before—Juba videos. Ghost stories passed around on USB drives. They started surfacing in 2005. No one in the classroom moved. Heavy breathing thudded through the camera's microphone. The lens steadied on a young Marine manning a turret. His right elbow rested across the machine gun. His left hand lifted a canteen. My heart hurt. The shooter's breath intensified, ragged and uneven. The familiar click of a bolt sliding a bullet into its chamber reverberated off the classroom's tin roof. More breaths cycled, heavy and erratic; the shooter's excitement was evident.

"Allahu Akbar," came the whispered chant with each exhale, delicate at first and rising with each moment, "Allahu Akbar . . ."

*Crack.*

The recoil from the gunshot jolted the camera, causing the entire scene to bounce. The checkpoint had erupted while the picture settled. Chaos in the street.

The rifle's report shattered the afternoon calm. The Marine in the turret was gone. "Allahu Akbar, Allahu Akbar," the shooter's whisper rose to a fanatical chant, intoxicated by blood, rage, and triumph. The screen cut to black.

"Make no mistake why you're here," the Chief Instructor cautioned. His tone was emotionless as he scanned our tense, pale faces. "*This* is your enemy. And he's hunting our Marines. Play the next clip," he commanded.

A black-hooded man entered the frame and sauntered toward a white plastic table draped with a green flag. A sniper rifle was slung across his back—the focal point of his grim attire. He paused, his hands resting on the table's edge, head bowed as if in ritual.

"Allahu Akbar, Allahu Akbar," he murmured. He turned toward a whiteboard in the corner of the room. The chant began low, rising with each repetition, gaining weight. "Allahu Akbar, Allahu Akbar." He uncapped a stubby, worn, dry-erase marker, raised it to the board, and etched one additional vertical line. A fresh kill. The camera pulled back. The board was nearly full. Dozens of lines. The screen went black again.

"*This* is your enemy, gentlemen," the Chief Instructor said. "And each one of those tick marks is your *reason*. Each one is an American life. A knock on someone's door. Two Marines in dress blues telling a family their child is gone. Never forget your reason."

# DARK HORSE

# 1

# TEARS AT FREMONT HIGH

## Seacliff

On weekends, my mother and I would day trip to escape the sprawl of Silicon Valley and head for the beauty of the Santa Cruz beaches.

She packed our gold four-door Saturn sedan with beach gear, folding chairs, a bagged lunch for me, and painting supplies for her. Mom always packed her easel last, closing the trunk with special care to avoid damaging its fragile legs.

The little car darted through the mountain curves as we headed out of San José. Leaving behind the dry heat of the city air, she rolled down the windows, inviting the wind to tousle my hair as I leaned my chin against the window's edge. Ignoring the rearview of the city in the side mirror, I poked my head farther out the car's window to take in the Santa Cruz Mountains along the curves of Highway 17. As the Saturn crossed the summit, the landscape shifted to dense, fragrant Coastal Redwoods and Douglas Firs; Mom asked, "Angelo, do you feel the temperature difference now?" I nodded yes and inhaled the moist, cool, pine-scented air.

Seacliff State Beach was our favorite. Tall eucalyptus trees lined sheer cliffs that descended into the expansive Monterey Bay. The beach had long been a gathering place for locals. Generations ago, it hosted jazz swing dance parties on the SS *Palo Alto*, the iconic cement ship anchored close to shore. The long-abandoned ship had sunk back into the sea, a grim relic of California's golden days. The moment we pulled into the sandy parking lot, I flung the door open, G.I. Joes clutched in my hands, and sprinted toward the Pacific. "Angelo-ooo," my mother called out, her cautionary words lost to the wind as the cold, wet sand squished between my toes at the surf's edge.

She would set up her easel on a narrow, sand-swept path that separated the beach from the parking lot. She secured the fresh, blank, birch panel in place and arranged her palette with dabs of color as she prepared to capture the day's shifting shadows and light.

Growing up without siblings taught me to be quick at making friends, and at the beach, it was easy. I would run and dig for hours with my fresh crew for the day. Burying G.I. Joes, setting up battles, and digging deep trenches to form moats around meager sandcastles in childish attempts to keep the waves at bay, the hours flew by.

My mother somehow managed to keep an eye on me while she painted. When the sun reached its highest point, the familiar cry of "Angelo-ooo" signaled the need to reapply my tropical-scented sunscreen and neon zinc. I ate my gritty sandwich while she rubbed lotion on my back. I looked at her painting to see how she had captured our day, her canvas now a vibrant representation of the picturesque shoreline. The hot, golden sand stretched along the kelp-washed beach, blending with the soft, fading shadows cast by the towering eucalyptus, reaching toward the bay's dark, frothy blue expanse.

The first in her family to go to college, my mother, Jerilyn Lightfoot, studied fine arts at San José State. While studying abroad during her senior year in Florence, she learned the techniques of the European Impressionists. Like the greats before her, she fell in love with plein-air painting and the freedom of capturing the natural world while surrounded by it, rather than a studio. This appreciation and observation of the beauty of the natural world impacted how she taught me lessons growing up. Nature was a priority in our lives: to see it, feel it, and experience it as an extension of ourselves.

## Boy Scouts

In fourth grade, my school hosted a club sign-up event where local community organizations pitched their programs to a fidgety audience of nine- and ten-year-olds. When the scoutmaster came to the stage to recruit for Boy Scouts, I naturally took an interest. Wearing an ill-fitting tan and olive drab uniform, he addressed our class, "As a scout, you will camp outdoors, learn knots, fire-making, survival skills, and individual responsibility." I heard nothing past "fire." I wanted in.

"Mommmmm," I burst through the front door of our house. Home for us was the back two rooms of Pantheon Fine Arts and Framing—my mother's art gallery and framing studio. Even then, houses in Silicon Valley were too expensive, but Sunnyvale had a loophole that allowed artists to live in business-zoned properties where they worked. The front three rooms of the hundred-year-old house were workspaces for framing, painting, and the art classes she taught at night.

My mom adored Greek and Roman mythology. Pantheon Fine Arts and Framing was named after the famed temple in Rome that was once home to the ancient gods and goddesses. Instead of the usual caterpillar bedtime stories that other parents read to their children, she told me the ancient stories of Perseus, Sisyphus, Icarus, and the other heroes of classical mythology.

After college, her first use of artistic talent was designing landscapes for flight simulators used by a military defense contractor. She continued advancing to work on projects that required top-secret clearance. However, all her success came to a devastating halt when a corporate raider, Paul Bilzerian, bought the company. Within months, the raider sold the division to make a quick buck, and she was left with a pink slip—plunging us into financial chaos.

Pantheon became Mom's opportunity for reinvention when she needed it most. Our setup was unconventional, but it worked. Mom was fighting for her dream of being an entrepreneur—even taking on a second job in retail at one point to keep the lights on.

Our little old house on Murphy Avenue sat next to a fancy French catering company called Mon Cheri. Every day, when I came home from school, Mon Cheri's cooking filled the air with the aroma of delicious Cordon bleu–style meals we couldn't afford. Through her challenges, I learned that dreams demand sacrifice and hunger, too.

"Mommm!" I shouted again as I ran into Pantheon's second front room. I was interrupting her conversation with a potential client. "Mommmm!" I tugged at her arm. She shot me a look that said, not now.

"Angelo, I'm with a guest," she said. "I'll talk to you in a bit—go start your homework." The client gave an understanding smile—witnessing a woman caught between her role as a mother and business owner. Defeated, I trudged to my room to play with my toys, avoiding homework at all costs.

That evening, as my mother prepared dinner with me, her restless and undisciplined chef's assistant, I paced around the kitchen recounting the scoutmaster's presentation, peppering my retelling with dramatic hand gestures and a singular focus on the word *fire*. I was determined to convince her that scouting was my destiny. She chuckled, amused by my excitement.

The next day, armed with the crumpled brochure I had fished from the depths of my Ninja Turtles backpack, she called the number listed. After a brief conversation, she broke the bad news to me: Boy Scouts was for ages eleven to eighteen, and I was only nine. I would have to start as a Webelos Scout, a transitional stage from Cub Scouts to Boy Scouts, but there wasn't a local pack due to a lack of parent volunteers. My dreams of learning survival skills and mastering fire-making were extinguished.

Unless . . .

After a few moments of contemplation, my mother called back. "Could a mom be a Webelos den leader?" she asked the Scouts representative at the central office in San José.

The man hesitated, clearly stunned. "We haven't had any moms volunteer before, but . . . I, uh, don't see a reason why it couldn't work," he replied, still sounding unsure.

We drove to San José a week later, where my mother filled out the paperwork to start our pack. Within a month, she rallied four other kids and their moms, forming a Webelos pack led mainly by women. For the next two years, every Tuesday night at 6 p.m., our Webelos den gathered in the front studio of Pantheon Fine Arts and Framing, a place where a group of boys learned the foundations of manhood—taught by their mothers.

## Orion

Two years later, as a full-fledged Boy Scout at the junior rank of Tenderfoot, I was off to my very first summer camp at Camp High Sierra in the Sierra Nevada Mountains. Boy Scout camp is a tradition in the scouting world, a weeklong adventure that marks your first actual break from the safety net of home and parents. I would spend it with a troop of boys, most of whom were older and seemed like towering giants to me.

When it was finally time to leave for camp, I was terrified. It would be the longest I had ever been away from home, and the thought of it gripped me hard. I was scared enough to beg my mom to let me quit.

"Mom, I can't do this," I sobbed. "I don't have any friends in the troop, and the older boys don't even like me!"

I meant every word. The idea of being alone in the woods for the first time was too much. And I still had what I considered a very reasonable fear of werewolves.

My mother drew me close to her. When my tears subsided, she took my hand and led me out of the gallery onto Murphy Avenue, away from the streetlights. Standing under the vast expanse of the night sky, she tilted her head upward to scan the stars. She cupped my hand and pointed upward with her index finger. "Ah, there—do you see that, Angelo? That's Orion," she said in a calm voice. "You can tell it's him because of his belt. See those three stars in a row?" I nodded, still sniffling. "Now, make an imaginary triangle using those three stars as the base. That bright star is his head; he's drawing back a bow," she continued. "That's Orion—the brave, cunning, and resourceful hunter and protector. I've read you his stories; I need you to be brave like him."

She knelt down in front of me and lifted my chin with her hand so our eyes met. With her thumb, she wiped the streaks of tears from my face and said, “Angelo, whenever you’re scared or feel alone, no matter where you are in the world, I want you to look up at Orion. That’s where our family goes when we move on from this world. It’s our connection to each other. We will always be with you wherever you go.” Her gaze softened, “Can you be brave like Orion?”

With a deep breath, my lip trembling, I nodded, “Yes.”

Our journey east took us deep into the heart of the Sierra Nevada Mountains. As we ascended Route 120, the road climbed sharply near Yosemite Junction. The evergreen forest gave way to a panoramic expanse of jagged, snow-capped peaks that loomed high above the tree line. It was another dramatic first for me—just enough to distract from the fear of being alone. That evening, I sat perched on an uneven log, arms crossed, and burrowed in an oversized Marlboro-branded coat I had borrowed from my father.

Still too nervous to join the other boys, I focused on the fire. The glowing embers captivated me, their deep purples and blues swirling upward before softening into wisps of yellow and orange. They floated skyward, blending with the cold, visible puffs of our breath and the campfire smoke curling up through our noses and into the night. As I followed the embers with my eyes, I noticed three flickering stars in a line above the smoky haze: Orion. I looked closer. I took a breath—everything was going to be okay—and exhaled.

### Baseball

By the time I entered high school, I had two great passions: Boy Scouts and baseball. During the third week of my freshman year, I noticed a flyer taped to a hallway door—tryouts for the baseball team. I wanted to play, but self-doubt crept in, as it always did.

“Should I try out?” I asked my dad.

“Of course, Angelo,” he said, as if it had been obvious all along. “It’s what you love. You should do it.”

My dad was a long-haul truck driver, and after my parents' divorce when I was three, the job kept him away more often than not. Like many fathers, he had to love his children from a distance—showing up when he could and making sure the moments mattered.

My Little League games were on Thursday nights. I'd scan the stands for him and catch sight of his pinstriped Weyerhaeuser work uniform. His sleeves rolled in tight one-inch folds, steel-toed boots firmly planted on the bleachers, and a pack of Marlboro Reds tucked into his chest pocket just beneath his stitched name patch: *Giuseppe*.

My dad grew up near Pompeii, and soccer was his native sport and favorite pastime. But, although an Italian immigrant, Giuseppe insisted I play baseball instead of soccer. He was determined to raise me as an "American boy."

My dad never understood tagging up, intentional walks, or even the game's basic rules. He didn't own a mitt, and I'm sure he couldn't throw a ball, so we never played father-son catch. But I'll never forget the San Francisco Giants game he took me to, where we witnessed the rare feat of an inside-the-park home run. He looked confused, unsure how it even happened—but we cheered like hell with the rest of the crowd.

Giuseppe loved America. There was nothing more American than baseball, so we both loved baseball.

## Fremont High

I started high school much like I had started Scouts—intimidated, alone, and painfully shy. The quirks of the district map assigned most of my middle school friends to our rival high school across the city—a place that felt as far away as the moon. Starting fresh, surrounded by ruthless and judgmental teenagers, only made the fear of not fitting in that much worse.

After my mom dropped me off in her gold Saturn, I trudged down a path lined with manicured red roses—the clear pride of the school's grounds crew. Tall hedges stood on either side like Roman praetorian sentinels, making the walkway feel more like a gauntlet. I stepped through the open gates and into a world I would come to both love and hate—one that would shape me and impact my life's trajectory.

Like most kids, I stumbled through the early days of high school, awkwardly trying to figure out who I was while pretending I already knew.

I stepped onto my first professionally maintained baseball field that Monday afternoon. The sight was overwhelming—the deep red dirt of the raised pitcher's mound stood like an island above the outfield's manicured emerald grass. Pristine white chalk lines stretched with detailed precision from home plate to the outfield, dividing the field into clean, symmetrical sections. The tall outfield walls, painted deep forest green, towered over me, dwarfing the short, three-foot chain-link fences I was used to. It felt like stepping into a dream, and I stood in awe of what this field represented.

Tryouts lasted two hours each day that week, with the final roster set to be posted on the gym's front door early Friday morning. I threw myself into the drills with everything I had, but it became clear I was falling behind. The other boys were bigger, stronger, faster. At just thirteen years old and still prepubescent, I was nowhere near my growth spurt—and it showed. My arm strength wasn't enough for a catcher or third baseman, my running speed drew chuckles from the coaching staff, and my swings lacked power. Every evening, I came home deflated, realizing the gap between the others and me wasn't closing—it was growing.

By the end of the week, the reality of being the new kid at a new school, with few friends and a passion I wasn't good at, felt like walls closing in.

Friday morning arrived. I made my way toward the gym through the thorny gauntlet of rose bushes. A group of boys jostled for position around the roster taped to the gym door, laughing and joking—their height forming an impervious wall. As I approached, a voice rang out from the cluster.

"Don't even bother looking, AJ. You're too small. Maybe you'll be good enough to play when you grow up."

I put my head down, walked past their jeers, swallowed hard, and fought back tears. Though I pretended not to hear, cruel laughter followed me down the hall. I waited for the first bell to ring, circling back around the gym and lingering until the others had dispersed.

Once the crowd was gone, I sulked up to the sheet of paper taped to the gym door, already feeling the weight of the inevitable. My eyes scanned the list—once, twice, a third time—each pass slower than the last. My name wasn't there.

The shock of it hit hard: my greatest love, my identity, my childhood dream—I wasn't good enough for any of it. I had been cut.

Years later, I'd find a small measure of solace knowing that one of the nicest guys on the team, Troy Tulowitzki, went on to play for the Colorado Rockies, finishing second for Rookie of the Year in his first season. Knowing I was up against that level of talent softens the sting now, but only just a little.

Not making the team shook me more than I let on. I searched for connection wherever I could, bouncing between different groups desperately trying to find my place. I became an outcast—focusing more on perfecting skateboarding tricks and hacky-sack skills than on my schoolwork.

During the second half of my sophomore year, I signed up for a drama class as an elective and found something unexpected: enjoyment. As I got to know the other kids in the class, I realized they, too, were a kind of social out-group—not because they lacked talent or charisma, but because they dared to love things that didn't align with what was considered "cool." The drama kids were quirky, fun, and unapologetically weird in the best way. They were also deeply intelligent, kind, and—most importantly—confident in who they were. For the first time, I felt like I'd found a place where I belonged.

Getting cut from baseball, while painful, forced me to open up to new experiences I likely never would've explored otherwise. And in doing so, I began to uncover parts of myself I didn't know existed.

Looking back, it's no mystery why I didn't exactly skyrocket up the social ladder. I checked every "uncool" box imaginable: I was 4'11" with a round baby face, didn't make the baseball team, stuck with Boy Scouts, joined the choir, became an actor, and spent a week during the summer between my sophomore and junior years at cheer camp—serving as Phillip the Firebird, our school mascot. I wasn't just climbing down the social ladder; I was tumbling down it.

But I was having a hell of a lot of fun figuring out who I was on the way down.

## Values

The summer before my senior year, our troop embarked on its annual trip to Boy Scout camp—my final one. After two years of Webelos and six years of Boy Scouts, I became a troop leader, achieved the Eagle Scout rank, and prepared to graduate high school in the coming spring.

That year, we ventured to Camp Royaneh, a scouting camp with nearly a century of history. For decades, thousands of scouts had made their pilgrimage to this extraordinary place, nestled among towering old-growth redwood trees and rugged cliffs of Sonoma County.

Our troop numbers dwindled over the years, as often happens when boys grow older, and life's other priorities take over. To help fill the gaps, my mother volunteered as an adult chaperone. She oversaw the troop at night, but during the day, while we hiked, fixed trails, built lean-tos, and scaled rock walls, she painted the stunning landscapes.

The scenery may have appeared wild and overwhelming to our untrained eyes, but through her artistic lens, I began to see the underlying structure in its chaos. She showed how nature's vastness could be abstracted into repeating, cyclical, and harmonious forms and patterns.

"The sun is not just a simple circle," she explained to a curious crowd of boys, her voice warm and inviting. "It's a living form of energy, radiating thousands of hues that shift and blend with each moment. To truly see it, you must allow yourself to feel its warmth." Inverting her fanned paintbrush, she pointed to the sky. "Clouds aren't just soft blobs drifting aimlessly; they're layered, stacked ovals with soft edges that shift as they stretch across the sky, each carrying its own story." She continued, "And trees. At first glance, they might seem like simple cones of green, but look closer. They sway and whisper, their branches stretching and curling like dancers in mid-motion. If you stand still long enough, you'll see their movement—the way their leaves catch the light and bend with the breeze. Mountains, too, are more than jagged triangles. Their peaks and valleys shift with shadow and light, changing with the time of day. Nature is always moving," she concluded, her voice softer as the boys drew closer. "The more you allow yourself to stand still and observe, the more you'll see its rhythm, intricacies, and soul."

Hiking up and down the steep mountain ridges, I noticed how the sun's shifting shadows danced across the trees, subtly marking the time of day. "Nature has no right angles, Angelo," my mother would often say as she explained the intricacies of the world around us. While many artists might reduce nature to simple, straight lines, she insisted that to a trained eye, nature was fragmented, disjointed, and imperfect—just like we are as humans. "You see," she would say, "we're not just observers of our environment; we're a part of it. And it's our imperfections that make us human."

At the time, I didn't fully grasp the depth of her words. However, through her patient teaching, I learned to respect and understand the natural world and to see the beauty not in its symmetry but in its flaws. Only later would I recognize this as the foundation of something greater—an introduction to values that shaped how I saw myself and my place in the world.

### The Origin of Empathy

Everyone is the same when you're in the woods. The pressure to hit the ball farther or tackle harder doesn't matter. There's no need to put others down to feel better. It wouldn't do any good anyway. It wouldn't speed up the tents going up or stop the rain. No one cares if you wear the right clothes or listen to the right music—and neither does nature. In the wilderness, basic human needs—food, water, and shelter—define everything. These needs are universal. Winning isn't about standing out; it's about helping each other and lifting others up.

One of my scout mates often lagged—physically, mentally, or sometimes both. Unlike the rest of us, he didn't have parents who were present like mine were. My mother held Webelos meetings at our house and took us to scout camp, while his grandmother raised him, relying on social assistance. My mom showed him kindness and patience, offering him a little more understanding than she gave the rest of us. She showed empathy and compassion but remained stern when teaching him life lessons.

As children, we often criticize things that are different or unfamiliar. However, I was reminded that adulthood demanded compassion and empathy for the things we did not fully understand. "Show compassion rather than judgment," Mom would say when she saw me slipping into the thoughtless traps of boyhood.

It wasn't until later that I learned his story in full. His parents struggled with substance abuse—back then, people just called them "addicts." His mother drank while pregnant, which made processing and learning more difficult for him. Looking back, I wish I had been more aware of his situation. But even then, we understood he needed extra help, so we provided it. We didn't treat him differently; he was one of us. He was family.

I realized that the Boy Scouts taught me more than how to appreciate nature or make a fire. It taught me how to see and understand my place in the world, recognizing the inherent dignity in every person. Being part of something larger than myself gave me a sense of significance—not self-importance, but the kind of worth that comes from belonging. I learned that belonging wasn't one-sided; it came with a duty. If I didn't hold up my end, there would be nothing to belong to. I embraced that challenge: the duty to do good for its own sake, or, as my mother often expressed it, "to make the world a brighter place."

The drive home from Camp Royaneh that Sunday was long and peaceful. Now old enough to drive, I was behind the wheel of the gold Saturn with my mother in the passenger seat. The calm mountain air whipped through the open windows, carrying the fragrance of pine and mountain wildflowers. Our roles, once so clearly defined, had shifted.

She had raised me from a young boy, using her art as a metaphor for how she saw the world. Now, I was beginning to see it for myself. I understood her landscapes—not just the brushstrokes, but the feelings they conveyed. I saw the world as she did: a tapestry of interconnected beauty and wonder. Her art and the natural world weren't simply mirrors of each other; they were intertwined, driving connection and making us feel more human.

By Monday, the tranquil beauty of the mountains gave way to the relentless buzz of cars, crowded sidewalks, and packed hallways at school. We were back in Silicon Valley. The world I returned to was a snarl of industry and innovation—a boomtown racing to create semiconductors, chips, and computers, technology that seemed to pull us further from the nature I had just left behind.

## End of Innocence

When I earned my Eagle Scout that summer, my parents gifted me my grandmother's 1986 Nissan Stanza. It had sat unused in her driveway for years, but now it was mine. With a top speed of forty miles per hour because of a busted transmission, highways were out of the question. Instead, I navigated the familiar streets of Sunnyvale and San José, the radio perpetually tuned to KFRC, San Francisco's oldies station—ironically, the only AM signal the ancient dial could catch. My friends quickly dubbed it the "grandma-mobile," with its boxy, chicken nugget–like color and shape. I didn't care; it was freedom.

I coasted into my senior year of high school—everything was finally coming together. Life felt like an incredible adventure. After a much-needed growth spurt, I reached a semi-respectable 5′10″ and 135 pounds soaking wet. I'd grown into a social butterfly, forging connections with the same charm I'd honed as a kid on the beaches of Santa Cruz. Theater, choir, and Boy Scouts had given me the confidence to defy social norms and chase my passions—strangely enough, pushing me into popularity.

By senior year, I was student body president, surrounded by close friends and brimming with excitement about the future.

I imagined myself as a modern-day Ferris Bueller, complete with spiked, frosted-tipped hair, embracing the thrill of teenage freedom. I made it a point never to let schoolwork get in the way of all the fun I was having. We skipped class for impromptu road trips over the mountains to the sun-soaked beach or spontaneous adventures in San Francisco. We planned multi-school parties and fueled our late-night escapades with gas station beef jerky and energy drinks.

One of our dumber stunts was mattress surfing—a wild spin on tray surfing. After sneaking out on Thursday nights, we'd hunt down old mattresses, cut a hole in the front, and hitch them to the back of a buddy's truck. Then, two or three of us would pile on, holding on for dear life as we hurtled down residential streets, sparks and laughter echoing through the night. We tested every limit of what it meant to be young, wild, and alive.

Six weeks before homecoming, my friends and I immersed ourselves in preparing for the festivities. We planned the parade and dance and looked forward to party hopping. I was even in the running for homecoming king. Everything in my life was firing on all cylinders—well, except for the grandma-mobile.

## The Opening Move

`11 September 2001 - Santa Clara, CA`

6:00 a.m. Pacific Standard Time. My alarm buzzed. With my eyes half open, I wrestled with the urge to roll over, surrender to my undisciplined teenage inhibitions, and fall back asleep. The routine was the same as always—just another day.

6:33 a.m. PST. I wandered downstairs, drawn by the faint hum of our living room TV. It was unusual to hear the news in the mornings; most mornings in our household were a discord of rushed footsteps, frantic reminders of the day's tasks, and mumbled goodbyes. But today, something felt different. Two muted gray towers filled the screen, black smoke curling into the sky like a strange signal. Reporters' voices stumbled, their words fractured and frantic. It all felt distant, surreal—like a movie I wasn't paying attention to.

6:52 a.m. PST. I left the house and slid behind the wheel of the grandma-mobile. Typically, the oldies station KFRC greeted the morning with upbeat tunes and the banter of the local radio DJs. Today, however, no music played; a national broadcast's raw and frightened tones overtook the station. The reports felt more ominous with every word. "What the hell is going on?" I thought to myself.

6:59 a.m. PST. The news came through like a wave, with voices on the radio escalating in panic. The World Trade Center South Tower had collapsed. I drove in silence, the air in the car heavy and suffocating. I willed the car to go faster to reach a familiar place where I wouldn't be alone. The world I thought I understood was crumbling, and I hadn't even made it to school.

7:07 a.m. PST. I pulled into the back parking lot. Typically, this was the spot for late-night donut runs and planning harmless teenage mischief, but today, it felt empty. Some kids headed home, but I followed the crowd that drifted inside the musty auditorium, not by choice but as if pulled by some greater force. Inside the seats were cold, stiff, and too close together, yet no one seemed to care. Administrators waved us in, their faces tense with a mix of fear and concern. I scanned the sea of familiar faces, searching for an anchor in the confusion. No one spoke; no one knew how to. We huddled, exchanging uneasy glances as a tech lowered the projector screen, and the flickering images brought the world's horror into painful focus. Reporters filled the silence, their voices cracking under the weight of what they described.

7:28 a.m. PST. The room let out a collective gasp—a sound of disbelief and fear so raw it felt like the walls themselves had absorbed it. The North Tower of the World Trade Center fell. We saw it happen live. The building folded inward, collapsing in a plume of smoke and ash that seemed to billow straight into the sky.

And then, silence.

We sat there, roughly sixty of us, as the hours crawled by. The auditorium became a makeshift shelter from the storm, but it offered no protection from the weight of what we were witnessing. Tears carved soundless paths down faces that had smiled so easily the day before. Voices were hushed, conversations broken into fragments, as if speaking too loudly would shatter what little peace we had left.

The world had shifted. We, young teenagers who believed we had all the time in the world, were left to face the truth: Time, as we knew it, had been divided into a before and an after by a "Where were you?" moment. The first of many for our generation.

# 2

# "DUDE, YOU'RE GONNA HAVE TO TALK TO MY MOM"

## A Different Path

In the days that followed, our American history and government classroom became a space for raw and difficult conversations. At the helm was Mr. Rafael Rojas, a Marine Reservist who approached teaching with the same no-nonsense discipline he no doubt learned in the Corps. He was my favorite yet most demanding teacher: punctuality, participation, and effort were nonnegotiable. He expected us to "give a damn," and after 9/11, it felt impossible not to.

Visibly frustrated, Rojas guided us through discussions that wavered between diplomacy and vengeance. Often boiling over with an unnerving thirst for retribution, the unprovoked murder of 3,000 Americans fueled our collective anger. Grief consumed us, but bloodlust wasn't far behind.

As a teenager inundated with hormones and lacking the maturity to process such complexities, I was confused—and angry. Rojas, the man who had attended my Eagle Scout ceremony just months earlier as more of a mentor than a teacher, dared to challenge our assumptions. A Marine, tough as nails, cautioning against all-out war? It felt like a betrayal.

"While violence is often necessary for certain forms of conflict resolution, it's not our only answer," he said, his voice a mix of anger and control. "Yes, we have a military for this purpose, and it will respond in kind. But it's crucial to understand that it was the Taliban who attacked us—not the Afghan people. Any military response must be measured, coupled with a diplomatic approach to dissuade future attacks and steer the population away from supporting the Taliban. Otherwise, this will happen again. We're in uncharted waters as a country, and we're all going to have a part to play." His final words were a bucket of water—extinguishing our rage.

Nothing in my world pointed me toward the military. I was a young, working-class kid from a family filled with immigrants with no real US military ties. I had no lineage of service. Yet, amid the chaos and grief, I began to wonder what my role was... Could I be part of defending my country? Could I become a Marine?

My history didn't matter. What mattered was the conviction growing inside me, a sense of purpose toward serving. The thoughts grew stronger each day, and Mr. Rojas seemed to sense it.

One day after class, he pulled me aside and said, "AJ, I think I have someone you should meet."

"Sure, Mr. Rojas," I replied, my curiosity piqued.

"His name is Staff Sergeant Walter Tinay. He's a Marine recruiter." I agreed, but there would be one big problem.

## The Recruiter

I wasn't old enough to be a Marine or even meet with a recruiter. I was still sixteen on 9/11, and the rules were clear: I had to wait. But that didn't change my resolve; it only made me more determined. Three weeks after the attacks, I turned seventeen, and then I met the man who would shape the rest of my life—my Marine recruiter.

Staff Sergeant Walter Tinay was a mountain of a man—the spitting image of what a Marine should look like. He was an enormous Hawaiian with a square jaw, jet-black hair cropped into an assertive flat top, bulging forearms, and a pristinely tailored and starched shirt. When he walked by, people paid attention.

I was first introduced to Staff Sergeant Tinay as Mr. Rojas walked me out of class one afternoon in late September. "Mr. Pasciuti, this is Staff Sergeant Tinay. We call him Tiny," Rojas said with more than a hint of irony. "But you can call him Staff Sergeant," he continued, correcting any potential for me to put my foot into my mouth or become this guy's snack.

"Afternoon, young man. So, you think you can become a United States Marine?" he asked, moving his giant paw toward mine.

"Uhh," I uttered, my eyes wide.

"Don't look at me, Mr. Pasciuti. Staff Sergeant Tinay asked you the question," Rojas said with a smile. Unbeknownst to me, I was undergoing a time-honored tradition of meeting a Marine for the first time.

"Umm-uhh," I continued to mumble, unable to manage anything other than make guttural sounds as a response.

"Well, AJ, not everyone can become a United States Marine. Why don't you swing by the office tomorrow after school, sixteen hundred sharp? Here's my card. Let's see if you have what it takes." Tinay's voice seemed to echo as a thin white card with a single red horizontal stripe crossed my vision.

Confused about whether he was asking me a question or giving me an order, I reached to grab the card as my nerves began to catch up. My hands shook as I mumbled, "Yeah, I'll see if I can make it." I tried to feign nonchalance as if that were even possible in the presence of a man of Staff Sergeant Walter Tinay's stature.

Rojas and Tinay entered the classroom, leaving me standing alone outside, trying to compose myself and make sense of what had just happened. Walking to my next class, I shook my head and wondered, "What the hell is sixteen hundred?"

### The Station

The next day, at 4 p.m. sharp, I opened the door to the Marine Recruiting station on Stevens Creek Boulevard in San José. A bell attached to the bottom of the door announced my arrival with a loud ring. Tinay stood from his desk to greet me. Across from him stood another towering square-jawed flat top. "Jesus, I must be out of my mind," I thought while flipping my frosted-tipped hair out of my eyes.

"AJ, thanks for stopping by; this is Staff Sergeant Milburne. He's a Force Reconnaissance Marine."

"Oh, cool," I replied with a quick nod, pretending not to feel the sheer intimidation of the scene and acting as if I had any idea what a Force Reconnaissance Marine was.

Both men sized me up as I approached Staff Sergeant Tinay's desk. As I sat across from him, his orientation and pitch were ready. Unbeknownst to me, this, too, was something Marines have gone through for generations—we all sit in front of a recruiter.

Laid out on the desk in front of me were fourteen color-coded, one-inch by two-inch plastic "benefit tags" with various words and phrases on them: Travel and Adventure, Pride of Belonging, Leadership and Management Skills. "AJ, do me a favor. Why don't you look at these dog tags and pick the top three things you're looking for?" Tinay instructed. His tone was different this time, softer and more welcoming. It helped to calm my nerves.

Still, it was one of those "Is this a question or an order thing?" I obliged and stared at the array of colors. In a bizarre, ironic way, we pick the values we most align with on the table, shaping his sales pitch to best suit my character. It's a genius way of gaining immediate trust and giving them what I would later understand as *buy-in* early.

I sat down, intent on choosing the best three tiles, thinking that if I picked the correct ones, they would see my superior intellect and ability and promote me on the spot. Boy, was I naive.

We sat for hours as they answered my questions. They showed me recruiting videos of Marines charging up mountains and a commercial in which a young Marine fights monsters on a chess board before saluting with his sword at the end.

It was nearing 7 p.m., er-uh, 1900, and by this time, I was gaining more confidence in my position. They wanted me, and I wanted to be one of them. I completed their dog tag selection, and I was feeling good.

We all stood as the meeting was ending. "One last thing," I cleared my throat as my youthful cockiness began to betray me. "I've heard that the Army and the Navy offer signing bonuses. What can you guarantee if I sign up to be a Marine?" I had taken the upper hand—it was time to use it to my advantage!

Unfazed and emotionless, Staff Sergeant Tinay locked eyes with me and then shifted his gaze to Staff Sergeant Milburne, who smirked back at Tinay. "Got him," I thought.

"Mr. Pasciuti," his gaze now back to mine as he leaned forward on the knuckles of the closed fists on his desk. "You want a guarantee? I tell you what. You sign those papers, and I can guarantee you thirteen weeks of boot camp."

He slapped the manila folder onto the table with a dull thud, then walked over and opened the office door. I was in. The teamwork, the belonging, the guns, the toughness, the danger—serving my country. I didn't know what the hell I was walking into, but I knew one thing for sure: I was *all-in.*

Over the next few days, I spent every free hour at the recruiter's office. I was like a groupie at the merch table—I bought buttons, stickers, posters, all of it. I was Mr. Marine at school. But my parents were another story.

I was still seventeen, and if I wanted to become a Marine and attend boot camp after I graduated, I would need both of my parents' permission. I was the only child of an artist mother and an anti-war American history buff Italian immigrant father. Staff Sergeant Tinay had his work cut out for him.

"Dude," I said, chuckling, "you're gonna have to talk to my mom."

## The Painter

"Hey, Ma! How are you doing?" I surprised her on the phone while she was at work; she now worked for the high school district office as a graphic designer.

"Hi, Sweetie, it's the middle of the day. Is everything okay—aren't you supposed to be in class?" she fired back, her motherly instincts kicking in.

"Heh, yeah, okay, fair question, I deserve that." I let out a nervous laugh. "So, there's this guy that's going to come see you." My left hand rubbed the back of my neck as I paced with my blue Nokia cell phone held to my right ear. "He's a US Marine," I said, my voice unsure and sheepish.

"A what?" my mother cleared her throat.

"Well, I've been talking with a Marine recruiter, and he told me he needed to speak with you and Dad before we went any further."

"Uh-um, okay. Sure, give him my number, and we can set up a time to chat." She tried to delay.

"Ummm, well, he's already on his way. He'll be there in ten minutes." Exactly ten minutes later, Staff Sergeant Walter Tinay—the chiseled, square-jawed, battle-hardened Marine—darkened my mother's office door.

"Angelo, what are you thinking?!" my mother barked, half-joking with me later that evening. "Did you see the size of that guy? They're going to make you a cook!"

## The Bull

"Absolutely not, Angelo," my father's response had been immediate and firm, his tone that of a man whose own father and grandfathers had fought in World War I and World War II—and not for the good guys. "Out of the question."

"Babbo, this is our country," I shot back. "You raised me to love this country. This is my duty. An 'American Boy,' remember?"

Giuseppe raised me as his American boy, encouraging me to play baseball over soccer. He also had me call him Babbo instead of Dad; it was the kind of cultural crossover that only children of immigrants can understand. While he never became a citizen, his love for America was undeniable. He listened to country music, was a passionate square dancer and aggressive bowler, devoured American history books, admired "The Duke" with a passion, and despised rap music with the same.

At that moment, my dad froze. His dark eyes searched mine, trying to see past the determination he already knew was growing. His voice softened as if pleading might change my mind.

"No, Angelo, this is different."

"No, Babbo," I said, my voice trembling. "It's not different. This is what you and Mom taught me—to care for others as if they were my own family, to never shy away from responsibility, and to know that our success as a people and a country is tied together. You passed those values to me, remember?"

Raised as an orphan alongside his brothers in an all-boys school in Pompeii after their mother went to prison for murder, he never truly knew love. Many of the priests charged with his care abused him, leaving behind deep physical and emotional scars. Still, he showed up the only way he knew how. He wasn't perfect—few fathers are—but he did his best. And through it all, his love for me was unconditional.

He drew in a deep breath as his nostrils flared.

"Enough, Angelo! I forbid it!"

"Babbo . . ." I stared at him, my heart breaking as my hands shook. I had never spoken to him like that before, never crossed this line. "I only need your permission now because I'm seventeen. When I turn eighteen next September, I'm going to join anyway. You can't stop me."

He didn't speak. He just stood there, staring at me, his face unreadable. I knew my dad as a passionate man, not an emotional one. I only saw him cry three times: once during a late-night long-distance phone call from his brother in Italy, sharing the news of his mother's unexpected death; once when returning to his orphanage in Pompeii, where he wept in a chapel at Christ's feet; and once when Italy's prodigal son of football, Roberto Baggio, sailed his final penalty kick over Brazil's crossbar, losing Italy the World Cup final in 1994—like a scene out of a Mafia movie—grown men, hearts broken, throwing food and drinks in despair and falling to their knees in agony.

Then, I saw it—his brows softened, and tears welled up.

He stepped forward, grabbed my hand, and pulled me into him. My head pressed against his barrel chest, where I could smell the faint scent of sweat, diesel, and the Marlboro Reds that were always tucked into his shirt pocket.

His arms wrapped around me with a protective and desperate strength, as if he were trying to hold on to me and stop time from moving forward.

Then his voice cracked. "Remember this, son," he whispered, his breath warm against my ear, "Pasciutis always come home."

# 3

-----

# "GET OFF MY BUS!"

## Melting Pot

8 July 2002 - 1900
San Diego International Airport, CA

At the San Diego International Airport USO, a group of about forty young men gathered. Nervous voices buzzed in the air. Introductions were exchanged over a few bursts of laughter, which helped break the tension. The group was a mix of young men, most from west of the Mississippi: A Mexican kid from LA, still wearing colors from his set, nodded to a farmer from Oklahoma with a tobacco can ring in his back pocket. A black kid from Vegas talked proudly about his hometown to a white kid from Bozeman. It was a cross section of America: long-haired surfers, Texas-sized belt buckles, disheveled, half-tucked plaid shirts, and an air of overconfidence.

As the chatter continued, a faded white school bus pulled into position. The group's mood shifted. One among us, self-designated as the leader, stepped forward and gestured for the rest of us to fall in line. We boarded the bus one by one and departed, the group's energy trailing behind.

The laughter and joking started again as the bus wound its way through the streets of San Diego. The bus passed San Diego Harbor, where towering naval ships painted in muted gray stood watch over the tranquil waters, exuding a command of authority even in the stillness of the setting sun.

The bus rolled through "Old Town." Spanish-style homes and terracotta-roofed restaurants lined the streets of San Diego's historic district; their charm beckoned tourists to explore one of America's most picturesque cities. We wouldn't be stopping.

We approached the front gate as the sunlight faded into a purple-and-orange dusk. Two Marine guards in camouflage fatigues with M16 rifles waved the bus forward in steady, deliberate movements that embodied the discipline that lay ahead. Above the guard shack, the words WELCOME TO MARINE CORPS RECRUIT DEPOT, SAN DIEGO were painted with an almost ominous precision. The bus fell silent.

### Headlights

Three minutes later, the bus rounded a final corner and stopped. The beam of the bus headlights illuminated four looming Marine Drill Instructors. The men were a force in their polished black shoes, which gleamed under the light, crisply pressed olive drab dress trousers and sharp khaki short-sleeved shirts that seemed molded to their frames, hands clasped behind their backs. Each man wore the same hat on their heads: an iconic "Smokey the Bear" campaign cover tilted forward at a precise 20-degree angle, casting a shadow over their faces and obscuring their eyes. In the light, the four men looked like statues.

The bus door opened. One of the four men broke the line and sauntered up the bus stairs. His heels clicked with menace on the hard rubber interior of the bus floor.

"Good evening, gentlemen. My name is Gunnery Sergeant Thompson. Welcome to recruit training," he said as he stood in the center aisle in front of us. "When we give you the command, you will fall out in an orderly fashion onto the yellow footprints painted on the ground as soon as you exit this vehicle. From there, we will begin your in-processing to recruit training. Do I have any questions?" Silence.

Gunnery Sergeant Thompson pivoted and walked off the bus. Now his counterpart, a younger Drill Instructor, walked onto the bus. When he reached the top of the stairs, he paused and pivoted. Then his voice erupted, "Get off my bus right now!"

The command sent a shock wave through all of us packed inside. Chaos ensued. As we tried to fulfill the order, the Drill Instructor charged down the bus aisle. His voice screamed at the tide of panicked recruits as we tripped over one another in the narrow space and attempted to get off his bus.

In the chaos, two more Drill Instructors appeared. Their voices boomed at the recruits as their arms sliced through the air. The scene spiraled into a frenzy, like a school of fish converging in terror from circling predators. We clambered over one another in a chaotic, desperate attempt to get off the bus without being picked off.

I finally broke free and stumbled off the bus. I spotted a pair of yellow footprints painted on the asphalt and planted my dirty, worn Vans within the lines. Frozen in place, my heart pounded; the only discernible sound was my breath, loud in my ears, with a metallic iron taste on my dry tongue. I locked into a "position of attention." I stood erect and as still as possible, as if my life depended on it. My world narrowed to one focus: Avoid attracting the gaze of the Drill Instructors, whose vision, like that of a T-Rex, responded to movement.

We had completed our first rite of Marine passage and awaited the next one.

"Gentlemen, it will be a long night and only get longer if you continue to fail to follow our orders." Gunnery Sergeant Thompson said with a sinister grin. "Upon my next command, you will assemble in a single file line and enter through this door alphabetically by your last name. These Drill Instructors beside me will work with me to properly 'motivate' you through the process. Do I have any questions?" Silence.

"Three, two, one, Move!"

### Frosted Tips

For the next four hours, we went through the motions methodically. We completed entrance paperwork, received rack assignments, were issued gear, and even made a scripted phone call home to inform our next of kin that we were alive.

The air remained tense throughout the evening. Every step was shadowed by lurking Drill Instructors who materialized out of nowhere, their eyes trained to catch even the slightest discipline slip. Eagerly, they responded with the weight and screaming chaos of a tradition honed over generations of Marines.

We were here to become Marines, and the Drill Instructors were the guardians of our transformation. They ensured that every correction served as a step toward molding us into a new version of those who had come before us.

"Got any moles, bumps, or bruises?" The barber asked, more out of habit than interest, as a toothpick rested between his teeth.

"Uh, what?" I stammered, but before I could process the question, the buzz of his electric clippers began their work. The barber ran over my entire scalp as swaths of my neck-length, frosted-tipped waves fell to the floor, remnants of a life I had just left behind.

I stared into the mirror, observing the transformation. It was more than hair being shed—it was a version of myself I had worked so hard to find growing up, and now it was falling away. My head now shaved before I ever shaved my face.

`17 July 2002 - Training Day - 3`

*To my family,*

*I'm stuck here in hell, and I want nothing more than to be home. I regret ever saying I wanted to leave. Boot Camp is harder than anything you could ever imagine. All of the videos don't even compare to what it's like here. Yesterday, they PT'd (physically trained) us until people dropped. Three people had to be carried away by a corpsman. Today, a guy scratched his nose and the Drill Instructors*

*IT'd (intensively trained) him until he puked on the floor and passed out in his own vomit. These men have no sympathy for anything. Truly brutes.*

*I have to get going now, it's time for lights out. Please write me often. I love you all very much and want to come home. I need motivation so please write often.*

*With love,*
*Recruit Pasciuti*

## Drill

For thirteen miserable weeks, we were stripped of our civilian identities and rebuilt as Marines. The transformation was merciless, defined by the constant screaming of Drill Instructors, the sting of criticism, and the weight of unachievable timelines and unrealistic expectations.

We shuffled between classes on military customs and courtesies, basic hygiene, casualty care, Marine Corps history, and the indomitable "Warfighting Ethos" that has always defined our tradition. Interspersed at various times were brutal sessions of weapons handling, hand-to-hand combat, and the foundational tactics of a rifle squad. But above all else, there was marching, hours upon hours of marching.

Close-order drill, an ancient practice used to maneuver armies since the fifth century, had long lost its battlefield utility. Yet, within the crucible of Marine Corps training, it remained sacred—a cornerstone of discipline and tradition. Drill Instructors would remind us, almost with reverence, that marching instilled obedience, confidence, teamwork, and camaraderie—qualities essential for every Marine. Our individualism was stripped away, and we were judged as a collective entity. This was a significant departure from the independence we had all known.

Our days blurred together in a haze of repetition and correction. Each morning, we would form up and execute endless movements: left obliques, column rights, parade rests—drilled until they seemed to become instinctual.

Hours were spent perfecting the ceremonial manipulation of our rifles, down to the faintest click of the ejection port cover during inspections. The sun rose and set with close-order drill as if the universe were mocking us.

"What's with all this marching? Don't these guys know we're going to war?" My rack mate, Recruit Rogelio Gomez from Dallas, Texas, muttered under his breath while tightening the fold on a rigid bedsheet during a stolen moment of peace.

We questioned the logic of it all and whispered in frustration to each other when we thought no one could hear—to us, the time seemed wasted, a pointless exercise when we should have been training for the realities of combat. But our protests went unheard. In Recruit Training, there was no room for dissent, only obedience.

`30 August 2002 - Training Day - 34`

*To my family,*

*Today was Friday, and it was fairly easy. We finished up "snap-in" week today. "Snap-in" week is where we learn everything about our weapon and its stances. We learned the prone (lying down), sitting (one of three positions), kneeling (uncomfortable as hell), and standing. In my opinion, standing was the hardest. Your body is so exposed and off balance. Very weird. Also, we learned about sighting in, zeroing, and our wind and elevation adjustments. A lot of math and quick thinking. Surprisingly, marksmanship is not just point and shoot. It's a whole world of muscle, mind, and body relaxation. You have to find your position and clear your mind. I find it relaxing.*

*Tomorrow we have a five-mile hump. Earlier this week on Wednesday we humped for about three miles. It was a very nice walk. But it was very embarrassing to have people from our platoon who couldn't walk a simple three miles. I know it's hard on some people, but fifty-five pounds isn't that much. I don't know. But at least we're weeding out the weak. Hopefully more tomorrow.*

*With love,*
*Recruit Pasciuti*

## The Transformation

As graduation approached, the early loneliness and homesickness I had carried as a typical seventeen-year-old kid began to fade, replaced by a deep sense of purpose and the unbreakable camaraderie of my fellow recruits.

The transformation was undeniable. I entered boot camp as a scrawny kid who barely managed three pull-ups. I struggled to grasp the precision of close-order drills and often questioned my decision to join. But by the end, I had become someone entirely new. A young man who had not only fallen in love with the Corps and the spirit of being a Marine—but who had also risen to lead one of our four squads through the final stages of Recruit Training.

The journey was marked by growth and unexpected recognition. My earlier achievement as an Eagle Scout earned me a meritorious promotion to Private First Class, validating the effort and determination I had poured into the process. For the first time, I felt like I had found my place in the world—where discipline, purpose, and brotherhood defined my existence. I couldn't have been happier.

## Graduation

`10 October 2002 - 1000`
`Marine Corps Recruit Depot, San Diego, CA`

The coastal California October air was crisp, the sky a brilliant canvas of blue, and the expansive parade deck stretched as far as an untrained eye could see—the stage where our transformation would be revealed. The slab of blacktop had carried the weight of generations. Lining its edges were the iconic, sun-washed, yellow-arched buildings. They had seen it all—kids like me stumbling in and then marching out months later as Marines.

My family had traveled hundreds of miles to witness this defining moment, and their faces were a mix of pride and anticipation as they searched the sea of recruits for me.

Overcome with emotion, my mother wept into my stepfather George's arms—each sob a potent blend of pride and relief. Nearby, my naturally stoic father stood with my stepmother, Gail, his head freshly shaved in a subtle show of solidarity—a wordless tribute to the journey I had endured. Though my parents had long been divorced, they shared this moment together.

As I marched across the deck, spine straight, eyes forward, I felt the full weight of their love and the moment's gravity. It wasn't just my graduation—it was theirs, too. Every step was a testament to their sacrifices, the lessons and struggles we had faced together, and the pride we now carried as one. The Marine Corps had changed me—but in that instant, it had changed us all.

Then, everything fell apart.

### Betrayal

Standing in our final formation, 500 young recruits, in a final display of acknowledgment and completing the transition, were given the command "fall out." The Company Commander barked the order in a booming and ceremonious voice. Five hundred men replied with a thunderous, "Aye, Aye, sir, Ooorah!" accepting dismissal from Marine Corps Recruit Depot San Diego and beginning the next chapter of our careers.

We were no longer recruits; we were Marines. As is tradition, our families came rushing forward to congratulate the Marine Corps' newest additions. We searched anxiously for our loved ones.

"Platooooon 1101, stand fast!" A booming voice commanded. We stood frozen.

"Plaaatoon 1101, ateaaan-Hut!" Eighty men followed orders without a second thought. They stood erect, eyes trained forward, anticipating our following command. Our families had found us and were going through the ranks, attempting to hug and kiss the young men they had missed so intensely.

Confused by our inaction, our families stepped back, bewildered, as Drill Instructors descended upon our platoon—the only platoon frozen in place. Drill Instructors snapped orders, correcting rebellious stragglers embracing their families, and ushered confused parents and loved ones out of our formation, many protesting along the way.

"What the hell is going on, Marine?!" one father yelled at the Drill Instructor.

"We've been asked to secure the platoon, sir," the Drill Instructor replied without emotion, carrying out his assigned task. "Platooooon, 1101, Forwarrrrrrd—March!" With a familiar whoosh and romp, our stiff-soled boots struck the concrete as they had thousands of times before. Our families screeched in disbelief.

"Left, right, left, right." Full thirty-inch steps carried us away from our stunned families. Our Troop Commander unexpectedly departed the parade deck and marched us to an unknown destination. Four minutes later, we approached our barracks, halted, and received our next instructions.

"When you receive the command to fall out, you will move immediately to your assigned rack and footlocker where you staged your gear this morning. You will not touch anything, you will stand at the position of attention facing toward the center of the squad bay, and you will not say a fucking word! Again, recruits, don't touch a thing. Fall Out!"

The same scene from our first arrival at Recruit Training unfolded during our unceremonious exit. Filled with panic and unsure of what was happening, eighty men flooded into our pristine squad bay. Each found his assigned rack and snapped to attention without hesitation. Silence.

*Thump, thump*—the sound of combat boots hitting the floor caught my attention. Conditioned to the polished *click, click* of a Drill Instructor's patent leathers, my senses heightened—this sounded different.

"I am the Officer in Charge of the Marine Corps Recruit Depot's Military Police [MP] Detachment." He paused for effect, letting his title convey the severity of the situation. "You are all under an official military investigation. These new Drill Instructors will assist my officers in searching through your personal belongings. You will cooperate with the investigation or be held accountable under the Uniform Code of

Military Justice. Are there any questions?" Silence. I started to shake. "Begin," the officer said.

Like untamed animals, the dozen new Drill Instructors plunged into us with a fury not seen since our first day. Starting at the first rack, three Drill Instructors surrounded their first victim. They shouted conflicting commands at the newly minted Marine. In shock, he crumpled to the ground. Now down on his hands and knees, he attempted to unlock his rotary combination lock on his sea bag. The three Drill Instructors followed him to the floor, still screaming.

In what seemed like an eternity, the young Marine remembered his combination. The lock opened with a click. The Drill Instructors pounced, ripping the sea bag from his hands and violently flipping it upside down, splaying the contents all over the floor as he moved to unlock his second sea bag. The sequence continued—the screaming, too.

Across the squad bay, more commotion erupted. Three additional teams of Drill Instructors, each accompanied by an armed military police officer, worked through each Marine. One by one, the Marines stood at attention. Their eyes darted as they tried to keep their heads still. Everyone was afraid to move as the Drill Instructors made their way down the line.

46 - 3 - 24; 46 - 3 - 24; 46 - 3 - 24—or was it 23? A wave of noise and spit hit the left side of my face. I moved as fast as my fingers would allow, spinning the silver and black dial: 46 - 3 - 24. I pleaded with the lock to open. *Click*. The bag flew effortlessly out of my hands as I shifted to my second bag. *Click, whoosh, boom.* My entire life, contained in two sea bags and one garment bag, now on the floor—jumbled with the lives of sixty of the eighty fresh Marines. I returned to my position. The storm rolled over me without incident.

A yell broke through the chaos in front of me as the Drill Instructor's voice shifted. Everyone's heads snapped toward the sound. A pitiful yelp escaped as a military police officer tackled one of our platoon mates and pinned him to his rack before taking him to the ground.

Twenty feet to my right, the same scene played out. They tackled another Marine and threw his sea bag on the floor. Hundreds of

$20 bills spilled out, scattering across the concrete at the feet of the Drill Instructor. A military policeman moved in, driving a knee into the Marine's back before yanking his arms behind him and snapping handcuffs into place.

"What's your combination?" The MP demanded.

"35 - 17 - 48, bbbbut it's not mine." He stuttered.

"Shut up." The MP dug his knee deeper into the Marine's back. When the Drill Instructor entered the combination, a second sea bag filled with $20 bills emptied onto the floor. It happened again. We remained frozen, knees locked, eyes forward.

They repeated the process until they checked every Marine's bag. Those who had stolen cash in their bags were escorted out of the back of the building through the showers. I never saw them again.

The scene was over as quickly as it had started. The officer returned to the center of the squad bay and told us that the rest of us were free to go. Our families stood stunned at the front door. "That's all, folks," he said.

I attempted to rearrange my belongings in my sea bag. *What have I just witnessed?* I thought. My world shaken. "We're Marines now," I muttered. "They shouldn't treat us like this."

Gomez, the Marine next to me, nodded in agreement. "What happened to everything we just went through?" he asked. "Marines don't lie, cheat, or steal; we treat each other with customs and courtesy. What was that? Was that all bullshit?"

"Were those Marines stealing from us?" I asked, the thought more absurd than I wanted to admit.

"Were our Drill Instructors?" Gomez added. "They had all of our debit cards."

"We had to turn in all our PINs to the guide, remember?" I shot back.

"I don't know, man; I guess so," he said, his voice hollow. "Let's just grab our things and get out of here, man." I nodded, finished grabbing my items, and met my confused family outside the squad bay.

No one ever gave an explanation, but after checking my bank account, I was a thousand dollars short.

## Camp Pendleton

Ten days later, I was hitching a ride from a boot camp buddy, sporting a freshly inked USMC tattoo on my left forearm. I passed through the Basilone Gate on the northern edge of Camp Pendleton, near the laid-back surf town of San Clemente.

Dressed in the olive drab, wool military equivalent of a business suit called "service alphas," I stood with my two sea bags, a garment bag, and a black plastic folder issued to safeguard my essential documents as I awaited my in-processing at the School of Infantry.

A handful of Recruit Training students had opted for the Military Occupational Specialty (MOS) 0300 infantry designation. We gathered near a half-broken A-frame sign with a faded message: INFANTRY TRAINING BATTALION—CHECK-IN—THIS WAY.

A buddy and I approached a bored-looking Corporal stationed at a desk and handed over our paperwork. Without looking up, he barked, "Go sit on your gear on the rocks outside."

"Uh, sir—er, Corporal—would you like our documents?" I stammered, trying to shake off the lingering habits of boot camp.

"I said, go sit on your shit outside!" he yelled, sharp enough to make us reel back out of instinct. Without another word, we pivoted and exited. Outside, we found our bags, sat down, and waited. And waited. And waited.

For hours, we sat, waiting and watching as more and more young Marines shuffled into the gravel lot, destined to suffer the same fate.

As the cool coastal evening fog hovered, the Corporal approached the now shivering group of Marines waiting on the rocks. "Get in a single file line by last name and make your way through processing," he ordered with a lazy gesture toward the doors behind him. My buddies and I shared glances—we had been through this dance before.

We slogged through in-briefs, rack assignments, and the breakdown into training companies. Corporals, who tried to emulate Drill Instructors but lacked both the authority and the conviction, wormed us through the rest of the evening's process. We'd meet our Combat Instructors tomorrow, but we had to get through tonight first.

As dawn broke, a scratchy recording of a bugle call, "Reveille," blared from strained speakers across the camp. This roused the barely rested Marines, who had only climbed into our racks a few hours earlier. We scrambled to dress, grab chow, and prepare for our first class—all within the next two hours.

Seated in a large, state-of-the-art indoor auditorium, the 120 Marines of Delta Company met their new chain of command and, more importantly, their Combat Instructors. These men were to the infantry what the Drill Instructors were to the Marine Corps. Guardians and guides. They were the keepers of the infantry legacy and were expected to take their jobs seriously.

After the initial brief, we broke into platoons to meet our instructors. Our platoon's cadre comprised two Corporals, one Sergeant, and a Staff Sergeant tasked with preparing us to deploy to the looming war in Iraq.

Something felt distinctly different from Recruit Training, not just the expected shift away from close-order drill. There was a significant, yet less tangible, change in tone. While our Drill Instructors, overzealous and often harsh in their methods, had demonstrated a genuine sense of purpose and care in transforming us into Marines, our Combat Instructors appeared, at best, detached.

If Recruit Training had been defined by constant yelling and endless marching, the School of Infantry was marked by cold indifference and grueling "humps" with a loaded pack.

We found ourselves plugged into the "Lance Corporal Underground," a nebulous rumor mill full of *sea lawyers* and young know-it-alls with no real beginning or end. At the time, the Marine Corps lacked a formal training curriculum or selection process for Combat Instructors. Viewed as a lesser role than Drill Instructors, there were no specific criteria for the position.

Compounding the issue, the Schools of Infantry were chronically understaffed and relied on loaned-out instructors, nearing the end of their enlistments, from nearby units. Many loaner instructors lacked the motivation or expertise to excel in the role. With rare exceptions, they seldom sent their best. "Doesn't matter anyway," our underground informant explained to us. "We're just a number; they don't care about us; they'll just make more of us bullet sponges."

Our training cycle lasted eight weeks. During this time, we learned the fundamentals of our new infantry roles: mastering rifles, machine guns, grenade launchers, mines, field craft, patrolling, and offensive and defensive tactics. Initially, everyone trained together, but midway through the cycle, we branched into specialized assignments: Rifleman, Machine Gunner, Assaultman, Mortarman, or Missileman. I was determined to become a Rifleman like my recruiter, Staff Sergeant Tinay.

Our days were consumed in overcrowded classrooms. Hundreds of students were packed into an oppressive, sterile auditorium of concrete floors filled only with unforgiving plastic seats. A Combat Instructor began each session with a rehearsed pitch about the topic and his teaching approach before launching into a two- to three-hour lecture. The presentation, delivered through an endless stream of PowerPoint slides, was met with blank stares from an audience in various stages of consciousness. This method, the so-called "informal lecture," became its own unique form of torment—a misery we dubbed "death by PowerPoint."

The Marine next to me leaned in, frustration evident in his voice. "What's with all this classroom and PowerPoint crap?" he muttered. "I thought we were preparing for war. We should be doing the job, not just reading about it on a slide."

I snickered in agreement. "Yeah, man, this is not what I thought grunt life would be like."

"I'm Ross Smith, but everyone calls me Smitty. I'm from Michigan. You?" he asked quietly.

"AJ Pasciuti, from NorCal. No one really knows how to pronounce my name," I chuckled.

"Pascweeti?" he attempted, his face twisting in confusion.

"No, Pa-shoo-tee," I corrected, barely holding back a laugh.

"Good to meet ya, Pa-shoo-tee," he said with a snort that caught the instructor's attention.

## The School of Infantry

Learning to be a grunt wasn't all that different from learning to be a Boy Scout: You started with the basics, gradually layered on more complex skills, and then applied them in scenarios requiring creativity and practical execution. The difference, of course, was in the nature of the instruction—and the grenade launchers.

After classroom lectures, our platoons marched in large formations to the dusty training areas on the northern side of Camp Pendleton. Walking in columns of two along dirt roads, we eventually arrived at brown barren patches of worn earth, where we staged our gear in neat rows. It was always dirt. Unless it rained, in which case it was mud. There was no avoiding it; dirt and sweat became part of the daily routine—we learned to love it.

As grunts, we were expected to carry our lives on our backs. Not just a task; it became a way of life. While Recruit Training used close-order drill to instill attention to detail, teamwork, and camaraderie, the School of Infantry had its own tools for delivering infantry life lessons: a weighted pack and a machine gun. Simple, brutal, and effective.

You learn a lot about yourself when you're hauling a fifty-five-pound rucksack, wearing an additional twenty-five pounds of combat gear, and lugging the twenty-five pound M240G 7.62mm medium machine gun straight up the aptly named Mt. Motherfucker. On these forced marches, or "humps," two hard truths emerge: The pack never gets lighter, and complaining wouldn't make the mountain smaller. So, you embraced the suck, kept pushing, and learned to suffer in silence.

Once we arrived at our range for the day, our platoons would sit on our packs in the sun, waiting, much like we did on that first day, patiently biding our time for our turn to perform the task we had learned earlier in the classroom.

"Stand by for your safety brief!" A salty Combat Instructor yelled and beckoned us to gather around. "Today, you're going to throw a live M67 high explosive fragmentation grenade," the instructor announced. "You've had the class, and now it's time for the practical application portion of your instruction."

Like kids at an amusement park, we lined up single file, a column stretching 120 Marines deep, ready for what felt like the "grenade ride." One by one, we entered a concrete-walled pit to face the instructor. With the same monotone delivery we had heard all morning, he recited the rehearsed commands: "Thumb clip, pull pin, prepare to throw, throw." It was functional and effective, but the instructor showed no engagement, as he had recited this for the thousandth time.

The School of Infantry operated like a well-oiled machine. It was a rigid and efficient system built for scale, designed to move Marines through training events while emphasizing only task completion. We were processed, not shaped. The system wasn't intended to invest in us as individuals but to move bodies through events: Attend the lecture, wait in line, complete the task, take the test, move on, repeat. It was functional and fast but created to meet the demands of wars based on attrition rather than precision. In that efficiency, something was lost. We were essential, yes—but only as tools. Interchangeable and invaluable. The deeper lessons—those that truly mattered—wouldn't come from a PowerPoint slide or a safety brief. They would come later—under fire, in situations where failure meant something permanent.

# 4

-----

# BOMBS OVER BAGHDAD

## Daywalker

20 December 2002 - 1600 - 3rd Battalion,
5th Marines Command Post, Camp Pendleton, CA

We drove up in an eight-passenger white "duty van." 3rd Battalion, 5th Marines, or as we learned to call it, 3/5, was one of the most famous infantry battalions in our Corps' history. From the trenches of the French hills in Belleau Wood to the rocky beaches of Okinawa, to the frozen mountains of Korea, to the sweltering jungles of Vietnam—3/5 was there. Always at the doormat to hell, always at the front, always the first to give her sons in service to America's mission. Three/Five was there. And now I was here.

I was about to face the next war. How would I react? How would I fare? How would I compare to the legions of men who had come before? Here I was, a kid, at the yellow-trimmed concrete footsteps of the home to one of the most famous units in our history. And I felt the weight of this history.

"Get off my grass!" a voice boomed above us from the second floor of the headquarters. "Hey, Marines! Stop—stop right there!" I stood frozen in an unfamiliar patch of grass, holding one of my sea bags and throwing one near my feet. "Who told you to put your bags on my grass?" the voice continued, searching for a target below.

Like leaping from a dropped grenade, our group scurried off the grass and into the nearby concrete walkway that would become our home for the impending ass-chewing. We heard the voice of our attacker echo as it spiraled down his hallway, down the stairs, and boomed out of the front door of the building toward us. We snapped to a familiar pose, frozen in fear.

"Who is in charge here?" he demanded. No one said anything. The group looked at me. I panicked. My new rank gave me away. I remembered being so proud only a few hours before when I received my second meritorious promotion, this time to Lance Corporal as the honor graduate from the School of Infantry. Now, sheer horror was what that new rank gave to me—sacrificial lamb. I inched my hand up. The wolf snapped toward the movement and narrowed his eyes at me. That was the first time I met Sergeant Major Joe L. Vines. Standing well above six feet, with chiseled muscles, deep shadowed veins on his arms, and the deepest darkest skin I've ever seen, topped with a screaming black high and tight haircut. "The Daywalker," so-called because he resembled Wesley Snipes in the Blade series. His eyes locked in on mine. "What's your name?!" He barked.

"Private First Class, well er uh, no, Lance Corporal Pasciuti, sir," I rasped.

"Who told you to walk all over my grass?" He demanded.

"No one, First Sergeant." I blurted. Unable to discern the sea of black chevrons making up his rank insignia over the black and green of his crisp, starched fatigues. A cardinal sin.

"First Sergeant?!?" He scoffed as he leaped toward me. "First Sergeant—young man, don't they teach you boys rank structure in recruit training?!?" Shaking his head in disgust, now face-to-face. "Get back in formation," he roared, and I fell back in line, safe from actual harm.

"Gentlemen, I am Sergeant Major Joe L. Vines," he paused. "Your Battalion Sergeant Major." He sneered. "We are a unit of discipline, and discipline will bring us success on the battlefield! You'll hear more from me as you go through your brief, so I'll let this young Sergeant finish checking you into the unit and take things from here. Remember, discipline requires obedience; do not do anything unless you're told," he commanded before pivoting away.

Our herd shuffled through the rest of the process relatively unharmed. I walked down one final hallway. The Sergeant pointed me to a door marked "India Co. Office." I sat on a red bench labeled "hot seat." My stiff wool service alphas rubbed into my thighs as my elastic shirt stays, meant to keep my shirt tucked in, pulled dozens of leg hairs from my skin, with my familiar black documents bag on my lap.

"Pas-sci-uti," an authoritative voice snapped. I bolted to my feet and awaited my next orders. Walking out into the hallway to meet me was the Sergeant who had guided me through the check-in process, "Welcome to India Co. This is your Platoon Sergeant, Staff Sergeant Gonzales; you're with 1st Platoon." Gonzales sported a slender build, light olive skin, salamander eyes, and a crisp high and tight. He frowned as he eyed me up and down with disdain. He said nothing and handed me a stack of paperwork to fill out. Sipping coffee and chatting with the clerk, I overheard them discussing my assignment as I completed my paperwork. 1st Squad, 1st Fire Team.

The days blurred together as the five weeks of preparation for deployment ticked by, each mirroring the last. Under the watchful eye of Staff Sergeant Gonzales, 1st Platoon moved with discipline. His muted, authoritative presence loomed over us, a Marlboro Light perpetually dangling from his lips, even as we laced up for our daily runs. Rain or shine, gas masks or not, whether in "boots and utes" or slick PT gear, Gonzales set a punishing pace, his lit cigarette trailing smoke just before he crushed it under his polished black combat boot and growled for us to move out. "Okay, gents, let's go."

My Squad Leader, Sergeant Pryor, balanced the grueling physical regimen with a fair hand. His easy demeanor countered Gonzales's intensity. Sergeant Pryor was a good role model who never held it against me that I was new.

Then I met Corporal Olsen, my four-man fire Team Leader. A red-haired warrior, he carried the M16 with an M203 grenade launcher as I did. I shadowed his every move, a miniature version of him in weapons and equipment.

The hum of preparation became almost rhythmic, a drumbeat of weapons and gear inspections, packing and repacking gear, and running patrol formations until muscle memory took over. The monotony of the routine offered a strange comfort, numbing my mind to the daunting future ahead.

Five weeks later, our battalion unceremoniously loaded dozens of white charter school buses on a cold, dreary evening in a nondescript parking lot in front of our now-empty battalion headquarters building. Families stood stunned, not sure of what to expect. Bundled up, cold, and teary-eyed, they could only watch and wish for a different reality. The fervor and fever of a nation preparing for war was now personal.

Strangers came together, pulled from every corner of the country by the common thread of their young Marines. The suffocating weight of the unspoken fear pressed down on them as they formed clusters, exchanging phone numbers and email addresses with people they had just met. There was an urgency in how they spoke, a recognition that these bonds might be the only thing they would have left when they went home and their Marines went forward.

Each family took turns with their Marine, standing stiff under the dim parking lot lights for photos that felt more like rituals than memories. No one said it, but they all knew these could be their last images.

The air brakes of the buses hissed a mechanical sigh, breaking the murmur of goodbyes. Doors folded open, and the Marines and sailors climbed aboard. This wasn't just a goodbye—we were leaving for war.

IRAQ—KEY CITIES AND REGIONS

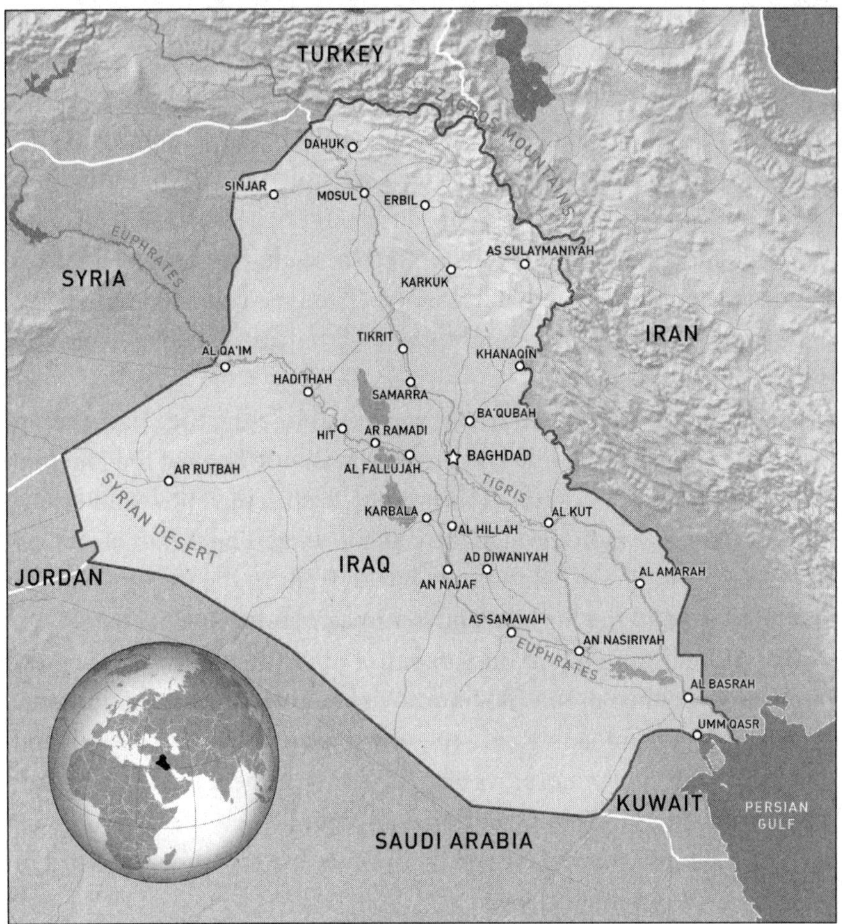


## Digging In

11 February 2003 - 0345 - Camp Doha, Kuwait

The sweltering wave of heat and the stench of jet fuel blasted our groggy platoon, now dressed in tan desert fatigues, as we walked down the exit ramp of the chartered commercial airliner onto the brightly lit tarmac. Like a small city in the middle of the desert, Camp Doha would receive almost all the forces staging in the region for the looming potential invasion.

Bright fluorescent lights shone brilliant white across the contrasting black desert. Stretching for miles, the airport operated like clockwork—landing areas were white, taxiways blue, and troop areas glowing a distinct muted orange. We unloaded our combat rucks within an hour of landing, each with one sea bag. We placed combat equipment and rifles in neat stacks as we assembled in two parallel lines, facing one another, to move our vast amount of gear.

We loaded onto ornately decorated local charter buses and drove to our first camp, where we unloaded. Then we reloaded onto a second set of white military-run buses, which drove us deeper into the darkening desert.

After another longer, quieter, and rougher ride, the sun began to break over our first Middle Eastern dawn. Gentle hues of red and pink emanated from the horizon, followed by flashes of yellow and orange darts as the sun fought through the cool morning. The flicker of civilization called softly from behind us, while in front us the vast open desert extended beyond the horizon and our imagination. North.

We pulled up to an endless expanse of white canvas, two-spired circus tents. Our platoon filed out to drone through our equipment's fourth and final unloading onto the soft, almost powdery Kuwaiti sand. The gentle hum of generators and the constant beeping from backup alarms on scurrying construction equipment filled the still morning air. Once we piled our gear neatly in rows, we stood by for word on where we would finally sleep.

Thirty minutes later, Staff Sergeant Gonzales gathered our Squad Leaders to review our racking plan. The large, hard-floored, expansive tents accommodated up to eighty Marines and provided essential shelter from the seasonal dust storms. 1st Platoon would occupy the left side of the tent. We rolled out our half-inch-thick foam mats on the cold plywood floors in a large U shape, leaving a communal area in the center. The following day, we began our preparations.

"Okay, gents," Staff Sergeant Gonzales began, taking a drag from the ever-present Marlboro Light and flicking the ashes down near his rifle. "We're packing our rucks and combat gear for a weeklong movement north. Our platoon is assigned to establish a defensive perimeter facing north at 'The Berm,' located in the middle of the division's lines. We move out tomorrow morning at 0800. It's a five-mile trek on foot, so drink plenty of water tonight."

The Berm was a wall of sand—fifteen feet high and twenty meters wide—marking the Iraqi-Kuwaiti border and separating two worlds. To the north lay the regime of a brutal autocrat, a landscape defined by desolation, despair, and martial law. To the south was Kuwait, a land of contrasting prosperity, civility, and opulence.

After a long sleepless night filled with anxiety, wonder, and multiple visits to the pisser, our platoon moved out in columns of two, loaded to the brim with a week's worth of supplies and entrenching equipment. We arrived at a nondescript tan piece of a plateau overlooking a second nondescript tan piece of plateau. "Okay, gents, Squad Leaders, set 'em in!" Staff Sergeant Gonzales shouted. Through rehearsed repetition, our platoon delineated our area of defense. Facing due north, we ensured our fighting positions created an interlocking field of fire, guaranteeing that any enemy unit who wandered in would receive maximum carnage. And then we dug.

We dug for hours, sweat streaking through the grime, with black aluminum entrenching tools carving "fighting holes" in the earth, each shovel stroke biting into the dry, unyielding sand. The positions had to be precise—six feet deep at a minimum, eight if the terrain allowed. Inside, the Marines sculpted shelves into the walls, not for comfort but for survival: grenade pits, water sumps, elbow rests, admin nooks, and, most important—firing positions.

Kuwait could be described with one word—dust. Dust wasn't just around us; it inhabited us. Dust lodged in the crevices of rifles. Dust accumulated on the hinges of our armored tracks. Dust ravaged the lenses of our old and worn-out PVS-7B night vision goggles. Dust wreaked havoc on engines—all of them. Dust gritted between our teeth with every bite and polluted our lungs with every breath. Dust wasn't just a temporary nuisance—it was a constant.

Each day felt as endless as the desert horizon stretching before us. Dig. Refine. Reinforce. Between shifts, we stood in our trenches, weapons ready, gazing at the nothingness of the beige canvas. The desert had a cruel way of magnifying its harshness. It reflected the sun's glare by day and drained the heat from our bones by night. Anticipation gave way to boredom and boredom to anxiety. The atmosphere was thick with tension and dread.

The only breaks in the monotony were the constant gas drills, random rehearsals for the nuclear, biological, and chemical attacks that felt almost imminent. These drills arrived without warning. "Gas, gas, gas!" pierced the routine with chaotic urgency. We donned our masks, passed the word down the line, and fumbled through rehearsals for a nightmare we prayed would never come: chemical warfare, sarin gas, oozing blisters, choking blood, adrenaline shots, nuclear scenarios—nightmare fuel. Yet the dust persisted.

### Selective Unmask

"Hey Pasciuti, put your gas mask on," Corporal Olsen said as he shook me awake. I was groggy from the one-hour sleep window our alternating watch allowed. Without hesitation, I yanked my mask from the Velcro pouch on my left thigh and slipped it over my face. Then, I rolled over and went back to sleep.

"No, Gunny, I won't!" A muffled shout nearby roused my attention, my eyes still closed.

"Give me your rifle, Marine." A second muffled voice, in an angry and booming tone, commanded.

Lying motionless on my side, I opened my eyes and witnessed two men standing outside their fighting holes, arguing. When low profiles and minimal movement were the norm, this was undeniably abnormal. One Marine stood with his back to his fighting hole after recently climbing out of it, while the other, larger Marine, loomed intimidatingly close to him. Gas mask canisters were on the front of their masks, nearly touching.

The two Marines were engaged in the grim ritual of selective unmasking—a harsh but necessary process that ensured our environment was free from contamination by nerve or blister agents. After we systematically reduced our protective equipment, the final and coldest step was for one randomly selected Marine to hand over his rifle, remove his mask, and breathe the air. If our canary in the coal mine was able to breathe and didn't die, then the troops knew the air was free from chemical agents—the all-clear was given.

"Gunny, I won't do it!" The smaller Marine, who had been selected to unmask, shouted back at the larger Marine. Using his right hand, the taller Marine grabbed the M16A2 service rifle from the younger Marine and then transferred it to his left hand to put the rifle behind his back. The younger Marine lunged forward to retrieve his rifle. The larger Marine stopped his desperate attempt to get his rifle back by planting the open palm of his right hand straight into the forehead of the smaller Marine. The larger Marine now had his hand cupped around the mask of the smaller Marine as he reeled back on his left leg and readied his next move. The kick from the larger Marine's combat boot struck the lower abdomen of the smaller Marine. He screamed as the Spartan-style kick sent him flying backward into his fighting hole. His body disappeared from my view as it crashed back down into his fighting hole with a heavy thud. I watched as the dust from the Spartan kick settled around the larger Marine's feet. He now stood alone with the M16 in his left hand and the gas mask he removed from the smaller Marine in his right hand.

"Who was that?" I asked Corporal Olsen.

"That's Gunny Jackson," he replied. "Don't fuck with Gunny Jackson."

## Combat Rehearsals

For the next four weeks, we cycled back and forth between our fighting positions on the front and our regiment's main camp, Camp Coyote, in Kuwait. Camp Coyote, near the central hub of the 1st Marine Division, bustled with constant activity—tanks, artillery, armored vehicles, satellite dishes—everything our division would need to cross "The Berm" and make its dash for Baghdad.

Our lives as grunts on the ground weren't too complex. We'd wake up, conduct our daily formation runs and calisthenics—most of the time in gas masks—and then head to chow. Showers weren't really a thing. We usually filled the rest of our days with one major training event, preparing us for what we'd most likely encounter once we crossed the berm.

Mass maneuver formations streaked across the Udari Range as hundreds of vehicles rehearsed delivering and unloading their infantry cargo. Rooster tails of dust filled the flat, desolate desert as the vehicles whipped through the sand in a single file line. On cue, they'd turn to face either the left or right flank, as if receiving fire from one side. Assault Amphibious Vehicles (AAV), which Marines called *tracks* because they drove using a tank-like tread instead of wheels—would pivot and confront the imaginary threat, providing ample space for one another and allowing the grunts in the back to spill out as soon as we stopped. Once halted, the vehicle commander would yell directions to our Squad and Team Leaders who would then relay them to us.

*Click, click, click*—the releasing hydraulic arms signaled that the one-ton armored ramp was moving, allowing for the deployment of anywhere from eighteen to twenty-four men. Once open, the troops would flow out in opposite directions, peeling around the side of the now-parked track. Aligning with one another, we would establish a "base of fire" and, with the help of the tracks, deliver an overwhelming barrage to stun our now-engaged enemy. Once in position, our commanders would decide our next moves and make specific calls for us to advance in various formations: staggered columns, wedges, ranger file, hammerhead left, and hammerhead right.

Back at Camp Coyote, all the days seemed to bleed into one. Commanders and troop leaders did their best to occupy our time, but there were only so many rehearsal drills or first aid classes one could handle in a day.

Most days were spent in our giant circus tent—waiting for word, or in my case, "working parties." As a junior Marine (or *boot* as we were called), my job was to do the unspeakable, all the work too arduous or disgusting for actual humans: filling endless sandbags, repeatedly cleaning our desolate camp, and worst of all—burning the shitters.

Plumes of thick black smoke wafted from the fifty-five-gallon barrels filled with human excrement and toilet paper, which we had doused in diesel and set aflame. Stirring with large metal poles or burning two-by-fours, our process was uncomplicated: Press play on the boom box, fill the barrel with diesel, light it on fire, endure the flames and smoke, and stir until the diesel burned off. We repeated this until we reduced the pile of waste to ash. Each barrel took hours to burn down, and dozens had to be torched daily. So all the boots had plenty of time to talk while Jimi Hendrix's "All Along the Watchtower" played—the only song that ever seemed to fit.

An old Navy term brought into Marine culture is "scuttlebutt." Originally used to describe a naval vessel's water fountain, the term evolved to refer to gossip, much like one would say, "heard it around the water cooler" in an office setting. We spent hours chatting. New guys from every unit in the 7,000-person camp would swap stories, trade whatever "intel" we had, and inadvertently spread rumors. "The Lance Corporal Underground" in the Marine Corps was strong, and it would've been foolish of commanders to believe it wasn't.

One rumor was so pervasive that it shook the entire 1st Marine Division. One smoke-filled afternoon, a Marine came running up to our group with some hot new "gouge" he desperately needed to share. "Jennifer Lopez," he huffed, now out of breath. "Jennifer," he wheezed, "Jennifer Lopez is dead—JLo is dead."

"What?" the group asked, confused by the urgency in his voice and the seriousness of his message.

"Like Jenny from the block?" one Marine corrected.

"Yeah, dude, I just heard it from another group. JLo is freaking dead, man!"

We were taken aback. How could this happen? Such an American icon had been removed from our lives, and none of us knew how. Because of our location, isolation from the world, and intelligence requirements that prevented outside communication, many of us went to war believing that one of America's finest talents was gone. The world seemed somehow different.

Back inside the massive white circus tent, boredom lingered as thick as the midday heat. Hundreds of troops lounged on thin foam mats or slumped in makeshift pallet chairs. We killed time playing cards while others reread the same old books. The air reeked of mildewed sweat and unwashed feet. The smell was embedded in the fabric of every piece of gear we owned. Fine particle "moondust" mingled with the constant haze of diesel exhaust wafting in from the generators outside.

A single boom box sat on a crate in the corner, providing our only escape. Its tinny, battery-powered speakers cycled through the same four CDs: the restless, drug-fueled lyrics of the Red Hot Chili Peppers' *Californication* and *By the Way*, the cinematic melancholy of the *Blow* soundtrack, and the raw, defiant energy of Audioslave's self-titled debut album. Played on an endless loop, these tracks became the soundtrack to our shared monotony as we awaited word to move out.

## The Talks

14 March 2003

"Okay, gents," Gonzales yelled, his head poking through the slit of our canvas tents as he entered, hard-soled boots knocking on the floorboards. "We've got a brief in an hour, on the other side of the camp." He continued, "Squad Leaders, get your men ready and in formation outside in fifteen minutes. Let's go!" He clapped his hands with the unmentioned sense of importance. This wasn't a standard formation; we were going somewhere different.

Crossing the expansive Camp Coyote took less time than usual. We headed toward the engineer and tank battalion locations and passed a newly deposited stack of supplies and equipment. Atop the arriving cargo sat dozens of bird cages, each filled with one pigeon. Sensing our distraction, Staff Sergeant Gonzales pressed us harder, in cadence, nearly at a run to our unknown destination.

Rounding one of our larger "chow tents," our platoon came to an uneasy halt, now standing in disbelief, as someone had assembled the 5,000 Marines and sailors of our regimental combat team. We moved like fish in an ocean to a made-up amphitheater in the sand. Fanned out at 270 degrees and filing back a hundred meters were lines scratched in the sand, each line identifying a unit. At center stage was one single M1A1 Abrams Tank. Like reasonable Marines, we ushered forward and found our patch of sand. "Sit, kneel, bend," echoed through the crowd as Marines from every unit fell into place for our brief.

General Conway, the top Marine in the country, climbed on top of the centered tank to deliver a speech that reminded us to maintain our humanity in the pending assault against the enemy. His fiery speech prepared us for our journey beyond "The Berm" and into Iraq. "Over your shoulders, Marines," General Conway said as he checked his watch. "Will be all of the might and firepower of Marine aviation." We then heard a rumbling off in the distance that grew louder and louder until it gave way to the roaring thunder of wave after wave of divisional air assets that flew right over our heads.

Aircraft of all varieties streaked just above us, creating our own private airshow. Troop transports, CH-53s, CH-46s, our famous and deadly AH-1 Cobra attack helicopters, UH-1 Huey squadrons, and our grand finale of air might, the F/A-18 Super Hornets and A/V-8 Harriers, all buzzed above us in a steady line. The display of raw air power drew cheers from the thousands of Marines.

That afternoon, we met our Division Commander, who spoke with a muted yet firm tone. He was not one to mince words. "My fine young men," General James Mattis, Commander of the 1st Marine Division, called us. "If you can't eat it, shoot it, or wear it, don't bring it." Then the General said, "Engage your mind, before you engage your weapon." His words reminded us of our duty to the innocent civilians of Iraq and, by extension, the United States. Finally, the General warned us, "Be the hunter, not the hunted."

That evening, each Marine in our 20,000-strong division was delivered an 8.5×11 letter emblazoned with the diamond-shaped insignia of the 1st Marine Division—a deep blue emblazoned with the red numeral 1. The red 1 was inscribed with GUADALCANAL in white, and the blue diamond background had five white stars, resembling the Southern Cross constellation under which the Battle of Guadalcanal took place.

The letter read:

*Commanding General's Message to All Hands*

*For decades, Saddam Hussein has tortured, imprisoned, raped, and murdered the Iraqi people; invaded neighboring countries without provocation; and threatened the world with weapons of mass destruction. The time has come to end his reign of terror. On your young shoulders rest the hopes of mankind.*

*When I give you the word, together we will cross the Line of Departure, close with those forces that choose to fight, and destroy them. Our fight is not with the Iraqi people, nor is it with members of the Iraqi army who choose to surrender. While we will move swiftly and aggressively against those who resist, we will treat all others with decency, demonstrating chivalry and soldierly compassion for people who have endured a lifetime under Saddam's oppression.*

*Chemical attacks, treachery, and the use of the innocent as human shields can be expected, as can unethical tactics. Take it all in stride. Be the hunter, not the hunted: Never allow your unit to be caught with its guard down. Use good judgment and act in the best interest of our Nation.*

*You are part of the world's most feared and trusted force. Engage your brain before you engage your weapon. Share your courage with each other as we enter the uncertain terrain north of the Line of Departure. Keep faith with your comrades on your left and right and Marine Air overhead. Fight with a happy heart and strong spirit.*

*For the mission's sake, our country's sake, and the sake of the men who carried the division's colors in past battles—who fought for life and never lost their nerve—carry out your mission and keep your honor clean. Demonstrate to the world that there is "No Better Friend, No Worse Enemy than a US Marine."*

*J. N. Mattis*
*Major General,*
*US Marines*
*Commanding*

Our division moved to our attack positions. The war was about to begin.

## The Reply

20 March 2003 - 1800
Assembly Area, Eastern Breach Site, Northern Kuwait

The desert sun hung low, casting long shadows across the horizon like a warning. Every instinct told us that war was approaching, yet no official announcement had been made. So, we continued to wait. Our hunger, like the boredom, gnawed at us; sharp aches grew as we carefully rationed our food, uncertain about when we would be resupplied. No one really spoke much about it; as we had learned early and often in our careers, complaining would change nothing.

1st Platoon gathered behind the hulking mass of the Assault Amphibious Vehicle. Ours had a name with a double meaning: the Higgins Boat. It was a nod to our driver, Lance Corporal Higgins, and to the boats of the same name that ferried Marines to foreign shores in World War II. Our new model boats were now enclosed with a protective roof, but the track unloaded troops as it did decades earlier by lowering a large steel ramp.

One Marine crouched by our small survival radio, which emitted a static-filled whine. The Marine cranked the handle until he tuned into a BBC broadcast. The words came over the radio, choppy but unmistakable: Our invasion was imminent. We shared glances among one another that acknowledged everything was about to change.

Soon after, the radios crackled, and the track engines fired up. We were moving out—north through the breach. The plan was straightforward: First Light Armored Recon (LAR) Battalion mounted in fast-strike Light Armored Vehicles, and Force Recon Marines in ruggedized Mercedes G-Wagons would scout and secure the breach. Behind them, 2nd Tank Battalion and 1st Engineers would clear the way, blasting through obstacles and creating a corridor. 1st LAR would hit hard and fast, catching any disoriented enemy units off guard, while the Abrams tanks, with their devastating 120mm main guns—the stuff of Iraqi nightmares—would deliver the final, crushing blows. It was a classic "hammer and anvil" tactic. The anvil was set, stunning and pinning down the enemy, while the hammer, already in motion, prepared to deliver the killing blow. Ultimately, the dynamic team destroyed twenty-seven Iraqi tanks and vehicles and killed over one hundred Iraqi soldiers.

Following in trace, our tracks roared north in a line, sand whipping in spirals behind us, plumes of dust and smoke marking our path. Like the spine of an ancient dragon, our convoy twisted and writhed across the desert night, racing toward "The Berm." Our first objective was the Rumaila Oil Fields. The name carried weight. Everyone knew what had happened there in 1991. Retreating Iraqi forces had torched the wells, turning the skies black with smoke for months. This wasn't just oil; it was a strategic artery; one Saddam couldn't be allowed to sever again.

Inside the troop compartment of our Assault Amphibious Vehicle track, the reality of being the new guy hit harder than ever. AAVs weren't built for comfort. Three narrow metal benches lined the interior, each topped with a thin piece of foam. Designed to carry a rifle squad of thirteen Marines with minimal gear, the space was cramped. Now packed for war with eighteen to twenty-four fully loaded Marines, the interior of the AAV was suffocating. Packs covered the exterior walls, containing everything we owned: sleeping systems, food, water, cold-weather gear, ammunition, and the vital extra pairs of socks.

We squirmed inside the cramped quarters, our backs pressed together, and legs tangled. There was no room to rest, and nothing to do but wait. When it came time to lower the exit ramp, we knew the drill: *Get out. Get on line. Make a decision.* Rush out fast, spread wide, rifles raised, and eyes scanning for threats. Form a line, find cover, anchor the base of fire, and decide how to hit back—all in seconds while the world spun in chaos. Until then, we rode in silence, swallowed by darkness, breathing dust.

As a boot—per usual—I was assigned the worst job: standing air sentry. While the others tried to wedge themselves into sleep, I stood atop the left bench, my shoulders and head exposed above the roof. I aimed my rifle outboard toward the vehicle's left side, gripping whatever piece of metal I could for balance as we lurched over the desert terrain. Next to me was Private First Class Charlie Graham, a tall, wiry Marine from Tampa, Florida. He had a nose that told a story, bent and crooked from years of hockey fights and a rough upbringing. He'd dropped out of college to join, and now here he was, another boot with a lousy job, waiting to see what other shit job came next.

Stars began to scatter across the expansive dark sky. I tilted my head back, searching for Orion. His belt gleamed above me over my right shoulder, pulling my thoughts somewhere distant, to a comfortable home, maybe, or the idea of it. Then, another light drew my attention. Three orange streaks sliced through the night, trailing northward. Moments later, the ground trembled with distant booms. Rocket-assisted projectiles—RAP rounds—fired by our artillery units shaped the battlefield ahead.

The opening salvo was followed by more. The sky filled with fire, streaks of light cutting through the darkness, each blast rolling across the desert like a violent eruption. Then came the faint glow of afterburners—dozens of them—etched against the black. Strike aircraft roared overhead, launching one of modern warfare's most extensive air campaigns.

Time blurred as streaks of light, punctuated by booms, appeared across the horizon. We had trained for this, and now it was happening. I watched it unfold—not in a classroom or training exercise, but in the desert, under the night sky—the same sky I had gazed at as a kid, dreaming of adventure. This was real, and I was part of it.

Bombs were falling over Baghdad.

"Crossing the berm!" I yelled into the darkness of the track below as we veered left, then right, grinding through loose desert dust. The track jolted through the gap without incident, leaving the boundary behind us. Fires burned nearby—just destroyed Iraqi tanks and armored vehicles laid in ruins motionless. Their smoldering cast an eerie glow through the dim green haze of my night vision goggles. The destruction transformed into bursts of light, flickering like broken phosphorescence. We were no longer in Kuwait. We had entered enemy territory.

Inside the track, the steady whine of the engine gave way to the sounds of preparation. Each Marine reached for his weapon, shifting it into "Condition 1." Rifles angled toward the deck, charging handles snapped back, bolts slid into place, and chambers filled with live rounds.

Grenadiers reached for their 40mm grenades with golden yellow tips, fingers tracing the familiar contours of the green casings in their pouches. One by one, the grenades clicked into the breeches of the M203 launchers with a solid, deliberate *thunk*.

The squad's movements were automatic, the muscle memory developed through hours of repetition. No words were necessary. Combat was no longer a concept; it was imminent.

Next to me on air sentry, Charlie Graham readied his M249 Squad Automatic Weapon, flipping open the feed tray and laying down a belt of ammunition—200 rounds, with every fifth one marked in red to identify it as a tracer round. The tray snapped shut with a click. His weapon was loaded, ready to spit fire into the night. Our squad was prepared. It was my turn next.

I grabbed my rifle and pulled the charging handle back with a swift jerk. The motion I had practiced thousands of times was supposed to be smooth and decisive. But something was wrong. The charging handle had stopped short. The bolt hadn't returned to its forward position—its return robbed by the grinding scratch of something in the chamber. My weapon was jammed.

"The dust," My heart sank, the realization hitting me. All the cleaning, all the time spent oiling and maintaining my weapon—it didn't matter. My rifle was jammed.

In a panic, my face shot up to meet Graham's eyes. He, too, noticed a distinctly different sound than a rifle going home on a full chamber. We locked eyes. Helpless, I pleaded with Graham directly to avoid the wrath of one of our senior Marines—a notoriously mean and short-tempered Southerner with a particular disdain for boots.

"No idea," Charlie Graham mouthed, shaking his head at me. He didn't have an answer. We both understood the stakes. My weapon wouldn't fire, and we were advancing toward the enemy. The thought of getting the attention of the mean-tempered Southerner crossed my mind, but he would turn my life into hell if I admitted my problem to him. The prospect of facing his wrath in the middle of the desert, in front of forty fellow Marines, felt worse than charging into battle against the Iraqi Army's 51st Mechanized Division with a jammed weapon.

I made my decision. I glided my fingers over the ejection port cover with a trembling hand. Then, with a gentle click, I closed it, concealing the evidence of my failure. I had been promoted from recruit training and was recognized as a high performer. The same had happened at the School of Infantry. Yet here I was, on my first deployment, my first actual combat operation, carrying a rifle that would not fire.

# 5

# THE MARCH UP

Hours later, Graham and I had my rifle back in working order and able to fire. We took the weapon apart during a break, cleared the jam, and put the rifle back together without drawing attention to ourselves. Thankfully, no one was the wiser.

Our track rolled north for five days along Highway 1 toward Baghdad. We made sporadic contact with the enemy. As planned, General Mattis's demanded pace proved to be too quick for the Iraqi army to react. The initial strike into Iraq, delivered through a decisive air campaign and targeted artillery, caused the Iraqi regulars to surrender at the sight of our advancing convoy.

First to fall were the Rumaila Oil Fields and the gas-oil separation plants, or GOSPs. The days blurred together, hours upon hours spent standing watch at the back of the track. For nearly eighteen hours a day, Charlie Graham and I faced the left side of the track, scanning the dusty horizon for any enemy movement that could slow us down. We stood under our combat load for hours, shifting our feet and knees as we sought reprieve from the weight while the rest of the squad idled below.

For hours, we talked about how and what we did before we joined and why we decided to leave to come here. We laughed and made jokes between full breaths of thick black diesel smoke from our track's exhaust, making the hours roll by more quickly. We were caked in dirt with half our faces black from soot, but we smiled anyway—we became inseparable.

The dust began to swirl.

OPERATION IRAQI FREEDOM, MARCH 20–29, 2003

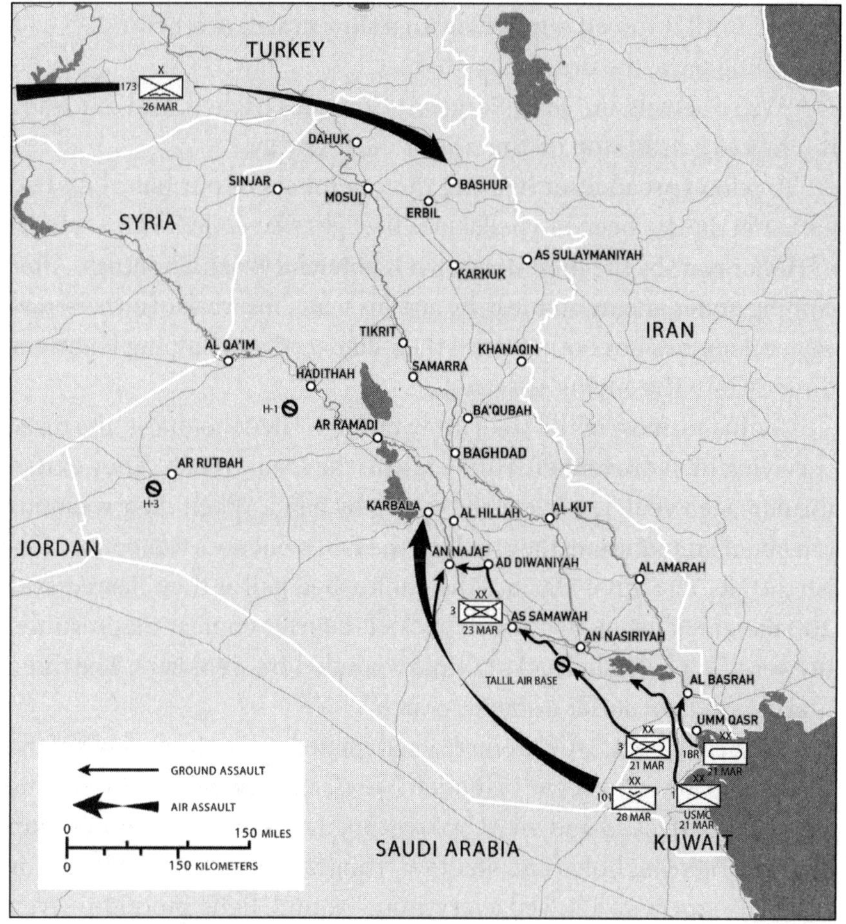

## Red Dawn

`25 March 2003 - 1200 - Highway 1, Ad Diwaniyah, Iraq`

I awoke in the cramped track as it motored along Highway 1, the few hours of stolen sleep fading as I lay still, eyes closed, trying to will myself back to sleep. Something was off. The air felt thicker, almost smothering. I opened my eyes to a dark haze of orange. Dust was everywhere—it consumed us and cloaked our world in a suffocating glow. As we rolled north toward Baghdad, the visibility reduced by the minute until it forced our convoy to a slow crawl. After five days of a punishing pace, the order came to halt.

"We're setting in," Staff Sergeant Gonzales barked, and our track lurched to a dead stop on the side of the highway.

Tension spread after hearing that members of our battalion had earlier in the day been in a hellacious firefight that ended with a "Medal of Honor run" by the then-unknown Lieutenant Brian Chontosh. After coming under enemy ambush, he and his team, in a rush of either bravery, recklessness, or both, turned their damaged and limping Humvees directly into the enemy's assault.

Confusing most of the Iraqi army through sheer boldness, the three surviving men drove their Humvee into the Iraqi trench. They exited the damaged vehicle to clear the trench by hand. When their weapons ran out of ammunition, they took up the fallen enemy's weapons to finish the job. The three Marines then unleashed hell as they cleared over 200 meters of an enemy trench in close-quarter combat that resulted in twenty enemy killed and multiple wounded Iraqi soldiers. The three Marines did not suffer a single scratch.

*Click, click, click.* 1st Platoon reacted immediately; the clicking of the track ramp lowering set us in motion like clockwork. Beneath a glowing sky thick with sand and wind, we wrapped rags around exposed skin and dug fighting holes and shallow "ranger graves" to huddle in for rest. The storm swallowed everything—sound, light, emotion—even our breath seemed muted against the constant roaring wind.

Shaky reports crackled over the radio net. An adjacent rifle company radioed that they could hear armored vehicles approaching their positions—danger close. The enemy tanks vibrated the ground as they approached the exposed infantry company, which had limited fire support because of the brooding storm. Quick to act, the battalion headquarters assembled a team of forward observers and air controllers to help direct fire and break the impending contact. Coalition air support and artillery worked together to identify and neutralize enemy threats through the limited range of available sensors, refusing to leave their fellow Marines stranded.

Artillery and mortar fire tore through the night for hours. High explosive and cluster munitions burst overhead, the canisters cracking open midair to scatter hundreds of smaller explosives. Sharp, rhythmic pops filled the air as their detonation unleashed a lethal swarm of violent shrapnel that ripped through anything and everything below. The nonstop barrage halted the advance of the enemy T-55 tanks and technical vehicles that moved along Highway 1.

Burying men and machines in the sand, the relentless storm raged on. Now tempered by the chaos of war, the entire 1st Marine Division stood motionless in their shallow fighting holes, enduring the futility of fighting against the inevitable. Then, as if summoned to finish what the sand could not, the rain began to fall.

For two days, the division was stalled. The most powerful military force on the planet, grinding its way through Iraq, was halted not by enemy resistance—but by nature itself. Days earlier, we had crossed the berm as Saddam's forces crumbled under our rapid advance. Now, nature had accomplished what every adversary the United States has ever faced had tried and failed to do—stop the advance of United States Marines.

OPERATION IRAQI FREEDOM, MARCH 29–MAY 1, 2003

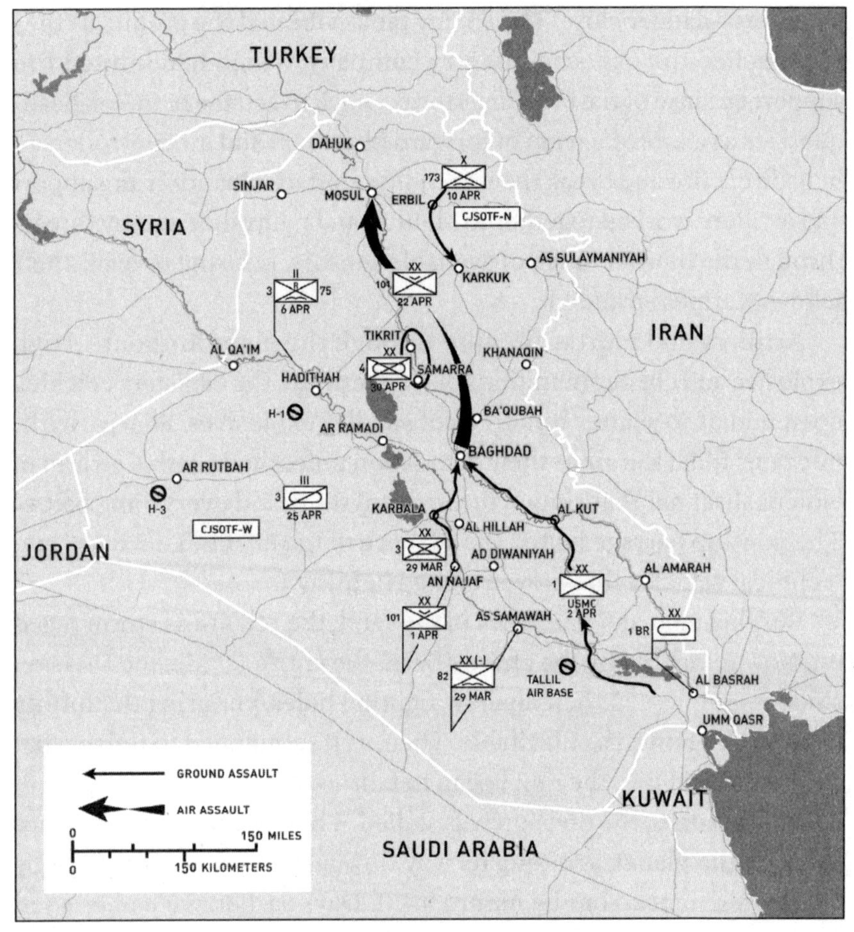


## Killing Fields

4 April 2003 - 0847 - Highway 1, Southern Iraq

Back in our tracks, roaring north, I was trying to sleep. My head rested on the buttstock of my inverted rifle. For once, I wasn't standing up on that damn bench as air sentry.

*Tink, tink, tink.* "Contact left!" Charlie Graham racked his Squad Automatic Weapon.

*Clack, clack.* Three bursts of five rounds ripped from his barrel—*brap, brap, brap.* The track turret jerked hard to the left; the Gunner dug his feet into the muted mint-green engine compartment for leverage. Grunting, he swung the turret and his body toward the target and depressed the trigger as he locked in. Rocket-Propelled Grenades (RPGs) streaked through the air. American .50 caliber machine guns fought back, hammering out a familiar rhythm. The RPGs detonated with loud, screeching thuds that sent shock waves through the reverberating metal. The constant *tink, tink, tink* of the bullets that struck our thinly armored vehicle filled the air. "We have to get out of this thing!" a voice yelled.

*Click, click, click.* The sound of the track's ramp lowering signaled its release. Sunlight and dust pierced through and swirled inside as it lowered. The air crystallized—fear, flies, adrenaline. Chaos.

The massive, matte green ramp, caked in months of desert grime, was our last barrier against the madness outside. It began to drop, and we shuffled forward inch by inch; the hydraulics groaned under our weight. Corporal Olsen leaned into it, one knee raised on the ramp, rifle at the ready, willing it to move faster. His shoulders rose and fell in a steady rhythm. He looked around, calm and sharp. The son of an LAPD SWAT Officer, he was born for this.

My wide eyes darted from man to man inside the track. Marines mixed hurried prayers with silent checks of their weapons. Some sipped water from their CamelBaks. The door reached just below level, and we poured out like a wave. The clang of our hard-soled boots struck the dense steel before giving way to the soft mud of the Iraqi soil.

Outside the dark cave of the track, the sun blazed high, blinding against the clear sky—broken only by the angry arcs of RPGs and the green and red tracer rounds. *Get out. Get on line. Make a decision.*

"Peel right!" Olsen shouted. We peeled right, moving as one, trained bodies navigating the chaos and fear. The mud, slick from the rain that had followed the sandstorm, grabbed my boots. I stumbled, crashing to the ground. My muzzle drove deep into the muck—my stomach dropping with it—plugging my barrel. I scrambled to my feet as the fight raged around me. My world was reduced to the crack of rounds, the smell of mud and oil, and the churn of men in the growing haze of smoke and dust.

From my knee, I looked up just in time to see two snipers from an adjacent track sprinting past. Crouched down to maintain a low profile, one carried a bolt-action rifle, while the other held an M16. Their eyes were narrowed, and their expressions fixed. Predators in their element, closing in on a chosen prey. Hunting.

One sniper veered left and angled himself near a ditch that paralleled the highway. He kept his profile low as he dropped a knee behind the cover of a crumbled wall. He was the shooter. Above the shooter's shoulder, just behind him, his spotter positioned himself in a way that looked like he was almost lying on top of him. The spotter oriented his binoculars on the battlefield below. Their target was the RPG position hammering our tracks. Its crew sheltered behind a makeshift berm. The spotter scanned the scene, observing the battlefield with precision. His free hand signaled toward the shooter's movement. The sniper positioned his rifle on a makeshift shooting platform formed by his buttpack and braced the rigid stock against his shoulder. He exhaled, slow and measured, his sights locked on the berm. A silhouette darted through a crack in the mud wall. A shot rang out. The RPG gunner was killed in an instant. With that chess piece off the board, our company was free to move.

I watched as the sniper cycled his bolt and ejected the spent casing into his hand. The shooter rose from his knees, ready to move. The sniper and his spotter did not stick around to celebrate; they were already on their way to their next position.

I followed close behind Olsen. When he dropped to the side of the road, I fell behind him. When he pressed himself into the dirt, I did the same. Olsen scanned the situation, trying to find direction in the thick gray haze. The rest of the squad fell neatly to his right and dropped individually. Pryor and Gonzales began discussing our plan of action. I frantically searched for something—anything—to clear my barrel. A stick, a rock. Nothing. Fear tightened my chest as the sounds of combat closed in: *tick, tick, pew, snap, snap*. Yelling. Chaos.

I fumbled with my cleaning kit, digging for the rods to fix my weapon. The squad moved. I looked down at the pieces from my cleaning kit scattered on the ground. My heart pounded. In a quick but clumsy scoop, I grabbed the pieces into my fist and ran after the squad. We sprinted toward a wadi—a shallow ditch that cut the road from the fields beyond. Down and in, slamming hard into the dirt walls as tracer rounds fractured the air overhead—*snap snap.*

Our tracks and tanks unleashed thundering combined-arms fire toward the enemy, which exploded in deafening bursts. The air was thick with smoke and heat, and each breath was a battle against the chaos.

My frantic hands worked to clear the mud from my barrel. The world blurred—the noise, the fear, the fire. At last, I broke free the blockage. "I'm up," I yelled to my squad as I sprinted forward, catching up as the sound of *snap snap snap* tore through the air.

"Contact front!" Sergeant Pryor's voice cut through the vortex. And then it began. Like unrestrained animals, we surged forward. Nearly 120 Marines stormed the berm to unleash a torrent of firepower. Standing, kneeling, and prone, we dug in. Our boot heels sank into the mud, bracing against the recoil as the dirt stiffened behind us. Fear evaporated. Chaos became clarity, and training gave way to rage.

Three rifle companies moved on line, assaulting forward with the full weight of the Marine Air-Ground Task Force roaring above. The Republican Guard—Saddam's elite—didn't stand a chance. Saddam may have chosen the location, but we set the rules—combined arms, precision strikes, the horns of a dilemma—a choice between two equally bad options.

This was what we were designed for—war on our terms. The vast field in front of us erupted as if the earth itself had decided to unleash its wrath. Behind us, the symphony of supporting arms roared to life. Fifty-caliber machine guns and 40mm grenade launchers fired in a synchronized rhythm, their operators working as our lives depended on them. Mortar crews in the distance initiated their calculated rain of destruction, interlocking fire on the enemy trenches as they zeroed in on their new objective.

Then came the artillery—no sound like it on earth. Too close to friendly troops to fire indiscriminately, the artillery crews and their forward observers had to be accurate—and they were. The first rounds screamed across the sky, tearing through the heavens with a haunting and unforgettable sound. They struck with surgical precision one after another, allowing the forward observer to adjust his readings. Satisfied with his corrections, the observer's voice cracked through the radio, a command as familiar as it was final: *"Fire for effect, over."* The distant booms of the artillery pieces thundered, followed by the unmistakable *wrrraaaaaccckkk* of shells ripping overhead.

Time seemed to warp—stretching and collapsing all at once. Soldiers often say that combat slows time, but that isn't entirely true. Sometimes, it slows, allowing you to see every detail in stark relief. Other times, it whizzes by in the flash of an instant, blurring events, people, and your sense of reality, almost making it feel as if it isn't even happening at all.

When the artillery rounds struck, the world shifted. In slow motion, I saw the projectiles hit the field, the earth buckling and cratering as if vomiting its own entrails. The explosion followed faster than I could process—fire tearing through the mud, a blur of heat, shattered colors, and fragments of earth twisting through the air like shrapnel from hell itself. The Marines surrounding me were screaming, their voices raw with a potent mix of fear and adrenaline—an experience unlike any I had known before. It was more than noise; it was visceral. It was primal.

"Hammerhead left!" The call echoed and passed through the line of Marines. Then, like the Roman legionaries of my ancestry, the patriots of my heritage, and every Marine who had ever set foot on hostile soil, we began our advance. In tight rank and file, we moved forward with purpose. Two platoons provided a punishing base of fire, pinning the Republican Guard, while command ordered our platoon—1st Platoon—to swing around and flank the enemy's left with our right. The plan was set. The assault had begun.

We were moving. Our squad fell in at the rear of the platoon. Charlie Graham and I held the tail. I felt the heat first—this bizarre, oppressive pressure—before the sound followed. *Woozt, woozt, woozt*. We hit the deck instantly as bullets sliced inches above us. A Soviet PKM machine gun had zeroed in; the unmistakable rhythm and sharp crack were distinctly non-American. Different from the deeper thrum of our 240G medium machine guns—it was a sound I'd come to recognize all too well over my career.

Dirt kicked up all around us. We scrambled for cover, hurling ourselves behind the berm, digging our helmets into the dirt, and facing each other. A gap separated us from the rest of our advancing squad. *Woozt, woozt, woozt*—the bullets chewed into the opposite side of the berm, inches from our heads—pinned down.

Panic weighed on my chest. I looked at Charlie, his face smeared with sweat and dirt. The nostrils of his battered nose flared with each breath he drew. A thick brown ring of grime caked his nose. The edges of his lips caked white with dried saliva; his apprehension was evident. Black sweat lines traced paths down his brow. He rolled onto his back to check for gunshot wounds; shoulders pressed hard against the berm. His chest heaved as he panted. We huddled together, time slowing, yelling over the noise as we tried to devise a plan, but the surrounding chaos drowned out everything. The PKM continued its ruthless barrage, the rounds chewing away at the deteriorating berm that shielded us. Fear took over—we were out of options.

A gap in the mortar and artillery fire barrages allowed the sky to clear. Unbeknownst to us, Staff Sergeant Gonzales recognized our predicament and noticed his split platoon slowing his advance. He got on the radio and devised a plan with the nearby Cobra Helicopters, circling and waiting for the command to strike.

With the plan in place and time running out for Graham and me, Gonzales lobbed a yellow smoke grenade into the field, marking the target and directing the Cobras' fire. Meanwhile, Graham and I provided suppressing fire trading volleys with the PKM's punishing bursts.

I rolled onto my back, slipping out of the PKM's line of fire just as the first Cobra gunship streaked over my left shoulder. Sleek and predatory, the Cobra prepared to strike. The heat from its engines poured over us as the two-bladed bird pelted us with dust, gaining thirty meters of altitude as it shot up above the fray before reaching its arch and tilting its nose down in anticipation. Its front cannon tracked left and right, the turret mirroring the pilot's head as he scanned for the target. Desperation—or maybe raw adrenaline—drove Charlie and me up the berm. We yelled, pointed frantically, fired tracers, and lobbed grenades from my launcher toward the enemy position, trying to direct the Cobra's strike.

*Vrrrrrt vrrrrrt vrrrrrt.* The front cannon roared to life. *Swoosh, swoosh, swoosh.* Hydra rockets tore from their pods, leaving bright white trails cutting across the blue sky before slamming into the PKM position.

Moments later, Dash 2 swept in, the second Cobra waiting in the wings. This one flew directly overhead, its nose-mounted machine gun already spinning and spitting its venom, raining hot brass and links onto the dirt around us. Explosions tore through the earth, cratering the ground and silencing the machine gun. The Cobra strafed the area, stitching it with devastating precision, ensuring nothing survived.

Charlie and I erupted in cheers, our fists pumping the air as adrenaline surged through us. Dash 1 circled back, the pilot surveying the destruction they had wrought upon the enemy trench. Nothing moved. The Cobras hovered over our shoulders for a moment, allowing us to regroup before moving forward.

Then, Dash 1 tilted, tipping its right wing as if nodding directly at us. No more than twenty meters above, the pilot saluted our squad before banking away, MARINES emblazoned in bold letters across the fuselage.

It was the kind of moment you never forget.

## Finishing the Flank

"Let's fucking go, Pasciuti!" Corporal Olsen yelled as Graham and I stared in disbelief at one another, snapping us back to the present. We caught up to Olsen and the squad, falling back into formation under the sharp edge of his voice. "What the fuck, Pasciuti?" It wasn't anger—it was something heavier, a mix of disappointment and care, the kind of tone that cut deeper than a reprimand. "Stay on my ass," he snapped, turning back to the fight. The aftermath of the Cobras' assault was unmistakable. The trench line ahead was a graveyard of smoldering craters, mangled weapons, and scattered remains. Green fatigues marked by a one-inch red triangle of Saddam's elite Republican Guard signified that we were in for a fight.

As the platoon pushed forward, finishing the flank, Olsen and I spotted enemy reinforcements—a squad of eight men sprinting toward the fight from an adjacent position. We dropped flat onto the edge of the berm. Everything sped up as we sighted in and discussed ranges, time threatening our element of surprise. "Grenades," Olsen said, already prepping his M203 Grenade Launcher affixed to his rifle. I followed suit, sliding a high explosive 40mm grenade into the breach. The distinct *thunk* of the grenade locking into place signaled I was ready. We opened our leaf sights in unison and sighted in, breathing wildly. "Three hundred," Olsen said.

"Roger," I replied, steadying my aim, mimicking his movement. Across the field, eight men ran, unaware of our positions and desperate to join the fight. Olsen fired first—*thunk*—and I followed a split second later, *thunk*. The grenades arced through the air like slow, lazy pop flies, tiny black dots against the horizon. We tracked them, breath held, and awaited impact as we watched the grenades fall slowly back to the ground.

The rounds landed with a crunch, the sound of the explosive round echoing across the flat field. The approaching enemy squad hit the dirt and opened fire in our general direction, spraying wildly. "Shit. Go three fifty," Olsen barked.

"Roger." *Thunk, thunk*. This time, the grenades found their mark. The advancing men moved directly into our volley and the fifteen-meter casualty radius of the 40mm grenades. Two of the eight crumpled. Unlike in the movies, the soldiers just collapsed, with no dramatic spins, flailing limbs, or end over ends, their lives extinguished in an instant.

The survivors dove onto a berm of their own and scrambled to take their last stand. With our ranges dialed in and their positions fixed, Olsen and I went to work. Methodically, we lobbed grenade after grenade, little golden eggs of death raining down on the trapped enemy. In desperation, they fought back with animal instinct, but Olsen and I had them cornered—their fate was sealed.

Olsen had trained me well, and I followed his lead without hesitation. We fired four more grenades each, the last volley leaving our barrels as the final two men broke and ran. The grenades landed at their feet. Their fight was over. Ours had only just begun.

## The Navy Cross

Gunfire erupted to our left—3rd Squad had made contact. Without hesitation, 2nd and 1st Squads sprinted in a line to reinforce, following a dirt path still flattened from the earlier artillery barrage. As we ran, we passed dozens of lifeless bodies in tattered green fatigues.

One of them moved—rolled from his stomach to his back. He'd taken rounds during 3rd Squad's pass but wasn't done. His hand reached for a weapon. I shouted something—though I don't remember what—panicked, and squeezed the trigger. Three shots. Center mass.

His body bucked hard, twisting and convulsing in pain. Desperate. His eyes snapped to the sky, then locked onto mine. Wide. Brown. Dying. There was no hatred in them—just confusion and fear. Almost pleading. No amount of training could've prepared me for that look.

Watching men collapse as Olsen and I struck from a distance with grenades felt surreal. Almost euphoric. But this—this was different.

This was raw. Personal. Up close. It wasn't a game. It wasn't a movie.

This was real. And it was awful.

"Let's go, Pasciuti!" someone yelled, snapping me back to the mission.

The thought of 3rd Squad pinned and alone drove us into an all-out run.

We hurried into position, getting on line to establish a base of fire. Ahead, I spotted 3rd Squad, led by Sergeant Nicanor Galvan—a short, stocky bulldog of a Marine with plenty of bark and one helluva bite, who had no patience for "soft-assed Californians." Galvan barked orders with his usual intensity as the squad directed fire toward a heavily fortified machine gun bunker that had them pinned.

The bunker's top was mostly sandbags and damp dirt visible from our position. Air support was unavailable, and artillery was too risky this close. 1st Platoon had to fend for itself.

Sergeant Galvan shouted to Lance Corporal Joseph Perez, their point man from Houston, Texas, who was closest to the enemy position. Perez was already lying flat on his belly, firing his M16, while a massive AT-4 rocket launcher strapped to his back made him an obvious target. Despite this, he continued exchanging gunfire with the position, desperate to buy time for the squad to maneuver.

Under the covering fire from our platoon, Perez rolled to his side. He yanked a grenade out of his pouch, pulled the pin, and shouted, "Frag out." With a skyhook shot, Perez launched the grenade into the bunker. The explosion shook the enemy's position, but Perez didn't stop.

He continued firing his M16A4, directing his squad's fire as they advanced. Then, with green tracers spitting around him, Perez stood and fired his AT-4 rocket into the bunker. The explosion obliterated the position, killing four enemy combatants and breaking their hold on our trench line.

As Perez moved to link up with 3rd Platoon on the left flank, a burst of enemy fire struck his torso and shoulder. The bullets spun him violently to his right side as he fell to the dirt. Dust puffed out of his flack vest where the bullets had entered.

"Corpsman, up," Sergeant Galvan shouted for our Navy medic as his squad echoed the call in a near roar, struggling to reach their fallen friend. Even while wounded, Perez directed the squad to take cover. He continued to provide accurate fire direction toward the enemy, enabling our squad to reorganize and eliminate any remaining resistance.

His actions enabled the platoon to break the enemy's grip on the position and seize control. Lance Corporal Perez didn't just hold the line that day—he defined it and lived to be awarded the Navy Cross.

## Spare Socks

With India Company's advance south through the field nearly complete and Lance Corporal Perez's MEDEVAC helicopter on the deck, the call came for us to withdraw immediately to the main area near our tracks on the highway.

Pockets of enemy resistance remained, harassing our movement throughout. As we neared the road, the ground shook beneath our boots. An entire artillery battalion had opened up—eighteen massive 155mm howitzers firing in unison. Each gun launched eight consecutive shells, each one nearly one hundred pounds, screaming through the sky and slamming into the earth with bone-rattling force.

The aftermath of the artillery barrage was grim. The trenches, vehicles, and bodies lay scattered, twisted where they fell, victims of the devastating "mixed" loads from our "shake and bake" missions. High explosive warheads combined with white phosphorus had obliterated everything in their wake.

White phosphorus, officially classified as a "marking" munition, was far more than that. The chemical ignited upon contact with oxygen, its sponge-like fragments burrowing into flesh and metal, burning uncontrollably. I was about to witness the human toll of what happened in combat when our munitions "marked their target."

The scene before me was the unsettling result. Men writhed in their final moments, their screams long faded. The ground was a patchwork of torn fabric, gauze, and blood—remnants of futile attempts to save one another. The air reeked of chemicals and charred flesh. The carnage was so fresh the flies hadn't yet settled in.

One body drew my attention. His uniform looked new, barely worn, but his lifeless, clouded eyes stared at the sky, almost gray. Dried blood and saliva framed his lips. A short, dark beard streaked with lines etched through the dirt on his face.

I didn't think about who he was, what he'd been, or the suffering he'd endured. It'd been forty days since my last shower, and my socks were disintegrating in my boots.

I needed his spare socks.

# 6

# “EVERY MAN IS IN CHARGE OF HIS OWN DESTINY”

## The Fall

May 2003 - Ad Diwaniyah, Southern Iraq

Our battle with the Republican Guard on April 4, 2003, was one of many our division fought during the march to capture Baghdad. As we pushed north, we fought at Al Kut, Hillah, Nasiriyah, and Najaf. Each fight felt fiercer than the last. As we moved closer to the Iraqi capital, many of Saddam’s loyalists fought to their deaths in a desperate resistance against coalition forces. Baghdad ultimately fell on April 15, 2003, only ten days after we had stormed the Republican Guard camp.

I struggled to understand the loyalty these men exhibited for the brutal reign of Saddam Hussein and his vile sons. It all seemed senseless to me that ordinary people, capable of reason, could sacrifice their lives for a leader who cared only for his self-image and power. What made his life more valuable than theirs?

In the end, their motives didn’t matter. If they chose to stand and fight, we fought through them. If they surrendered, we guaranteed their safe return to their homes. The choice was their own.

However, once Baghdad fell, it was as if the bayonet stuck in the Iraqi's back was removed, and the myth of the strongman fell apart. Freed from the dictator's threats, the Iraqi army dissolved overnight. Saddam, their leader, fled into the shadows until, months later, US Special Forces found him cowering in a hole and pulled him out.

In early May, President Bush stood on the deck of an aircraft carrier in front of a banner that read "Mission Accomplished." A triumphant message that would later prove to be embarrassing. America and her Marines believed the war had ended.

But it was only just beginning.

*June 2003*

*To my family,*

*Here I sit another lonesome night. As the world passes me by I sit...and wait. Wait for what, I don't know. My heart sits heavy in my chest. Full of sorrow and longing for what was.*

*Days seem to dwindle by, slowly wasting away. My mission is done, the war is won, the people are free. But what am I? Memories of home slowly fade into a mist of what used to be. Soon to be replaced with an unwanted vision of...*

*When I think of home, I miss the small memories. The touch of a hand, a smile from a loved one, a hello from a friend. In a world so full of people, I've never felt so alone. But I'll make it. I have to. So many people are counting on me. I will come home. I will make more memories for the ones lost before. My life will start again. I will pick up and start. I'll continue to love family. I will eventually leave this place, but this place will never leave me. Lessons, I've learned a few. Friends, I've lost them too. Growing up, needless to say, has already happened. Mountains, I've conquered; deserts, I've crossed. Life, I'm ready to live it.*

*I know now, in hindsight, what this war was for. Yesterday, an old man approached me as I was patrolling through the city of Diwaniyah. He came, obviously speaking a foreign tongue. As he drew closer, he opened his arms, still speaking to me, and grabbed me. I drew back, alarmed and angry, because he touched me as*

*I stepped back and I saw him sobbing. He then grabbed me and practically fell into my arms, hugging me. My translator quickly ran to my side to see what was going on. As the man continued to sob words into my shoulder, the translator processed the words, and then he started to cry. He said the man was so happy to see us. He said he'd been waiting for us for so long. "We were his saviors." As the translator told me this, I started to cry because I had finally realized what good we did. It hit me like one huge wave of emotion.*

*So there we were, three men on a busy street in a war-torn country, crying. The simple look on a hungry child's face is enough to make you lose your bearing and burst into tears. We have stopped that. Soon, children will not have to worry about hunger. We've done good. And I couldn't be prouder to not only say I was there, but I DID IT. I stopped all of that. I helped to bring that man to tears. This life has changed because of me. I've come to a realization as well. I came here to help these people, yes. But I can't help feeling greedy for what I've gotten out of this. If I could sum it all up in one word, it would be appreciation. My life will never be the same. War is not all bad. Well, let me rephrase. War is hell, I've been through it. But when wars are fought out of need and righteousness, the outcome is immeasurable. My only hope is that someday Americans will realize this. We have to endure hardships to reach happiness and good.*

*That being said...I'm out of words. My thoughts are on paper, and I feel good. Another day is done. You could look at it as another day closer to home. But I don't...Soon I hope...soon.*

*With all my love,*
*Amatangelo Pasciuti*

## A Fate Worse Than Death

Months before returning home, our rifle company faced a series of personnel changes. Combat replacement Marines filled the vacancies left by Marines whose contracts paused due to the war, creating an opening at headquarters.

I was sitting on my worn, sweat-stained green cot in the dusty squad bay of Ad Diwaniyah when one of the most feared men in the company walked in: Gunnery Sergeant Rickey Jackson.

Gunny Jackson was a formidable figure, an intense and intimidating man who commanded respect wherever he went. Born into the depths of poverty in southern Georgia, hardship and struggle marked his early life. The Marine Corps offered him a way out, a chance to transform his life.

Gunny Jackson looked as though he was forged from steel. His pecs, lats, and traps merged into his neck, which bulged as it brought the entirety of his muscle mass together. His presence alone held power. This was not someone who could be taken down. His existence was a testament not only to his physical prowess but also to the relentless drive and determination that propelled him from poverty into a position of leadership and strength.

As tough as any infantryman could be, Gunny Jackson embodied the spirit and resilience of a "Marine's Marine." His purposeful voice carried a thick Southern drawl reflecting his roots. When he spoke, people listened. The last time I saw Gunny, he had spartan-kicked a Marine into a hole.

"Pasciu–, Pasca–, ah, hell–P-shoot!" His voice shot through the squad bay like a grenade going off. "Where's this Lance Corporal P-shoot?" Conversations stopped. Every set of eyes turned to me.

"Aw, crap," I thought. The squad bay fell silent. "Yes, Gunny!" I shouted and jumped to my feet out of instinct.

"Well, get over here, Devil Dog!" His tone left little room for hesitation. I jumped over a cot and scrambled toward him.

"Yes, Gunnery Sergeant," I replied with my face level to his barrel of a chest.

"Where you from?" He barked down at me.

"Uh, uh…California," I stammered, unsure where this was headed.

"Up north, right? That place with all that silicone crap?"

"Uh, what? Oh, wait, Silicon Valley. Yes, Gunnery Sergeant," I said as I nodded my head.

"Good. That means you can type," he declared. "You're the new company clerk. Grab your shit and get it over to the Company Office. You're done with 1st Platoon." He snorted, turned his broad shoulders, and started to walk away.

"Uh, what, but Gunnery . . ." he snapped his head back and glared at me, not saying a word.

"That wasn't a request, Devil Dog," he said, flashing an almost sinister grin. I slunk back to my rack to pack my gear. No one uttered a word. I was exiled—marooned on an island of spreadsheets and daily rosters, betrayed by my ability to use a computer. My platoon mates avoided eye contact as if I had some kind of contagious admin virus. As if looking at me too long might land them behind a desk. I'd been sentenced to a non-combat role—a fate worse than death for an infantry Marine. My warfighting days were over.

### Return Home

After four additional months of stability operations across central Iraq and finally settling in a town called Al Diwaniyah, 3/5 was flagged to return home. As I boarded a strangely familiar chartered 747 on the tarmac at Kuwait International Airport, I looked out over the same hazy skyline that had welcomed me so many months earlier. I was leaving the Middle East; I would never be coming back.

3rd Battalion, 5th Marines, returned home from Iraq two years to the day after the attacks that had prompted so many of its Marines to enlist. Stepping back onto US soil was a surreal mix of relief, disbelief, and detachment. After months immersed in carnage, anger, and violence, you sort of become numb to it all. The suffering you witness no longer feels real; it becomes a distant, detached image as if you're watching a movie rather than standing face-to-face with human pain.

But now I was home, with time to reflect on everything I'd been through. Combat leaves its mark, often taking pieces of you that never return. Innocence, goodwill, and the belief in humanity's basic decency are stripped away, bit by bit. Returning to civilian life's normal rhythms after witnessing the worst of human nature is a jarring transition.

On one hand, you feel an overwhelming gratitude for being alive, a thirst for life, and a deep respect for its fragility. On the other hand, there's a sharp cynicism—a recognition of a shared humanity with your enemy and the bitter reality of killing or being killed. The brutality is overwhelming, and its logic is painfully simple: stimulus and response. There's no room for thought or emotion—only reaction.

We were conditioned to sharpen our instincts and respond faster and more decisively. When the time came, we executed with crushing efficiency. Close-up firefights, sniper shots, artillery barrages, and air strikes—we did our jobs. We dedicated ourselves to ending the lives of others and succeeded. And then we just came home. It was over.

## "We'll See"

Back at Camp Pendleton, CA, in October 2003, Lance Corporal Gregorio Sanchez and I were walking back to our desk job to finish some company paperwork when a flyer on the wall caught my eye. It read: "Scout Sniper INDOC—9 Feb. Meet at Pull-Up Bars at 0400."

In the Marine Corps, an INDOC—or indoctrination—was the initial step, essentially a tryout for a specialized role. In this case, it was for the Scout Sniper Program. At the top of the flyer was a crude sketch of the Grim Reaper, the unofficial mascot of the snipers.

Short, stocky, and a hard worker, Sanchez had endured the same fate as I had. Yanked from his rifle platoon and sentenced to clerical work by our company First Sergeant, we bonded over our shared resentment for our boss and the job, as well as our quiet desperation to escape it.

He pointed at the Reaper's skull and said, "Those guys are crazy."

"Yeah," I nodded in agreement, but seeing the flyer made me think back to the snipers I had encountered at the beginning of Operation Iraqi Freedom when we crossed the berm—how they floated above the battle. Going to war had been a transformative experience for me in 2003, but as I considered what lay ahead in 2004, I knew I couldn't stick it out behind a desk and remain off the battlefield. I made a mental note of the February start date of the INDOC. As Sanchez and I walked back to the office, I was already contemplating learning more about the sniper program.

Sanchez and I were filling out paperwork back at the office when Gunny Jackson walked in to check on us.

"Hey Gunny," Sanchez said, laughing, "Pasciuti wants to take the sniper INDOC!"

I shot a betrayed look at Sanchez and a frightened one toward Gunny Jackson.

"Oooh, is that so?" Gunny Jackson teased. "You want to do all that snooping and pooping stuff, all sneaky sneaky?"

Gunny Jackson and I couldn't have been more different. He was nearly two decades older than me, but like my high school teacher Mr. Rojas, he saw something in me.

Harsh and rough around the edges, Gunny wasn't the most emotionally available guy—but he played a crucial role in helping me process the weight of what happened in Iraq.

I had just turned nineteen. I'd fought in my first war. I'd taken my first life. And I had no idea how to carry it.

I was already suffering from what would eventually be called PTSD, though I didn't have the words for it then. Gunny was the only person I opened up to about it, and for some reason, I felt like I could be honest with him.

"Well, yeah, Gunny, I think I do," I said with a nervous smile. Gunny was one of the few people who didn't laugh or dismiss me when I told him about my dream of becoming a sniper.

"P-shoot, are you willing to do whatever it takes to follow your dream?"

"Yes, Gunnery Sergeant," I said. Jackson raised his right eyebrow, a mix of suspicion and intrigue in his expression—an emotion only a six-foot-tall, 240-pound Southerner with a tough upbringing could convey with such subtle menace.

"We'll see," he replied. "Meet me here tomorrow in green-on-green PT gear at 1100 sharp; from now until this INDOC of yours, your lunch hour is mine."

For the next four months, we worked out every single day. Whether on long trail runs or in the gym, I followed Gunny Jackson every day at lunch like a lost puppy. He lifted heavy weights; I lifted lighter weights. I wheezed behind him on long trail runs. He and his wife, a fiery Latina Marine whose tenacity was equal to Gunny Jackson's in every way, took me under their wings. Sprinting, lifting, vomiting, and more sprinting, the Jacksons had an interest not only in me as a Marine but also as a person. I was still little more than a boot, but Gunny didn't hold it over me. It was the first time I was treated as a human being in my career.

## Worthless

8 February 2004 - 2200 - Oceanside, CA

I tossed and turned in bed, unable to sleep. In six hours, at precisely 4 a.m., I was supposed to be standing in line for the Scout Sniper Platoon assessment and selection. Doing so would violate a direct order.

Forty-eight hours earlier, I had stood rigid at the position of attention, six feet from my company First Sergeant's desk, facing him. To my left, Gunnery Sergeant Rickey Jackson sat on the office couch, his sharp eyes on my face. The tension in the room was palpable as I made my case. The sniper INDOC was only two days away, and I was requesting permission to leave my office if I passed the selection.

The First Sergeant didn't share my enthusiasm. He cut me off mid-sentence, his nasal voice adopting the sharp tone of a yapping poodle. "You're my office bitch. If you go, who's going to be my bitch? You're staying the fuck here. Now, get out of my office."

Later in life, I understood that people often forget what you say but always remember how you made them feel. And that man made me feel worthless. My chest tightened.

"But First Sarge—" I tried again.

"I said dismissed, Motherfucker. Now get the fuck out of my office."

The weight of his words struck me like a punch to the gut. My dreams and months of preparation were shattered in an instant by a coward who had never taken a chance himself and was shielded from debate by a system that permitted only obedience.

Swallowing my frustration, I muttered the required farewell. "Good afternoon, First Sergeant," pivoted and left the tiny office. Jackson, silent throughout the entire exchange, didn't intervene. He just watched as I floundered alone—I was furious.

By Friday afternoon, as the office emptied, and the day faded into a chilly winter evening, I was left alone to close up. Jackson reappeared and gestured for me to sit in an old swivel chair before rolling one over for himself. "Don't speak," he said, raising a hand. He sat across from me, our knees nearly touching, carefully choosing his words.

After a moment, his sharp eyes locked onto mine. "P-shoot," he said, in a deliberate tone, "Every man is in charge of his own destiny." He let the words linger in the air before continuing. "If you're not here in this office on Monday morning, then I'll know where you're at." In a sense, he, too, was giving me an order, one he could not openly give: Disobey the First Sergeant and take charge of my destiny.

Monday morning at 7:30 a.m., my chair in the India Company office sat empty.

## Sniper INDOC

`9 February 2004 - 0400 - Camp San Mateo`

"Stand by for gear inspection!" A voice boomed in the dark, puffs of air rising from his frigid breath. Illuminated only by a dim headlamp, the grim Sergeant read a script from a laminated sheet of paper, now damp from the drizzle.

"Let's go—drop your shit!" another voice barked from the darkness. Like a pack of hyenas, the Scout Sniper Platoon circled the forty or so young men standing in a loose formation beneath the pull-up bars at Camp San Mateo inside Camp Pendleton.

In unison, the frantic group spread ponchos on the damp grass, unloading the contents of their freshly packed rucksacks onto them.

"Attention to detail, gentlemen," the voice read from his clipboard script. "As a Marine Scout Sniper, the smallest detail can mean your life. We're conducting a snap gear inspection to ensure everyone here has every item on the gear list. If you don't, you're out." Each item on the thirty-point gear list was held up to the glaring intersection of two Humvee headlights, their beams crossing through the misty darkness. No piece was too small to escape judgment—a single missing pair of earplugs was enough. Too afraid to move, we watched as seven frustrated men protested while they packed up their gear and walked away.

"Welcome to the Scout Sniper Platoon, INDOC!" The man with the clipboard spoke again. "Until we inform you otherwise, you will be under observation for assessment and selection into the Scout Sniper Platoon. If you are selected for the platoon, you will be trained as a PIG, which is what we call a Professionally Instructed Gunman—a sniper in training." He continued, "If you prove yourself as a PIG, you'll have a shot at sniper school to become a HOG—a Hunter of Gunmen. But first, you'll have to make it through this INDOC. Over the next five days, we will test you physically, mentally, and tactically to see if you have what it takes to become a member of our platoon. Remember, this is an all-volunteer platoon, and this assessment is no different. We will push you to your physical and mental limits while you remember three beautiful words that will make all the pain disappear: DOR—Drop On Request."

Three hours in, after two back-to-back physical fitness tests and enduring both physical and mental "training," the sun finally crept over the ridge, illuminating the misty valley in a fiery red glow. "On our way to the pool," the lead sniper called out. "The great equalizer."

Wait—pool?

Nobody said anything about swimming. I thought snipers needed steady hands, not gills. Sure, I'd spent weekends at California beaches, but that mostly involved boogie boards and sunburns—not combat swimming.

I was in over my head, out of my depth. And soon, quite literally, I'd be underwater.

"Let's go, keep it tight!" the lead sniper yelled as the roughly thirty men tread water in a tight box formation at the deep end of the frigid pool. Ninety minutes into our loosely "regulated" swim session, we began to lose men. Men typically quit in pairs. One would break, allowing the next man an easier exit by quitting with someone rather than alone.

Between swim drills, through the haze of churning water, I caught sight of an argument breaking out near the entrance to the pool deck. Two men were yelling, but their words were drowned out by the noise and splashing. Judging by the way everyone else scattered, they had to be high-ranking.

*Is that Gunny Jackson?!* I panicked at the thought—just as a random hand grabbed me and yanked me underwater. *Sharking*. A delightful little tradition in which a random hand drags you to the bottom of the pool mid-swim to test your composure.

I struggled and pulled, frantic to reach the surface, desperate for air, and eager to witness the unfolding scene. Gunny Jackson was nose-to-nose with our First Sergeant, now backing down from his attempt to pull me from the INDOC.

The realization hit me almost as hard as the random wave of water smacked into my face and throat. I went under, choked hard, and clamored to the surface, another hand grabbing me down, the light in my eyes beginning to fade. Then release. I darted for the surface and its precious air. Hacking furiously, my body sending visceral signals of flight through my veins—I was done. I swam for the wall. DOR.

Crawl after sluggish crawl, my hands reached the side wall of the pool deck. Like a sailor marooned on a foreign shore, I flopped my elbows blindly onto the concrete edge, panting as my heart roared. Upon opening my eyes and recognizing my surroundings, two desert-tan boots, sweat-stained and frayed after nearly a year in Iraq's punishing sand, confronted me. "I recognize those boots," I thought as my head shot up in fear.

"What are you doing on the side over here, P-shoot?" A stern and familiar voice questioned.

"I'm quitting, Gunny; I can't do it." My voice, heavy with shame, bounced off the water.

"Like hell you are, P-Shoot!" He crouched down, his eyes ablaze. "Look at me! Welcome to 'the suck,' P-Shoot! You asked for this! Now swim your little scrawny ass out there and finish what you started." He snorted something about "wasting his damn time" as he walked away. I swam back into the formation.

### The Scout Sniper Platoon

I didn't exactly shine during the INDOC, as I remained a solid 135 pounds at nineteen years old. My ruck run times were slow, I lacked land navigation skills, and my weapons knowledge was limited. This was playing out much like other tryouts I had encountered in my life. I was in way over my head, and I felt familiar walls closing in.

I had one bright spot on my résumé. Although I was smaller, slower, and different from the other guys, I came with high recommendations from my company. Gunny Jackson and my first fire team leader, Corporal Olsen, spoke to the platoon on my behalf. They described me as a phenomenal shot with the M203 grenade launcher, quick to learn, and possessed excellent field skills. They let me join the platoon as a PIG. But that was only the beginning.

Life in the Scout Sniper Platoon felt similar to the sniper INDOC—rough. PIG life is not a good place to be. While your friends in the line companies may revere you, the HOGs in your new Sniper Platoon act as your judges, juries, and executioners. A no-nonsense approach was the only acceptable demeanor. Above the doors was a quote from Hemingway, something about hunting men, paired with a large "Happy Hunting!" sign. We were here to perfect the craft of killing, and the HOGs of the Scout Sniper Platoon had mastered it. I had witnessed two of them in particular.

Corporal Blake Cole and Sergeant Jimmy Proudman were a tight partner pair. Blake embodied the witty, blunt, and near cavalier attitude of a Southern California surfer, complete with hair to match, although he actually hailed from the south side of Chicago. Jimmy was a red-haired, sunken-faced, steely-eyed hunter from South Texas with an unhealthy obsession with death metal music. They were the only familiar faces I recognized. Although they looked different, I remembered: These were the two snipers I had seen sprinting past at the Republican Guard training camp.

This was the team that inspired me to become a sniper, and they were like gods to me.

### The Awakening

America's insidious and disproven justifications for entering Iraq were overshadowed by the confusion surrounding our reasons for staying. By late 2003 and early 2004, unrest erupted from a tangled web of cultural misunderstandings, perceived disrespect, and the destabilization of Iraqi society following the invasion. For many Iraqis, particularly in Anbar, the disbandment of the Iraqi army represented a pivotal moment. The army, closely linked to the nation's identity, was a source of pride and a symbol of sovereignty. Many Iraqis viewed its dissolution as an act of humiliation, stripping Iraq of its self-respect and security.

Rising religious strife had further complicated the situation. The newly empowered Shia majority, long oppressed under Saddam's Sunni-dominated regime, sought vengeance, intensifying frustration among a population already angered by coalition actions. The lack of sufficient aid to restore a fractured government stood in stark contrast to the overwhelming aggression of American military forces. Without a clear geopolitical or military strategy in place, the shift from being seen as liberators to being viewed as occupiers happened swiftly, fueled by growing resentment among the local population.

Seizing the opportunity, Al-Qaeda capitalized on the instability, escalating the civil war. What started as the ousting of a dictator had devolved into a conflict fueled by sectarian hatred and foreign manipulation. America found itself again ensnared in an unwinnable war of its own making.

Geopolitics aside, I had seen their faces—the Iraqis whose lives we had helped to change for the better. I wasn't naive about the cost or complexity of it all, but I couldn't shake the memory of their hope. I was determined to do my part, to hold the line and protect the chance at a better future that we had fought to give them.

Through our last impossible war, the world learned how to defeat a superpower. And like that war, the enemy we faced now wouldn't be wearing uniforms or standing out in the open. Intelligence reports painted a grim picture—they were dug into abandoned civilian homes, forcing us to come to them. The fight had shifted—now it was on their terms.

It was not the first time Marines had gone from house to house and room to room to root out a dug-in enemy. The Battle of Hue City during the Vietnam War was one of the bloodiest urban battles in Marine Corps history, with over a month of brutal, close-quarters combat. Like Hue, this kind of street fighting drove casualty rates through the roof. The enemy had the advantage of concealment and time—they fortified positions, mined entryways, and turned bedrooms into machine gun nests. Entire city blocks became kill zones.

As a sniper in training, my job would be to slip into these same abandoned houses and find angles of overwatch for our troops. All while trying to avoid walking into a trap set by nearby Al-Qaeda fighters.

Before returning to Iraq, we needed to train for the type of urban door-to-door war we were about to fight. While we were able to keep up with basic skills in the lead-up to deployment with motorized patrols, live-fire ranges, and platoon assaults at Camp Pendleton, the base at the time lacked connected buildings in the form of a town for us to hone the close-quarters battle skills needed to raid houses and homes in a large city.

In the aftermath of Fallujah, the Marine Corps eventually built "combat towns" on base so this type of training could be integrated into the School of Infantry. But we couldn't wait. Instead, we headed to a movie studio in San Diego.

The lot had a mock main street set, which we used for urban training. Studios had retrofitted the buildings with Iraqi-style facades, complete with state-of-the-art pyrotechnics and Hollywood makeup artists who made simulated casualties look disturbingly real. Actors portrayed both Al-Qaeda fighters and Iraqi civilians.

We patrolled the streets of the movie set, interacting with men and women playing the roles of local Iraqis. Their reactions shifted depending on our behavior. If we were aggressive or disrespectful, they responded with anger and hostility—just like they might in a real-world scenario.

"Listen up, PIGs, we just got new word." Our Platoon Sergeant, Staff Sergeant Fritz Sleigher, a no-nonsense natural-born leader who didn't ask for respect but exuded it, briefed us on the situation in Iraq. His tone indicated that it wouldn't be good. "We've already been talking about the insurgency growing overseas for months," he began. "Our sister battalion, 2/4, is in the thick of it, and they're getting hit hard." He paused, "We've got a new threat on the battlefield—IEDs, improvised explosive devices. They're homemade bombs, and they've been tearing our guys apart. None of our vehicles have real armor, so we're wide open to these things. Fertilizer and fuel, old artillery shells, you name it, they're rigging it to blow. Remote detonation and pressure plates on the road—there's no single way to spot them. The enemy is only limited by their creativity and resources."

The room was dead silent; the implications sunk in. "Two/Four's already lost several guys to these damn things." He looked around the room, gauging the apprehension before delivering the next blow. "And if that wasn't bad enough, 2/4 just lost a sniper team. Ambushed. All four dead on a rooftop. We don't know what happened just yet. The enemy videotaped the bodies of the four Marines they killed and sent it out to the damn Associated Press. It looked like they were in a walled rooftop compound in Ramadi. When they missed their check-in, a quick reaction force was sent out to find them and found their bodies on the roof. This was the Sunni stronghold we have talked about. The insurgents took the team's kit. Scout Sniper Corporal Tommy Parker's sniper rifle was missing."

When I read his obituary, I learned that Tommy Parker had enlisted in the Marines right after high school, just like me. At his memorial, they spoke about how he had needed his parents' permission to join, since he was seventeen. The reverend said he was a hero not for how he died, but for his decision to serve. The photo tribute featured pictures of his two-year-old daughter, whom he had left behind in his hometown of Heber Springs, Arkansas.

**THE SUNNI TRIANGLE**

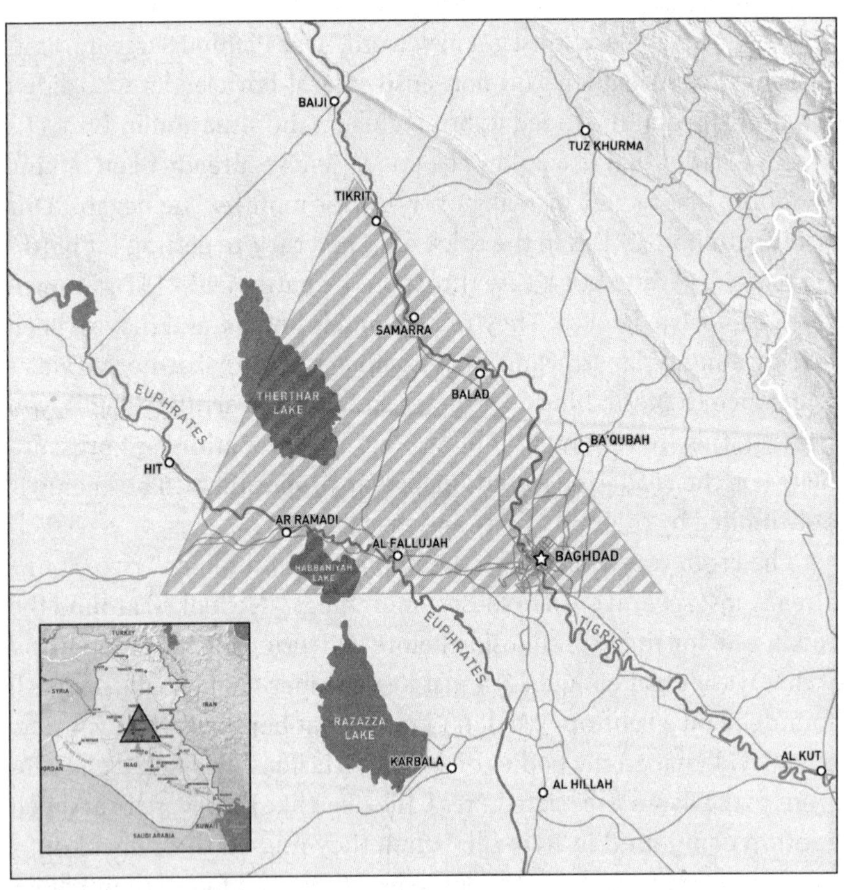


## PIG Life

Our infantry battalion received new orders. We were heading back. The insurgency had gained enough strength to warrant the reintroduction of combat troops, a calculated measure to stabilize the region and prevent the fragile democracy from descending into further chaos. Three/Five was en route to Fallujah—the heart of the newly designated "Sunni Triangle," a deadly nexus connecting Baghdad, Ramadi, and Fallujah, dominated by Al-Qaeda-aligned Sunni rebels.

The maps were unsettling, to say the least. The city ahead was roughly the size and scale of Jersey City, New Jersey—only with 250,000 to 300,000 civilians crammed into just fifteen square miles. It was a dense, tightly packed urban jungle—block after block of concrete, alleyways, multistory buildings, and narrow streets—all potential kill zones.

Rumors of a large-scale battle spread through the Lance Corporal Underground.

With deployment approaching and the sobering reality of returning to a mission we believed was over, our unit ramped up its training. Gone were the illusions of victory and the haze of post-war celebration. We faced a harsh truth: This wasn't the war's end. It was only the beginning. And this time, we wouldn't be fighting the remnants of the Iraqi army.

The Al-Qaeda network had embedded itself deep within the Iraqi conflict, exploiting the fractured alliances and sectarian strife that defined the landscape. Religious divisions poisoned negotiations and undermined fragile promises of cooperation among warring factions. Meanwhile, Al-Qaeda recruited zealots from across the globe—fighters eager to die for the chance to kill infidels and secure their place in paradise.

This new enemy was unlike anything we had faced before—ruthless, unyielding, and fanatical. Reports from the units deployed described drug-fueled firefights where insurgents, riddled with NATO rounds, would continue to charge, undeterred, driven by a near-supernatural resolve. For them, surrender wasn't an option. And for us, the knowledge of what awaited captured Marines—torture, mutilation, and beheading—meant surrender to them wasn't an option.

As the Sniper Platoon increased its pace to match the feverish vibe, I fell farther behind. I struggled in an environment that demanded nothing less than excellence. Being a Marine Scout Sniper left no room for mistakes and no tolerance for weakness, and it required a willingness to embrace immense suffering as a constant. Yet, my physical limitations kept me sidelined from opportunities, regardless of how much I tried to compensate for them.

I was always last—last in ruck runs, last in land navigation courses, last in daily PT. This automatically put me on everyone's radar, and not in a good way. My fieldcraft, marksmanship, communication, and reporting skills were on par with my peers, but none of that mattered. The stigma of being the runt stuck with me, an unshakable mark in a brotherhood that valued ruthlessness and precision above all else.

## Losing It All

In late June 2004, the day I had dreaded arrived. "Pasciuti, get in here!" Staff Sergeant Sleigher's voice echoed from the loft's stairs. I stood outside the building, waiting for my performance review board, the last chance to defend myself and avoid dismissal from the platoon. The administrative review felt more like a sentencing, and I knew this was my final opportunity to advocate for my place among the snipers.

I ran up the stairs, my eyes flicking toward the Hemingway quote stenciled on the wall. The words barely registered as tunnel vision took over. As I reached the ragged plywood floor above, the rickety wooden stairs creaked beneath my boots. Five Marines sat in judgment at a long table, expressionless. At the center was Staff Sergeant Sleigher. Among the Marines were Blake Cole and Jimmy Proudman, the snipers I had witnessed in Iraq. I felt the weight of their disappointment and hung my head in shame.

"Pasciuti, you're a smart kid, what's going on here?" Sleigher's voice cut through the tension.

I snapped to attention and responded, "I have no excuse, Staff Sergeant." I understood that attempting to explain would be seen as a weakness—a fatal flaw in this room.

"Don't give me that," he said, his voice abrupt. "You're comparable to the other PIGs in every metric except your physicality. You're last or nearly last in every physical domain we assess. Ruck runs, pool PT, all of it. You're a liability if you can't keep up. You understand that, right?"

I held my ground, silent—my lips pressed tight. There was no point in arguing. I knew this wasn't a conversation, but the conclusion of a decision already made.

"I have no excuse, Staff Sergeant. I really do want to be a sniper," I said, my voice steady despite the rising lump in my throat.

"I understand that Pasciuti," Sleigher replied, his tone softening. "But you're going to need to do more than just want it. As of today, we are releasing you from the Scout Sniper Platoon. You will be moving to Headquarters and Service Company—they need a new company clerk." My mind reeled as I blinked, refusing to believe what I had just heard.

"No, Staff Sergeant, please. Can I go back to India Company, back to the infantry?" I asked, my voice edging toward desperation.

"Unfortunately, no," he replied. "We have a position for your skills in Headquarters Company." My fate was sealed. I was out. Stripped of my dream, I was sent back to being a company clerk.

# 7

-----

# A NEW DAWN – FALLUJAH

### A Second Chance

13 August 2004 - 1630 - 3rd Battalion, 5th Marines Command Post, Camp Pendleton, CA

Losing the Sniper Platoon crushed me. The same damn thing that had always haunted me shattered my dreams of what I could be as a Marine: I wasn't big enough, and I wasn't strong enough. I was back in the Headquarters and Service Company office, even further from combat than when I was India Company's clerk. On the eve of what the Corps called our generation's Hue City, a fight promising to be brutal and historic, my role was reduced to paperwork.

A shadowy figure entered the door as I was cleaning the offices on a lazy Friday afternoon in August, before heading to the barracks for the weekend. Sergeant "Memo" Sandoval from the Scout Sniper Platoon approached me. We had known each other briefly while I was in the Sniper Platoon, and he was a recent transfer from the Marine Corps Shooting Team in Quantico, VA. He had joined our platoon and would lead Team Four—the general support team for the battalion—handling various tasks across the battalion's broad battle lines.

"Grab a seat, Pasciuti," Sandoval said as he pointed to a stained maroon swivel chair and indicated that I should sit down. "How are you doin', Bubba?"

"I'm doing okay . . ." I trailed off.

"We've got a unique opportunity I think you'll want to hear about," he said, pulling up another chair beside mine.

"What can I do to help?" I asked, trying not to sound too eager.

"We're bringing a lot of reconnaissance equipment on this deployment—cameras, computers, radios—and we're having difficulty managing it all."

My ears perked up. "How can I help?"

He leaned forward, his voice steady. "We want to bring you back to the platoon. On a probationary status, of course. You'd manage the tech and radios for us during the deployment. You'd be on my team—'Banshee 4.' We're general support, but you'd be part of the fight."

I stared back, expressionless, as I processed the unexpected request. *Back in? Could this be real?* My head spun.

"Think about it," he quipped, tapping his knees as he stood.

At the door, he turned back. "Monday morning 0700 at the sniper loft."

Somehow, I was back in. For once in my life, my Silicon Valley background was paying off. This was it. My last shot was to prove I could be something and make my mark as a Marine.

## The Gambit

`11 September 2004 - Camp Doha, Kuwait`

Orion hung low in the familiar night sky, greeting us as our battalion landed in Kuwait for the second time. It had been exactly one year since we returned home from Iraq and three years since the attacks that had changed everything. The date of our arrival was not lost on us. We had just said a second, more painful goodbye to our still-stunned families. During the flight, we felt a mix of determination and apprehension, realizing that this time, the fight would be even worse.

Through experience, I understood the human mind and body must undergo a metaphysical transformation to prepare for the carnage we were sure to face. This transition wasn't about becoming a soldier or a Marine but about returning to something more primal, something rooted in survival. Compassion and warmth fell away, replaced by a steeled focus. I thought of the wolf and its prey. *Does the wolf feel for the caribou calf in its jaws?* I asked myself.

We were good men sent to do bad things to worse people. The transition had started long before we left, creeping in during the weeks leading up to our departure. Each passing day chipped away at the person we were at home, carving out the animal we needed to become. The moment we landed in Kuwait, the change was complete. The hot, putrid stench of jet fuel and the harsh fluorescent glow of the reception lights on the tarmac served as a Pavlovian reminder that everything had changed. We were here to kill or be killed. Nothing more existed. Our minds and souls hardened to the horror we would undoubtedly face; we had transformed into predators once more.

## The Camp

Uday and Qusay Hussein, Saddam Hussein's sons, had claimed a sprawling vacation community on the shores of an artificial lake near Fallujah. Lined with date palms and covered bridges, it was purpose-built to be a retreat where Saddam's ruling Ba'ath Party elite could escape Iraq's relentless heat. Instead, it had become a playground for two of the most sadistic men in the regime. Torture chambers and rape rooms were tucked among boat docks, go-kart tracks, and Ferris wheels.

By late 2003, Saddam's two sons had been found and killed. Coalition forces shifted from active combat to stability operations and the Army's 82nd Airborne turned the camp into a staging area. The site's strategic location made it an ideal hub, while larger troop bases were being built nearby. When the 1st Marine Division took control, it was renamed Camp Baharia and became the primary transit point for combat units preparing to assault the city.

The camp surrounded the lake with groups of small beige brick bungalows. Each bungalow housed four to eight Marines in its narrow quarters, the cramped space balanced by the simple comfort of having a solid roof overhead. The scene had an almost ethereal charm. The milky blue-green water, sourced from the Euphrates, shimmered in the sunlight and was framed by tall palms and well-kept paths that connected to the shore.

Marines made the most of their time. Letters home often included requests for baseball mitts or fishing gear, distracting the monotony between missions. The lake wasn't exactly bursting with fish, but catching them wasn't really the point. For many, it represented a small piece of something familiar. We caught a few, but no one dared to eat them. The stories of what the two brothers had done here were too vivid. It was said that bodies were dumped into the water by the dozens. The lake's beauty concealed an unsettling reminder of the place's past and why we told ourselves we were there. It was a chance at democracy for the fledgling government, so accustomed to the "steel" boot of autocratic rule.

By October, Baharia bustled with activity, a peculiar blend of preparation for brutal urban combat and the unnatural beauty of the surroundings. Marines cleaned weapons, checked gear, and rehearsed tactics against the backdrop of a paradise once designed for decadence and power—a strange purgatory before stepping into the inferno that awaited us in Fallujah.

## Politics of the Battlefield

The 1st Marine Division was back in Iraq and locked in on Fallujah. Months earlier, in April 2004, orders had come down to take the city after a shocking and brutal act of violence. Insurgents ambushed and killed four Blackwater private contractors, then set their mutilated bodies ablaze. Dragged through the streets, they were eventually hung from a bridge—a clear message to the world: The United States was not welcome in Fallujah.

Tensions in the region, already simmering, boiled over. Al-Qaeda operatives seized on the fallout from the prisoner abuse scandal at Abu Ghraib, a catastrophe of negligence and cruelty that devastated coalition efforts. The sadistic images from Abu Ghraib showed the world America at its worst. When leadership and discipline broke down, they gave way to juvenile boredom and a twisted hunger for dominance over others. The damage was irreversible. We were supposed to be the beacon on the hill—a shining example to the world. In one flash, all the good we had done was buried beneath the weight of those photos. The hearts and minds we had bled to win abandoned us overnight. A straight line could be drawn from the actions of the soldiers at Abu Ghraib to the hundreds of American flag-draped caskets that followed.

With an effective propaganda campaign, Al-Qaeda rallied support from across the Muslim world, turning Fallujah into a stronghold teeming with Islamic militants, "The Mujahideen." These fighters, driven by ideology and the promise of martyrdom, were determined to kill as many Americans as they could on their path to paradise.

Within days of the mutilation of the Blackwater contractors, hawkish politicians demanded immediate action—they wanted Fallujah taken. Senior Marine Commanders pushed back. Using lessons learned from Vietnam, the Marine Commanders argued for a more measured, sustained counterinsurgency campaign built on special operations, civilian engagement, and surgical strikes. They also warned that successfully clearing the city would require a significant increase in combat forces.

But their objections fell on deaf ears. While commanders urged restraint, politicians wanted blood. Under pressure from Washington, Marine leaders assembled a force of just 2,000 and moved to encircle and seize the city. The Marine Commander's only request: "Just don't pull us back."

The Marines hit hard and fast. The Mujahideen were caught off guard and were quickly overwhelmed. Marine snipers, supported by combined arms, stifled enemy movement. During the battle, a single sniper, Corporal Ethan Place, eliminated thirty-four enemy combatants, twenty-one on a single day. Adapting to the unemotional reality of combat, the sniper aimed not for the high-center chest—a traditional target—but for the pelvic girdle. The new tactic was a response to fighters often drugged with amphetamines to dull pain or fear, turning them into something like "terrorist zombies." Shots to the pelvis shattered mobility and caused massive blood loss, rendering the enemy incapable of continuing the fight. Corporal Place, the sniper who pioneered the technique in Fallujah, ensured each shot was lethal or at least left his targets immobile for follow-up shots.

Despite the Marines' initial success, the operation came to an abrupt halt. The same commanders who had cautioned against a rushed assault were now ordered to cease their attacks and withdraw. Reports of civilian casualties—many of which were exaggerated or entirely false, fueled by Al Jazeera's propaganda—triggered political backlash in Washington.

The American politicians who had demanded ruthless retribution suddenly lost their resolve. Swayed by media narratives and public pressure, they chose to end the offensive, lacking the courage to see it through.

The decision handed the Mujahideen an unearned victory, both strategic and symbolic. Fallujah remained under their control, and the withdrawal only bolstered the insurgency. The Marines would return, but the delay would come at a devastating cost. This retreat allowed insurgents from around the globe to pour into the city, strengthening its defenses and turning Fallujah into a more formidable and hostile stronghold. This decision guaranteed that the next battle would be bloodier, sealing the fate of hundreds of coalition forces in the inevitable struggle to reclaim the city.

## The Eve of Battle

`7 November 2004 - Camp Baharia, Iraq`

Pantera's "Walk" blared from four massive speakers bolted to the roof of an Army Psychological Warfare Humvee. Typically, those speakers blasted messages to break the enemy's resolve or influence the local population. Today, they were for us. The brutal bass riffs reverberated through the air, exciting every Marine as they worked in anxious silence. The tension from the weight of it all was electric. Charged energy coursed through every conversation, each ending with a firm handshake and a hug. "Good luck."

All of 3/5 seemed packed into a sprawling dirt lot, a chaotic scene of preparation. Thousands of Marines spread out their gear, checking and rechecking for final inspections. The rip and crackle of ammunition boxes being opened echoed off the hard-packed dirt. Riflemen tore open cardboard boxes, pulling out 5.56 green-tip rounds and stacking them in magazines. Nearby, machine gunners uncoiled belts of 7.62 ammunition from brown wooden crates, carefully threading them into feed trays. Heavy machine gunners loaded .50-caliber, armor-piercing along with high-explosive grenade rounds, the metallic clinks of the massive cartridges—their sheer weight a guarantee of destruction. Rockets and missiles followed, with anti-tank rounds and shoulder-fired "fire-and-forget" systems pulled from thick Styrofoam cases like weapons from another world.

The grenades came last. Each Marine was issued a combination of the four—fragmentation, incendiary, smoke, and non-lethal flash-bangs—for the unlucky civilians caught in the wrong place. Taped and placed into pouches with deliberate care, close at hand for when the inevitable chaos broke loose.

Radios beeped their shrill encrypted tones as operators darted between vehicles and tents, ensuring every frequency, crypto fill, and time sync was perfect. Those little gadgets were the lifeline of our operation, and every transmission was secure and untraceable.

Later that afternoon, the ground began to tremble—the first sign of the seventy-two-ton M1A1 Abrams tanks rolling into position at the front of our convoy. The deafening whine of their jet engines announced their arrival, guzzling gallons of JP-8 fuel and spewing a thick acidic exhaust that lingered in the air.

The tanks prowled with the arrogance of predators, daring anything to challenge them. Their hulking desert-tan frames boasted scaled reactive armor, exuding raw power—annihilation. Paired with patrolling infantry, the Abrams radiated menace, threatening overwhelming force and the fury of their 120mm main cannons. More than just weapons, they were a *promise* to the Mujahideen.

Metal music pulsed through the setting sun, sending energy waves through the lot. The heavy riffs sliced through the clouds of smoke from cigarettes and chewing tobacco. Around us, the arsenal of war lay stacked and ready, a raw force unmatched since Vietnam. The preparations were complete. Platoons posed for photos in front of their matte green Assault Amphibious Vehicles, aware these might be the last taken of them alive. The same tracks that had carried us to Baghdad eighteen months ago would now bring us straight into hell—again.

## SECOND BATTLE OF FALLUJAH, NOVEMBER 7, 2004–DECEMBER 23, 2004

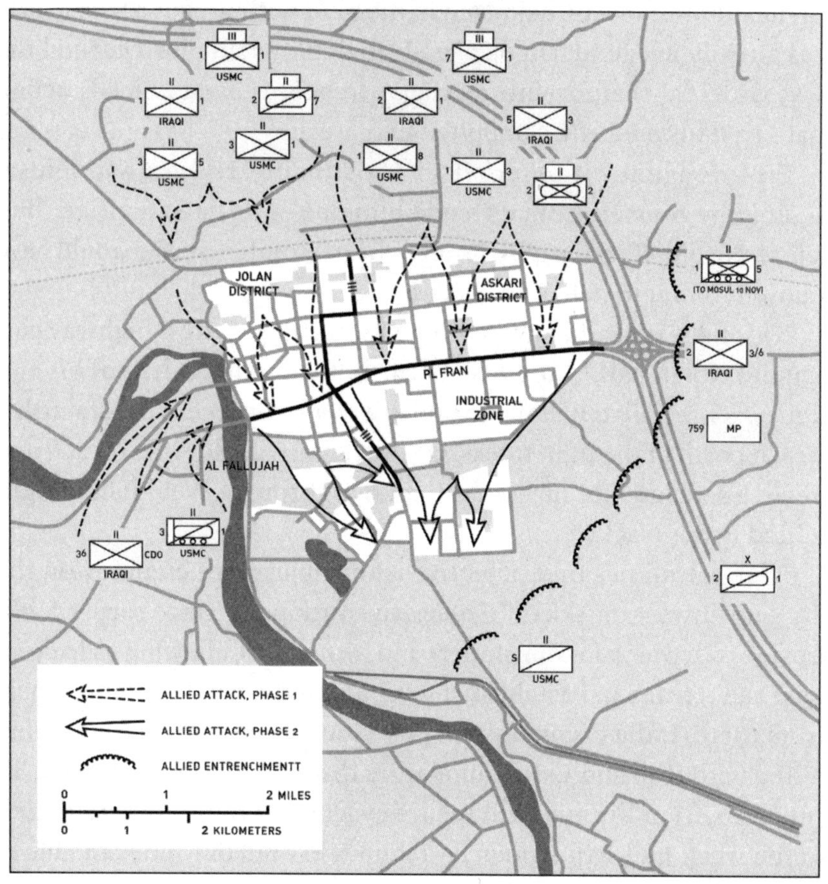

### The Final Brief

"Alright, gents. Light 'em up," Captain Brian Chontosh yelled, signaling the obligatory company huddle. One hundred and fifty Marines, sailors, Iraqi soldiers, interpreters, and journalists shuffled into a loose semicircle around him. Chontosh stood 6′2″, his balding white head caught the faint glow of a setting sun, his reddish-blond stubble giving him the look of a man who didn't have time for anything but his motto: physical discipline and mental toughness. Captain Chontosh wasn't just our commander; he was a leader, a Marine's Marine.

He was raw, unpolished, and exuded more "enlisted" than "officer" despite the rank on his chest. A lion of a man, always with a cigarette or a pinch of chewing tobacco tucked in the corner of his mouth. He carried himself like he belonged in the mud with us, not above us. He was already a legend. On our last Iraq deployment, he'd earned the Navy Cross for charging into an enemy trench, a chaotic, bloody action that saved his men and catapulted his career.

We loved him with every fiber of our being. His grit and refusal to separate himself from us made him one of us like no officer had before. He didn't just inspire loyalty—he personified it. We would have followed him into hell. And we did.

"Our fight is south, toward Route Fran, the east-west highway cutting the city in half," Chontosh began before taking a drag of his cigarette. "Three/Five will move under cover of darkness to establish a breach north of the train tracks. On order, we will blow the breach and create a safe lane for our tanks to punch through. We'll follow right behind in our tracks."

"Our battalion's first objective is the apartment complex on the city's northwest outskirts," Chontosh continued. "Once secured, it'll provide overwatch for our snipers and heavy guns, allowing us to dominate the terrain and establish a foothold in the northernmost block. From there, India Company will push south, house to house, moving online with Kilo and Lima Companies through the Jolan District. To the north, friendly units will secure evacuation routes for casualties. To the west, 1st Light Armor Battalion will hold our flank and block enemy reinforcements. To the east, 3/1 and the Army's 2nd Cavalry will push through the city's center. Everything south of us is Indian Country."

Commanders leaned over large maps; their alphanumeric grids illuminated by red-lensed flashlights. Platoons and squads studied smaller strip maps, yellow-coded to mark objectives, hazards, and targets.

"Remember, gents—violence and control. We'll meet back up once we hit Fran. Let's go get 'em." The sun sank low, its golden light fading into the final moments of what could be called normal. This was it. The following sunrise wouldn't bring calm but rage—rage for the slaughtered contractors, rage for the mess we'd made, rage for the duty we had to fix it. We weren't here to debate politics or question motives. We were here to fight.

This wasn't the America of polished speeches, thousand-dollar loafers, and endless committee hearings. That America wouldn't have dared to step foot here. This was the coalition—soldiers, sailors, airmen, Marines, and allies, all duty-bound by necessity, each man or woman relying on the other to stay alive. Backgrounds didn't matter. Rank, class, and money meant nothing. The only currency here was the ability to move, think, and fight as one.

Politicians started this war, but we were here to end it. We would set things right through bloodshed, carnage, and the unwavering resolve of America's Marines. The Iraqi people needed relief from the oppression of the insurgents. Our mission was clear: Take the city or die trying. The survival of Iraq and our brothers alongside us was all that mattered. Everything else was just noise.

Fallujah was ready. So were we. Two hours after sunset, the sky opened up with rain as the barrage began.

`7 November 2004`

*To my family,*

*Today, we go in. Later this afternoon, we'll load up and move toward our attack positions outside Fallujah. There is a feeling of mixed emotions in the air. A lot of the men are nervous but do their best to try and hide it. Some turn their fear into raw emotion, using it to heighten their senses and reactions. All the men are ready. All well-trained entities waiting for the call to answer. Today, we woke up knowing that this day would swing the war on terror and, in turn, change history. We are all honored to be part of such an event. Our only hope is that we are not forgotten. Our sacrifices and pain are not in vain.*

*I was told by a great man once that as long as the living carry on the memories of the ones lost, the lost will never truly die. Someday, someone will read about our endeavors and wonder why we did it. We do our job for the faint glimmer of hope that we give. We don't do this because we are war junkies by any means. Democracy gives freedom to the oppressed. It gives a chance to people with only their hearts to give. We do this for our hope. Someday, after this is all over, we will look back on our time and know. Know that we did the undesirable. We did the job that no one wanted to do. To give hope to the people no one wanted to help. When we look back at our lives, no matter what we become. We will know that we were a part of something great. We changed the world. If not for many, but for a few.*

*If we pass in this war-torn country, we will know that we did good and we died for something great. Freedom. I don't know what the future holds for me. If something should happen, I only hope my memories and morals live on.*

*To my family and friends. I love you, and I will carry your memories with me no matter where I go.*

*From the men of 3/5 Scout Snipers: Pray for us and let no one forget.*

*From me: I love you all.*

*Your son,*
*Amatangelo Pasciuti*

## The Apartments

8 November 2004 - 0800 - Northwest Fallujah, Iraq

*Crack, Crack, Crack.* Bullets whizzed by Memo and me as we bolted from the cover of a ditch near our battered, bullet-riddled Humvee. We sprinted toward a side stairwell on the far western edge of the apartment complex, desperate for actual cover from fire and higher ground. Kilo Company, leading the assault, had drawn concentrated fire, and the open street left us dangerously exposed. We were "Banshee 4," one-half of the general support team now attached to Kilo for the seizure of the apartments, and we had to move.

Since Memo had brought me back into the platoon, he hadn't just taken me under his wing; he'd politicked his way into making me his partner. I managed the platoon's communications and reconnaissance assets, and once the other teams were set, I was free to operate alongside him. Our unique role, assigned as general support across the battalion, granted us the freedom to maneuver anywhere in the battlespace where precision fire was needed.

*Snap, snap, snap.* A second burst kicked up dirt near my boots.

"Let's go, Bubba," Memo shouted. We needed to get to cover fast. As we scurried across the street, he transitioned from his M16 to the Benelli shotgun slung across his back, loaded with breaching rounds. Our way in was a rusted metal side door. A fire team of four men had just made entry—gunshots rang out moments later. We rushed past the fire team and their first enemy KIA (killed in action) and made our way upstairs.

We'd solved our first problem. Now came the next. Inside, the only light in the expansive complex came from a dim reflection of the sunlight on the stairwell. Long, empty hallways stretched in both directions—now dark from the cut power. The upper floors of the building were eerily quiet, and we didn't know if we were alone. Memo and I moved cautiously, stepping through the uneasy silence, weapons at the ready. The stairs gave us a straight shot to the upper floors, but every crunch of debris on the stone steps tightened my stomach.

Reaching the fourth floor, we picked an apartment overlooking a vast expanse of open dirt—empty and flat like a football field, stretching along the city's northern edge. I stared at the barren ground, and my heart sank. "Our guys have to cross that," I said. "They'll get picked off!" I whispered, fighting the urge to yell.

"Yeah, got it," Memo said under his breath, already scanning the windows. "Let's set up here."

"Okay, Pasciuti. You're in there. Your sectors of fire are south-southeast. You may see 3/1 and 2nd Cav on your far left," he said while crouched in the back of the room, surveying the now billowing city in front of us. The smoke from burning buildings obscured the muted rising sun in the cold, storming gray sky above.

"I'll take this room, south-southwest, and cover India and Lima's movement," he added.

"Roger, sounds good," I whispered. "What about security?"

"There's no time," Memo shot back.

## First Shots

It didn't take long for our first target to appear. The Mujahideen were scrambling, caught off guard by the division's near-total encirclement of the city. The precision strikes of aerial and indirect fire dismantled their command structure, and we cut off their reinforcements. Their communication networks were in shambles. The feint attack days earlier had lured them into reinforcing the wrong side of the city, leaving them scrambling to reposition on the north side. One by one, loitering aircraft and snipers like us eliminated those dashing through the open streets.

Movement caught Memo's eye at the far left of his field of view behind the scope on his M40A3 7.62 sniper rifle. It was subtle, just a shadow slipping into Memo's sector. "Hey, Pasciuti, did you catch that?" he asked.

"Yeah, I see him—behind the metal fence, right?" I replied from the next room in my own shooting position overlooking the city.

"Roger. He was moving through the courtyard. I've got him at about 400 meters. Looked like an AK. I've lost him behind the fence, though," I said, squinting at the rusted sheet metal fence that obscured my view.

"Yeah, I got him," Memo confirmed. "He's turkey-peeking, popping his head over the fence." A pause. "There he goes!" Memo shouted as the figure's AK-47 appeared above the wall, spitting rounds blindly into the field toward the apartments. "Here's the plan, Pasciuti," Memo instructed. "Aim six inches below the top of that metal fence where it meets the brick wall. When he pops up to fire again, I'll call it, and you'll take one well-aimed shot. Got it?"

"Got it," I replied as I positioned my massive rifle on a makeshift shooting platform made from a plastic dining table, now layered with thick blankets to provide the elevation I needed to stay seated behind the rifle and shoot over the edge of the external wall.

I exhaled, focusing my breath and mind on the designated spot. I didn't need to see the man to kill him, not with the weapon I held: the Barrett .50 Caliber Special Application Scoped Rifle (SASR). Typically, the SASR was meant to destroy light armored vehicles, penetrate bunkers, or even take down helicopters, but its capacity for destruction wasn't limited to materials.

The ten-round external box magazine I was using was loaded with one of the most terrifying bullets in the United States inventory: Raufoss rounds—armor-piercing incendiary bullets designed to melt through metal and detonate inside troop compartments. These terrifying projectiles were engineered to penetrate armor. Their copper jackets, crushed on impact, would ignite a classified mixture of explosives and zirconium powder. The resulting reaction melted through metal, followed by a hardened tungsten core penetrator designed to punch through the molten wreckage and devastate whatever lay inside—inflicting maximum carnage.

I focused on the spot Memo had designated. Shadows shifted on the ground below the fence, and the faint hint of movement confirmed that he was still there. "Now?" I asked, my pulse pounding in my ears.

"Hold," Memo whispered back. The seconds dragged on, the anticipation building. "Wait for it," Memo mumbled, almost sensing my nerves. "Here we go. One more second." The man's AK-47 reappeared above the wall, this time with a head aiming behind it. He was becoming bolder and exposing himself for longer. He wouldn't live long enough to learn from his mistakes. "Now!" Memo hissed.

I exhaled, steadying my crosshairs and blurring the target beyond the reticle. My right index finger tightened on the trigger, willing it to break and unleash the devastation of the round. In what can only be described as a punch in the face, the firing pin slammed forward, triggering the primer on the back of the round to ignite a sequence of explosive pressure, propelling the bullet forward through the barrel. Hot, concussive gas blasted from the muzzle brake, sending shock waves of heat, sound, and force back toward me.

The tiny concrete room magnified everything. The pressure from the explosion was mind-numbing.

Memo watched through his scope in the adjacent room. He followed the projectile's trajectory as it tore through the air and smashed into the targeted fence. As expected, the thin steel door was no match for the round but fulfilled its intended purpose: igniting the incendiary portion of the bullet.

"Holy shit!" Memo shouted, the need for stealth forgotten. "You got 'em," he declared, pointing out the streaking, hot orange flash that engulfed the figure behind the wall, sending his arm tumbling and his AK-47 flying. My second shot hit the gate's lock, blowing the door open and revealing the now motionless body at the foot of the gate.

## Pairing Up

The metallic squeak from the door below gave them away. First, we heard the grating sound of its hinges—a telltale sign that someone had entered the building the same way we had. Then came the footsteps, crunching on shattered glass in the hallway. The sharp echoes bounced off the polished concrete walls, amplifying each step as it traveled upward toward our position on the fourth floor.

Memo and I scrambled as quietly as we could and pressed against the interior wall of our apartment, which provided a clear line to the stairwell. The soft thud of boots on the stairs grew louder, echoing our earlier movements.

"Wait for them to expose themselves fully," Memo whispered. I nodded, pulling an M67 fragmentation grenade from my pouch. If our opening volley didn't kill them, I was ready to send the grenade tumbling down after them. Behind my M16, my breaths slowed—*inhale, exhale, inhale, exhale*. Every sense sharpened at the sound creeping up the stairs. My vision waited for a flicker of movement as the tension climbed with each step. The boots were nearly at the top. The wait was excruciating, each second stretching longer than the last.

Then, movement. Through the vertical iron rails of the stairwell, I caught a flash of a shoulder, followed by a weapon edging into view. Then came the unmistakable outline of a helmet. I froze, my mind racing. "Wait," I thought, "a helmet?"

Before I could act, Memo shouted, "Hey, you've got friendlies up here."

"Shit, thank God," a voice below exhaled, full of relief.

"Come on up!" Memo yelled.

Two men appeared, slinging their tan painted M4s as they rushed up the stairs. The attack outside still raged, and we didn't have time to waste. As they approached, a flicker of recognition passed between us. Coincidentally, we knew them, though only in passing. They were Navy SEAL snipers attached to 3/5 for the push south into the city. One of them was a then-unknown Chris Kyle.

They were doing the same thing we were, and by sheer chance, they chose the same position we did to set up and cover the infantry's advance. There was only one problem: They were too late.

"Damn, that's a great spot," one of the SEALs said, looking around. "Got any room on your side?"

"Nah, we've got two windows, and they've both got guns on 'em," Memo replied, always quick with a solution. "Why don't you take the room across the hall? There's a bed and a crib you can set up on in there."

The SEALs moved into the neighboring apartment and set up their rifles, adding their firepower to ours. Three snipers and one PIG (me) worked together, decimating targets for the next six hours until the sun sank below the horizon. The SEALs covered the sprawling open fields and protected the western flank of 3/5's advance into Fallujah. We were grateful to have them there.

The following day, the main assault began. With the breach cleared by a coordinated airstrike of eight 2,000-pound GBU-31 bombs, 3/5, along with 7,000 soldiers, sailors, airmen, and Marines advanced south.

# 8

-----

# THE COST OF DEMOCRACY

## The Carnage

10 November 2004 - 0813
Jolan District, Fallujah, Iraq

A thirteen-man Marine squad moved along the wall, their boots scraping over fractured asphalt scattered with remnants of the city's destruction. The drizzling air carried a thick, acidic cloud of carbon and dust that hung heavy in the windless street. Hot breath, nylon straps, and gear scraped against the ten-foot cinder block wall as the armed men inched forward. A tan-gloved hand reached out, unlocking the gate. The metal door creaked open just enough for a waiting Marine to throw an M67 grenade into the courtyard.

India Company had already taken fire from the building; insurgents were now barricaded inside. The distinct metallic ting of the grenade spoon echoed across the street, sharp against the quiet that followed the last volley of gunfire. For a moment, all movement stopped—every Marine braced—waiting to gain momentum.

The grenade's purpose was twofold: killing or stunning anyone near the entryway and signaling the platoons across the street to unleash a barrage of suppressive fire, ensuring no insurgent at the windows survived long enough to counter. The mission: gain a foothold—by punching our way in. Once we owned the courtyards, we'd begin the perilous next steps, clearing each room and killing anything inside.

The shock wave pulsed outward, rattling against the oblong courtyard walls. Mud, shattered debris, and noise erupted into the air. Marines from across the street unleashed their fire into the building, accompanied by the constant *thwack* of bullets striking stone and the echoing cracks of rifles. The noise was deafening. The fight was on.

Lance Corporal Charlie Graham lunged forward, blasting through the still-vibrating metal door. His stubbled, tired face was already slick with sweat and a familiar dread. His helmet sat crooked on his head because of the chaotic entry, but he moved with purpose, the rest of the squad flowing behind. The squad's strength lay in its numbers and unyielding violence. Coursing forward, the squad slithered into the courtyard, their rifles spitting hatred into their prey as they encircled the house's front entry.

The overhead fire rained debris down on the now-surging Marines—they needed a second grenade. One Marine readied to open the door, the other to roll the grenade inside under the covering fire of the squad.

The first circle of hell had to be taken.

*Thumb clip, pull pin, prepare to throw, throw—Ting.*

November 2004

> *To my family,*
>
> *We prepare, guns ready, to enter the first circle of hell. Eye contact is made with a friend who you see as a true soulmate. A bond only made in the perils of hell. He gives you the go-ahead. You reach into your pouch. Hands clammy from sweat and bitter cold. Shaking. Your button releases. Pouch is now empty, right hand full. With a little bit of a fight, the pin is pulled. You reach back with all your might and heave the ball of death. Strength comes unknowingly from the depths of your body. "Frag" is thrown. Time slows down. The seconds seem to take an eternity.*

*One...Life's past flashes by. Memories of home, sounds of the innocent laughter of youth. Happier times, family's faces, hopes long gone, and dreams too far to reach.*

*Two...Thoughts seem to drift, anywhere but here.*

*Three...You start to remember why you are here. Your mission. Your purpose.*

*Four...It all seems wrong; fear collides with confusion and doubt.*

*Five comes too quick...Boom!*

*You come spiraling back to reality, knowing your one purpose is to kill. Flashes of hot red light and metal erupt, cutting through the false curtain of peace. No going back now. You're in. Intense feelings excite your senses. Chemicals in your body boil. This is only the beginning. You cross the border, cross into the house of the devil. Eyes sharp and focused for movement. Breath is held, heart pumping. First door is kicked, opening with full force. A wave of blinding smoke and searing gasses hit, causing eyes to close and nostrils to burn. "Must push on!"*

*Second room. "God could this be it?" Heavy breathing pelts your back, your soul mate waits on your move. "Go!" Like an explosion, Marines pour into the room covering every tangible direction. Room is clear. Again we move on, throats tired from constricted and rapid breathing. Like a smooth ocean current we glide stealthily into a maze of uncertainty. Like a deadly ballet, we float from room to room expecting the worst. "No man left behind" is our creed and we all question our ability to grace fire for a fallen comrade. It must be done.* Crack! Crack! Crack! *The familiar sounds of an M16A4 explode from an adjacent room. You fear the worst. "God no!" One more friend gone, one more body bag filled, one more mother crying into an American flag.*

*Your son,*
*Angelo*

The second room on the left side of the entry hallway exploded as the door swung open. Flashes of light and concussive pressure pulsed from within, chaos spilling into the hallway. Inside, two Marines fought for their lives. An insurgent, crouched behind a bed, screamed as he sprayed the room with gunfire, hitting one Marine before being engulfed by the team's return fire forward.

Recoiling like a wounded animal, the squad regrouped in the hallway, pulling back to triage the heavily wounded Marine. "Corpsman up!" echoed through the line, half in anger, half in raw, choking fear. The sound of his armor's Velcro and plastic gauze bandages tearing open mingled with the wet, gurgling breaths of the Marine on the edge of death. His blood and sweat and piss-soaked uniform left streaks across the tiled floor as they dragged him toward the relative safety of the courtyard, where a second corpsman was waiting, surgical gloves already on.

The house fell silent as the squad pressed forward. The only sounds that remained were the crunch of boots on broken plaster, the heavy, hot breaths of adrenaline, and the faint gurgling gasps of an insurgent dying in the corner. A small fire flickered in the kitchen, feeding on scattered rags and charring rice bags as the Marines crept through the smoky haze interior.

With the first floor cleared, the squad gathered at the base of the stone stairway leading to the second floor. Every rifle was pointed upward, aimed through the gaps in the iron railing. Vulnerable on the exposed stairs, the Marines moved with care, backing up step-by-step to keep their weapons trained on the second-floor hallway. The first and second men led the ascent, their footsteps deliberate, while two others stood ready to yank them to safety if they were hit.

Kneeling at the top of the stairs, the Marine steadied himself as he began to "pie" the hallway, angling his weapon to cover the space while exposing as little of his body as possible. Breathing heavily, he took a long sigh, the barrel of his rifle inching across the threshold.

The pressure hit first, a burst of air that shook the constricting walls, followed by flashes of light and sound.

*Thwack, thwack, thwack, thwack.* A Russian PKM medium machine gun snarled to life; its belt-fed rounds ripped down the hallway—narrowly missing the Marine's face. He flew backward, yanked by his collar, tumbling down the steps as the squad below retaliated, their gunfire pouring into the hallway. Dust, smoke, fear, and madness swirled as the squad scrambled to regroup and counter.

*Get out. Get on line. Make a decision.*

"On my mark," the Squad Leader hissed. "You four lay down cover fire—upstairs and down the hall. Keep your heads down. You," he gestured, "Hug the wall and get a grenade around the corner."

"Go." His rifle spoke before he could. The fight was back on. Wave after violent wave, Marines and Mujahideen collided—each clash more brutal than the last.

Like the ocean tides Marines had navigated for over 200 years, the Marines remained unstoppable.

A single wave might break. But the tide always surges forward.

And so did we.

A grenade exploded down the hall, engulfing the Gunner and his screams as the peak of the rising tide washed into the second hallway. Without time or momentum to waste, the squad surged almost simultaneously into the three rooms on the second floor. The cheap balsa wood doors and Chinese locks splintered under the weight of the Marines' heeled boots. Every room cleared increased the probability that the next room was full of awaiting jihadis—explosions, gunfire, yelling, screaming—death.

Brave Iraqi interpreters stood shoulder to shoulder with their Marine brothers, facing the same fury, the same bullets, and the same death. They had volunteered to fight alongside a foreign military—fully aware of America's history of walking away from its allies when the smoke cleared. Still, they chose hope over fear—democracy over religious oppression.

In the chaos of battle—amid gunfire and shouted commands—they did more than translate. They *pleaded.* They shouted to the Mujahideen, offering them a chance to live—a chance to surrender.

"Give up or meet your god."

The insurgents answered with gunfire. The Marines answered back—honoring the interpreters' courage the only way they could. By arranging the meeting.

## Street Fight

Outside, the fight raged. The battalion had run headlong into a stronghold of jihadi resistance, fighting block by block through the Jolan District. Fighting on a coordinated line, Lima and Kilo Companies pressed south shoulder to shoulder, clearing houses one by one. The enemy's defensive line, a last stand for many Mujahideen fighters, made every inch an agonizing, bloody effort.

Deciding that the risk outweighed the reward, Captain Chontosh ordered his engaged platoons to fall back and bring in the heavy guns. Two M1A1 Abrams rumbled into position from an adjacent street and moved to the front. Two Assault Amphibious Vehicles equipped with .50 caliber and MK19 automatic grenade launchers flanked them, pulverizing every window.

The tanks, shielded by the squads, pivoted down the street, the growl of their engine turbines cutting through the echo of bullets flying from rooftop to rooftop as they careened into the outer gate. Marines scrambled to avoid the dominating threat.

One of the Abrams adjusted its position, lowering its 120mm main cannon to target the house's central stairwell—the building's spine. A direct hit would shatter the structure's core, reducing the house to rubble and ensuring no one inside would survive.

As the Gunner depressed the internal trigger, the tank behemoth rocked back. Igniting the powder of the massive shell inside, it sent the explosive projectile cascading out of the rifled barrel and slamming into the center of the house just fractions of a second later. The explosion seemed to stop time. The new houseguest's pressure blew every unbroken window out of the building as fire, dust, debris, and the men's souls spewed into the chilly sky.

The Marines allowed themselves only fifteen minutes to regroup. Sitting on commandeered couches, drenched in sweat and debris, they sipped water, reloaded magazines, and lit cigarettes with shaky hands. One house down, eight more before the end of the block, thousands more remaining in the city. The Marines had their work cut out for them.

The days fell into a bleak, monotonous rhythm.

By nightfall, the Marine platoons sought shelter in a half-destroyed house—what remained, anyway. Before they could rest, they moved the dead Mujahideen into a separate room, sealing away the carnage as best they could. Then they collapsed, worn down to the bone.

The young men sprawled across cold floors and broken tiles, the only light coming from the soft orange glow of kerosene heaters and the dim red beams of headlamps. Lying on their backs, they smoked cigarettes and talked in hushed voices—stories of home, of who they had been before, and who they hoped to be if they ever made it out of this mess.

On some nights, there were laughs; on other nights, just silence. And sometimes, a soft whimper in the dark—barely audible—a sniffle for a lost brother or the quiet tremble of someone trying to brace themselves for another day in hell.

At sunrise, the young warriors roused from an uneasy sleep, consumed whatever meager breakfast they could manage, and prepared for the day's exchange of death. By 8 a.m., the opening act would begin with the deafening roar of F-18s slicing through the sky, their payload released in precise pairs. The 500-pound warheads slammed into the ground, sinking momentarily before exploding in a geyser of fire, rubble, and dirt, launching debris hundreds of feet into the air.

The artillery executed a methodical barrage to rake the enemy's positions from near to far. Each crunch of the heavy shells aimed to shatter more than just the enemy's will to fight. It was deliberate, relentless, and impersonal. An ominous prelude to what awaited inside the rooms. The carnage would shift from the distant screech of ordnance to the intimate brutality of close combat, measured in inches and fractions of a second. The losses were beginning to take their toll.

## Human Suffering

The human suffering defied comprehension. The air hung heavy with crushed dust and decay as lifeless hands protruded from collapsed rubble, frozen in futile attempts to claw toward survival. Dried blood crusted under their fingernails was the only evidence of their struggle. Bodies lay shattered and contorted, some half-twisted across courtyards, others dangling from windows or strewn across the pockmarked streets oozing.

Two corpses told a tale of desperation. Their flesh, devoured by flies and swarmed by mosquitoes, reeked of rot and decay. Behind them lay a long, charred stretch of asphalt—a path of panic marking their frantic, hopeless flight. The evidence was undeniable: the night patrols of the KC-130 gunships hunted and chased them down.

The gunships ruled the dark; their propeller engines droned a constant hum over the city. They hunted with patience, announcing their presence only with the distant *brrrrt, brrrrt* of 30mm cannons or the heavy, jarring *boom, boom* of grenades and artillery raining down from the sky. These men had tried to escape, but the gunships allowed no way out. Trapped in the open, their paths cut short by a barrage of projectiles, they fell in the middle of the street. The story of their final moments lingered in the air like the stench of their bodies.

The hardest part of fighting an insurgent hell-bent on death is coming out alive. The Marines had to show unimaginable bravery, creativity, and dedication. When every instinct screamed to turn and run, to save themselves and go home to their families, they had to override it. The squad lived, breathed, and survived as one. Marine casualties were mounting rapidly, and each death or morbid injury served as a reminder to each of his own fragility. Wanting to run from but choosing to run toward. The Marines had made a promise to one another, and life or death was nonnegotiable.

The bond we shared was beyond explanation. Each loss tore through the men who, only hours earlier, had woken up next to the fallen Marine or had shared a cigarette in a rare moment of calm. Now he was gone. Their last goodbyes often came with the cold, emotionless zip of a black body bag or the chaos of a MEDEVAC, with tires screeching as the vehicle rushed toward the nearest field surgeon, guns still firing.

The brutality felt so cold. Death was everywhere; its stench mingled with the choking odor of human waste, fear, and black exhaust smoke drifting through the streets. Each man grappled with the loss, the fragility of life, and the overwhelming reality that he could be next.

Many spent their final moments lying on their backs, writhing in pain, and slipping in and out of consciousness. They held onto the bloody hand of a friend or a Navy Corpsman who understood there was nothing left to do but provide comfort as the young Marine began his journey beyond the stars.

December 2004

*To my family,*

*All my life I've been raised with a belief in a higher power. This being my second war has brought me to question myself even more. Too many times I've seen wonderful young men cut down in their prime. I find myself questioning the reasoning behind the reality. I don't know how much else I can put into this . . . I don't know if I believe anymore. How can I look up to a power that would rip my friend Shane Kielion, a young father from this world merely three hours after the birth of his son? Think of the mother. The best day of her life, turned into a violent nightmare. Think of the son. Every day he will be haunted by the knowledge of his birthday. The day a hero gave his life for his son's freedom. I met, reacted to, and came to love every fallen Marine in our battalion. Some of the best men I've ever known. All gone, but why? Is it a constant dance between good and evil, where sometimes the devil gets his way? Or are some men meant to die for a higher purpose? I know God does not kill man; I know that man kills man. But why did these men have to give so much? Why couldn't God protect them? Who will protect me? Where can I find answers? I just don't understand. How can someone who loves us so much stand by and watch our nation's best feel so much pain? I may just be looking for answers where there are none. I mean no harm or disrespect in my thoughts. They are just simple questions with complex answers.*

*It is said never to underestimate your enemy, nor to fail to understand his reasons for fighting. To be honest I've tried to understand their thoughts but fall short continuously. Why do foreigners come to this country for the sole purpose of killing an American? What have we done that would cause so much hatred? Why do they feel they must fight a futile jihad. I feel I'm arguing a moot point. No one knows why we die or what happens when we do. All I can do is cherish and hold the memories of our brothers close. Learn from what they had to offer, and respect what they gave. I will never forget my friends.*

*Your son,*
*Angelo*

## The Chance

Three/Five and the remaining 7,000 soldiers, sailors, airmen, and Marines fought their way south to Phase Line Fran. The coalition killed hundreds of insurgents, rescued countless hostages and civilians, and destroyed tens of thousands of munitions stockpiles. Torture rooms revealed unimaginable horrors: decapitated bodies, women discarded in the streets with their faces and breasts mutilated, the charred remains of children. The Mujahideen were proving worse than Saddam.

The division's initial push south drove it to its objective in just two weeks. The relentless pressure from coalition forces—constant bombardments, special operations raids, and snipers in the streets—left the insurgents with no place to escape. By December, only brutal pockets of resistance remained.

I was now a member of Banshee 2, Sergeant Blake Cole's sniper team. Cole was the same Marine I had seen eighteen months earlier, sprinting past me during the gunfight with the Republican Guard.

India Company faced some of its most violent battles during the initial push into the city, and one of those fights left a gap in Sergeant Cole's team. Our platoon's corpsman, Hospitalman Third Class James Pell, had been severely wounded while leaping from roof to roof. Sniper Platoons often operated with a specially selected Navy Corpsman who went through the same training as any PIG but whose primary role was to provide medical coverage when necessary. Not every team had a corpsman assigned, but those who did benefited from the extra insurance of lifesaving skills when operating far from traditional units. With Doc Pell wounded, Blake's four-man team was reduced to three, and I was pulled from Memo's team to fill the gap.

"Listen here, Pasciuti," Blake said. Strawberry-haired and cocky, he sat on an ornate Persian rug with his gear off, warming his feet by a commandeered kerosene heater. An unlit cigarette dangled from his lips as he turned to face me, planting his sweat-stained socks on the muddy rug. "I don't give a fuck about what happened before or why you got kicked out of the platoon. I ain't got time for that shit." He exhaled and leaned forward slightly. "Doc Pell getting hit really fucked us. You've got big shoes to fill." He paused, sizing me up. "Scardino and Powers vouch for ya, so you're good in my book. Stay tight, stay close, and don't fuck up. I'll teach ya everything ya need to know."

Without waiting for a reply, Blake flicked his silver Zippo lighter across his leg, lit his cigarette, and leaned back, signaling the end of the conversation and tolerance for my presence. "We're inserting again tomorrow night. India Company's going back in—we're going with them," he added as I stepped toward the door.

"Copy that, Sarge—" he cut me off.

"And none of that Sergeant shit, it's just Blake."

"Copy that, Blake," I replied, correcting myself as I left the room. I was back on a sniper team, back in the fight, and back in the most dangerous city in the world. The rest was up to me.

## Change of Command

`10 December 2004 - Jolan District, Fallujah, Iraq`

"Powers, Scardino, Pasciuti; come on over here with me," Blake called, motioning us into India Company's new command post. The building, one of the few undamaged structures in the heart of the Jolan District, had become a makeshift headquarters. Inside, a broad-shouldered

Captain Len Coulman waited with Blake around a large black and white satellite-imaged city map.

"This is Captain Coulman," Blake introduced. "He's India Company's new commanding officer. Captain Chontosh got called back to Quantico to teach infantry officers. Captain Coulman's been with the company for a while and is just now taking over."

"Good afternoon, sir," the three of us replied in unison.

"Hey, guys, good to meet you," Captain Coulman began. He was a bear of a man from Chicago stepping into a role previously held by a leader whose reputation bordered on legendary. Captain Chontosh had commanded with grit and charisma, earning the unwavering loyalty of his men. Now, all eyes were on Coulman, waiting to see if he could measure up under the enormous pressure.

"I just wanted to thank you for what you guys do," Coulman continued. Our faces twisted confused glances because thanking young enlisted was not a normal practice. "Our boys out here really appreciate it when you're around. Makes them feel a bit safer knowing you're here." Stunned, we mumbled a collective thanks.

"Blake tells me you're going out ahead of our lines tonight." Coulman said.

"Yes, sir," Lance Corporal James Powers replied. "I'll be taking point." Powers continued, "We'll step off from here at around 2300 and patrol approximately 500 meters ahead of India Company's forward lines." Powers's sharp, cold features, and Texan drawl stressed his certainty.

"Then we'll find a suitable house to cover the long axis of the roads as you head south," Lance Corporal Anthony Scardino added. His laid-back, almost lazy Tulsa twang—reminiscent of Matthew McConaughey's—contrasted with the seriousness of his words.

"We'll catch 'em as they cross the roads, moving to alternate positions," I added, finishing the thought. The three of us, thick as thieves when I was first in the platoon, were finally back together.

"Looks like you've got a solid team here, Sergeant Cole," Coulman remarked.

"Best in the battalion." Blake shot back.

## The Night

Six hours later, we stepped off into the cold December Iraqi night. The frigid night air remained stagnant, and the streets were empty. The soft hum of the KC-130 purred above as dogs barked in the distance.

Our four-man sniper team slipped through the shadows of the lifeless streets, partially illuminated by flickering orange streetlights. Our greatest asset—stealth—enabled us to operate in small numbers and challenge the conventional reliance on overwhelming firepower. Like a dagger, our purpose was precision.

Our target was a two-story house overlooking the approaching advance. Enemy snipers had already taken the lives of several of our Marines from the rooftops, and our commanders needed those positions neutralized. We would serve as a blocking unit, ready to engage any maneuvering insurgents.

Powers entered the courtyard first, his steps careful and slow. Blake entered next, I followed, and finally Scardino. The cold, unmoving air wrapped around us, and nothing—not a word or scrape of gear—made a sound. Blake approached the door, the glow of his night vision goggles casting a pale mint-green hue across his face, his breath frosting with each exhale. The door clicked, and the faint creak of its hinges broke the stillness. We froze.

A distant *pop, pop, pop* rippled through the darkness, faintly echoing gunfire. Packs of hungry dogs barked again, fighting over scraps of human remains. My radio emitted a sharp crypto *beep*, which I muffled with my gloved hand. We waited—one minute. Nothing moved.

Blake nodded his rifle, signaling for Powers to move forward. The door pivoted open, and we stepped inside, pressing into the darkened house. It was quiet. A steady drip from a faucet into a metal sink echoed softly from another room. We waited—three minutes.

Blake adhered to sniper doctrine with a near-religious dedication, "Sniping was equal parts art and science. Every move is deliberate, and every decision is informed by an understanding of our environment," he reminded us in classes while still back at Camp Pendleton.

*Stop, Look, Listen, Smell, Plan.*

"Every environment has a rhythm, a flow, and a baseline that humans, as intruders, disrupt. Nature adapts, waits, and observes. The key to survival is outlasting nature or your enemy—allowing the baseline to reset and integrating instead of imposing."

Now kneeling in the front room of a pitch-black house—we waited. Creeping up the stairs, Blake led the team in a familiar procession. Step-by-step, we ascend the stairs together. We waited again—two minutes.

Blake took command of the hallways as he popped around the corner, allowing Powers, Scardino, and me to get into position. Then, in pairs, we crept toward the rooms, hoping every one was vacant.

We regrouped in the center of the main bedroom, kneeling in a practiced formation, each facing outward, watching and waiting. The house returned to its stillness as distant gunfire and barking dogs faded into their own pattern. We waited again—ten minutes.

With the baseline reestablished, we positioned ourselves, set claymores on tripwires, conducted radio checks, and determined our sectors of fire. We waited for dawn and the inevitable, ritualistic scream of F/A-18s overhead, their roar signaling the start of another day.

## The Cost

`11 December 2004 - 0820 - Fallujah, Iraq`

A muted dawn broke over the smoldering Iraqi city. War raged, and it was almost time to begin again. No prayers emanated from the mosques.

Almost immediately, the day turned to hell. The first house the Marines entered that morning swarmed with insurgents. Both defensive lines had unknowingly spent the night facing each other. The result was catastrophic. Intent on death, the remaining enemy aimed to take as many Marines down with them.

The gunshots came first—a single *crack*. Then two in response—*pop, pop*—before the blasts erupted into what sounded like 300 in return, ricocheting and punching through the brick walls. Surprise caught both sides. This fight was violent and personal. The squelches from the radios came next.

Our sniper team was blocks away, deep in uncleared territory, and it was broad daylight. We couldn't move—exposed and isolated, trapped in place.

The contact came too soon. The enemy didn't need reinforcements. They were already there.

We could only listen. Helpless. Pinned by sunlight and empty streets, we sat there as the radio crackled—call signs shouted, gunfire echoed in the background, screams through static. We heard it all in real time. The confusion, the desperation, the pain. We couldn't do a damn thing.

No shots to take and no ground to cover. Just sitting in the stillness while our brothers fought and bled, one block too far away.

The most brutal kind of torture—watching a war unfold by sound, knowing each second might be someone's last.

India Company was in contact, and the familiar sequence began to unfold.

*Get out, get on line, make a decision.*

Assault Amphibious Vehicles roared into position, circling the block as two Abrams tanks barreled forward from the flank. Mortar teams adjusted fire while India Company scrambled to gain high ground on rooftops overlooking the insurgent stronghold.

The Marines pulled their wounded as they fought to withdraw, dragging their brothers through the rubble.

AAVs and tanks raked the building with machine-gun fire, the Abrams rocking back with each earsplitting blast. *Boom.* The first round struck, sending dust and debris cascading through the air. *Boom.* A second impact collapsed the front of the house into rubble. Two more 500-pound bombs streaked in for good measure. Another house was destroyed, and another compound was cleared. The fight continued.

I lost another close friend that day—someone my age—who had been there for me during my darkest moments recovering from the last war. Greg Rund was the smile of India Company—the cheesy grin that pierced through the ugliness of it all. A known class clown and a survivor of the Columbine High School massacre, he kept India Company together by being that same beloved class clown for us.

He died as the two-man in a stack, rushing to the aid of another wounded Marine trapped alone in a room. When every instinct screamed to run, to live another day, to save himself, Greg made a choice. Greg chose his brothers.

Two solemn Marines dressed in pristine dress blues arrived at his mother's home that evening in Littleton, Colorado. Interrupting her birthday celebration to deliver the news no parent should ever hear.

India Company lost its smile.

Mop-up operations continued for another two grueling weeks as insurgents clung to every inch of ground, demanding a price for each step the Marines took. The city became a battlefield of attrition. The fight raged on, blow after bloody blow, a grudge match where no ground was yielded without bloodshed and bombs. The cost of progress was measured in young men's lives.

The city was finally cleared of insurgents on December 21, 2004, and civilians were allowed to access their homes two days later. Three/Five and the 1st Marine Division prepared the city for its first elections since before Saddam's reign of terror on January 30, 2005.

Three/Five gave nineteen of her sons to the Battle of Fallujah, and the coalition gave eighty-eight more. Hundreds more wounded. The personal cost was incalculable.

Democracy was restored.

## The Dawn

January 29, 2005

*To my family,*

*Tonight, as I sit down to write this letter, I try to think of where I am at. Not only on a physical level, but on a spiritual and mental level as well. Physically right now I am lying on history. Tonight I will sleep on the actual table that will host Iraq's first legitimate election in over three and half decades. Fallujah is one of the many cities that will participate in the elections. History will be made tomorrow. Not only for the fact that the recently hostile and terrorist-ridden city of Fallujah will hold elections. But for the fact that Iraq is one step closer to being freely controlled and governed. Tomorrow marks the beginning to the end of terror. Come sunup, Iraqis from all walks of life and differences in beliefs will come together with one common goal: freedom.*

*In retrospect, Iraq today is very similar to where the United States was over 200 years ago. So similar in fact, that our histories run almost parallel. First, escape from a radical and tyrannical leader through a vicious war. Second, small "baby steps" toward the goal of a government of and for the people. Third, the slow and precarious steps to hold on to the newly given responsibility. America (contrary to popular belief) was by no means born overnight. America was merely an idea confined to the imaginations of fearless diplomats. Iraq is no different. The necessity of our being here is far from a question. Iraq is the first step to creating a righteous government in the Middle East. I for one am proud to say that I have a hand in bringing this, in a sense, infant from birth (the overthrowing of the self-destructive government) through its first breaths of life. And for being here to witness its first steps toward maturity. Most days tend to be like Groundhog Day, the monotonous and repetitive scheme of everyday life. But not tomorrow. Tomorrow their future begins.*

*Spiritually, I am finally sound. I chose to open my eyes, my heart, and most of all my mind. I'm reading a book by Harold Kushner called* When Bad Things Happen to Good People. *Kushner discusses Thornton Wilder's unique way of looking at a beautiful tapestry: "Looked at from the right side, it is an intricately woven work of art, drawing threads of different lengths and colors to make up an inspiring picture. But turn the tapestry over, and you will see a hodgepodge of many threads, some short and some long, some smooth and some cut and knotted, going off in different directions." Kushner then explains that "Wilder offers this as his explanation of why good people have to suffer in this life. God has a pattern into which all our lives fit. His pattern requires that some lives be twisted, knotted, or cut short, while others extend to impressive lengths, not because that one thread is more deserving than another, but simply because the pattern requires it. Looked at from underneath, from our vantage point in life, God's pattern of reward and punishment seems arbitrary and without design, like the underside of a tapestry. But looked at from outside this life, from God's vantage point, every twist and knot is seen to have its place in a great design that adds up to a work of art." Although his explanation of the metaphor may not answer all of life's complex questions, it helped to ease some of my pain of losing my friends. Nothing will bring my friends back, and the voids made by their deaths will never be filled. What I've realized we all must do is learn from their sacrifices. Rethink what means most to us in life, be mindful of what we take for granted, and truly figure out what kind of "thread" we want to be.*

*Mentally, I am unsure to say the least. Not unsure of myself or my abilities, but unsure of the future. Home is a goal fast approaching, but with it comes fear and doubt. I find a fear of acceptance. I'm not sure if people understand my journeys and experiences. Can they accept? Can they relate? Do they understand that ours was a just cause? Or simply the question of everyday life going back to normal. Old relationships become a flicker of a memory, with the understanding that as people grow older, they can sometimes grow apart; but never expecting such a rapid rate. In my journeys, short as they may be, I've realized that even though times and people change, family stays vigilant. Family is the fuel to my fire, my reason for preservation. Throughout my life and all its awkward equations, the only unchanging factor is family and its undying love. I understand fully and deeply respect my family for enduring these uncertain times.*

*As for the rest of my life, I am again unsure. My future after the Corps remains a mystery. Love is a gamble in which I am too scared to throw the dice again. I understand my age, but I also realize I don't live the average life of a twenty-year-old. My companions and I live in a world so full of stress and uncertainty. The idea of (in comparison) the minor stress of a deadline at work or a mid-term school exam seems so, well... desirable. In no way do I mean to cut down or degrade anyone. No one will ever know our day-to-day lives, and I suppose that's a good thing. The life lessons learned and maturity gained are immeasurable, but come with a high price. Home, the once distant memory, is now a rapidly approaching reality. Only two months until we begin our new journey. Our journey home.*

*Your son,*
*Angelo*

# 9

# PIG HUGGER

### The Test

27 June 2005 - 0730
Scout Sniper School, Camp Pendleton, CA

I stood by the pull-up bars, staring at sniper instructor Staff Sergeant Dave Slafsky, who appeared uninterested. "When I say begin, you will proceed with your pull-up evaluation for the PFT (Physical Fitness Test). Each pull-up must start from a dead hang, motionless at the bottom, and move to a chin-over-bar position with no hip movement," he explained. "Only valid pull-ups will count. If we repeat a number, it means you haven't met the requirements."

Scout Sniper School at Camp Pendleton had a history of training dozens of legendary snipers, each earning a place on our wall of honor. Our sniper instructors were guardians of the badge and the gatekeepers of this shadowy world. Each was selected from the fleet as the top sniper in their platoon, and the standards among these men were some of the highest I had ever seen. They were a notoriously strict cadre with zero patience for two things: weakness and repeating themselves.

"Begin," Slafsky ordered, his face blank.

I tightened my core, engaged my traps, and pulled myself upward—fear and anxiety willing me over the bar.

The pull-up bars were outside, next to the old World War II–style Quonset hut. With no insulation, the building accentuated the contrast of the coastal weather: frothy, humid summer afternoons juxtaposed with frozen, dreary mornings, the icy dew crackling beneath our boots. It sat at a parking lot's end, a desolate area ringed by rolling hills and rocky ridges, perfect terrain for aspiring snipers.

As snipers in training, they called us PIGs (Professionally Instructed Gunmen). Each of us had passed an INDOC in a Sniper Platoon, earning the potential to go to sniper school. All Marines in a Sniper Platoon had to pass an INDOC, but not all Marines got a shot at sniper school. If we made it through the school, we would graduate and earn the right to be called HOG (Hunter of Gunmen), gaining the Military Occupational Specialty (MOS) 8541/0317 Scout Sniper. HOGs were always in short supply. There were only about 300 snipers in the entire Marine Corps—a reflection of how brutally difficult the course was. More than half the PIGs training alongside me wouldn't become HOGs.

"One," Slafsky said.

I lowered myself and paused at the bottom to regroup.

"Two, three, four...eight, nine, ten, ten, ten." Confused at the bottom of what should have been my twelfth pull-up, I glanced at Slafsky. He remained unmoved.

"You didn't hit a dead hang," he said.

There was no time to protest; my arms were burning, and I was losing my grip strength. I continued to pull as my forearms betrayed me.

"Eleven, eleven, eleven—eleven," Slafsky counted. "Nice job. I won't even bother learning your name," he snapped, recording my score as I fell from the bar.

The Marine Corps PFT comprised three events: twenty dead hang pull-ups, one hundred crunches, and a three-mile run in 18:00 for a perfect score of 300 points. Any score below that standard would reduce the individual score. Each event's points were then added to create a composite total. I needed a minimum of 225, a first-class PFT, to get into sniper school—and I was off to a terrible start.

My pull-ups earned me only fifty-five points out of one hundred. I needed to be near perfect to pull this off.

Next were the crunches. The pacing instructors considered errant hip movement an infraction, resulting in repetition of the task and a sapping of energy.

"Eighty-six!" the instructor yelled at the end of our allotted two minutes.

"Eighty-eight." I corrected—every point counted.

"Roger, eighty-eight!" He yelled as he paced on to the next student.

*Shit*, I thought to myself. I felt the familiar walls closing in.

After some quick math in my head, I realized that, in order to obtain a total passing score, I would need to complete the three-mile run in under 21:00 minutes.

*Good, I can do that*, I thought to myself.

"3, 2, 1, go!" a sniper instructor yelled as thirty men in ill-fitting olive drab gym shorts and matching cotton tees began the three-mile sprint. Designed as a hybrid distance between sprint and endurance, the three-mile run hurt more than any other event. The only option was to sprint as fast as possible, for as long as possible, before your legs gave out—hopefully after you crossed the finish line.

I followed the winding course over rolling hills and multiple tight turns. Just before the 1.5-mile checkpoint, I took a wrong turn and wandered through a dusty lot, searching for other runners. Nothing—the clock was ticking.

I faced a choice: rush back and risk cutting the course short or correct myself and hope to salvage my time. Finally, a Marine streaked by, and I chased him to the correct turnaround, far behind my intended pace. It was a dead sprint back.

"20:58, 20:59, 21:00, time!" an instructor shouted as I crossed.

Twenty-one minutes exactly. My score was 226. I bent over, hands on my knees, attempting to spit away the dryness. I scored a 226—I made it—but just barely.

## The Inquisition

*Wrap, wrap, wrap.* I smacked my palm against a two-foot by two-foot piece of fire-engine red plywood with a small pig's hoof painted in the center.

"PIG at the hatch!" I called out to the instructor, who had just shouted my name from down the Quonset hut hall.

"Get in here, Pasciuti!" barked a voice I'd never heard before. I ran through the door, coming to a stop six feet from the desk, centered at attention. The two men were unfamiliar to me. They were older than any instructor I had encountered during my first week, and from their expressions, it was clear they had questions I might not want to answer.

"How many crunches did you do on your entrance PFT?" asked Staff Sergeant Roger Dickinson, a Northwesterner with a sharp jaw and a short blond fade. He sat at his desk, not smiling.

"Eighty-eight, Staff Sergeant," I said, as my eyes narrowed, and my head tilted in confusion.

"It says on this sheet of paper you got an eighty-six." A second voice cut in from my right. A muscled Staff Sergeant with light eyes, buzzed black hair, and a demeanor that dared anyone to cross him.

He was a Reconnaissance Marine. The patina gold Master Parachutist Wings and Combat Diver bubble on his chest gave him away. The shiny insignia contrasted with the faded and worn woodland camouflage fatigues. The Jump Wings and Dive Bubble served as a sort of business card—letting everyone know they were dealing with a killer. Known for their disdain for weakness, Recon Marines demanded excellence in every domain. The fact that we were even having this conversation about a bare minimum PFT score incensed the seething Staff Sergeant.

"According to this sheet, it's eighty-six," he repeated, his callused knuckles wrapping on a weathered clipboard, glaring over at the seated Staff Sergeant.

"Get out of my office; get back in the classroom," the seated Staff Sergeant sighed, shaking his head. I rushed out, my mind racing. Two crunches. Two points. That was the difference between me sitting in that classroom and getting sent home.

Behind that door, they argued about my fate. They had already admitted me to the course, and they had turned away better-qualified Marines. Their math error had cleared me for sniper school. They had a dilemma: own their mistake up the chain of command or force me to quit, ensuring I'd never know the truth.

"What was that about?" whispered my sniper school partner, leaning closer.

"My PFT score," I said under my breath.

"What are they arguing over?" he asked.

"The rest of my life," I shook my head, looking up at the unfazed instructor explaining Ballistic Theory to a focused group of twenty-three other Recon Marines, Navy SEALs, and infantrymen from across the country.

Down the long hall, shouts erupted behind the closed door. Through the thin walls, we heard furniture scraping and instructors yelling back and forth.

"This is bullshit!" A door slammed shut. Our marksmanship instructor paused, flashed a grin at the outburst, and kept teaching. Nobody came for me. They had made their call. I was a marked man.

## PIG Love

"Get in here, PIGs!" a deep voice with an Appalachian drawl said, carrying a particular swirl of dread and strange excitement. My partner and I stepped into the instructor's hooch—a damp space lit by harsh flickering fluorescent light that washed over the stink of sweat, dirt, and stale chewing tobacco. Layers of faded beige paint clung to the rusting Quonset hut walls. Weathered desks lined the perimeter—almost holding the walls up, while random bits of burlap covered the duct-taped carpet. This place was objectively a dump, but to snipers, it was the 1st Marine Division Scout Sniper School—hallowed ground.

Standing with our arms behind our backs, we were introduced to our tactical instructors. Staff Sergeant Dave Slafsky, tall with light brown hair and a pale complexion, sized me up.

"Oh great, we get the physical specimen—this'll be fun," he said, sounding half-bored and half-amused. "You sure you don't want to quit now and save us all a lot of trouble?"

When I said nothing, he shrugged.

"All right, listen up. Each instructor mentors two teams. You two, you're with me and Corporal Payne. This is Payne's first-time teaching, so he'll shadow me. You'll receive lessons from different instructors, each with their own specialties—feel free to ask them anything during class. Outside of class, see us. We'll show you everything you need to know."

He stopped talking as I felt a presence beside me. I turned to my right, well up and to my right. Glaring down at me was one of the most menacing men I had ever seen—Corporal Wesley Payne, a 6′3″, 220-pound athlete. The son of a prominent attorney from West Virginia with a forehead like a Mack truck and a jaw like a cinder block—he looked more like a black Terminator than a Marine. He said nothing, only stared.

Corporal Payne held the same rank as I did, but that was where the similarities ended. He was a sniper from 3rd Battalion, 1st Marines (3/1) who had fought in Fallujah, pulling shrapnel from his own skull during combat, earning his second traumatic brain injury and first Purple Heart, only to continue the mission after his Team Leader went down. He embodied courage and professionalism. And now, Corporal Payne was back at Camp Pendleton teaching at sniper school. He was as bright as he was big. There was no stopping him—ever. One look at him told me that rank didn't matter here—there were only PIGs or HOGs.

"Start pushing, Pasciuti," he ordered, voice flat. My partner and I dropped to the floor.

"How many, Corporal?" I asked with a smirk.

"Until I get tired, smartass. From now until graduation, you'll be with Staff Sergeant Slafsky and me—between classes and for one hour afterward. Part of being a sniper is being strong; the other is being resilient." He continued, "We're going to build both of those here every day—we're going to make sure you never struggle with a PFT again."

"Yes, Corporal!" I grunted as sweat collected on my nose.

"Part of success—both as a sniper and in life—is visualization," Payne said, crouching next to me while I strained through another push-up. "You've gotta see it before you do it. Visualize the bullet's path, start to finish."

He nodded toward a mirror across the room. "You see that mirror over there? Says *Scout Sniper* across the top."

"We do that so we never forget what we're aiming for. Not just the goal—but who we represent."

Then he looked at me, dead serious.

"I want you to go home, grab a marker, and write *Scout Sniper* on your mirror. That way, every morning while you're shaving that nasty little PIG face of yours, you're staring at what you want to become."

"You got that, Pascweeti?" Payne leaned in. "And what kind of name is Amah- Ama-whatever? Pas-eee-uti?"

"It's Italian," I said, already regretting it. "It means *beloved angel*."

"Whaaaat?!" Slafsky and Payne burst into laughter. "All right, Pasciuti," Payne smirked. "Our sweet little angel—get outta here, piggies. Back to class."

My partner and I scrambled to our feet, laughing as we left the room. Even though this was serious, we were having the time of our lives. We were in sniper school.

While I would have preferred a different environment to build a relationship with my instructors, I recognized that the time I spent with them was valuable. I focused through every grueling push-up and bead of sweat—even as their two huskies came over to lick the salt dripping from my face. I realized that, in their eyes, I would reflect their teaching.

They were shaping me into who they wanted me to be. I was all ears, and all eyes, and sweat.

## Fire Hose

First, we learned marksmanship. We dove into internal, external, and terminal ballistics, trying to grasp the physics shaping a round's path from when the primer ignited until the bullet stopped inside its chosen target. The sheer volume of information was mind-numbing.

I laughed to myself as I recalled telling my high school math teacher that I'd never need to know the radius of a circle. Three years later, I was eating my words.

"This, gentlemen, is a minute of angle—a way to measure a circle," our marksmanship instructor said as he scribbled circles on the board. "This concept of radius will influence everything you do from now on. In math, there are constants. In sniping, there are also constants."

Sniping linked precision to predictable results. Accurately calculating wind became the single most significant determinant of hitting a target at a distance. Gravity and its effects were given, but the wind shifted during a bullet's flight. Yet, no classroom could teach the wind.

We settled down behind our optics in fields of tall grass, watching as sweeping gusts rippled across the landscape. The expansive valley and swaying stalks reminded me of my mother's plein-air paintings. From November to March, dark shades of green crept across the slopes—the cold coastal air heavy with moisture that would slow my rounds.

In the summer's baking sun, the lush slopes faded to golden brown, as the tall wheat-colored grass flowed in waves above the green valley floor. Over time, we could see and feel seasonal patterns emerge—nature's thumbprint.

We studied how nature influenced the bullet's flight path. Every variable mattered: hot or cold, humid or dry, elevated or at sea level, or swayed by the Earth's rotation. When applied correctly, math allowed a sniper to defy nature—if only for a moment.

Alongside ballistics, we learned every detail about our rifles—their weights, manufacturing processes, and inherent limits.

Each morning, we rumbled down Basilone Road in an old canvas-topped flatbed diesel truck. The road was named after the World War II Marine who earned the Medal of Honor at Guadalcanal and was killed in action on Iwo Jima—earning the Navy Cross. He was an ordinary kid from an ordinary background who trained in these same hills before he gave his life for his country. Every man in the flapping canvas truck was prepared to do the same.

We stopped at a dew-soaked mountainside range where a flat, dark green meadow stretched a mile into the valley. The 1,000-meter known-distance range was where we would start, offering us a chance to learn the fundamentals in near-perfect shooting conditions.

Here, we laid the groundwork for everything that would follow. We recorded every environmental factor we could in our data books: altitude, temperature, humidity, barometric pressure, light, and wind, working to identify patterns across various ranges and firing positions.

Large red range flags flanked the meadow, snapping in the breeze and providing visual cues to match subtle wind shifts with what we saw and felt. We established the mental framework necessary for a scientific, repeatable understanding of how bullets behaved in flight over known distances, constructing what snipers referred to as DOPE, or Data on Previous Engagements.

It demanded more than just marksmanship fundamentals; it involved recognizing patterns, observing the minute details in our environment, applying the math we had studied, and training our minds to react. Consistency built confidence. Confidence built speed. And speed made all the difference when lives were at stake.

"Listen up, PIGs!" our marksmanship instructor yelled while holding a single 7.62 caliber sniper round. "From here on out, you are responsible for every one of these you shoot," he said, waving it across the circle of students. "You own it." He continued, "You are responsible for its flight and ultimately its actions," letting the message sink in. "Let's go—get on your guns," he ordered, clapping his hands.

From the known-distance range, we transitioned to the unknown-distance range, a makeshift battlefield filled with scattered man-sized steel targets meant to simulate the complexity we would inevitably face in combat. Twenty targets were spread across a field 500 meters wide and 1,000 meters long, each spray-painted with a number on its chest.

When called up, each student had five seconds to scan the field, locate their assigned target, and estimate its distance with their sniper partner. Through whispered breaths and quick scribbles in our data books, each team had to associate what they saw through their scope with the DOPE we had built at the known-distance range, make the necessary adjustments, and compose themselves before pulling the trigger.

"Five, four, three, two." *Bam* "Hit! Lucky shot, PIG!" our instructors encouraged us. Thousands of small decisions conditioned us to overcome our fear of failure and foster a bias for action.

For the first six weeks, we trained on the range in the mornings and shifted to field skills in the afternoons: survival, advanced navigation, and trapping small game to survive alone if necessary. We constructed sniper hide sites in the hills and spent hours observing from them while drawing field sketches and range cards through telescopic lenses. We learned to patrol in small teams of two or four Marines, avoiding natural lines of drift—where nature directed us through the path of least resistance but where our enemies would likely be. A thirteen-Marine squad relied on numbers and force, but as snipers, we survived on stealth.

In the evenings, we learned about mission planning and sniper employment. We dissected each step of a sniper mission, from receiving the warning order to establishing final firing positions: route planning, terrain analysis, fire support coordination, communications, medical evacuation, food, water, ammunition, and extraction. We also analyzed how snipers integrated into an evolving battlefield, identifying where a single radio call or well-placed shot could best fulfill the commander's intent.

"What you do off the gun—planning, reconnaissance, coordination—is just as important as what you do behind the scope," Corporal Payne said as he lectured on sniper employment—the intersection of history, doctrine, and creativity.

"Snipers need to be able to think. You're not just a killer; you're a chess player. You exist to take pieces off the board. You want to be a killer, go be a machine gunner instead. As a Scout Sniper, you exist to help accomplish the commander's intent through reconnaissance, observation, and, *if needed*, your bolt gun.

"Contrary to what Hollywood tells you, snipers never work alone. We are the last step of a long math equation that ends in something—or someone—needing to be killed. The rest of the unit will work to get you where you need, with what you need, and cover your ass while you're there." He continued, "Your most valuable asset isn't your bolt gun; it's your voice. If you think critically, act professionally, and build strong relationships," he paused and glared, "you have *the start* of being a successful sniper.

"You are above no one," he closed.

After qualifying on known and unknown distances in week six, only eighteen of twenty-four students remained. Our individual skills phase ended, and our instructors began combining each skill set into complex scenarios. I was finding my groove. The method of instruction built not only competence in our defined skill, but confidence in ourselves. What had been theoretical mission planning and patrolling classes turned into real exercises. We received our mission order at noon, planned until 8 p.m., briefed on our mission, set off into the night, and conducted the operation until morning. Bite-sized "mini missions" helped frame functional concepts and allowed time for debriefing and reflection as we evolved into what they wanted us to become.

Each week brought more complex assignments until we reached Hell Week—our seven-day patrolling exercise designed to physically and mentally reduce every student to rubble and then grind them even further. Food was foraged if in season, sleep was stolen in twenty-minute chunks, and water was our only resupply—along with more missions. We moved from the north side of Pendleton, where two-man teams patrolled for twelve hours at night and rested during the day. All to carry us to the south side of Pendleton, twenty miles away, only to turn back and head north to complete a live-fire mission, where missing was a droppable offense. This was capped off with a thirteen-mile escape and evasion movement through the isolated slot canyons of the coastal rolling hills—a cloud of riot control (CS) gas wafted into the sky, marking our progress and pushing us beyond any limits we ever thought we had.

## Stalking

Stalking defined sniping, and sniping was stalking. The two could never be separated. Sniping wasn't the caricature of a boogeyman in a ghillie suit; it went deeper. The camouflage paint wasn't just for concealment—it was a ritual, our transformation into predators. Hunting the deadliest game—another human being—required more than just marksmanship. It demanded embracing the mindset of an animal, stepping into a realm where killing became not just necessary but instinctive, a feeling reinforced by the sensation of recoil.

The sniper became a part of the environment, melded into it, and studied it as if it were a living, breathing entity. Nature was always moving. It was in this space—where creativity met necessity, that art met science. Stalking forced constant adaptation and demanded experimentation until every move and decision executed the mission. Commanders despised it because they couldn't quantify it. It didn't produce easy metrics or tidy after-action reports. Like any art, it resisted control, existing beyond the structures of conformity.

Sniping was never just a science. To think like a sniper meant coloring outside the lines, seeing possibilities where others found rules, and embracing the freedom that could mean the difference between success and failure—life and death.

The rifle might have been my weapon, but the ghillie suit felt like my shield. Rooted in Scottish Highlander tradition, it was named after a Celtic woodland spirit. British snipers first wore it during the Boer Wars and World War I to gain an edge in brutal battles of attrition. My own suit started as desert camouflage utilities reinforced with heavy brown canvas on the chest, elbows, and knees to endure the friction from constant crawling. I draped and attached a layer of tattered fishing net across the back, then ripped up dozens of burlap sandbags and old olive drab shirts into ragged strips, tying them in small patches that added depth and enabled me to attach vegetation.

We dunked our suits in filthy water and buried them for weeks, allowing the stench of rot to replace any human scent. When I pulled mine from the dirt, it reeked of sweet, earthy, pungent decay—perfect to vanish into the battlefield.

Sniping wasn't just about being the best shot in the world; that skill was expected. It involved enduring the environment, suffering longer than your enemy, and outlasting your prey. Our ghillie suits gave us the ability to do just that.

### Turn the Map Around

"Get in the class PIGs." Staff Sergeant Slafsky yelled. His voice carried an edge.

We filed into our musky classroom, partner by partner, settling into cold chairs. Slafsky hooked up a laptop, and a briefing entitled "Counter-sniper Operations" flickered onto the projector.

The video opened on a Marine slouched in a sandbagged guard post—bored, but alert. The desert wind blew dust across the frame. Just another day in Al Anbar. Then the footage froze.

Slafsky stepped in front of the screen, his usual sarcastic tone gone, "Here's what we know. Multiple enemy sniper teams are operating throughout Al Anbar Province. One name keeps surfacing—Juba."

He let the name hang in the air.

"Word is, he's one of their best. Moves in plain sight. Hides among the population. Doesn't take long shots—gets close, within 200 meters. One or two rounds, always to the head or high chest, which suggests he's well-trained."

"Some units are describing him as a ghost." He paused.

"Snipers don't believe in ghosts; we believe in patterns."

He pressed play. Our class sat silent, afraid to move. We watched the Marine faithfully stand at his post until the end. A single rifle crack reverberated out of the small classroom speakers. The Marine collapsed behind the sandbag wall to die alone.

"These teams are killing Americans," Slafsky said, scanning the room. "They target guard posts or convoys, focusing on turret gunners or vehicle commanders. Coalition forces have tried using camouflage netting and acoustic trackers—but that only works if someone gets shot first. I'd say that's a big problem," he added.

We replayed the videos in slow motion, searching for patterns. Under Slafsky's guidance, we exchanged ideas on how to stop these snipers. Then he posed the question that changed my perspective on the fight: "How would you do it? Turn the map around—if you were him, how would you hunt Americans?"

He took a breath. "Snipers and Recon are called 'cowboys' because we see the battle from a different perspective. To be an effective hunter, you need to get inside the enemy's mindset. What patterns do they use? Which routes do they take? How do they blend in with the population? Each answer should lead to more questions. He is only limited by his creativity and resources," Slafsky continued. "A fancy gadget won't save you. You have to think faster than him."

He eyed us. "Yes, we're 'cowboys' because we adapt and think differently. Don't let that intimidate you. Use what you learn here. Apply the basics better than your enemy, suffer longer than he does, and we'll get him. After all, cowboys won the West."

## PIG Hugger

As the son of an artist, and shaped by scouting's wilderness fundamentals, stalking should have come naturally to me. I understood the techniques and knew how to apply them. My problem was patience. Too afraid of failure and shame, I let my anxiety get the better of me as it caused me to rush through nature and our stalking lanes.

Three weeks before graduation, we had one final graded stalk. I needed a perfect score—a 100. Saying I was cutting it close would be an understatement. To be flawless and achieve this, I had to move undetected across a 1,500-meter stretch of flowing low grass and coastal shrubs under the watchful eyes of two sniper instructors perched behind advanced Leica rangefinders with 10× binoculars. These optics, made for controlling artillery and aerial ordnance, were incredibly expensive and crafted with the finest glass in the world. Dave Slafsky, one of the cadre's top observers, known as the "PIG Killer," was on the glass, and I was being hunted.

After crossing the 1,500-meter exposed field, I crept within 200 meters of the observers and set up my final firing position. This concealed shooting platform allowed me to remain hidden even after taking my shot—critical for a sniper's survival. I would then fire a blank 7.62 round to simulate eliminating one observer. Meanwhile, a patrolling instructor—a walker—traveled the stalk lane in radio contact with the observation truck. If an observer spotted something in the brush, he would direct the walker to that location. They would attempt to vector in on the shooter from there. The walker remained neutral, offering no guidance to either party.

If a student fired without being spotted, the walker would approach the shooter while the truck went "blind" until the walker was in position. The walker's task was to get within ten meters of the hide site, allowing the student to identify one of his preselected targets and fire a second shot—this time under direct observation. If the observers detected no trace, the walker would approach and remove the burlap veil from the shooter's head, confirming the sniper's location by touch.

Talk about pressure. It felt like game seven of the World Series, being behind in the count and not just needing a homer but a grand slam. I took my first shot. *Bam*. The 7.62 blank smacked against the boiling air. A small branch shifted in front of my muzzle.

"Shit," I muttered.

"Freeze 'em," crackled the walker's radio in the distance.

"*Freeze*!" echoed across the field.

Nobody moved. The observers were certain they had a kill. I was just under 200 meters from the truck. It was September in Pendleton, and the Santa Ana winds had sucked every bit of moisture from the air. It was 102 degrees, and I was covered in cotton, thick canvas, dried mud, sweat, and layers of burlap strips woven into whatever vegetation I could find.

It wasn't just hot; it was Africa hot. I was out of water and had to take a leak. My first shot stirred a bush, and one observer in the truck noticed the slight movement. A perfect score would be impossible if they could walk on me.

*Crunch, crunch, crunch*—the dry crack of long-dried coastal reeds revealed the walker's presence coming toward me. His footsteps grew louder as I pressed my face deeper into the buttstock of my rifle, forcing a line of sight on the observers in the truck. My thick veil and the mud-covered underbrush concealed my panicked eyes as if closing them could eliminate the danger approaching me.

"Okay, I'm within ten meters," the walker spoke into his radio, off to my four o'clock. I recognized the voice. When I opened my eyes, Corporal Payne stood there, waving a walking stick through the air, his head angled toward the walkie-talkie on his shoulder strap. Under my veil, I could feel my pulse hammering in my eardrums—my own tactical instructor had come to insert the final dagger. The observers held up white index cards covered in random letters and numbers. "Yankee, seven," I murmured.

"PIG says Yankee seven," Payne relayed.

"Roger, have him shoot," the observers replied.

So far, I had scored an 80. I had moved into position undetected, closed to within 200 meters of the observers, taken my first shot, and correctly identified my target. Now, to pass, I needed to take a second shot under direct observation, without being detected.

"Fire on the T of two," Payne said.

Five, four, three, two—*Bam*. Exhaling in dreaded anticipation of what lay ahead, I squeezed the trigger. The same damned branch shook again, sealing my fate.

"Three steps forward." The observers needed to bring Payne within a foot of me, and they were closing in.

"PIG at your feet," snapped the radio. I held my breath.

"Negative," Payne replied, chuckling in his Appalachian drawl—a near miss. I was in the predator's jaws.

"Seriously, we just saw that bush move. Fine, take one more step forward," Slafsky barked sarcastically through the radio. Payne's boots crunched on the caked mud, his boot tips digging into my right rib cage. It was over.

"Who is this?" he asked, not moving his lips.

"Uh, what—Pasciuti, it's Pasciuti," I whispered, breaking protocol on the stalk lane, a violation that could get me dropped. Payne said nothing.

"PIG at your feet," echoed Slafsky over the radio. The jaws snapped shut. Silence. Payne's weight shifted.

"PIG at your feet!" the radio demanded again.

"Negative," Payne answered.

"What?!" Slafsky sounded furious. He had one attempt left.

"Fine, Payne, you've got to be kidding me, baby step forward," Slafsky said.

Payne stepped forward, his left boot pressing into the arch of my back, while his right sunk in behind my chest, gaining him four inches of height in the process. I was dinner.

"Negative," Payne said into the radio, pivoting to face the truck.

"So, you're telling me there isn't a literal PIG under your feet!" Slafsky fumed.

"Negative, that's three tries. You missed him, Slafsky," Payne said, blocking the radio to stifle protests.

"What's the PIG's name?" Slafsky yelled into the radio, loud enough to be heard without it.

"PIG's name is Corporal Pasciuti," Payne answered. Silence.

"Consider yourself hugged, Pasciuti, don't fuck it up," Payne muttered down to me, lifting his boot off my cracking back and stepping into the brush. Payne had crossed a line. I was more than a student to him—I was his reflection.

Twenty years later, I discovered Slafsky had done the same for Payne.

## HOG's Tooth

20 September 2005 - 0900

Scout Sniper School, Camp Pendleton, CA

"Please take your seats, ladies and gentlemen; the ceremony is about to begin," a speaker crackled to life inside a small, faded, red-walled auditorium. Families from around the country gathered at the School of Infantry for a thirty-minute ceremony. The ceremony marked the transition of their Marines from infantry Marines to Scout Snipers.

"Thank you again, ladies and gentlemen," Staff Sergeant Dickinson from my first week adjusted the microphone while wincing under the tension of his thick, starched tan and olive drab service uniform.

"'Live by the gun, die by the gun,' is more than just a saying here at sniper school; it's our way of life. For every bullet you fire that takes a life, there's a bullet somewhere meant to end yours."

"The origin of the HOG's tooth dates back to World War I—our first major sniper war. When an Allied sniper would hunt and kill an enemy sniper. He would take the last bullet chambered in the enemy's rifle and wear it around his neck—the bullet intended for him."

"By wearing the bullet meant to take his life, he could never die."

The Staff Sergeant held up the 7.62×51mm NATO sniper round to show it to the audience and continued, "This is a HOG's tooth. When a sniper graduates from this school, they transition from being a Professionally Instructed Gunman, to becoming a Hunter of Gunmen. In honor of that tradition, today we present that round to them."

"And now, the graduates of scout sniper basic course 4-05," the Staff Sergeant said.

"First up, the Class Honorman—the Marine with the highest GPA across all our academic tests."

"Corporal Pasciuti is your Class Honorman," he said abruptly.

I shot up from my rickety swivel seat—part shock, part fear that I had misheard. Snapping to attention, I broke ranks and jogged to the stage, heart pounding.

But he wasn't finished.

"Corporal Pasciuti is not only the Class Honorman—he was also selected as the Instructor's Choice."

That one hit harder.

The Instructor's Choice wasn't just about scores or stats. It was about grit. It was about who they'd trust with their life in a gunfight. Every sniper instructor cast a vote for the Marine they'd want beside them in combat. And they picked me.

What the audience didn't know was how much I struggled at first. I wasn't the fastest, strongest, or most skilled coming in. I fumbled through early evaluations, constantly playing catch-up, constantly second-guessing myself. But I refused to quit. Every failure fueled me. Every critique sharpened me. I listened without ego, learned without attitude, and clawed my way up with nothing but determination to prove to the world I was worthy.

I blinked, rocked back on my heels, trying to take it in.

They had given me the only thing I ever wanted in life—a hand-up, rather than a handout. That honor, that recognition, meant more than any ribbon or certificate. The sniper instructors had seen something in me worth betting on. Through their brutal standards and tough mentorship, they helped shape the best version of who I could be.

Earning their respect was the real graduation.

"Honorman Corporal Pasciuti will be awarded his HOG's tooth by another Marine Sniper, and true to our legacy, a Marine Sniper from the last war will indoctrinate you into our ranks."

I bowed my head as a grizzled Vietnam veteran with tiger-striped fatigues and gray hair approached me. The old sniper paused when placing the green parachute cord lanyard with a hole drilled through one single 7.62 sniper round.

"Carry on the legacy, young man—happy hunting." The old veteran whispered in my ear.

# 10

# ENTER JUBA

### The Green Beret

An Army convoy rolled to a slow stop on Route Michigan. The east-west road connected Fallujah to Ramadi, cutting through the Sunni Triangle—the heart of the Islamic State's resistance network. It was another blistering day in the Euphrates River Valley. The Humvee's air conditioner had likely quit, as they usually did. The engine just couldn't keep up with the added weight of the armor.

They were probably on their way back to Ramadi after a long night of hitting high-value targets. The lead vehicle came to a stop—an Iraqi-style traffic jam clogged the two-lane highway. The convoy took a security halt, waiting for an Explosive Ordnance Disposal (EOD) team. That was the norm—two, sometimes three, hours on the side of the road. The limited number of EOD teams always meant long waits, turning the waiting itself into a form of torture.

Inside the vehicle, the only fresh breath of air came from a narrow crack in three inches of bulletproof glass. Eventually, the heat drove him out of the truck. One by one, his teammates followed. They knew they would be there for a while.

The door swung open, and he placed his dusty tan combat boot onto the scorching asphalt. His gear dug into his collarbone, but he barely noticed. The wear on his kit told the story—months into a long deployment. The sweet, pungent scent of sweat rose from his chest as the burdensome armor prevented his skin from breathing or ever truly drying. A shower would be the first thing on his list once they got back to base.

He bent at the waist, stretching out a spine compressed by years of carrying gear, then turned to face the front of the vehicle. One elbow rested on the roof, the other on the open door. His feet gently kicked debris off the road.

The EOD vehicles heading toward the suspected IED cut through the traffic. Civilians, familiar with the routine, cleared the road without being asked. A crowd formed as they shifted along the shoulder, and the EOD Humvees crept forward.

A shot rang out, its sound concealed by the whine of diesel Humvee engines. The bullet tore through the air at over 2,700 feet per second—faster than the speed of sound. It reached its target in less than half a second.

The round punched into the soldier's right abdomen as he stood perpendicular to the shooter. It slipped between his armor plates, slicing through both lungs as it ripped a path through his body, narrowly missing his heart.

He collapsed to his knees. A crimson spray spat from his mouth. His lungs had collapsed. Each breath came as a desperate gasp, a losing battle against the rising dark tide. The rumble of passing Humvees drowned his cries. No one noticed his desperate fight for life.

He was alone.

Driven by desperation, he clawed at the ground as he pulled toward the front Humvee tire. With a shaking hand, he grasped the rubber in a final attempt to hold on. His body slumped against the wheel, barely upright.

His eyes darted from side to side—a silent, frantic plea for help. He tried to call out, but his voice failed, strangled by the blood choking his throat. Tears mixed with sweat and dust as they rolled down his cheeks. He convulsed once, then twice, then went still.

His life ended there, alone and afraid.

"No, wait, stop. Run that back a bit," I blurted to my sniper team. We found ourselves crammed into a small, stifling room at our forward operating base (FOB). My team and I huddled over our ten-inch Panasonic Toughbook screen. Our eyes were glued to a video, watching the final moments of a Green Beret's life. The urgency in the room was palpable—we needed to reverse-engineer the enemy sniper's tactics, and we had to stop him fast.

My team, Banshee 2, our four-Marine sniper unit, was poring over a new intel dump from our battalion. It contained a fresh batch of Juba videos recently posted on the Al Jazeera Network, and we were determined to analyze every second.

"Okay, yeah. That's it right there. After the shot hits, the camera rolls away without bouncing. He's not walking…he's shooting from a car!" I nearly leaped off the green, cigarette-stained Iraqi couch.

We occupied a position in Amiriyah, a small town about thirty kilometers south of Fallujah. The town served as a crucial gateway, linking the rural stretches of Iraq to the larger urban centers where our main Marine units were based. Our platoon of forty-five infantry Marines hunkered down in a sprawling 5,000-square-foot compound, tasked with securing the area and maintaining vital supply lines. But right now, all that mattered was neutralizing the sniper who was picking us off, one by one.

After our evening meal of reheated boiled ham and tray rations of mashed potatoes, our Team Leader, Jimmy Proudman, gathered Gabe, Tony, and me. We descended into the videos, each meticulously spliced into a single file for us to dissect. It was a somber scene, one we dreaded yet respected intensely. There was no laughing, no joking, just silence, cigarette smoke, and consideration—we were about to watch Americans die.

The black-hooded man from the Juba videos returned. Same plastic table, same green flag, same whiteboard. This time more vertical lines. Each line represented the end of an American life. A mother from Tampa, a father from Philadelphia, and a teenager from Cleveland—each struck down in a moment of unexpected chaos and violence—hundreds of clips, each one more unsettling than the last. We sat in silence, our eyes glued to the screen to absorb every frame. We watched them because we needed to delve into our adversary's twisted psyche.

The unimaginable torment was not just watching hundreds of young Americans in their final moments; it was realizing you had become numb to the videos because you had seen so many of them. So we took breaks and tried to shake off the weight of what we had witnessed, knowing we had to go back in and face it again. We did not like it, but we understood its purpose.

In each video, our shooter left "target indicators"—subtle clues and hints that, if we were sharp enough, we could piece together. It felt as if he taunted us, daring us to catch him. He paraded his actions not just out of arrogance, but as part of a sinister game. Call it hubris or foolishness, but our sniper wanted his exploits broadcast to the world so he could flaunt his skill and challenge us to come after him.

He shot with accuracy, but he was also patient. He knew how to conceal his position even from short distances, within a few hundred yards. We were dealing with a professional. Some claimed he even won an Olympic medal shooting for Syria—that idea was quickly dismissed by anyone with common sense; his skills were not.

He could shoot to kill but he could also shoot to wound, which sometimes instilled more fear among the troops. It was his way of asserting he was God here—that he alone determined which Marines and soldiers would live and which would die here.

I gave Juba credit. He clearly understood the old sniper proverb: *Kill one and terrorize a thousand.* But Juba had taken it a sadistic step further: Turn the camcorder on, kill one, upload footage to the internet, *terrorize a million.*

His twisted proverb was working. Marines were dying from single, well-aimed shots throughout the Al Anbar region—their final spasms of death uploaded by Juba for the world to see.

I didn't care whether Juba ever shot in the Olympics. I wasn't out here to win medals, and the Marines were notoriously bad at handing them out anyway. I was here to stop this guy and get Tommy Parker's rifle back.

Marine snipers had our own literary inspiration. Painted above our Sniper Platoon's loft entryway, we paid homage to the most dangerous game. Hemingway's assessment that he referenced in his short story "On the Blue Water" that "There is no hunting like the hunting of man."

And we were out for blood.

USMC EUPHRATES RIVER CAMPAIGN

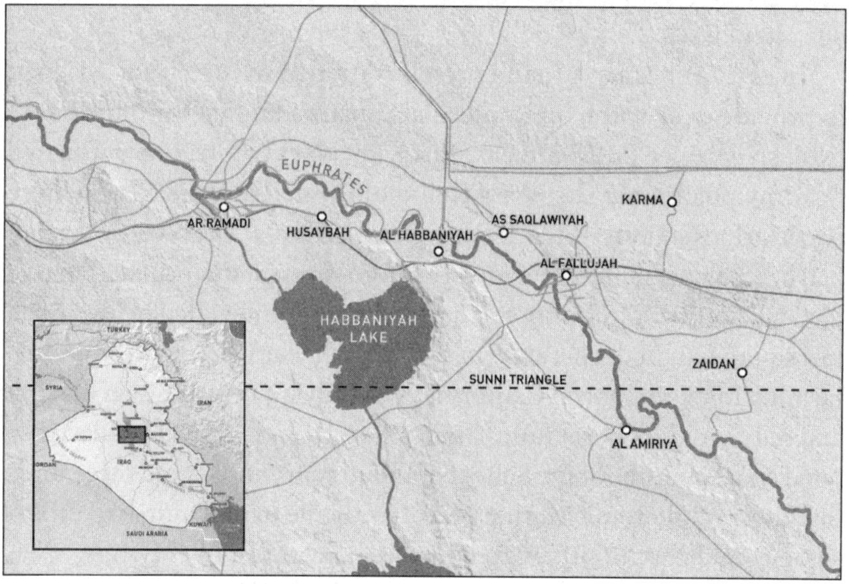

## Sandstorm

On January 11, 2006, 3rd Battalion, 5th Marines arrived in Iraq for the third time in three years. Our chartered flight touched down, and we rolled through the usual motions: disembarking, collecting our gear, and preparing 1,500 Marines for combat. This time, I didn't bother to look at the horizon or care to watch the dawn.

Within two weeks, we began conducting missions south of Fallujah, which we had captured a year and a half earlier. We extended beyond our established boundaries in the cities and patrolled the rural towns and fertile valleys on the enemy's home turf dotted along the winding Euphrates River. After regaining control, we aimed to collaborate with local nationals and government agencies to secure the environment for the newly elected administration. The mission also included eliminating any insurgents plotting against it. Unlike during our previous deployment, 3/5 now covered hundreds of square kilometers, and the opposition was fierce from the start. Insurgents, aware of the arrival of fresh troops, tested our resolve. Our unit killed dozens of fighters in those initial weeks, but not without sustaining our own losses.

In early February, I found myself stationed in Amiriyah, assigned to provide overwatch on Route Zinc, an area known for improvised explosive device (IED) attacks. Just a few days before, one detonated near my position at the intersection of Route Iron and Zinc, where two Marines—Smitty and Chavez—lost their lives. They were on a foot patrol when a remote-detonated IED tore through their squad. Chavez died instantly, while Smitty collapsed, shrapnel embedded in his throat. His squad fought desperately to save him. Javier Chavez, from a small farming town in Central California, was only nineteen and on his first and only tour. Corporal Ross "Smitty" Smith and I had formed a close bond since our time at the School of Infantry, having served three tours together. While some Marines serve as the head of a unit, and others serve as its heart, Smitty was our soul—he was just twenty-one.

The fading desert sun dipped below the horizon, casting a sandy pink haze through my scope. In the distance, a dark vortex of a sandstorm loomed. Closer, I noticed two men by the roadside. One glanced left, the other right, then looked over his shoulder. The man on the left took out a shovel and began to dig. The man on the right kept watch. Then, the digger lifted his caftan above his knees to work faster.

I grabbed the radio. "Diesel 6, this is Banshee 2. I have two military-aged males digging adjacent to Route Zinc. I will continue observation, but my visibility is fading."

"Copy, Banshee 2," came the response from command. The two men worked quickly. The man on the right knelt, pulled out an object about the size of a two-foot by two-foot cardboard box, and placed it into the hole dug by the man with the shovel. Both men appeared anxious, their lips pursed as they rushed to complete their task while the winds of the sandstorm began to swirl. I felt a heavy weight in my chest. Everything fell silent. For some reason, I didn't alert the command. Instead, I continued to observe the two men.

Conflicting thoughts swirled in my head: 2nd Platoon is counting on me; if I don't kill them, Smitty and Chavez would have died in vain. What if 2nd Platoon can't reach them in time and no patrol is available? Should I wait? Should I continue to observe? Or should I act?

War is gray; it's never black or white. To us, they were terrorists; to them, they were Mujahideen, freedom fighters. They fought for their cause, just as I fought for mine. You must be as violent as necessary to ensure your return and the safety of your brothers, yet not lose yourself in the violence.

The struggle for your soul was a constant battle while deployed. You must return with your dignity, honor, and moral compass intact.

Yet, in those fleeting moments of calm between the chaos and the gunfire, I longed for any action to change the trajectory of events—a raised hand, a step back, anything to validate the hope that we weren't merely killing machines. The desire to return home unbroken, to preserve a semblance of the person I once was, clashed with the brutal reality of my duty.

Returning from war wasn't just about physical survival; it was about emerging with your spirit intact. We were warriors, yes, but we were also human beings yearning for peace amidst the violence. The internal battle—the fight to remain humane while facing inhumane circumstances—was as harrowing as any combat we endured. In the end, the most significant victory was not just coming home, but coming home whole.

"Banshee 2?" Captain Coulman's voice interrupted my thoughts.

"Roger. Sorry, Six, yes, the two men are still digging: I'm losing visibility. Six hundred meters, I have a shot," I replied to Captain Coulman.

"Banshee 2, cleared to engage." Captain Coulman trusted me completely.

With a focused mind, I laid my cheek on the back of my rifle stock, ensuring that my face fit into the natural cheek weld, honed by thousands of repetitions.

I breathed in as the cold winter air churned into my lungs through my nostrils. I observed the wind, watching for debris and dust that swirled in the path of my projectile. The wind was momentarily calm, likely the calm before the impending storm, lightly blowing toward my face—minimal wind call.

I pursed my lips and slowly released hot, stale air from my mouth to clear my mind and calm my heart rate. I checked that my vertical scope turret's range was correct—DOPE was set. My final breath came more slowly as my body tingled. Adrenaline and norepinephrine flooded my system. I had chosen the man on the left and would work from left to right. With the crosshairs trained on his chest, I could see his face. He was an average-looking man in his thirties with dark hair, a thin beard, and his white caftan still tucked up around his knees. His lips wrinkled as he focused intently on his efforts. Through my scope, I saw my target clearly one last time. I exhaled. My focus moved to my crosshairs, pinned to his chest, blurring the target himself and ensuring my aim did not drift. I slowly squeezed my trigger. Four pounds of pressure was all that was needed to break the trigger and end this man's life.

The gun recoiled. The first shot reverberated in my ear. My 175-grain bullet sliced through the air at 2,700 feet per second, taking just over a second to travel and strike the first man square in the chest.

The second man was in my sights before the first could hit the ground. I racked my bolt to the rear to load the next round into the chamber. In that split second, the man on the right recognized something was wrong and turned to watch his friend with the shovel fall. I fired, hitting the second man in the shoulder. The round spun him partly around before he collapsed to the ground. My sights returned to the first man lying next to the hole he had been digging, shovel by his side—dead. I racked my bolt to the rear to feed the next round into the chamber. The second man, now back in my crosshairs, crawled on his belly. Was he trying to wriggle into the hole for cover? Was he planning to detonate the charge?

Four more pounds of pressure, letting fly the last shot, ending the engagement—and his life.

"Diesel 6, this is Banshee 2, both targets neutralized."

I remained concealed in my position as the storm rolled in and the sun continued to set. After the initial shock of the situation faded, a few locals moved toward the deceased men in a slow procession. Following Sharia law, the two men needed to be buried by sunset to give their souls a chance at heaven. I watched quietly as sand flung into the air, masking the fading purple and orange horizon—the two bodies were shrouded in large white cloths. In those silent, storm-brewing moments, only interrupted by the sound of the winds whipping into a frenzy, I grappled with the gravity of my actions.

Adherence to the rules of engagement provided legal and operational clarity, but the emotional burden remained mine to bear. I quietly observed the entire burial out of a mix of curiosity, respect, and responsibility. I see the sandstorm today just as I saw it then: a metaphor for the chaos of war. Every decision we made as snipers was a tightrope walk between duty and humanity.

## Knife to a Gunfight

`9 April 2006 - 1400`
`Euphrates Riverbank, thirty kilometers south of Fallujah`

"Diesel 2, this is Banshee 2—radio check," I whispered into my handset.

"Got you loud and clear. How're you guys holding up out there?" a voice crackled back.

"We're good. It's h—" I unkeyed the handset as sweat rolled down my grease-painted face. From behind the veil of my ghillie suit, my eyes widened in alarm. I fixed my gaze on a narrow row of red-brown mud houses that lined a farm field. I heard something that grabbed my attention—a scrape of a sandal and indistinct chatter.

Overhead, a cluster of date palms swayed in the breeze, blending with the thick reeds and brush that concealed us below. My team slept beside me on the cool ground of our shallow hide site, their rifles resting across their chests. By midday, the Iraqi heat had driven most locals indoors, so we scaled back our security, leaving only me awake to monitor our surroundings.

For months, we patrolled the Euphrates River valley, hunting IED emplacers and terrorist cells. On cool, damp nights, our six-man element slipped past our forward lines, crossed village streets, and melted into the dense vegetation along the water. The farmland drew its life from the river; for us, it offered concealment—while for our enemies, it promised something different. We monitored adjacent roads and crossing points from hidden positions on the bank, setting ambushes near makeshift docks and using suppressed rifles to eliminate anyone ferrying weapons or supplies. More than a few took their final breaths in the shallows of the Euphrates.

India Company and our team had decimated the area's resistance, leaving only the IED makers. So, we pressed deeper into unfamiliar territory to find and eliminate them. By April, we had advanced to the rural northern edge of town. This was quite literally the enemy's backyard.

I set my rifle down on the dirt beside me as I reached for the radio handset. The only thing I had on me was the knife I'd been using to pick at my nails. A faint noise caught my ear—I froze mid-sentence. Two men appeared around the corner of a narrow alley, heading straight for us. One had an AK-47 slung across his back, while the other carried a small black box.

Fifty meters out, I glanced to my right without turning my head, hoping to see someone awake. No luck. At forty meters, I clicked my tongue in our predetermined pattern to rouse my teammates. Thirty meters, my eyes remained locked on the men—they showed no sign of noticing us. Twenty meters, they kept coming. At ten meters, I had no choice but to act.

In a surge of adrenaline, I sprang to my feet, grabbing the only weapon I had in my lap—my Strider knife—while letting my rifle clatter to the ground. I threw myself at them, yelling loud enough to snap my team from their tepid sleep. I was their worst nightmare, death personified, charging toward them at full speed in a ghillie suit; there was just one problem: I didn't have a gun.

Tony shot up first, unleashing a volley of machine-gun fire from his M249 Squad Automatic Weapon past my left side. The heat rushed by my shoulder, splitting the now fleeing men into two paths—one bolted left, the other right. Tony's second burst struck the man on the left, spinning him in a dusty circle before he vanished from view.

My target was gone, so I pivoted to the second man fleeing down a dirt path. By then, Jimmy and two other snipers had steadied themselves in a stable seated position and fired two suppressed rounds each. The man died mid-stride.

The black box I saw turned out to be a video camera. When the camera flashed to life in our hands, in front of an enormous flag adorned with crossed swords, we witnessed two figures in dark jumpsuits disassembling old artillery shells and showing how to rig the fuses. This was part of a training clip for local insurgents. Not only had we located the bomb maker, but we also uncovered the instructor.

For eight more weeks, we worked with India Company and local police, aiming to secure the town and its surrounding villages. We maintained a firm approach to keep the insurgents at bay and support the fledgling democracy. By May, new orders arrived. India Company had to end our mission, dismantle our base, and consolidate with the battalion in another area. The drawback of using combat troops for stability operations is that once the situation calmed, we had to pull back. The progress we had made with local sheiks and governors vanished instantly, leaving them to fend for themselves.

Our next mission was to relieve an Army National Guard unit and secure the primary route between Fallujah and Ramadi, marking our return to urban combat. Our little hunting trip by the river had come to an end.

# 11

# TO CATCH A SNIPER

## Red Pushpins

25 May 2006 - 1600
Camp Habbaniyah, eighty kilometers west of Baghdad

After spending five months fighting in the suburbs south of Fallujah, we arrived at an old World War II–era British Royal Air Force base called Camp Habbaniyah. We were taking over from an Army National Guard unit that had endured a grueling twelve months and was heading home. However, in their final month, they pulled back, ceased their patrols, and left the streets to the insurgents. Their decision—borne of fear and exhaustion—was a choice to protect themselves rather than maintain mission readiness.

The consequences of their withdrawal were evident. The area had turned into a playground for insurgents who exploited the vacuum to plant IEDs and establish sniper positions. I understood the Guard's fear. The weight of twelve long months, the constant threat of death or injury, and the longing for home were powerful forces. However, pulling back and dropping their guard felt like a betrayal of duty. Combat leadership wasn't just about avoiding casualties. It was about responsibility; about confronting the danger head-on to protect others. The enemy didn't care about our unit rotations or our fatigue. They only saw opportunity.

After being promoted to Team Leader, I took over Banshee 4 for the final phase of the deployment.

Reality hit fast.

Jimmy Proudman and I set up a briefing with the National Guard's intelligence section to get up to speed. Around a cluttered table at the base, our teams gathered with our Battalion Infantry Weapons Officer, Gunner Mike Musselman.

Gunner Musselman walked us through every major incident the National Guard unit had faced. No fluff. No filters. Just the hard truth of what we were walking into.

We pored over a stack of manila file folders filled with vague reports, often written reluctantly after serious incidents in which an American was wounded or killed. A Toughbook laptop lay open, displaying digital map files and statements, while a pin board on a five-by-five-foot table covered with a map dominated the center. Dozens of colored pins dotted the map, each representing a unique event: IED strikes, IED finds, weapons caches, small arms attacks, and sniper attacks—explicitly marked with a single red pushpin.

The sniper attacks stood out as an anomaly; each of us quietly realized that we had never hunted a sniper before—at least, not a real one. There were rumors in Fallujah of an Olympic sniper named Mustafa, but nothing was ever confirmed. Most attributed it to the usual scuttlebutt, similar to the widespread, albeit false, belief among US and Coalition forces that J. Lo had died before our entry into Iraq. But these were not rumors. This was real. We could see it, touch it, and would eventually witness it.

The red pins didn't just represent sniper strikes; they represented American deaths. Each man around the table fell silent as the gravity of the situation sank in. We started reading the detailed reports—each one as gruesome and heartbreaking as the last. The frantic radio calls, the descriptions of how each attack unfolded, the communication logs, MEDEVAC reports, grid locations, and ultimately casualty reports all told the stories of lives lost. Each statement served as a blunt reminder that a man or woman from a place not so different from my own had embarked on a similar journey and call to service, but had faced a different end.

As snipers, we understood that what we did to the enemy went beyond a simple strike from a distance. We decimated the enemy's concept of safety and security. Every soldier maintained a space they protected as their own—a safe place filled with personal mementos like a letter from home, a photo of loved ones, or a cherished memory of better times. As snipers, our job was to kill more than people; it was to destroy those dreams. The flash from the end of a muzzle erased not just a life but every semblance of safety the enemy thought they had. Those red pins did the same to us. They stole our sense of security, and Jimmy and I were determined to set things right.

I found myself mesmerized by the map, dotted with so many red pushpins. One of the Army guys, preparing to leave Iraq, approached me, snapping me back to the room and said, "There's a big sniper problem out there. Be careful." I nodded, already fully aware of the gravity of his words. I received the message loud and clear. We were in the presence of a deadly adversary whose shadow loomed over every pin on that map.

Once the National Guard unit departed, my team and I quickly got to work. Our mission was to regain control and remind the enemy that *the Marines had landed*, and we weren't backing down.

I noted the locations of several recent sniper attacks. I assembled two small teams and, in the middle of the night, we visited every site in the area where a fellow American had been shot.

For weeks, we hunted an unpredictable adversary. We chased rumors pinned to a map—pushpins marking thin leads, whispers passed along by exhausted infantry patrols, fragments of sightings, and ghost stories. Most were dead ends, just noise and static. We even interviewed locals with the help of our attached interpreters, hoping someone might finally crack. But no one wanted to be seen talking to us. Too dangerous.

One evening, weighed down by the oppressive summer heat, a gaunt Iraqi man met us at the doorway of his cinderblock home. Sweat dripped from his brow as he glanced over his shoulder and whispered, "La, la, qanaas," shaking his head.

"What'd he say?" I asked our interpreter.

"He says there's a sniper that hunts these streets. And if they help us…he'll kill them." The man didn't wait for our response. He quietly shut the door. He wanted to tell us more, but not at the cost of his family's lives. Another trail had gone cold.

Still, we knew he was out there watching the same streets, stalking the same alleys. He knew we were hunting him, too. That much was clear.

Night after night, we prowled the grid of city streets and swampy reeds tucked next to the Euphrates River. I dragged my team route by route, house by house, every pushpin stamped in my mind. We were always a few days too late—just enough time to imagine the shot, the scream, the aftermath. That was all he left us; scenarios to replay in our minds.

With multiple outposts between Fallujah and Ramadi, the area was ideal for his craft. Marines were tasked with acting as peacekeepers, posted in towers and at checkpoints, patrolling the same routes day after day. Predictable. Vulnerable. He didn't need to be lucky—just patient.

As the days bled together, frustration turned to obsession. He was close and I could feel it.

But the closer we thought we got, the farther he slipped away. And he wasn't our only adversary.

We worked out of a half-finished, crumbling shell of a building just south of Route Michigan, which we called OP Falcons. It sat on a small rise, giving us a commanding view of the valley and the road below—our battalion's attempt to stop the IED emplacers who were tearing our ground patrols apart.

From our vantage point, 700 meters back from the main road, we had a decent line of sight, though not a perfect one. A small hill and a row of houses just below us created a blind spot. Dead space. One we couldn't see into, no matter how many hours we spent glassing it.

I was behind a spider hole, posted up on a stack of sandbags, scanning west toward Ramadi—another long, blistering shift in the windless heat. Sweat poured from my body, and my mind wandered.

*Boom.*

An explosion echoed in the distance, jolting me back as the shock wave crawled up our hill. Dust rose in a slow, nauseating cloud. The familiar voice of the radio crackled—two Marines injured. *Urgent.* Their track had hit an IED as they were passing in front of our position.

"Where'd it come from?" the infantry platoon Lieutenant asked as he ran toward my position, desperate for answers.

"I don't know," I replied, scanning frantically. "I can't see anything to the north." My stomach sank. "Shit...it's our dead space."

The enemy had discovered the one gap in our coverage and cut in like a scalpel. We were meant to be the overwatch, the angels on their shoulders—providing insurance against the men who hunted them. They identified our weakness and slipped right in, planting a bomb almost under our noses.

To the northwest, at the edge of our battalion's battlespace, another track from the same platoon raced toward the IED strike. Those wounded Marines were their brothers. Without hesitation, they left their assigned position to assist with the evacuation.

Their arrival was chaos—the whine of tracks, Marines shouting, blood staining the concrete of our dusty compound. The MEDEVAC bird was on its way, but first, we had to keep them alive. Our corpsman, HM3 AJ Barth, dove in, gloved hands moving fast, cutting away uniforms soaked in blood, working deep into torn flesh to stop the bleeding.

I tried to help, crouched beside them, feeling useless. "Back off, let me do my job!" Barth snapped. So I stood there, helpless, as the wounded Marine writhed and moaned, shards of metal lodged in his body.

The *whomp whomp whomp* of the CH-46 reverberated through the dry air. Dual rotors kicked up a storm of sand and dust as it landed behind our small outpost. Two more corpsmen sprinted off the ramp and into the swirling heat, working with a sense of urgency that only comes from trying to beat death.

They loaded the stretcher; the bird roared back to life, and we stood there, blasted by grit and regret as it lifted off—carrying away our brother's fate.

Then silence. The chaos was over.

The second track that raced in to help cleaned the blood from their troop compartment, reloaded, and headed back down the narrow path toward Route Michigan, returning to the position they had left behind.

Ten minutes later—*Boom.*

Another explosion, same stretch of road, only farther away.

The IED was waiting.

They left a gap in the line to save their brothers, and the enemy exploited it. The first blast drew them out, and the second finished the job. "We need a corpsman!" the radio screamed back to life.

We weren't fighting amateurs. Our enemy was patient and cunning. He studied us, tracking our habits to strike at will. They were limited only by their resources and imagination, and we had underestimated them, and our brothers paid the price.

"Fuuuuuuuck!" I screamed, crouching down with my head in my hands. "They're fucking toying with us!" My fists clenched, rage choking my throat.

We were being hunted, one by one, and bleeding out in a game we were supposed to be winning.

A few nights later, at 2 a.m., I stood in the middle of the intersection where another US soldier had been shot. We noted the direction of the suspected trajectory based on the written report—roughly west-southwest. Although often inaccurate because of the chaos of the situation, the calculation was all we had to go on. Observing in the dark, I asked myself, "Where would I shoot from to hit the person standing here?"

As I stood in the darkness—squarely in the middle of an Iraqi street, at the spot where the man had taken his last breath—an eerie feeling washed over me. As if taking a panoramic photo, I slowly turned 270 degrees and looked at all the potential buildings and houses. To hunt the killer successfully, we had to *turn the map around*. We needed to get inside his head, uncover his habits, learn more about him, and figure out where he preferred to position himself for the kill.

I knew this because I had killed, too. A sniper's job was deceptively simple in concept, yet endlessly complex in execution. We were the hunters of men—granted the power to act as judge, jury, and executioner.

My mission was to kill.

But more than that, it was to save lives—by killing. As contradictory as it sounded, that was the grim truth of our purpose. If I didn't end the lives of those who meant us harm, they could kill us—or worse, kill the innocent civilians we were there to protect.

And if that happened, I had failed. Failed my team. Failed those we supported. Failed the very reason we were there.

## Target Indicator

"Any idea where the shot came from?" asked my partner, Corporal Gabe White, a mountain-bred soul born in California's high country, cut from the same cloth as the old 49ers: part wanderer, part woodsman, and the kind of man you'd want beside you when the trail got steep. He pulled me out of my thoughts and back into the reality of the Habbaniyah street, where I stood on the spot marked by a red pushpin. Beyond the glow of the streetlights, it was pitch-black, but my night vision goggles helped me scan the shadows. The street glowed in a light green hue as I thought to myself, *If I were going to take a shot at me right here, right now, where would I be hiding?* I looked left. I looked right. A building. A house. Then an irregular hole in an exterior wall. I pointed upward and nudged my shoulder against Gabe's; I had a hunch. "Let's check out that house right there."

Silently, we patrolled to the building and knocked on the door. The home was occupied. We only needed a minute; I tried to explain to the family in hushed tones using broken Arabic. I climbed the stairs. Nothing of interest was in the bedroom overlooking the intersection, so I headed to the roof.

The roofs of Iraqi homes are not sloped like those in the United States. They are flat, with a small three-foot brick wall along the perimeter. Often, these roofs are covered in tar, like that found on top of a New York City brownstone. I quietly moved to the corner of the roof and took off my NVGs.

The faint glow from the open door leading to the roof was enough for me to recognize the scene. We first noticed a brown, wood-beaded mat neatly laid out, the same type of mat that New York cab drivers sometimes sit on in the driver's seat.

I knelt to examine the mat more closely. I followed the directional line it suggested and noticed a spider hole—a small four-to-six-inch opening in the wall. I laid down on the mat as if I were taking the shot myself. The field of view aligned perfectly with where I had stood moments before. This was the spot.

I had found his sniper's firing position. As I pushed myself off the mat, I noticed two muted gold-colored metal objects. Two brass shell casings. The first rule of any US military sniper school is never to leave your brass behind. We consider this a target indicator—anything that reveals your presence to the enemy. This had to be the position for an enemy sniper because no US-trained sniper would be that careless.

I picked up the spent brass and rolled the cartridges between my fingers. Using an infrared flashlight, I examined the ballistic markings on the casings. And there it was, stamped on the bottom of both casings. The letters "LC" glared back at me. Most US military rifle ammunition is produced at Missouri's Lake City Army Ammunition Plant. It hit me like a bullet: this sniper was using a US military-issued weapon, the M40A1, to kill US Marines and soldiers. My mouth dropped open. I looked at Jimmy and said, "Holy shit."

## Tommy's Rifle

In a sense, I had been hunting for Juba since I started sniper school back at Camp Pendleton. It was there that we studied the attack on Corporal Tommy Parker and his team from 2nd Battalion 4th Marines (2/4). They were operating from a rooftop observation post in Ramadi in June 2004. A quick reaction force investigated the team after they missed their radio check-in, only to discover that all the team members had been violently murdered. All their equipment, including the Team Leader Tommy Parker's M40A1 sniper rifle, was stolen. Later, the insurgents would make a propaganda videotape of their attack and distribute it to news outlets worldwide. I recalled learning about the ambush that day in 2004 at Pendleton. Our Platoon Sergeant, Staff Sergeant Sleigher, came in with a wretched look on his face.

He explained what happened via an intelligence debrief. Staff Sergeant Sleigher made us watch the footage. The four bodies strewn on the roof were shot countless times. Their Kevlar vests were gone. Boots gone. Blood everywhere. Weapons gone. There were signs of some struggle, but the Marines were clearly caught off guard.

As a Marine, I wanted to avenge Tommy's murder, but I also wanted to make sure I learned from the incident, so the same thing didn't happen to me and my team.

It turned out that the rooftop was a location they had used before, which was a glaring red flag for any sniper. But Corporal Parker's sniper team was ordered by his command to that rooftop in the city of Ramadi—they didn't have a choice. The enemy knew they were there. It was what snipers called an overt position.

Sometimes snipers operate from openly visible positions. For instance, snipers stationed atop the White House deter attacks by signaling our counter-sniping capability and swift, precise response to hostile actions. However, operating from a rooftop in Iraq within enemy territory during combat is an entirely different matter. Commanders often fail to recognize or, worse, deliberately ignore the fact that a sniper's security lies in their stealth rather than in their numbers.

We later discovered that construction was underway on the ground floor of the building—meaning access couldn't be controlled. The roof, already in a fixed and exposed position, became even more vulnerable with the added movement below.

All of it added up to an avoidable tragedy.

Tommy's rifle in enemy hands fueled increased sniper attacks and, subsequently, more gruesome videos we had to endure. This was not something we took lightly.

## Open Palms

16 June 2006 - 0430 - Habbaniyah, Iraq

My point man, Corporal Brett Stidfole, approached the weathered, rusted metal door, its surface pitted and sun worn. Brett glanced back at me, and I gave a firm nod. He carefully lifted the handle, the door creaking slightly—a sound that seemed to echo louder in the stillness of the predawn. We all held our breath, our ears straining for any hint of movement. Silence. We were in.

Three days earlier, Sergeant Jimmy Proudman—Team Leader of Banshee 2—and I had briefed our battalion on a mission we'd been working on. Fueled by fresh intel that a sniper was using a stolen Marine sniper rifle, and frustrated by the enemy's ability to exploit gaps in our lines with IEDs, we designed a plan to draw one of them out.

A bait mission.

Whether it was fatigue from losing too many Marines to an invisible enemy or the distraction of being just weeks from rotating back home, the brass shut it down.

Denied.

After the brief, a visibly frustrated Captain Coulman pulled us aside.

"I don't give a shit what they said in there, Pasciuti," he growled. "This is a good plan."

"What do you want to do, sir?" I asked, unable to hide the grin breaking across my face.

He paused for a moment, weighing the risk. He knew what it meant to disobey a direct decision from higher.

"We're going to run it," he said. "Just make sure you guys don't miss."

Our eight-man team slipped through the courtyard, each member finding cover and positioning themselves for maximum tactical advantage to cover our next move. As we secured the perimeter, my focus narrowed to the front door. I could feel the tension in my chest, the responsibility of the mission heavy on my shoulders. I conferred with Stidfole—another nod, another unspoken understanding passed between us. It was time.

I approached the front door and cautiously raised my gloved hand. I knocked on the door with the carbon fiber knuckle protection of my Oakley combat gloves. The carbon shell produced a distinct *ping* against the metal door. I waited for five seconds, then knocked again. I wanted whoever was inside to know that my presence at their front door in the middle of the night was intentional. I was not going away. I knocked a third time, and just as I pulled my hand back, the door cracked open two inches. Behind a sliver of light, I could make out a man's face. His eyes—wide with tension—locked with mine.

Quickly, I needed to show the Iraqi homeowner that I meant no harm. I put my index finger vertically to my lips, signaling him to be quiet, with both my sniper rifle and my M16A4 slung behind my back. I then presented my open palms to him and smiled as if it could have lightened the situation. He acknowledged my gesture and slowly opened his door. I had earned his trust by showing my vulnerability. This man was not my enemy, and I needed him to understand that. We entered and waited as he roused his family members. One by one, his children, his wife, and the grandparents assembled in the foyer.

Sgt. Kevin Homestead, a Squad Leader with Kilo Company, was on the mission to provide outward security for the house and watch for any potential ambushes. Kevin and his team moved in to assist the family and guide them to a safe location with food, water, and sleeping supplies. I handed over the remaining movement of the family members to Kevin and his squad members. Kevin and I shared a look, "with respect." Kevin knew what I meant and nodded approvingly.

Kevin, like me, strived to understand the civilian men and women caught in this terrible situation, and he worked diligently to show them we were not monsters, just men from a distant land on a mission to hunt our enemies. I had no doubt that Kevin's men would ever cross any lines. He trained them well. Two armed guards from Kevin's team would watch over the family while we went to work. I made my way upstairs to the main bedroom.

Sitting on the edge of the still-warm bed, I moved a nightstand toward the window to use as a bench. I placed my rifle on the nightstand and examined the window. Its angle would help conceal the barrel of my rifle and provide me with an ideal line of sight. I cracked the window open four inches toward the street and started setting up my position.

There was a screen behind the window that would conceal any movements behind me. I used the corner of the window drape to cover the rifle. Anyone looking up at the second floor from the street would see a typical view of an open window and a hanging drape. I was in position. My team confirmed that Banshee 2 was ready at their west-facing site. I glanced at my watch. It was 5 a.m. We were back on schedule.

I grabbed my Leica Vector Combo 10× binoculars and rangefinder, and a handheld GPS unit known as a DAGR. As the morning light crept over the Iraqi horizon, I settled in and began studying the streetscape as it fell into its natural rhythm.

During standard overwatch, most of my time wasn't spent behind the rifle. Instead, I stayed "out of the gun," scanning with wider-lensed optics like my binoculars. They offered a broader field of view, lower magnification, and the ability to catch subtle movements my sniper scope might miss. It was about seeing the whole picture—before zeroing in on a single point.

I began to create my range card, which detailed significant features and reference points. I kept it next to me, measuring distances of 100, 200, and 300 meters. In my line of sight, roughly 250 meters away, a man in a white caftan was going through the motions of setting up a roadside market. He was lifting the canvas covers of the food stalls. Next to the market was a chai tea shop that would also open shortly. The market resembled every other market I have seen in Iraq—nothing out of the ordinary.

The trap was set to spring at 7:00 a.m.—designed to draw out a potential sniper or IED team. As a bait mission, the goal was to convince the enemy that this area was unguarded and vulnerable.

At exactly 0700, we'd pull the M1A1 Abrams tank—normally stationed in that sector—away to simulate a response to an urgent incident on the far side of town, mimicking the same conditions that had followed an IED strike weeks earlier.

We knew the risks. Jimmy and I were clear from the start—we'd never use live Marines as bait.

So when the armored vehicle pulled away, it sent a clear message to the enemy: this area was exposed. Unprotected. A gap in our defenses—exactly the kind of opening they had exploited before.

Only this time, it was intentional.

It was still early—5:56 a.m. The local mosque began its somber symphony of melodic and guttural prayers over the loudspeakers. I would have to wait a while before this town, located south of the Euphrates River, came to life. I was on the gun, waiting and watching when, at 7:05 a.m., our platoon corpsman, HM3 Barth, tapped me on the shoulder.

Dark-haired and similar to me in both build and features, Barth and I were nearly inseparable. He was from Youngstown, Ohio—and like me, his name was AJ.

We even shared the same birthday.

"Hey, AJ. You need to get some rest. Why don't you come off the gun." Doc got mad when we didn't listen to him.

Just like any Navy Corpsman, Doc Barth was our "team mom"—a strange, sacred mix of medic, therapist, and brother. The relationship between Marines and their corpsmen wasn't just built on duty—it was absolute trust.

Navy corpsmen were nothing short of guardian angels. The ones who ran toward the chaos when others hit the deck. When a Marine went down, it wasn't the Lieutenant or Squad Leader they cried out for—it was Doc.

For generations, those final, desperate moments on the battlefield were filled with calls for mothers... or for the corpsman.

The respect we held for them was immeasurable. It didn't matter what your rank was or how tough you thought you were. If Doc told you to drink water, you drank. If Doc told you to rest, you rested. If

Doc told you to shut the hell up and stop being stubborn, you nodded and zipped it.

Doc knew best—always.

So when Doc Barth shot me a look and told me to get some rest, I didn't argue. I got off the gun, rolled onto the bed behind me, and let exhaustion take over. Because if Doc said I needed it, I probably needed it an hour ago.

Two hours later, at 9 a.m., Doc Barth gave my thigh two purposeful squeezes to subconsciously let me know it was a friend waking me and that we were safe. I could already feel the temperature beginning to rise. It would be another hot day. I made a feeble attempt to stay hydrated, sipping on my bathwater-temperature water.

I was ready to get back on the gun. Doc Barth briefed me on the limited activity he observed during his shift before slapping his thighs in the most Midwestern way possible, standing up, and declaring, "Well dude, I'm gonna go take a shit." Doc got off the gun and headed downstairs to take care of business. As he left the room, he poked his head back in and smirked, "Try not to kill anyone while I'm gone."

As I settled back into position, the low drone of a diesel engine and the rumble of tracks on pavement gave way to the unmistakable sounds of an Assault Amphibious Vehicle headed our way. I shook my head—this wasn't right.

When it rolled into view, my stomach twisted, and my already dry mouth smacked open. It was one of ours. India Company. They weren't supposed to be here. Our own guys had just stumbled into the kill zone we had set for the enemy. A head popped from the turret—Sergeant Cyle Burton, a Squad Leader with India Company. We had done three deployments together. The bedroom felt hotter around me.

"Red One, this is Banshee 4," I radioed, maintaining a steady voice. "We're running a mission here."

Burton's response was routine. "Roger, Banshee 4. Just letting the engine cool. Be out of your way in five."

"Good. Five minutes—we can do that." I returned to scanning.

Sniper school taught me to survey using a "fifty-meter overlapping strip search," sweeping right to left—opposite the way we read. This forced our brains to notice anomalies in an environment, a *disturbance in the baseline.*

On my third pass from near to far, something caught my eye: a gray four-door sedan parked near a roadside market—standard issue for Iraq. Since I'd already seen the driver exit, cross my field of view, and sit at a chai shop, I thought the car was empty.

A silvery glare from the rear passenger panel piqued my interest.

I snapped left, dropped behind my rifle's scope, and cranked the magnification ring on my Schmidt & Bender. My field of view tightened from a 3× broad field of view to a 12× lock on the object.

A Sony Handycam was positioned in the sedan's rear triangular window, its lens aimed directly at Burton's vehicle. *Major Disturbance.*

My mouth dried as sweat trickled down my temple. Burton was either about to be shot by a sniper, or his AAV was seconds away from detonating into a fireball.

"Red One, Red One, this is Banshee 4. Button up. You're about to get hit," I hissed into the radio.

Burton's response came back, confused. "Say again, Banshee 4?"

"Button up. Now! You're being videotaped." The alarm in my voice snapped him to attention.

Sergeant Burton whipped his head left and right before dropping inside the track. A second later, his arm shot up to grab the hatch. Still on the radio, he barked to his squad, "Brace for impact!"

I was alone.

Hot flashes shot up my spine and into my now throbbing ears.

I frantically scanned the area for indicators; my rifle swung from left to right.

Something was wrong. Deeply wrong.

They had slipped past us. Somehow.

Was it an IED? A sniper? Had they been here before—did we fall into *their* trap?

Every shadow stretched into a threat. Every movement flashed like a weapon.

*AJ aboard the USS* Comstock *in 1996, meeting a USMC sniper for the first time.*

VE LEFT) *Inspiration: US Marine and history teacher Mr. Rojas shakes AJ's hand at AJ's Eagle Scout nony, summer of 2001, San Jose, CA;* (ABOVE RIGHT) *Recruiter: Staff Sergeant Walter Tinay and AJ iuti after USMC boot camp graduation, October 2002.*

*Head Bonk: AJ says goodbye to his father, Giuseppe, before deploying to Kuwait, February 2003.*

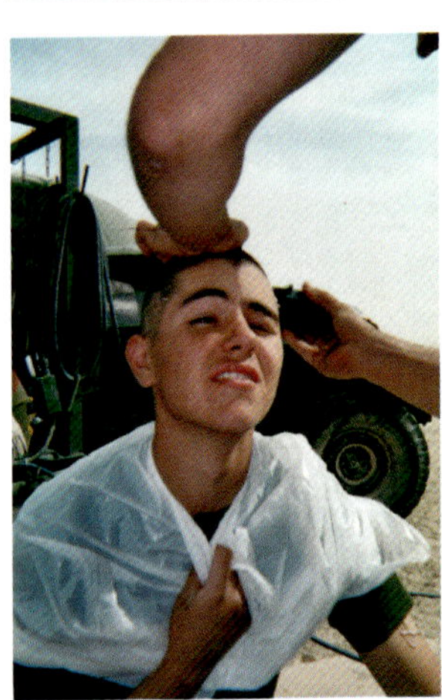

(ABOVE) *Boots: (left to right) AJ Pasciuti, John Henry, Charlie Grahan February 2003.*

(LEFT) *Buzz cut: USMC barbershop. Kuwait, February 2003.*

(BELOW) *AJ reads a letter days before crossing the berm into Iraq, March 2003.* (JOHN MAKELY, BALTIMORE SUN)

*Udari Range near the Kuwait-Iraq border, February 2003.* (JOHN MAKELY, BALTIMORE SUN)

*Snakes Biting: AH-1 Cobras nduct a rocket and gun run ıst Iraqi Republican Guard, April 2003.* (JOHN MAKELY, BALTIMORE SUN)

*Sergeant Pryor and Corporal Olsen recover after a brutal firefight against the Republican Guard, April 2003.* (JOHN MAKELY, BALTIMORE SUN)

*AJ and Charlie Graham clear Iraqi military buildings en route to Baghdad, April 2003.* (JOHN MAKELY, BALTIMORE SUN)

(ABOVE LEFT) *Babbo: AJ's father, Giuseppe, wearing AJ's modified patrol ghillie suit before Fallujah, September 2004.* (ABOVE RIGHT) *Giants Fan: Each Marine was allowed to bring one personal item to w while on downtime in Fallujah. Camp Baharia, November 2004.*

(ABOVE) *The Marine sailors of India Com gather for one last p before entering the c November 2004.*

(LEFT) *Bench Rest: A uses an unorthodox shooting platform w engaging insurgents in Fallujah, Novemb 2004.*

*Banshee 2: (left to right) James owers, Blake Cole, Tony Scardino, asciuti. Jolan District, December 2004.*

*Iraqi Elections: AJ and Blake Cole at an overt sniper position providing security for the first Iraqi elections in decades, January 2005.*

*urning Home: After llujah, AJ meets his rying mother, April 2005.*

(ABOVE LEFT) *Honor Grad: AJ shakes the hand of Vietnam Sniper Jim Gularte at sniper school gradua* *September 2005;* (ABOVE RIGHT) *Spider Hole: AJ peers through a small window observing Route Michigan—connecting Ramadi and Fallujah—June 2006.*

*Banshee 2: (left t right) Gabe Whi AJ Pasciuti, Jim Proudman, Tony Scardino. Amiri Iraq, February 2*

LEFT) *The Rifle: AJ holds Corporal Tommy Parker's M40A1 sniper rifle, used by Juba for two* *s, now back in American hands, June 2006;* (TOP RIGHT) *Partners: AJ and Kevin Homestead hold* *ecovered M40A1 after killing Juba and his spotter, June 2006;* (ABOVE) *Banshee 2 and 4: The teams* *onsible for hunting Juba down (rear left to right): Jimmy Proudman, AJ Pasciuti, Brett Stidfole, AJ* *th, Jarred Ramsey (front): Gabe White, Tony Scardino, June 2006.*

(ABOVE) *Bearshark Platoon: Hawthorne, Nevada, September 2009;* (RIGHT) *Recon Sniper: Staff Sergeant Matt Ingham zeroes his M40A5. Rodriguez Live Fire Complex, South Korea, May 2009.*

(BELOW) *Who Dares Wins: SAS, SBS, Royal Marines, and US Marines pose in front of a historic mountain range. Helmand Province, November 2009.*

*ands with his Assistant*
*Leader, Joe Gillooly.*
*Zad, December 2009.*

*ndu Kush: AJ pauses for a*
*oto while descending from*
*the white mountains. Now*
*Zad, December 2009.*

*: AJ and Matt Ingham cooking an Italian meal for their teams on New Year's Eve, December 2009.*

(ABOVE) *Bearshark & Scarface: Members of 3rd Platoon pose with one of Scarface's UH-1Y Hue Note: Scarface painted 3rd Recon's emblem on t nose. (Rear left to right): AJ Pasciuti, Joe Gilloc Scarface Pilot, Toshi Coenen, Dillon Garretson, Tylor Johnson, Nick Jacobs, Efrain Martinez, P Peters, Kevin Kinkade. (Kneeling left to right): Randall Hutchcroft, Dan Castaneda. Helmand Province, March 2010.*

(ABOVE) *Angela's Letter: AJ stands with the letter received from a high school student. Helmand Province, May 2010.*

(BELOW) *Marjah: Paul Peters (left) and AJ rest during a break in the fighting. Marjah, Februar 2010.*

(ABOVE LEFT) *Heavy Hover: Special Amphibious Recon* *·psman Lee Boujie (left) and AJ Pasciuti (right) vector* *I-53 Super Stallion into a hover while conducting fast-* *ıg operations. Petra, Jordan, May 2012;* (ABOVE RIGHT) *Bottom Up: Nick Sabbato climbs from a rigid-hulled* *'atable boat while conducting a Visit Board Search and* *eizure, December 2011.* (MIDDLE) *Top Down: Members* *of the 24th Marine Expeditionary Unit's Force Recon* *toon slide from an SH-60 Seahawk while conducting a* *'sit Board Search and Seizure, November 2011.* (RIGHT) *ıck Friday: The Force Recon Platoon get in the holiday* *spirit by pretending to wait outside the ship's store on* *Black Friday. USS* New York, *November 2012.*

(ABOVE) *High Boat: Basic Reconnaissance Course students (ropers) struggle under the weight of the U*
*Combat Rubber Raiding Craft, Coronado, CA, 2015.* (MASTER SERGEANT HALSEY GREEN, USMC RET.)*;*
(BELOW) *Row: Basic Reconnaissance Course students (ropers) practice paddling the USMC Combat Rubber Raiding Craft, Coronado, CA, 2015.*

*Blake Cole (left) and AJ reunite while training in Hawaii's Pohakuloa Training Area. Both became Marine officers: Blake through the Marine Enlisted Commissioning Education Program, attending college while on active duty before earning his commission as a Marine aviator, and AJ as a Chief Warrant Officer, Infantry Weapons Officer—known as a Marine Gunner.*

HT) *Attack at Dawn—Company nmander Mike Davidson (right) assesses the enemy disposition while conducting a heliborne company attack—Mount Bundy Training Area, Darwin, Australia—August 2019.*

OW) *Trinity—The Trinity team poses for a photo following the final company attack of a four- ıonth training exercise. (Left to right) Jeremy Moon, Ben Reid, Vill McCabbe, Ben Shorthouse, te Rollins, Dean Long, Terrance ploe, Pete O'Brien, AJ Pasciuti, Jay Baker.*

(ABOVE LEFT) *IMC—AJ briefs the first class of the Infantry Marine Course—School of Infantry, Camp Pendleton, CA—January 2021;* (ABOVE RIGHT) *Ender's Game—IMC students were taught chess by thei instructors as a means to stimulate an adaptive mindset and develop military strategy.*

*Warfighting—IMC students study* Marine Corps Doctrinal Publication 1, *"Warfighting." Historically only officers or senior enlisted personnel receive education on the Marine Corps' warfighting philosop This was the first time that entry-level enlisted students were educated rather than simply trained. Scl of Infantry, Camp Pendleton, CA, January 2021.*

*l Reload—IMC student conducts a magazine change while under the instruction of Federal Air hals. School of Infantry, Camp Pendleton, CA—March 2021.* (LANCE CPL. ANDREW CORTEZ, US MARINE ;)

*Hunt—AJ Pasciuti, Mark O'Connell, Dave Delong, and other instructors before hunting students on final mission. School of Infantry, Camp Pendleton, CA—April 2021.*

(ABOVE LEFT) *The Letter: AJ references Angela's letter during his retirement speech. School of Infantr Camp Pendleton, CA, May 2023;* (ABOVE RIGHT) *Finally Home—AJ and his mother, Jerilyn Lightfoot, smile at the end of a long journey. School of Infantry, Camp Pendleton, CA, May 2023.* (BELOW) *The Ri AJ poses with Tommy Parker's M40A1 sniper rifle. After Tommy Parker's death, Juba used the rifle tc hundreds of US and coalition service members. The M40A1 was returned to its rightful owners in 200 In 2024, the rifle went on display at the National Museum of the Marine Corps in Quantico, VA, wher continues to be exhibited today.*

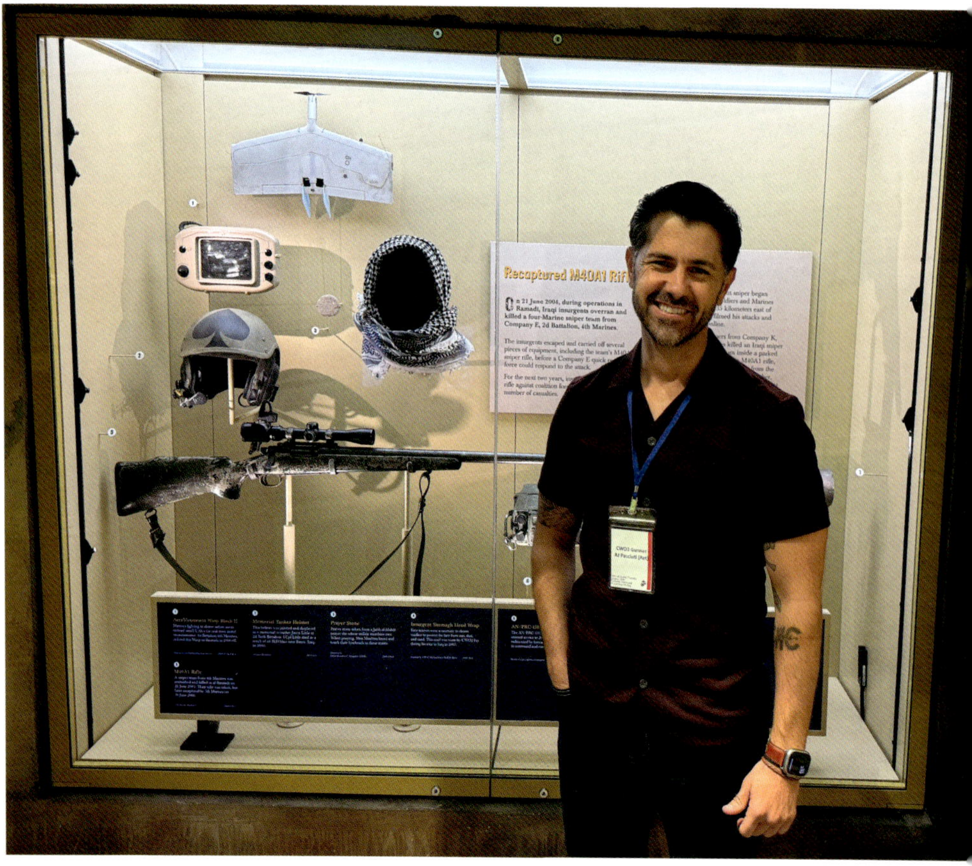

My heart pounded like a drum as my mind raced—spotters, trigger men, ambush routes, hidden angles. It was all spinning faster than I could piece it together.

Eight kilometers away, at OP Cubs, India Company Commander Captain Len Coulman—Diesel 6—listened to the nightmare as it unfolded through a squawk box connected to the radio. Cubs served as a makeshift command post while India Company was on rotation. The radio net was our primary lifeline. Banshee 4's call lit up India Company's frequency. The company staff snapped to, relaying the message. Coulman and 1st Platoon crowded around the radio, hanging on every word. 2nd and 3rd Platoons, no doubt, did the same.

Each platoon jumped to an "alert" status without hesitation. No one had any idea what was going on, but we weren't about to let ourselves become victims. A squad was alone on patrol. A fight was coming, and no one was going to let them face it alone.

Sweat trickled from my right brow, sliding past my temple. My mouth, filled with American tobacco caked in who-knows-what chemical that permitted it for export, felt like sand. I could hear my breathing and focused on keeping my rhythm to control my racing heart. Hot, stale air swirled around me as I centered my breath and cleared my mind.

No one was coming; there were no good options.

The radio crackled—muffled voices, bursts of static, encrypted beeps. Confusion and nerves reverberated through the company. I couldn't make out the words. I didn't need to.

The fight was here.

I breathed in.

*Calm yourself, pay attention, look for disturbances.*

I exhaled.

My eyes darted back and forth across the scene, scanning for anything out of the ordinary—shadows, errant trash, men sitting at chai shops.

Nothing.

"Be patient; wait for movement," I told myself as I took a deep, slow inhale.

The radio calls continued in vain.

I brought my scope back to the Handycam and scanned the rest of the car. Tinted windows blocked any chance of seeing inside. My rifle stayed trained on the camera, perched on the divider between the cab and the trunk, nestled into the dim, triangle-shaped window on the rear passenger side—the only untinted window.

If anything was going to happen, it was going to originate here.

Captain Coulman came over the radio, looking for clarity. We'd worked together for two deployments. I was his sniper in Fallujah, and now I was his sniper in Ramadi.

He knew my voice and sensed the urgency.

Calm and composed, Captain Coulman cleared the net. "Banshee 4, give me an idea of what's happening out there?"

### Juba's Hand

"Red One rolled up for a routine stop. I've got a positive ID on a Sony Handycam that's open and recording the track. I had them button up. Something is about to happen."

Coulman and I agreed I needed to hold my position, cover the engagement, and supervise the infantry sweep. Firing now would compromise my position. Worse, I couldn't confirm whether the sedan was occupied.

I heard Cobra and Huey gunships in the distance, and I radioed Coulman the option, "Let's see if we can grab a Hellfire."

"Roger." Coulman worked over our air frequency. We waited. Nothing.

*Silence is the loudest sound on the battlefield.*

Coulman's voice returned, abrupt with frustration. "Rotors are a no-go. Section's bingo on fuel. They're headed back to base."

No air support. My mind raced. I shifted to the next option.

"India Fires, India Fires. This is Banshee 4. Request immediate suppression on grid thirty-eight Sierra, Lima Bravo, five, five, three, six, niner, eight, zero, seven. Enemy vehicle in the open. Danger close. Friendlies protected—200 meters. South-Southwest."

"Banshee 4, this is India Fires, stand by."

Our fire support section rogered up, repeated the grids back to me, and sent the message to the artillery battery.

I waited, determined on the gun, my cheek dug into the buttstock, eyes trained on the camera in the sedan's rear window. I watched for movement, my finger on the trigger.

The radio crackled. The voice was flat.

"Banshee 4, this is India Fires. Immediate suppression denied. Target is in a No-Fire Area."

Rules of engagement restricted fire within 500 meters of culturally significant sites. A mosque sat 400 meters north of me. The mission was scrubbed.

Sergeant Kevin Homestead stepped in, having caught the last transmission. "Hey, I'm here to help."

"Thanks, but we're on our own," I replied. We were out of options.

Coulman's Chicago accent cut back in. "Banshee 4, this is Six. Any update?"

A high-stakes, three-way standoff. No one moved. Each waited for the other to make the wrong call—the fatal mistake. The air crackled with anticipation; each passing moment brought the potential for chaos closer. One wrong move would undoubtedly unleash a torrent of action, locking every entity in a deadly dance.

Burton's men had no choice but to sit and wait, their fates in someone else's hands. The agony of it must have been unbearable.

Something was off.

Juba must have sensed it.

Burton's sudden dive to cover had to have spooked him. The walls were closing in. He was caught in his own trap. There was no escape.

India Company scrambled a reaction force—Marines donning combat gear, locking mags into their rifles, and loading into vehicles. The cavalry would be here soon.

Coulman's voice hit the net again. "Banshee 4?"

I didn't hear him.

"Banshee 4?"

That's when I saw it—a hand—movement in the sedan's backseat.

A person sat in the rear, adjusting a camera. I had my proof: someone was in the vehicle.

"Banshee 4, this is Diesel 6!"

I exhaled, steadying my optic. The hand slid forward again, slow, deliberate, creeping past the dark tint. Brown, ashen fingers curled around the screen, the thumb pressing buttons—his left hand.

I couldn't see his face. I'd have to make a judgment call.

"Six, this is Four. I've got movement," I said.

Coulman's voice cut through the radio, "Pasciuti, take the shot!"

## Juba's End

"Breathe in," I told myself—maybe aloud.

I brought my scope back to the Sony Handycam, dialed to 12× power. The tinted windows obstructed much of the car's interior, but the silver camera sat nestled against the dim, triangular window on the rear passenger side door.

Indecision gnawed at me.

The politics of the modern conflict flashed through my mind. If I pulled the trigger and was wrong, I'd end up in prison. If I hesitated and Marines died, I'd have to bear that weight forever.

I exhaled, assessing my shot.

A layer of tempered glass stood between me and my target. The bullet's path could shift, and civilians were nearby. I drew my final breath as his left hand worked the camera; his head had to be hovering near the flip-out screen.

I made my decision and slowly exhaled.

Four pounds of pressure. *Boom.*

My first shot smashed through the glass to clear a path for my next two rounds, which followed close behind.

*Boom. Boom.*

Two more rounds followed, tight in a two-inch space above the camera and below the edge of the window.

Chaos erupted.

The family inside the house screamed. I heard movement on the street through the open bedroom window. The residents had no idea a sniper was in their midst. The men from Homestead's team rushed to calm them, but the house next door caught the panic and joined in.

"Kevin, get on the gun," I said, dropping to a knee.

Homestead took my spot, rifle trained on the scene. He wasn't a sniper, but he grew up hunting and was a competent shooter. I trusted him.

I grabbed the radio. "Red One, I need you to move your track to that sedan now."

Kevin scanned the scene as I shifted to command and control. We still weren't out of the woods—an ambush was possible, and that car needed to be secured.

"Kev, anybody touches that car, you shoot," I told him.

The net buzzed with encrypted beeps and frantic transmissions. I broke in.

*"BREAK, BREAK, BREAK! ALL STATIONS CLEAR THE NET, THIS IS BANSHEE 4!"*

"Red One, get to that vehicle now. We'll hold security until you arrive."

Burton responded, "Roger, Four. We've got to head east 200 meters to cross the wadi."

His track peeled out, throwing asphalt, racing east.

I switched to Coulman to update him while observing the situation unfold and helping to coordinate company assets.

Then Kevin tapped my shoulder. "Look," he said, his voice tight.

The man who parked the car—the one who had calmly walked to the chai shop earlier—was returning as if nothing had happened.

I didn't hesitate. "Kevin, the moment he touches that car, plug him."

"Breathe in," I said, steadying Kevin.

Six paces. The man walked with an air of arrogance.

Brown prayer beads swayed rhythmically in his right hand as his sandals slapped against the dusty pavement. He brushed his hands across his thighs, wiping away the crumbs from his last meal. Heavyset, balding, and with sloped shoulders, he looked nothing like a fighter—more like someone who never missed a meal.

But his movements were too smooth, almost rehearsed.

"Exhale," I coached. Kevin's stale breath hissed through pursed lips.

Four paces. The man glanced over his left shoulder, surveying the street.

A flicker of satisfaction danced in his smug smile—a routine operation. Park the car. Walk away. Wait for the sniper to take the shot. Then chaos. Then the getaway.

Not today.

"Breathe in, focus on the crosshairs," I said, watching his chest slowly rise.

Two paces. He wiped his hands again, adjusting the beads entwined between his fingers and extending his right hand toward the sedan's front passenger door.

The prayer beads swung. The door cracked open.

His expression dropped. He saw Juba.

"Exhale—*slow, steady, squeeze,*" I whispered.

Four pounds of pressure.

*Boom.*

Kevin's shot struck the man two inches above the sternum, shattering his rib cage. The impact sent him stumbling back; he collapsed into the crease of the open door. As he fell, his body twisted, exposing his vulnerable left side. The suddenness of the attack left him sprawled and in shock.

"Hit him again," I yelled.

The street erupted. More screaming.

Four more pounds of pressure.

*Boom.*

The second shot tore through the side of his chest, sending a shock wave through his body. He crumpled to his knees, gasping as pain radiated from the wound. His breath hitched. His hands searched for support as his world narrowed.

I took Kevin's spot on the gun.

The man, now mortally wounded, clawed across the passenger seat, dragging himself toward the driver's side, trying to escape—or reach his weapon. I didn't care.

The broken glass I had shattered earlier, and the open front passenger door, were my only vantage points into the vehicle. I didn't have a clear line of sight. I had to stop him from moving.

*Boom*. Right knee gone.

*Boom*. Left knee torn away.

His movements stopped.

"Banshee 4, Red One, approaching now!" Burton's voice shot in.

"Roger, Red One, you have two hostiles at the target; the status of both is unknown. We've got you from over your left shoulder," I reassured Burton.

Burton's track streaked into position. The ramp dropped, and Marines poured out as fire teams moved to secure the street. Burton and a machine gunner approached the sedan.

I radioed, "Burton, you've got a man in the front seat. We've hit him a few times, and I'm unsure of his status." Burton's squad surrounded him as he moved closer to the sedan.

"Roger, Four. He's dead." Two bullet holes left fresh dark blood stains on his white caftan, prayer beads in his hands, clutched to his chest. "We're checking the back now," Burton radioed.

Burton swung open the rear door. His team aimed, ready.

"Yeah, you've got another one," Burton said. "He's dead too."

I exhaled.

The first shot was perfect. Juba was slumped over, soaked in blood, hands limp in his lap. The round sliced through the seam where the window met the roof, shattering the glass before punching through his forehead.

He never heard it.

"Burton, look in the back window," I directed. "You'll see a small silver Sony Handycam."

Burton pivoted between the car and me, blocking my view. He crouched, reached inside, and retrieved the camera. Lifting it into the air, he gave it a quick shake so I could see.

"Four, this is One. Good copy on the camera," he said, voice edged with excitement.

"Roger, One." I replied.

Burton turned back to his team, barking orders, directing the search for intel. Then he stopped.

"Hey, Four—there's something else in here," he said. "Looks like a rifle. One of ours."

I froze.

"What?" I craned my neck to get a better look back behind my rifle.

Burton reached in, both hands grabbing the weapon. He turned, lifting it above his head.

Through my optic, I recognized it instantly.

McMillan stock, Schneider barrel, Remington 700 short action. My stomach leaped into my throat faster than I could jump to my feet. I glanced back at the team in disbelief. I knew exactly what it was, but I needed to hear it.

"One, this is Four. Read me the first series of digits from that rifle." I asked.

My team leaned in, silent and waiting. Each USMC sniper rifle carried a similar and familiar letter-number combination, starting with one letter followed by six or seven numbers.

Burton read it out. "Remington Model 700. Serial number: E6546973."

No one spoke. We knew. Corporal Tommy Parker's M40A1.

We got it back.

# 12

# "WE'VE ALREADY BEEN OVER THIS"

### Losing Ray

26 June 2006 - Camp Habbaniyah, Iraq

"Hey, AJ, can we chat outside?" Memo Sandoval, now our Platoon Sergeant, said as he set his hand on my shoulder. His face showed restrained pain.

The blaring Iraqi sun blinded me as I opened the squeaky, metal-grated door and stepped into the oppressive heat. I wore only my olive drab running shorts and sneakers. We were back at our platoon headquarters for a few days of rest. In less than a month, we'd rotate out. Our relief unit was on the way.

"There's something I've got to tell you," Memo said, extending a stateside pack of Marlboro Reds. This wasn't good news. I flicked my silver Zippo, lit my cigarette, and waited for a name I knew I'd recognize. "There's no easy way," Memo said, his voice trembling. "Ray's gone." He cradled his forehead in his left hand as a thin line of smoke floated from the cigarette in his right. He knew that Ray and I were close. I remained silent; the cigarette's cherry crackled as I inhaled nicotine and toxins as if they could somehow grant me clarity.

Staff Sergeant Ray Plouhar was one of the kindest men I had met in the service. He was from Lake Orion, Michigan, and I first got to know him when I joined the Sniper Platoon in 2004. He was a HOG who looked out for me, even though we served on different teams. Raised rural, blue-collar, and big-eared, he understood what it felt like to seem small and knew how to stand up for himself and others. We stayed as close as we could to one another in Fallujah the previous year and always shared a big hug when we saw each other. He even promised my mom he'd bring me home safe.

"How?" I asked, exhaling smoke and brushing away a single tear before it fell.

"IED," Memo answered. "Hit the Colonel's convoy. Ray was in the lead vehicle. Word is he died on impact." Just weeks before heading home, I'd lost another brother.

Before he was killed in the line of duty, Ray had become infamous within the Marines for reasons beyond his control. While Ray was posted to recruiting duty in Flint, Michigan, in 2003, a film director who claimed to be making a minor documentary about high school career choices approached the Marines about filming recruiters in Flint. Ray was serving as a Marine recruiter at the time in Flint and was ordered to give the filmmaker and his crew full access. Ray did so and allowed the film crew to join him on visits to shopping malls and schools because he always saw the good in people. What the Marines and Ray did not know was that the filmmaker was making a big-budget anti-war feature film. When the film released to theaters, it portrayed Ray as an overzealous Marine who preyed upon vulnerable young teens to get them to join up and fight an unnecessary war. Nothing could have been further from the truth. Ray genuinely cared for those recruits and cared for us even more.

The real backstory of how Ray became a recruiter reflected what a selfless man he was. In 2001, when his uncle needed a kidney to survive, Ray immediately offered one of his own. To remain with the Marines during his recovery, he took on the role of a recruiter, which was less physically demanding than being a sniper. This decision wasn't about choosing an easier path; it was about buying time—staying in the fight until he was medically cleared to rejoin a battalion in combat.

Ray was so much more than the man portrayed in the film. He confided in me several times about how humiliated and deeply betrayed he felt by the production team he had allowed into his life. Ray left behind two young sons, Raymond and Michael. At his funeral, the Marine Corps presented his wife, Leigha, with his Purple Heart. His father-in-law remarked, "Ray chose to go where others would not and could not go." Yet, in the end, Ray went to his grave burdened by a wrongful shame that was never his to bear.

I let the next single tear roll down my cheek, crushed my cigarette into the desert sand, exhaled the putrid smoke, and mumbled, "What the fuck is this all for?" Then I went inside.

Three weeks later, we were home—and I was drunk.

## The Animal and the Alcohol

The hardest part about turning into an animal was becoming human again.

The instincts that kept me alive in hell didn't belong in society: violence, callousness, and rage.

America and her Marines struggled with the unintended consequences of brutal combat. The mental and emotional toll of war carved deep, often invisible wounds. Yet the Corps did not recommend—or require—any real assessment or counseling for PTSD, psychological trauma, or substance abuse for those returning from combat. Mandatory briefings were given to a half-listening crowd before we boarded planes home. No real action followed for those who had seen hell and would now be left to live with it.

My three tours in Iraq, completed in just three years, left me drained in ways I didn't comprehend. I had witnessed unfathomable death and destruction, but also more courage and sacrifice than I could ever have imagined. One of the hardest but necessary parts of the homecoming ritual was visiting the families of fallen Marines.

While I was deployed, my mother and stepmother made it a point to attend every funeral of a close friend who died while I was away. A comforting—and equally heart-wrenching—act of solidarity, born from the unbearable weight of having a child at war.

They stood among the mourners, comforting families they barely knew, feeling every loss as if it were their own. The agony they must have felt, watching another mother weep over a flag-draped coffin—her child given in service to our country—knowing the mother would have given anything to take her child's place, wondering if they were next.

It's impossible to describe when a mother or father hugs you like their own son, and the best you can do is hug them back and sob, knowing you can't replace what they lost. The tears, the stories, and the big-bellied laughter over recounted childhood memories always dragged everyone back to the day we lost him.

The reality of the grieving family before me and the haunting memories of their child's death tore at me as I held a mother's hand in silence. The dirt, dust, blood, cries, and chaos seemed to reappear in those rooms as if they were floating in the air. The only thing that numbed the pain was booze.

Like any group of early twentysomethings, alcohol permeated our childish, tough-guy culture. The Marine Corps was founded in a bar called the Tun Tavern in Philadelphia in 1775. Drinking was hereditary and ingrained in our Marine DNA long before we first set foot on the yellow footprints at boot camp. We drank together. We drank alone. We drank when we were joyful. We drank when we were angry. But we always drank the most when we remembered the ones we had lost.

We lived like we wouldn't see twenty-five. Between all the funerals and the way the war had escalated; we figured we were next to die. I was spiraling out of control, unable to stop. My own family told me they were more worried about me driving around Orange County on a Friday night than they ever were when I was over in Iraq.

## The Favor

4 February 2007 - Super Bowl Sunday,
Laguna Beach, CA

Prince's electric halftime show thundered through the downpour, setting the stage for Peyton Manning and the Colts to claim their first championship in three decades. When closing time approached at a bar in Laguna Beach, I decided to drive over to a friend's place for the after-party. I had no business getting behind the wheel.

Southbound on the Pacific Coast Highway, I rolled in my lifted red pickup, music blaring like a chump, trying to somehow attract women. Thirty minutes later, I sat on the sidewalk—handcuffed—my career was over.

By no fault of its own, the Marine Corps resorted to the only tool it understood: punishment. In a hollow attempt to curb substance abuse, the Corps enforced a policy of zero tolerance for any infraction: half-pay, restrictions, and the worst outcome for me—reduction in rank. That would kill any chance of reenlistment and end my career. Right after being hand-selected by my mentor, Wesley Payne, to teach alongside him at the coveted Scout Sniper School on Camp Pendleton, I just blew twice the legal limit. It was discipline without understanding—accountability without healing. We were just kids who had walked through hell and were left to cope with it on our own.

"Sergeant Pasciuti reporting as ordered, Sergeant Major," I said. Monday morning brought the weekend's disciplinary reports. My arrest report was on it. The newly promoted Sergeant Major sat with his seat leaned back, his head resting on his index finger. We knew each other. He was India Company's First Sergeant on our last deployment. The Marines in Juba's crosshairs were his men. When we arrived back at the base with 2/4's rifle we recaptured from Juba, he hugged me, promising to return the favor. My future was in his hands.

"What were you thinking, Pasciuti?" His loud voice was wrapped with more hurt than anger. "You're one of this battalion's leaders. People look up to you. Do you understand that?"

"Yes, Sergeant Major," I said, staring at the bookshelf behind him. I couldn't meet his eyes; I was too embarrassed. Plus, I could tell this was a one-way conversation. The hail of expletives hit like a flash-bang. "You dumb mother... Jesus, you could've killed someone, you idiot." He continued, enraged. "All the atta' boys in the world get wiped away with one awe shit. This is your awe shit. You're back at square one."

"What am I supposed to do here, Pasciuti?" he said, still fuming.

"I have no excuse, Sergeant Maj—."

"You're goddamn right, you don't." He cut me off. He drew in a long, heavy breath, gritting his teeth in anger. And slowly exhaled. "Pasciuti, you remember that favor I owe you?" His voice softened for the first time. My eyes darted from his bookshelf back to his narrowed, enraged eyes. "Consider us even," he growled. "Now get out of my office... and don't fuck this up!" he yelled down the hall as I sprinted out, afraid he might change his mind.

### Sniper School Instructor

August 2007 - Scout Sniper School,
School of Infantry, Camp Pendleton, CA

"Well, look who it is!" Sergeant Wesley Payne greeted me as I walked through the doors of the sniper school. "My favorite PIG has returned as a HOG—the sniper killer." Payne had been my greatest advocate for an instructor position. He took me under his wing during my training and then pushed for me to instruct beside him, teaching other snipers how to think.

"No, Wes. Thank you," I said as we hugged. I was now a sniper instructor. Like Payne and Slafsky before me, I would teach mission planning and employment. I would hone my craft while mentoring the next generation of snipers.

I worked with some of the finest Marines I'd ever known. A rugged assembly of the toughest men from diverse backgrounds. From Long Beach to Long Island, the Oregon Coast to Puerto Rico, and everywhere in between. We all brought something different. It was the intersection of experiences from all our lives. The city kid and the country boy depended on one another because sniping crossed both worlds. We recognized we were not a homogenous group and had different strengths and weaknesses. But together, we shaped hundreds of the most competent warriors the Marine Corps had ever seen. I became friends with many, only to lose some during the war—and even more after.

"Okay, PIGs, grab your guns!" I shouted, leading them into a narrow alley by our neighboring Quonset hut. "Today, we're painting rifles," I said while holding reeds and tall grass in one hand and a matte tan spray paint can in the other.

"Nature has no right angles." I reminded the class.

"See those sharp edges on the barrel and stock? We want to break up that outline. Layers of color create deeper shadows, and shadows give us dimension. Painting your rifle has nothing to do with looking cool. Nature is fragmented, disjointed, and imperfect—your weapon should mirror that. When stalking the enemy, remember we aren't observers of our environment—we're part of it. Your rifle must be, too."

The thousands of hours spent in that dilapidated, condemned tin hut, whether as a student or an instructor, remain some of the most pivotal experiences of my life—often learning more from the students than I ever imagined.

## Help Line

"Do you want to kill yourself?" A preoccupied voice inquired over the phone at my local clinic.

"No," I blurted, a reaction to the faceless voice on the line—never having it said out loud.

"Then, we won't have an appointment for another four months." The impatient clerk responded.

"No, I don't want to kill myself. Well, I don't know…I'm just struggling a bit, that's all. It was a burial…in Iraq…I shot two guys…I can't stop thinking about it; I just don't know if I made the right decision," I recalled.

"What? I'm sorry, man, there just aren't enough mental health providers. We only have one on the base. If you're not a harm to yourself, I can't get you in."

"Oh, okay," the phone clicked off before I could finish.

I hoped leaving my infantry unit would give me a fresh start, pulling me away from the cycle of deployments and combat. I didn't realize that my old platoon was the biggest tether holding me together. As an unmarried instructor, I felt like the odd man out. In the six months after leaving Iraq, with a $25,000 reenlistment bonus, I bought a snowboard, got another tattoo, picked up a DUI that almost ended my career, and sank $10,000 into debt.

More isolated than ever, I was unable to sleep without pills or function without alcohol. My spiral continued. One humid morning, Wes pulled me aside into the sniper instructor's office loft. I had shown up at 9 a.m. to teach, unshaven and still drunk from the night before. Wes yanked me from class into the office and said, "I'm from West Virginia, I've seen addiction." I hung my head down, "I don't know what to do." Wes cut me off.

"You need help. What about your court card from the DUI? You have to go to AA for that, right?"

"Yeah, I haven't gone yet," I admitted. The idea made me nervous. I was only twenty-two. I told myself I was too young to be an alcoholic.

"Find a meeting. We'll go together."

Three days later, Wes drove me to my first AA meeting. We pulled into a parking lot behind an old strip mall. Spilled coffee and remnants of dried creamer stained the sign-in sheet for our court cards—proof of mandatory attendance for civil sentencing. I introduced myself to the group:

"Hi, my name is Angelo, and I'm, uh...I um...I'm an alcoholic." From that moment on, I replaced one addiction with another—my nightly meetings. For months, I white-knuckled through the steps with a sponsor and a process I only half-believed. Over time, though, I connected with a community of people wrestling with the same demons. It was one of the most welcoming places I had ever known. We were a regular assortment of outcasts—doctors, lawyers, taxi drivers, waitresses, felons, reformed neo-Nazis, or just dumb kids. Our pasts didn't matter—we were on the same path. I will always remain a *Friend*. Wes Payne taught me to never give up on someone. If you are ever dealing with someone with substance abuse, don't give up; you might just be the one to save their life—like Wes Payne saved mine.

I worked through private channels for mental health counseling. Whether it was real or imagined, we believed that seeking treatment could brand us as weak and unfit for deployment. If you wanted to keep your security clearance, you paid for help out of your own pocket or went without the help.

With compassionate care from private mental health professionals and mentors—and, somehow, a bowling league—I was getting back on my feet. Six months later, I was still sober and had taken a part-time gig as a waiter at the Cheesecake Factory four nights a week. It was against the Marine Corps' rules to moonlight, but it was known as a "sober job" at AA meetings—it helped keep all my waking hours occupied. So, by day, I taught Marines how to suck the eyeball out of a rabbit. By night, I waited tables in a pressed white uniform, hawking over-caloried cheesecake to tourists. I didn't care. I was happy, and no longer buried in debt—just broke.

### We've Already Been Over This

Sitting at my desk, I heard a car door slam and heavy footsteps approaching the HOG hatch. "Hey, who are you, sir? That door's for snipers only," one of my buddies warned the intruder.

"I don't give a shit what your sign says; I'm here to see somebody!" The voice carried a familiar twang. I knew that voice. I leapt to my feet and burst into the hallway.

"P-shoot!" barked Gunny—now First Sergeant Jackson—as he brushed my buddy aside. We hugged there in the corridor.

"How the hell are you, Devil Dog?" he asked, clapping me on the back while steering me outside toward his little red pickup.

"I'm doing better, First Sergeant," I said, boots kicking small rocks. "I had a rough patch for a while, but I'm getting back on track."

He raised an eyebrow. “What’s up?”

“Well, Afghanistan’s heating up again, and there’s talk of a plus-up,” I said. He nodded, waiting.

“I want to get in the fight,” I told him. “I’m thinking Recon.”

“Damn, P-shoot,” he said with a grin. “You sure do love to get your ass kicked. So what’s holding you back?”

I shrugged. “The swimming, mostly. I don’t know if I can hack it.”

He chuckled. “Well, I can’t help you there. How long before you go?”

“Five months,” I said.

“Then it looks like for the next five months, you need to fall in love with the water—or don’t. That part’s up to you.” He paused, looking me in the eye. “We’ve already been over this, P-shoot. Every man is in charge of his own destiny. I’ll tell you what: I’m coming back in six months. If you’re not here, I’ll know where you’re at.”

## Becoming Recon

07 July 2008 - Reconnaissance Training Company, Camp Pendleton, CA

> *To quit, to surrender, to give up is to fail. To be a Recon Marine is to surpass failure: to overcome, to adapt, and to do whatever it takes to complete the mission.*

Six months after my conversation with First Sergeant Jackson, I found myself fighting to stay conscious at the bottom of a fifteen-foot pool on Camp Pendleton. I was twenty-three years old—a Sergeant, a sniper instructor, three combat deployments behind me. And yet, I’d chosen to start over, to take on the brutal selection for the elite Amphibious Recon Battalions.

There was just one problem: I was a terrible swimmer.

The Basic Recon Course had a 17 percent success rate. It chewed up and spit out even the strongest Marines. For me, it felt like an impossible task. But when faced with the impossible, I turned to something familiar—something Wesley Payne had taught me years earlier.

I went home, grabbed a marker, and wrote my next mission on the bathroom mirror:

*Recon Marine.*

Different mirror, same ritual. See it every morning. Say it out loud. Then make it real.

Recon Marines, born from the Pacific Islands–hopping campaigns of World War II, had a legacy of overcoming impossible challenges. Recon Marines and Navy Underwater Demolition Team swimmers set the standard. On moonlit nights, grease-painted raiders paddled rubber boats to shore and slipped into the frigid water. Six-man teams worked to take photographs, conduct hydrographic surveys, disarm mines, and silently eliminate sleeping Japanese soldiers.

In Korea, Recon Marines drove jeeps onto icy shorelines, sabotaged tunnels, and destroyed rail lines deep behind enemy lines. In Vietnam—facing a hellacious enemy—they cleared tunnels and called in airstrikes. Hand to hand, in the mud, face-to-face. When grenades ran out, they hurled rocks. In Kuwait and Iraq, I witnessed Recon Marines roaring across the desert in customized Mercedes G-Wagons, their feet dangling off helicopters during nighttime raids. These guys were Detachment One—an elite experimental unit of Force Recon Marines and enablers, which became Marine Special Operations Command.

> *Forever shall I strive to maintain the tremendous reputation of those who went before me.*

The instructors divided the four-month Basic Reconnaissance Course, which included a bone-crushing curriculum, into three phases: Individual Reconnaissance Skills, Long-Range Patrols, and Amphibious Operations.

During the first phase, we focused on two critical elements: physical fitness and mental resilience. Every morning, we spent four hours at the pool, where I had completed my sniper INDOC years earlier. I still hated that place. Broken heaters meant cold showers and an even colder pool. We hit the water at 0700 on the dot, wearing full fatigues to add more drag. Our only relief came when the sun finally burned through the marine layer around 0900.

Every session began with a 1,000-meter warm-up swim, followed by a 25-meter underwater swim and a 60-minute tread—mental resilience. Then we tackled combat strokes, CPR, and lifesaving fundamentals, followed by more treading—this time with bricks and sharks. Your mind goes to a funny place when you're blacking out. The light almost fades into pulsating circles around your eyes; then you wake up feeling near euphoric and confused at the top of the pool deck—a corpsman's wet hand slapping your gray face. Eight weeks, every day, rain or shine. Did I mention that I hated that place?

By 1100, we dried off, boarded our white buses, and returned to the classroom. Lunch came to us in a sad box of stale breaded cold cuts, a sugary juice box, and a banana—though most of us relied on MREs (Meals, Ready-to-Eat). At noon, we studied the skills we needed as long-range scouts: advanced navigation, tracking, patrolling, long-range communication, and survival. As a sniper, I was in my element and I was outperforming the entire class—except for one other Marine.

His name was Matt Ingham. On paper, we were practically twins—identical résumés, the same schools, the same quals. But there was one glaring difference: He was an East Coast sniper.

And in our community, the East vs. West rivalry was alive and well—part playful, part dead serious. Think Biggie vs. Tupac, but with ghillie suits and bolt action rifles.

The West Coast was the best coast. Obviously.

More importantly, he was outpacing me, and I resented him for it. Matt had a quiet, contemplative demeanor, and a slight frown that made him appear perpetually annoyed. He stood five feet eleven inches tall, broad-shouldered and fit, complemented by sandy brown hair. He was also brilliant, and wanted to graduate at the top of our class, just like I did.

The patrol phase felt similar to sniper school, with heavy rucks, radios, antennas, bugs, brush, hunger, and camouflage face paint. The only difference was the scale. Six-person teams could stay in the field far longer and travel farther than two-person teams. If you want to go fast, go alone; if you want to go far, go together.

Matt led an adjacent team, and our competition continued. His leadership style, much like mine, inspired open and honest dialogue. He guided our classmates with patience, sharing whatever knowledge he had. We pushed each other, and over time, we became friends. His unique canine tooth stuck out slightly, causing his lip to catch in a mild snarl whenever we argued—usually ending in laughter, as I nicknamed him "snaggletooth" or "rock-biter."

We became inseparable.

Our final phase took place on the Silver Strand in Coronado, California—an entire month of amphibious work in the water. Each morning began with a two-kilometer open-water fin where I pushed a loaded combat ruck, my rifle, and extra gear, wearing military SCUBA fins that felt like 2×4s and nails.

After our fin, eight Marine teams hoisted 322-pound Combat Rubber Raiding Crafts over our heads and carried them on our shoulders for the entire three-mile slog of asphalt and sand to the training area in the Pacific Ocean.

Along the way, we passed the Navy's BUD/S compound—where SEAL and Recon students shared that special kind of bond forged through collective misery. The new coalition of instructors wasted no time marching us straight back to face the icy grip of the California surf, SEAL and Recon students shoulder to shoulder in shared suffering.

Fun fact: SEAL boats weigh about 170 pounds. Ours, over 300. Just saying.

That month echoed the amphibious tradition of the Corps, dating back to World War II. Over 80 percent of the global population lived near coastlines, and when war erupted, Recon Marines had to be the first ashore. During our culminating event, we launched boats and swimmers from hovering aircraft into the choppy waters of San Diego Harbor at night, then navigated eight raiding crafts to a link-up buoy five miles off the coast. Our teams assembled, conducted final comm checks, and moved in two wedge formations toward the shore. A mile out, we swapped our engines for paddles, slipped onto the beach, and left footprints that vanished with the tide—like the Marines of our lineage.

> *Exceeding beyond the limitations set down by others shall be my goal, sacrificing personal comforts and dedicating myself to the completion of the reconnaissance mission shall be my life. Physical fitness, mental attitude, and high ethics—The title of Recon Marine is my honor.*

Two weeks later, Matt and I graduated from the Basic Reconnaissance Course—I was the Honor Graduate, and Matt was number two—by .05 percent. I never let him forget it.

The next stop for Matt and me was Okinawa, Japan. Afghanistan was heating up, and our new unit, 3rd Recon Battalion, was going.

# 13

------

# THE FLIP OF A COIN

## The Rock

`1 October 2008 - 0630 - Camp Schwab, Okinawa, Japan`

I yanked open the blinds to my barracks room window and took in my first Okinawan sunrise. Blue-green hues shot through the pink, humid morning sky and stretched across a rugged green bay. The crystal-blue water lapped at the coral and rock-laced sand in the distance. A small island dotted with still palm trees and gnarled lava rock sat offshore, and beyond it, a sprawling bay overlooked the luxurious resorts along the Okinawa coast. I had arrived the night before and woke up to find I was in paradise.

Okinawa itself had a brutal past. Though the island had become part of Imperial Japan, the Ryukyu Kingdom remained united, and many islanders still saw themselves as distinct from the Japanese. Considered "the doorstep to Tokyo" in World War II, it was the final island in a chain stretching from Australia across the Pacific and home to the war's most bloody battles.

The largest amphibious operation ever conducted, Okinawa had to be earned. 183,000 Americans stormed ashore, surpassing the Normandy landing by 30,000 troops. A "typhoon of steel" raged for eighty-two days. Okinawa became hell on earth with naval barrages, sweeping air raids, and uncontrollable fires. Inconceivable amounts of bravery and resolve helped the Allied forces break the back of the Imperial Army, as victory in the Pacific was on the horizon. Yet, the devastation to the island was staggering. With over 200,000 dead, including 94,136 Japanese soldiers and 94,100 civilians, many of whom died by suicide—Okinawa became sacred ground.

I was ready to start a new day with a unit that had an old history.

### The Team

3rd Reconnaissance Battalion was located in the northern, jungle-covered region of the island at the tip of a small peninsula near a fishing village. The remote base, which housed only a few units, was nestled where the coral met the jungle. The jungles became our backyard. Established for the invasion of Guam in 1944, 3rd Recon Battalion specialized in jungle and mountain warfare. In March 1965, they were among the first combat troops to arrive in Vietnam. Their history was filled with the mud of many shores and continuous conflict.

Matt and I reported to the unit and received our assignment to Bravo Company, 3rd Platoon. As new Staff Sergeants, we each had our own teams. My first team member and Assistant Team Leader (ATL) was Sergeant Joe Gillooly. Born in Kennesaw, Georgia, his father was a retired Marine Drill Instructor while his mother was a proud descendant of the Taino People, an indigenous tribe originating in the Caribbean before settling in the Americas. Joe enlisted after 9/11, just like I did. However, due to what I jokingly referred to as a character flaw, he chose pushing papers over infantry, almost immediately regretting his decision.

For the next four years, he was determined to become a Recon Marine, even hanging a recon poster in his tiny gray cubicle. Through years of dedication and hard work, he graduated from BRC in the class after mine, becoming my ATL. With a shaved head and a square jaw, Joe had a goofy laugh that revealed his kind nature, standing in sharp contrast to his imposing stature. He was green in reconnaissance, but he was intelligent and eager to learn. His role involved mastering the nuances of being a Team Leader, managing the team's logistics, and serving as a strict disciplinarian—he was dad, and I was mom.

Over the next few months, the rest of our teams came together, with some members newly graduated from Recon School and some transfers from other units. With our rosters finalized, our next step was to study the evolving war in Afghanistan. We were a jungle-based unit preparing to deploy to Afghanistan. To train in the temperate mountains, we needed to travel, so we did.

## The Work-Up

Over the next year, Bravo Company expanded into five platoons, each comprising twenty-four Reconnaissance Marines. Matt and I were the two Team Leaders in 3rd Platoon. A troop cap imposed on the Afghanistan surge changed our deployment orders. Only one reconnaissance company from the battalion would deploy, supplemented by two reserve recon platoons.

We bounced across the Pacific, training in locations that prepared us for Afghanistan's mountainous terrain. Our first proving ground was six cold, rainy weeks at the Rodriguez Live Fire Complex in South Korea. Nestled in the mountains near the DMZ, the Army's premier live-fire training site demanded our full attention. Long-range mountain patrols, ambushes, crew-served weapons, close-quarters combat—Rodriguez had it all.

Matt and I constantly competed. In a recon platoon, the number-one team is called when failure isn't an option. This designation was primarily symbolic, but we both wanted it. Our platoon had yet to designate a top team, and we fought for it right until deployment.

At night, after the commotion of training faded and the tempo died down, Matt and I would link up for a walk and a dip of tobacco—our ritual reset. It was just the two of us, in the dark, beneath the stars, away from the noise. I always called him "Number Two," a little jab I liked to throw his way since I'd edged him out at Recon School. Without fail, he'd respond with a light punch to my gut and a smirk. That was our rhythm. Brothers through and through.

Being a Recon Team Leader wasn't easy. We weren't merely teachers and guides—we were still students, in a way, constantly learning, adjusting, and figuring things out as we went. Our job was to shape our teams—combine hard-earned experience with just enough room for experimentation and creativity. It was a tightrope. The pressure wasn't just personal; we had to balance loyalty to our men with the company's never-ending demands. That tension lived in every decision we made. Those quiet walks were our way to decompress. To vent without judgment. To remind each other that we weren't alone in the fight.

Matt and I couldn't have been more different. He was steady and calculated, always thinking three moves ahead. I was loud, fast, and unpredictable—always charging toward the next challenge as if it owed me something. But somehow, our contrast worked. His calm balanced my chaos, and my fire kept his gears turning.

We'd argue—hell, we'd go at it like siblings sometimes—but beneath it all was respect, trust, and ultimately, love. The kind forged under stress, built from shared burdens. We leaned on each other more than we'd ever admit out loud.

Leading a recon team demanded everything. Exceeding the limitations set down by others was the standard. With 120 Marines in the company and all eyes on us as two of the most experienced members of the unit, the pressure never let up. Our own leaders expected a steady hand, while our junior Marines needed inspiration. And we carried that weight together.

Our rivalry pushed us to work harder, train smarter, and lead better. Each of us measured ourselves against the other—but never at the cost of our bond. Through every mission, every fight, and every high and low, we knew we made one another better. That's what brothers did.

He was always better than me. I just never let him know it.

## Coin Flip

28 September 2009 - Hawthorne Army Depot, Nevada

Our next stop was Hawthorne, Nevada—an isolated town in Mineral County, about thirty miles from the California border and the Sierras. The only real development there was a sprawling 226-square-mile Army ammunition and training depot that crept into the Sierra Nevadas. Hawthorne was perfect for where we were about to go: rugged mountaintops with jagged red cliffs that plunged into vast expanses of moon dust and desert rock.

Leading up to deployment, we began a barrage of training exercises designed to sharpen our razor's edge—desert patrols in armored vehicles, deep reconnaissance, mountain survival, rappelling, helicopter raids, close air support, and long-range shooting.

Matt and I continued our walks in the harsh and desolate Nevada landscape while our teams remained neck and neck throughout the final stretch of training. Over the last nine months, we each had our slip-ups and learning moments during evaluations, but neither let the other get too far ahead.

The night before we headed back to Okinawa, we had one last decision to make.

"Okay, boys, here are the rules," Captain Kevin Kinkade announced. Our five platoons were crammed into an old Army ammunition warehouse that reeked of asbestos and guano. 3rd Platoon gathered in one of the less crap-covered corners. Kevin reminded me of Charlie Sheen's character in the Vietnam War movie *Platoon*. Although he was born into a good family north of San Francisco and attended excellent schools, he was motivated by a call to service and chose the Naval Academy as his college.

The Naval Academy produced two types of officers—jocks and nerds—and Kevin was a nerd. Recon's background as an information-gathering force meant we had both infantry and intel officers. Kevin, an intel guy, ended up with our recon platoon. We called him "Squirrel" for his frequent attention shifts, fluffy blond hair, and unintimidating demeanor. He was a great leader who had a tough job and cared deeply for his men.

"Now, while I'm happy to have the problem of having the two best teams in the battalion, Gunny and I just can't seem to agree on who gets the title of Team One. So, we're going to flip a coin!"

The platoon erupted in playful jeers, each Marine hollering why their side deserved the top spot. Matt and I eyed each other.

"Alright, boys," Kevin shouted back, smiling at the group. The anticipation was killing us. We'd sweated together all over the Pacific for nine months, waiting for this final moment.

"Once I flip this coin," Kevin said, "I'll let it hit the ground. Nobody touches it until I do. Understood?" He looked both of us in the eyes as our teams crowded closer. "Ingham," he said, "call it."

Matt conferred with his team, then looked back. "Tails never fails!"

My eyes darted to Kevin's outstretched hand, a tarnished quarter on his thumb—heads facing up. He dropped his hand and flicked the coin into the air, our heads moving in unison as we tracked it until it clinked against the concrete floor. It bounced once, ricocheted off a wall, then slid under a dusty green cot. The platoon scrambled forward, one Marine diving under the cot to shield the result.

"Gentlemen!" Kevin barked while using his elbows to keep us back. "The coin is heads!" My team roared in victory, drawing attention from the rest of the company. Matt protested, claiming a redo based on the wall's interference. I gave no quarter—meaning I literally took the quarter to prevent any chance at a second flip.

"Ahhh, looks like you're still number two," I chuckled as I walked toward him to shake his hand. Matt shook his head in disgust, kicked at the ground, and bumped my fist.

"Lucky bounce," he snarled at me as his lip caught on his tooth.

"One last thing!" Kevin shouted, pulling us back in. "We've decided on a call sign as well," he said as our eyes widened. "We've gotten a lot of great suggestions from the boys and had a hard time deciding, so we came up with one on our own."

"Our call sign will be Bearshark." He announced proudly.

"What the fuck is a bearshark?" I blurted.

Kevin grinned, “Great question, Team One,” he said, winking at Matt. “We asked ourselves which animals were the most badass creatures on the land and in the ocean, so we put them both together and came up with... *Bearshark*.”

“What—was Bear-Killer Whale already taken?” I snapped. “That’s the dumbest name I’ve ever heard.” I kept arguing while Matt, meanwhile, dropped to the floor in laughter. He loved it and sprang to the Captain’s defense. Always scheming, he saw an opening.

“I think it’s perfect,” Matt said. “It’s a combination of all of us. Tell you what—give me Team One, and I’ll let you pick the call sign.”

I rolled my eyes. “Fine, Bearshark.”

AFGHANISTAN—MAJOR OPERATIONAL CITIES

## A Different Kind of War

October 31, 2009 - 2338 - Camp Leatherneck, Helmand Province, Afghanistan

Afghanistan. Just the mention of the country's name evoked crushing military defeats suffered by the world's greatest superpowers: Great Britain, Russia, and now maybe us. Afghanistan's history was as complex as its people. Landlocked at the base of the Western Himalayas, the country's position in the middle of ancient trade routes made it the crossroads of Asia. Over the centuries, enormous armies crossed the frozen Hindu Kush and scorching deserts to fight for passage or control, from Alexander the Great, who clashed with Persia, to Genghis Khan, who left his mark during the Mongol expansion.

The Afghan people reflected their terrain as harsh realities molded them into sturdy, resilient tribal communities shaped by the unforgiving landscape. Frigid Himalayan ranges melted into brutal deserts, with fertile valleys yielding wheat and opium in between that fed both families and war efforts.

The British spent most of the nineteenth century trying to control Afghanistan during the First and Second Anglo Wars. This was during the height of their empire and the period of their greatest military strength. The results were disastrous. Thousands of British soldiers perished at the hands of fierce Afghan fighters protected by their rugged native terrain.

In 1979, the Soviet Union's invasion prompted the United States to support Afghan resistance fighters, aiming to drive the Soviets out. When the Soviets eventually withdrew, a civil war erupted between American-backed militias and the Taliban. The Taliban rose to power in the mid-1990s and imposed a regime of strict fundamentalist religious rule.

Similarly, a fundamentalist group rose to power alongside veterans of the Soviet-Afghan conflict. Led by the aristocratic heir Osama bin Laden, the fundamentalists believed that the United States was waging a war for religious dominance, so they established a base for the group within Taliban-controlled Afghanistan. Following the September 11th attacks, the Taliban refused American demands to expel bin Laden and Al-Qaeda.

The United States launched its campaign on October 7, 2001. The first to deploy were CIA and Special Operations teams to rally tribal militias and capture or kill high-value targets. A wave of American and coalition forces followed. Task Force 58—a joint USMC and Navy command led by future Defense Secretary General Jim Mattis—invaded the south and cut off the Taliban's escape. By November, coalition forces had defeated the Taliban, tracking its leaders to Tora Bora, where Special Operations Forces (SOF) overwhelmed the Taliban and Al-Qaeda loyalists defending Osama bin Laden. Although Al-Qaeda and the Taliban surrendered, they bought just enough time for bin Laden to escape. Our operation was a success, but bin Laden's escape cast a shadow: America's most wanted fugitive was on the loose, and he had begun to regroup.

By 2007, the Taliban had returned to full force. They threatened NATO's efforts to stabilize the country. In 2009, after campaigning to reduce deployments and end the two-front wars, President Obama ordered a surge of 17,000 troops. Third Recon was part of that surge. A story of sweat and blood, written by millions of warriors over thousands of years, continued. Our next war began again. But this time, it would be different. Would we be predator or prey?

### "Who Dares Wins"

`November 2009 - 1038 - Undisclosed location, Southern Helmand Province`

"Contact left!" someone yelled over the radio.

My head snapped to the streaking RPGs wobbling through the air from a rocky dune about 300 meters off my ten o'clock. British .50 calibers and grenade launchers roared in response. From my spot in the turret, I swung my Heckler & Koch automatic grenade launcher into position, racked the handle, and pressed the butterfly trigger with both thumbs. I sent eight rounds ripping toward the berm—*brap, brap, brap*—each 40mm shell tracing an arc toward the dune.

Six days earlier, a convoy of sixteen vehicles rolled out of Camp Bastion: thirty SAS and SBS troops, joined by twenty-five Afghan Special Forces. I was a US Special Operations Attaché assigned to a joint drug and weapons interdiction effort. I had arrived in Afghanistan a month before my unit as part of the advance party and volunteered to tag along with the Brits.

Our mission was to cross the desert for two weeks, raiding known smuggling routes while gathering intel. Southern Afghanistan's opium and black tar heroin fed the Taliban's war machine—ironically funded by the very countries they fought.

The British knew desert warfare better than anyone. Like Lawrence of Arabia in World War I and the SAS Long Range Desert Group in World War II, they understood every nuance of the Mars-like expanse. We traveled in open-air Jackals—British-made, light-armored, long-range dune buggies, without relief from the scorching midday sun or the biting evening winds.

We drove sixteen to eighteen hours each day, interdicting vehicles and chasing leads from our Afghan interpreters. Every four hours or so, we formed a security circle for the British tradition of "a cuppa." Using purpose-built hot water spigots from their engines, the Brits always had hot water ready for a cup of tea. Even war couldn't break British traditions.

We had intelligence of a local warlord with a nose for opium, and we were closing in. The RPGs that had just shot over my head were a good indicator that we'd found the right spot.

"Contact lef'. Tree hunnert meeters but aff tae lef'side, o'er tha berm," came a voice through the radio from the SAS Troop Sergeant Major, a Scotsman whose thick accent was often the butt of British snobbery. Even he admitted that he was difficult to understand, and the stress of an RPG skimming past his head distorted his already unintelligible accent even more.

"Uh, AJ, did you get that?" the SAS Troop Commander asked, hoping my American *accent* might decipher the Scot's shouts.

I shot a glance at my driver—a Royal Marine Commando with "boot" inked on his neck. I once asked him about what I initially thought was a derogatory term, and he explained that Royal Marines were called "Boot Necks" in the 1700s when they wore strips of boot leather around their throats to protect against sword slashes. This echoed the American Marine tradition of referring to ourselves as "Leathernecks" for the same reason. Both names originated when our nations were enemies, yet today, we fought alongside each other as allies in a different war. But that was a story for another time; we needed to figure out where the RPGs were coming from.

I keyed my mic and let out a laugh. "That's a negative."

"Rog-O, got it," the commander said. "Okay, gentlemen, let's get on line, get some pressure on them, and make a decision." He said with perfect British polish.

In unison, the convoy shifted out of its column and formed four-vehicle wedges, with each unit shielding the others while delivering combat power on all sides to guard against ambush. The enemy fighters scattered, abandoning their dead and speeding away in Toyota Hilux trucks toward the Pakistani border. Air support circled overhead as we pursued in our bucking desert rigs. It felt like an old Western, with the British-led force pushing hard after the fleeing Taliban. A few small pockets of fighters slowed us just enough for the primary target to slip across the border—two white pickups with green Pakistani flags marked the border checkpoint about 500 meters beyond our reach. NATO forces couldn't cross into Pakistan.

Frustrated by the escape, we questioned a handful of farmers near the border about the missing warlord. We dismounted; rifles slung. One farmer stood with his wife—covered from head to toe in a faded dusty blue burqa—and their three children: two boys around twelve and a tiny girl no older than three, her blonde-red hair hinting at generations of invasions. She peeked from behind her father's leg with wide, piercing blue-green eyes. When I reached into my cargo pocket for a few Jolly Ranchers and knelt down, she began trembling, urine trickling down her dusty leg and pooling near her little black feet. I saw myself as a liberator and a protector, but to her, I was a nightmare.

We knew our inquisition wouldn't produce answers because the Taliban blended into these villages, and we were just tourists. Our makeshift band of desert raiders climbed back into our jackals and headed north toward Camp Bastion, where most of the surging NATO forces would soon arrive. On the way, we conducted four more raids, torching bundles of processed opium and seizing weapons, money, and drugs bound for Iran or the Taliban pockets.

Our last stop held significant sentimental value for the SAS. They guided us to the site of the first SAS raid since World War II—Operation Trent. Two months after 9/11, British forces parachuted into the remote Registan desert under the cover of darkness, carving out a runway for the follow-on attack. Aided by US air support, the SAS assembled one hundred operators on Kawasaki dirt bikes and Land Rovers to destroy an opium factory and a local Taliban headquarters. The SAS troopers killed over seventy Taliban, while suffering only four minor injuries, making the mission a resounding success. A painting immortalized that operation, depicting the battle with a distinctive camelback-shaped mountain in the background. Years after the daring raid, the SAS returned to a place already etched in their history books. We stood and took photos for their journals and memories back home, celebrating another successful mission by the SAS.

## Now Zad

By mid-November, our recon company had arrived at Camp Leatherneck and began preparations for immediate combat operations. They assigned 3rd Platoon a hunter-killer mission forty miles north in Now Zad. Initially under British control in 2006, it was a labyrinth of mud-brick structures and narrow alleys, earning the reputation as the most perilous location in Helmand. A small hand-painted sign declaring WELCOME TO APOCALYPSE NOW ZAD greeted us at the entrance to the remote base. The Taliban had poured fighters into the area for years, clashing with British, Estonian, and now American forces. By 2008, the town, once home to 35,000 residents, lay deserted. The only

## HELMLAND PROVINCE DETAIL

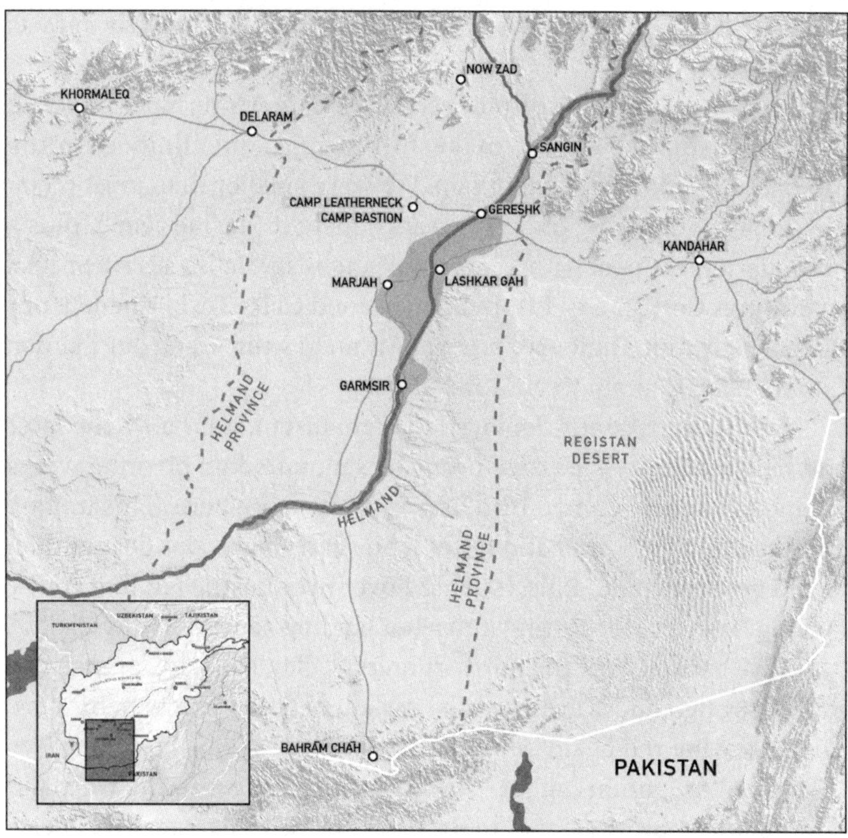


movement came from wild dogs and vultures that fed on the dead Taliban abandoned in the streets after years of fighting.

When Matt and I went on missions, we were silent professionals who understood that only our skills could keep us alive. However, to get on the missions, we had to be consummate politicians who used our voices to persuade senior leaders to let us go outside the wire. So, we worked our angles with company leadership, emphasizing our sniper experience to secure the mission. With support from mentors advocating for us and a solid briefing by Captain Kinkade, we got the green light. Our orders were to head north to support a Marine rifle company under constant attack. Our objective: Find and kill the Taliban. The only problem, we'd be working with a unit we'd never met in one of the most inhospitable places on the planet. If things were going to work, we'd have to be perfect. If they didn't, they'd most likely unravel in an instant.

The heavy, humid heat from the MV-22 Osprey's turbines punched at me as I stepped off the makeshift tarmac and climbed up the ramp. 3rd Platoon was loading up. We were smaller than most recon platoons—comprising only two teams of eight Marines each, plus a headquarters element with a communications specialist, a Navy Special Operations Corpsman-Hospitalman Second Class Toshi Coenen; our Platoon Sergeant, Gunnery Sergeant Efrain Martinez; and our Platoon Commander, Captain Kevin Kinkade.

The Osprey, recently deployed to Afghanistan, was half-helicopter and half-plane. Two massive propellers mounted on pivoting wings enabled the aptly named bird of prey to fly anywhere. This unique aircraft could fly farther and faster while carrying troops deeper than any helicopter could. Plus, it could hover over hostile landing zones, making it perfect for getting into a hot landing zone like Now Zad.

As we banked over the north-running valley, a blazing orange sun broke through and warmed the snow-dusted winter sky behind us. Long, glowing red beams stretched down the snaking corridor. Two 5,000-foot mountain ranges—towering black ridges to the west and dusty tan-and-brown slopes to the east—formed a narrow gap. Locals referred to the western side as the Black Mountains, their onyx-like stone dominating the horizon. Opposite stood the White Mountains, highlighted by chalky red patches and moonlike dust. Between them was a small, fertile valley reminiscent of California's high desert. Tiny villages dotted the foothills, each enveloped by the long shadows of the setting sun.

The Ospreys dropped in one by one as their escorts of Cobras and Hueys circled patiently above. As I shuffled down the greasy ramp, I went to bump fists with the crew chief; he waved me close, leaned in under the repeating blasts of rotor wash, and yelled over the roar, "Good luck!" while unfolding my knuckles to shake my hand.

## NOW ZAD OPERATIONAL MAP

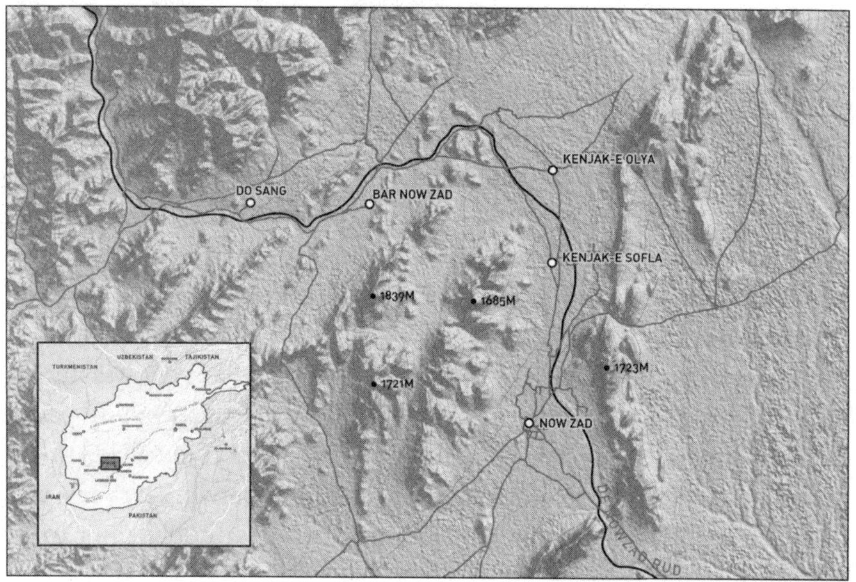


## FOB Cafferata

```
December 2009 - Now Zad Valley,
Helmand Province, Afghanistan
```

Forward Operating Base Cafferata was located at the mouth of the valley and bordered by the town. They named the base after Hector Cafferata, a Marine who earned the Medal of Honor in Korea in 1950 for standing alone and holding back hundreds of enemy fighters. Reluctant to seek glory, he once said, "I did my duty. I protected my fellow Marines. They protected me. And I'm prouder of that than the fact that the government decided to give me the Medal of Honor."

Like him, the lone rifle company defended the farthest reaches of Allied lines. One hundred fifty Marines manned mortars, missiles, armored trucks, sniper rifles, and foot patrols. And, like him, they fought valiantly.

For five weeks, we conducted mission after mission. On stormy nights, we'd load into Mine-Resistant Ambush Protected Vehicles

(MRAPs) with our anti-armor teams, moving north through deep wadis and dry desert washes, then slipping off the vehicles to begin grueling fifteen-kilometer climbs into the craggy mountains. The southern end of the Hindu Kush brought an unbearable cold. Freezing rain lashed through the valley as we advanced north. Sharp ice crystals, like frozen needles, turned exposed skin into frostnip. For hours, we trekked across the rugged terrain, weighed down by 120-pound rucks and forty-five pounds of weapons and gear. Our legs strained in mountaineering boots, a small perk of recon—infantry Marines had to wear their standard-issue parade boots.

Armor was nonnegotiable. A mandate required every Marine to wear full plates at all times, with no exceptions. The 120-pound packs dug into our bulletproof plates, and the heavy helmets only added to the misery. We relied on stealth, but risk-averse commanders far removed from the realities of combat considered moving without armor to be a liability.

Thanks to the military-industrial complex, our rucks were packed with reconnaissance and radio gear, each powered by different, incompatible batteries. We carried an M240B machine gun, a sniper rifle, and grenade launchers attached to suppressed assault rifles. There were no tents, sleeping bags, or fires; we needed to remain concealed and ready to fight.

At night, we huddled in pairs behind rock outcroppings, relying on our layers and our brother's heat for warmth. With two Marines on watch at all times, there was little chance for sleep—or food. Our recon equipment took precedence, and most of our water froze. For four to eight days, we survived on our only food that wouldn't freeze: jerky, trail mix, and stolen chow hall Clif bars. If I never see another Clif bar, it would be too soon.

"Ya out there, Bearshark?" a female voice crackled over the net. Our attack helicopter squadron—Scarface—was running a night patrol. Over time, we'd developed a bond.

"Hey Betty! This is Bearshark One. Great to hear from you," I said. "We're doing alright down here, just a bit brisk," I joked.

"Got anything for us to check out?" she asked, cool and direct.

I only knew her by her call sign. "Betty" was a Marine Huey pilot and one of the best. We first met at a planning conference where air-ground integration was not just helpful but a matter of life or death. She was tall, sharp, and carried herself with natural intensity. With her blonde hair pulled into a loose bun, dusty flight suit, and squared posture, Betty didn't need to prove anything; she was already doing the job.

Confident without arrogance, humble without hesitation, and professional to the core. In one conversation, Betty shattered outdated notions about women in combat.

Because the truth was simple: She wasn't a *female* Marine—she was a Marine, and a damn good one.

Emails couldn't foster the type of trust required in the fight. That trust was built face-to-face when you looked someone in the eye, shook their hand, and knew—without question—they had your back when it mattered most.

Betty had that presence. If anyone still doubted the role of women in combat, it was only because they hadn't worked with someone like her.

Night after night, the Cobras and Hueys prowled the valley. From our mountain hide sites, we watched them hover and circle on station, scanning the terrain below for hours at a time. We got to know the voices behind the call signs, and they kept an eye out for us. They dropped small unauthorized resupplies on quieter nights—chewing tobacco, energy drinks, and more Clif bars in green parachute bags. The cans often smashed against the rocks and exploded, but it was the thought that counted.

"Bearshark, we're bingo on fuel," Betty radioed.

"Copy that, Scarface. You guys take care," I replied.

"Stay warm, Bearshark One. Scarface out."

Outside large operations, our two teams took turns in the field. One team forward while the other rested, resupplied, and planned. We welcomed the returning team with "five-star" feasts of bartered frozen steaks and pasta sent from back home. We cooked over a fifty-five-gallon drum we had cut in half using some Boy Scout ingenuity to turn into a barbecue grill. Over the fire, we smoked cigarettes, laughed, argued, and joked about the cold. We were a family.

As Christmas approached, so did our care packages—well, sort of. Because of our remote location and enemy threat, our resupplies, along with our mail, were delivered by parachute drop from Marine C-130 cargo planes. Two nights before the holiday, a massive coalition effort was underway to ensure frontline troops got their mail.

Under the green glow of my night vision goggles, I watched the C-130 bank over the valley floor, low and slow, its propeller tips flickering green and white with static electricity. Out of its belly fell four pallets of supplies and mail destined for a makeshift drop zone near FOB Cafferata. Three drifted beneath the pillowy gray outline of their parachutes—one, not so much. After the C-130 engines faded, I heard frantic flapping overhead. A fouled chute sent the pallet rocketing from 1,500 feet and smashing into a burst of green-hued moon dust, skidding to a mangled stop about a hundred meters away.

"Please don't be the mail," I muttered, bracing for disappointment.

We picked through the wreckage of our outpost's one and only mail drop—what was left of it, anyway. A shredded pallet sat in the hard dirt like a crime scene, surrounded by mangled USPS boxes and envelopes that looked like they'd been through a monsoon...and a fistfight.

One package was addressed to my platoon. It came from my old high school's leadership class, which had gotten my address from my mother. They wanted to send us a piece of home. Inside, they had painted a poster with WE LOVE OUR TROOPS in bold letters. Their names and heartfelt messages fanned out around the edges. As requested, I presented the banner to the platoon. Matt, known for his stoic demeanor, uncharacteristically asked that we tape it to the wall by our firepit.

I tipped my head and squinted, surprised to find an ally in emotional stuff like this from Matt.

"Reminds us why we're here," he said.

Four days after Christmas, Matt's team returned from a seventy-two-hour recon patrol. They had found something big—the enemy's local command and control area.

# 14

# THE WORST DAY OF MY LIFE

## The Divide

Afghanistan was not Iraq. In Iraq, we operated in a largely homogenous environment; cross-unit cooperation occurred, but infrequently. By the later years of the Iraq War, most units commanded extensive battlespaces with their own resources, conducting independent operations. Afghanistan presented a different scenario. Our limited numbers forced us to adopt a multifaceted approach. Transport helicopters facilitated combat patrol insertions, artillery Marines doubled as infantry, and logisticians became Troop Commanders. For the first time, Americans had to rely on NATO air support.

Once the traditional barriers separating units fell away, we discovered that the coalition's true strength lay in its unity—the coalition itself. No unit could operate in isolation, and no mission existed as a standalone effort. Relationships were everything, and ours with the infantry unit was terrible.

From our arrival, we felt like outsiders—isolated by assigned living quarters away from the combat troops. We appeared different, acted differently, had unique equipment, and carried ourselves in a way they didn't understand. Worse, we had no prior working relationship with the unit that now owned us operationally.

Recon Marines followed a principle centered on the speed of trust. Upon completing Recon School, a young Marine became part of the team and were immediately trusted. Despite lacking experience, leaders never considered newer Recon Marines inferior. We were equals in our personal responsibility to one another, working toward a collective task. Although rank and experience mattered, we always gave trust, even to those at the lowest level. To do otherwise would be an indictment of the recon pipeline itself.

Matt and I knew the infantry didn't work that way. That was our mistake. We should have known better. Whether too young, too proud, or both, we failed to establish a solid command relationship where our new commanders would trust our judgment. The infantry and the broader Marine Corps had a certain way of doing things. Some things seemed illogical, but many made sense.

We refused to budge on what we saw as irrational cultural practices—uniform regulations that offered no tactical advantage. Non-standard boots, rolled sleeves, and the absence of rank insignia sent their hyper-focused command into a frenzy.

Typical pre-mission gear and personnel inspections had a purpose: making sure weapons worked, radios had batteries, and every Marine knew the plan. That made sense.

But in Now Zad, before every patrol stepped off, leaders from their unit would swarm the squads, zeroing in on Marine Corps uniform standards we saw as irrelevant in the operational environment. They circled like hyenas, ready to pounce on the smallest infraction. Where we tried to build camaraderie and ownership, they drained morale with every visit.

Our defiance divided us from them, suggesting we considered ourselves superior. My perspective has shifted now. I have realized that not every issue can be blamed on others. We chased the concept of who was right and refused to acknowledge that both parties made mistakes. We wound up dwelling on our differences rather than seeking common ground. In the end, we were one another's only hope for survival, and our egos wouldn't let us talk.

The notion that poor working relationships gradually improve over time is illogical. We should have engaged in a private dialogue with their command, involving leaders from all levels, to foster clear communication and identify shared objectives. Instead, we chose to argue rather than listen, shouting our individual truths at one another to defend our perspectives.

The era of General Mattis's Rehearsal of Concept drills in the sand, shifting large elements without relying on a single PowerPoint slide, had passed. We had moved into a technological landscape but faced a pivotal moment where integrating high-tech solutions was still relatively new. The unit focused on perfecting the briefing format, rather than identifying potential flaws in any strategy. Extended mission briefings transformed into presentations with over one hundred PowerPoint slides. While drones were increasingly employed to "verify" the observations of reconnaissance units or check on our patrols instead of scouting ahead—or trusting the guy on the ground.

Throughout December, our fractured relationship only worsened. Dangerous movements, mandatory reoccupation of hide sites, multiple denied extractions following compromises, and literal yelling matches over radio nets. My skin crawled as our relationship crumbled. The situation grew unsafe. We initiated discussions with our higher command about pulling our platoon out.

Despite our concerns, the platoon continued to operate in the Now Zad valley. Stopping wasn't an option—not with the young infantry Marines still vulnerable. So we adapted. We teamed up with an element from the battalion's Scout Sniper Platoon—a few of them my old students—and ran reconnaissance patrols northwest of town, past the Black Mountains. Bearshark, Bounty Hunter, and Scarface owned the nights. Taliban intercepts called the snipers and us *tree people*, never knowing where we'd be, only that we were always watching. They hated us for it.

On one of those patrols, Matt identified a crucial pattern. Bar Now Zad—one of our major objectives—bustled during the day with black markets and Taliban activity, yet several vehicles returned to a village named Do Sang each night. This detail supported other intelligence reports indicating that while the Taliban were active in Bar Now Zad, their leaders lived in Do Sang. This changed everything.

### Tails Never Fails

The plan came together fast. Lima and Kilo Companies would be helicoptered in to secure a foothold and methodically clear Bar Now Zad and Do Sang house by house. Bearshark's mission had two main components: one team would directly assist Lima Company, providing overwatch of their movements to the east of Bar Now Zad, while the other would act as the Aerial Reaction Force. It was a new concept, UH-1Y Hueys working with a twelve-man recon team to intercept and interdict any escaping vehicles.

Then, twenty-four hours before H-hour, the plan changed. The ARF concept was scrapped by the infantry command. Instead, a team would insert into the remote hills overlooking Do Sang to cover the infantry's landing. This new mission wasn't ideal—too close of an insert, too near the proximity of town, and there wasn't enough time to remain clandestine. But even worse, they would be alone.

Any team that went in would be in for a fight. Matt and I knew it, and both wanted that fight.

"My team's rested. We've got the legs," I shot at Gunny and the Captain.

"So what? We were just there—we know the terrain better," Matt fired back.

"Bullshit, man. I can do a map recon," I snapped. Neither of us was backing down.

Then Matt smirked, that snaggletooth showing. "Tell you what—let's flip for it."

"You've gotta be kidding me," I said, flailing. "No way. This is ridiculous. I'm not flipping a coin for this mission."

Matt laughed. He knew I couldn't walk away from the challenge. I rolled my eyes and shook his hand. "Fine, your pick," I said as Kinkade found a coin.

"Tails never fails," Matt grinned.

This time, Matt won.

## Keep Pushing

10 January - 2300
FOB Cafferata, Now Zad Valley, Afghanistan

A hovering drone's thermal feed bathed the operations center in flickering shades of black and white. On the large canvas screen, I watched two Hueys tear through desert canyons, flying fast and low—no more than twenty meters off the deck, banking hard between ridgelines.

After winning the coin flip Matt's team was first in—eight Reconnaissance Marines and five attachments.

My team waited in the command center and watched. Our insert would be by ground, driving up the eastern side of the battlespace and departing thirty minutes after Matt's team touched down.

Knowing they were in for a fight, their group included Captain Kinkade, a signals intelligence analyst, two Afghan National Army Commandos, and one Afghan interpreter.

The plan was simple, at least according to the PowerPoint. Two false landings at separate locations to confuse any enemy observers. A third landing allowing Matt's team to exit the still-spinning aircraft, followed by a final false insertion at a random site to conceal their true location.

I watched as the first landing zone kicked up dust, obscuring the drone feed. The Hueys touched down, rotors still spinning, and held for twenty seconds—just as planned. Then thirty seconds passed. Then a full minute.

The birds weren't moving. No heat signatures emerged.

Something wasn't right.

Confusion spread through the command center. Last-minute plan changes and miscommunication compromised the insert, leading the helo pilots to believe mistakenly that only one landing zone existed.

Matt's team faced a choice—get off now in the wrong place—or risk the entire operation.

The Hueys lifted, pelting sand and dust over the Marines, crouched in two tight circles on the barren rock. No dummy drops. Wrong landing zone.

And I could only watch.

## Trapped

The first thing I remembered was the light. Then the pressure. Then the sound. Then the dark.

*"Are you okay? Are you okay!"* I came to, shouting, trying to account for my team.

Through the explosion of swirling brown smoke and dust, I spotted Corporal Nick Jacobs, my point man, and team sniper, seated across from me—dazed and wide-eyed. Blood trickled from his nose. A Montana kid on his first deployment, he was made for the outdoors, but no one was made for this. Slumped beside him was Corporal Tyler Johnson, a tough, scrappy Marine from Minnesota. His attitude led him to the Corps and was also why he was on my team—to shape it into something productive.

Then dark again.

Thirty minutes after Matt's haphazard insertion, my team loaded into the MRAPs. Six armored vehicles, operating under Combined Anti-Armor Team (CAAT) Black's call sign, carried us fifteen kilometers north in a convoy. Similar to Matt's element, my large team consisted of eight Recon Marines, our Platoon Sergeant, Gunnery Sergeant Martinez, our Special Operations Corpsman Toshi Coenen, two Afghan Army commandos, two signals intelligence Marines, and one Afghan interpreter. They would drop us off near a small village nestled between the White and Black Mountains. From there, we'd disappear into the broken terrain, making our way toward Bar Now Zad under a waning crescent moon, guided by the stars. We would arrive at our observation point just before dawn.

An ill-advised six hours of pre-raid reconnaissance was all we had before the young Marines approached in the bellies of the swooping gray helicopters. Our job was to isolate the northern approach, block reinforcements, and cover the assault force clearing the town.

Matt's objective was located eight kilometers to my west, on the western edge of Do Sang. My team was assigned to cover Bar Now Zad to the east, with Bounty Hunter—one of our sniper teams—positioned between us to bridge the gap. Three reconnaissance elements had the task of covering twelve linear kilometers of mountainous terrain—it felt impossible. So, we would have to adjust, move closer to the towns, and cover key friction points. That meant risk. Our exposed forward slope would leave us without cover. We had no choice. We had to get close.

After the infantry entered the town, our teams would cover where we could from the hills, directing close air support and covering the infantry squads from maneuvering Taliban. Once the two towns were cleared, the two recon teams and single sniper team planned to consolidate with all our forces in Do Sang and stabilize the area for the next week. At least, that was the plan.

*"Are you okay? Are you okay!"* I choked through the haze.

"Yes," both men responded again.

The patrol had tripped a hidden pressure plate in a deep wadi, triggering eighty-five pounds of homemade explosives. Our Wisconsin-made 38,000-pound Oshkosh was thrown fifteen feet into the air by the explosion, sheering off its entire left side before slamming back down. The V-shaped hull was our only salvation, deflecting the blast outward and preventing us from being ripped apart.

We were alive—for the moment.

I fumbled for my headlamp and clicked it on; the red lens cast a Mars-like glow on the still-swirling dust inside the troop compartment. Above me, I heard a whimper, followed by a groan. Jacobs and Johnson jumped from their bench, hauling our wounded turret gunner back from the roof's edge. Soaked in blood, shrapnel scattered across his arms and face. It wasn't fatal, but it was serious. His eyes fluttered as he drifted in and out of consciousness, his face a mask of blood and shock.

"You guys good up there?" I yelled to the drivers.

"Yeah, we're good!" they yelled back.

The radio crackled. "Bearshark One has hit an IED on insert, status unknown."

I grabbed the handset. "We're good," I answered, my face still numb.

"Bearshark, you'll need to stay in the vehicle. We've got chatter—Taliban says you're in a minefield. They've planted smaller ones—toe poppers—around the larger IEDs. EOD is en route."

"Shit," I thought about the delay in the mission's timing. The distinct smell hit almost as soon as the scream.

"Fire!" yelled the driver. He scrambled away from the engine, crawling toward the turret opening in the vehicle's center.

"Let's go, get him out," I barked as we grabbed the wounded, semiconscious Marine. We pushed him up through the turret, where the shaken but alive drivers grabbed his vest and hauled him to safety.

Flames shot up from the front of the vehicle. I snapped a look at the fire suppression systems—fractured from the blast—and then down at my modified ghillie suit. Burlap and fire don't mix.

The fire spread fast, blocking the turret access and forcing Johnson, Jacobs, and me into the corner of the warped vehicle.

"You two, go!" I ordered. Johnson, all brute strength, wrenched at the twisted rear door, pushing hard against the warped metal. The door gave just enough. Jacobs and Johnson slipped out.

Then, without warning, the mangled vehicle shifted, and I heard a loud thud. The door slammed shut. I was sealed inside—alone.

A hundred yards away, my team sped toward us across the open wadi, and the confirmed minefield. First by vehicle, then on foot. They closed in to establish a perimeter and triage the wounded.

Inside the wrecked MRAP, I scanned the smoke-filled compartment for anything to extinguish the fire. The interior was a maze of shattered boxes and scattered gear.

I was running out of time.

The flames licked at the communications equipment, melting the green and yellow buttons.

The ammunition was next in line.

Jacobs and Johnson shouted outside, straining against the bent door. They tried to force it open with their weapons, but made little progress.

I was out of options—I was not going to allow myself to burn to death.

I grabbed my pistol, feeling its promise. I thought of Orion—where my family went—I'd be there soon.

"Hold it open!" I heard a scream. Barreling back toward the burning wreck, the newest member of my team, Lance Corporal Chris O'Connor, saw the situation and sprinted from his vehicle, tossing his weapon aside as he tore a fire extinguisher free from its mount.

Jacobs and Johnson threw everything they had into prying open the door, creating just enough space. O'Connor dove forward, shoving the nozzle through the gap and releasing a jet of white powder suppressant, dousing the flames creeping toward my burlap back.

My team arrived seconds later, each man risking his life to pry mine free.

## Reinsert

Two hours later, Explosive Ordnance Disposal had cleared up to our position and helped us move to a compound at the western edge of the wadi.

"Bearshark, we're going to need you to continue to push into position." The call came back in. I was arguing with the Operations Officer again over *his* assessment of *my* team's disposition.

"My team is combat ineffective. Our entire lead element was hit, and we're severely concussed. My corpsman is with one of my Marines now. We need to roll this mission twenty-four hours. Bearshark Two's insert was klicks off course, and even if we had operational vehicles, we'd arrive at our position past dawn."

"Negative, Bearshark One. CAAT Black will return to base to refit, and you will continue from your position on foot."

"On what?!?" I hissed back while my point man and I traced a finger on our map, showing our objective and drawing a line to our current position.

We'd have to drastically alter our planned route, adding a second mountain pass and five unplanned kilometers. The only way we'd get into position in time to provide overwatch for the assault was to run the eleven kilometers we had left on our perilous movement.

## Tumbling Stars

11 January 2010 - 0547
Three kilometers east of Bar Now Zad, Afghanistan

I sipped water between breaths, shooting half-dried blood out of my nose as I took a knee at the edge of a wadi, facing our second mountain climb. I was the leader, and my team was watching. I looked up toward the sky, searching for Orion. The stars seemed to almost circle around me. Streaks of wobbly white lines traced their way across the dark sky. Pain flashed through me, and fear pressed at the edges of my mind, but I buried both. Finally, in near desperation, I found his belt, only to see him spinning too. My team needed strength, and I had to give it to them, even if I had to fake it. I leaned over my rifle and threw up on the cold rocks.

The frigid mountain air hung low as the sun's rays crept over the horizon. Pink and orange hues cut through the fire-red illuminated rocks. Our team was on the backside of our last mountain pass, pressing through our final stretch for our hide site. We'd made good time but had to enter our most dangerous phase—slipping fifteen people into a clandestine position on the forward slope of a small hill, 500 meters from the edge of town, in broad daylight.

By 0900, we had established our position. Our assault would begin within the next ninety minutes. I called in to report our location and confirmed Bounty Hunter and Bearshark Two's locations. Matt was too far to reach with line-of-sight communication, so we relayed through our air frequency. I could hear the irritation in his voice.

"Hey P, we've got guys moving, two by two," Jacobs whispered. I looked up to a small valley to our north and saw eight men moving in pairs, separated by fifty meters along a dirt path. Fighters—young, well-kept, and moving with purpose. Yet we couldn't act. They knew our rules of engagement as well as we did. Moving in pairs, no weapons meant no action on my part. Hamstrung by the rules meant to protect unnecessary deaths, we watched our enemy maneuver freely.

Miles away, Matt saw the same thing, only worse. Closer to the primary objective, he saw over forty fighters moving into the area—two by two. The Taliban knew we were coming. Tipped off by spies, our errant dummy drops, or the infantry battalion's irrational desire to shoot missiles into the target city the night before, they prepared their defenses. We were walking into an ambush.

## The Dilemma

`11 January - mid-morning - Bar Now Zad, Afghanistan`

"The . . . usin . . . ildren to . . . robe our line . . .," Matt's broken transmission crackled over the net, relayed to one of the AV-8 Harriers circling 20,000 feet above, trying to slew its sensors to spot weapons and justify declaring a Troops in Contact (TIC).

Limited aviation across the region meant air support wasn't simply requested—it had to be earned. Priority was tiered and reserved for units actively engaged with the enemy. Matt, a specially trained air controller, understood the protocol and the politics, and he knew how to navigate the system.

A TIC served as a crucial lifeline. It signified that Marines were in danger. It meant every jet and helicopter in the region would abandon their tasks to respond. But urgency wasn't enough. It had to go up the chain of command. It needed approval. He was doing everything possible to force a decision that would bring help.

"We . . . e got . . . methin . . . goi . . . on . . . here. Ban . . . eee Two . . . decla . . . an . . . minent TIC," Matt said. His ordinarily steady voice wavered.

We fought in Afghanistan with rifles in our hands and rule books in our pockets.

The rules of engagement were clear—outlined in briefings, reinforced during training, and memorized in bullet points.

Yet, in the mud and dust, clarity was always the first casualty.

War is never black and white. Yet, the governments that sent us here insisted it should be. They drew imaginary lines in the sand from the safety of their air-conditioned offices—lines the enemy had no intention of honoring.

In the name of restraint, we gave up our greatest weapon—aggression.

We had prepared for war, but we fought with one hand tied behind our back.

Each unit grappled with the irony of loyalty to either the men or the mission. Attack too soon and face a judge. Wait too long and face a mother.

This burden rested solely on the young shoulders at the front.

The Taliban faced no such dilemma.

"We...ne...addition...air...support...now," came the barely intelligible call.

"Hey Bearshark, we're bingo on fuel. We're going to have to hit the tanker. We'll be back as soon as we can," the frantic Harriers radioed. They had no choice; they were out of gas.

The command had disregarded Matt's request. No one else was coming.

The planned gap—meant to give aviation time to refuel before the assault—left our recon teams alone, exposed deep in the enemy's backyard.

And we'd tipped our hand.

*Brap brap brap.*

Two distinct machine guns echoed in the distance over my left shoulder. The fast-paced M240B unleashed hundreds of rounds, desperately trying to halt the assault, closely followed by the deeper, slower thuds of a PKM. *Bomp bomp bomp bomp.*

Whoosh—*boom.*

Rockets and RPGs slammed in the distance.

My heart sank. A deep aching pit formed.

Matt's team was in heavy contact. We were helpless.

"No!" I yelled. My team jumped to their feet.

The distant booms and gunfire continued. Green and red tracers arced across the sky, hitting rocks and deflecting into the air.

Scrambled voices over the net became frantic as my signals intel Marine and interpreter grabbed my arm.

"The Taliban is attacking your team right now," the interpreter said, his hands trembling. He was a civilian, but this country was his home, and he valued a free Afghanistan more than his own life.

"They said they're getting the first team now and will move to the second one next." He pointed to the base of the mountain below.

Eight Taliban gathered at the foot of the mountain—weaponless. We were next.

No time to rest. No time to think. Twenty-four hours without sleep. The IED still echoed in my ears. My head still spun. I had just run eleven kilometers across unforgiving mountains, my lungs burning and my legs throbbing—arriving only forty minutes before the assault.

I faced a choice.

Stay in position—do my job, protect the Infantry Marines advancing into danger.

Or break from my post and rush to the aid of my best friend, who might already be dying.

One choice meant betraying my duty. The other meant abandoning my brother.

There was no right answer.

I had seconds to decide.

War is never black and white.

Moments later, the distinct rumble of the enormous rotors of the CH-53 Super Stallion washed over the floor of Now Zad Valley.

The assault wave had begun.

Alongside them raced Scarface, a mix of Hueys and Cobras splitting off toward Matt's position to our west. They scrambled to save the teams they knew—Marines they'd spent countless frigid nights with hovering over the dark valleys.

A bond that ran deeper than most understood.

Streaking in over our right shoulder, the CH-53s touched down 750 meters to the north. A platoon of Marines hurried down their ramps, quickly dispersing into the town as sporadic gunfire rang out through the streets.

Clinging to my radio's air frequency, I listened as the firefight unfolded, caught between two worlds, with my eyes focused on my sector, keeping the Marines in front of me safe. Matt's broken voice crackled through the radio, yelling—gunshots echoed through his microphone as he desperately called out to Scarface, swooping down the valley.

"Bearshark, where are you? We can't engage—Bearshark, do you copy?"

The panic in the pilot's voice split through the static. A camouflaged team was sprinting through open terrain, weaving through rock and dust, and death. Taliban were closing in from all sides—and Scarface couldn't fire. Too close and too risky; the snakes couldn't bite.

"Scar…eep c…oming towa…us, danger clo—"

Scarface tore down the valley, engines screaming, skimming low over the mud rooftops of Do Sang. They banked hard into the wadi, trying to split the kill zone—trying to reach Matt's team.

And then—nothing.

My stomach dropped. My head spun. I stared at the handset, waiting for something—anything.

A call sign. A breath. A voice I knew.

## Break Contact

I heard him before I saw him, his engines thrusting against the cold. A black dot screeched high above, cutting through wispy clouds, shining a frigid blue. Scrambling to lose altitude and join the fray, his afterburners scorched holes in the hearts of any Taliban.

"Bearcat, Bearcat, this is Wraith, over." The steady-handed Harrier pilot punched in.

"Wraith, this is Bearshark." Kinkade's panicked voice filled the gray. "There are fighters everywhere. Can you get into the valley?"

"Copy, we're inbound to you for a flyby. Keep your heads down. Wraith, out."

Watching the gray Harrier streak past my head at near supersonic speed was like seeing a ghost punch through the sky. My brain caught the shape first—sleek, low, and fast. My mind couldn't fully register what it was seeing. No propeller. No visible flame. Just a flat, deadly blur slicing through the air like it was ripping open the horizon itself.

Then came the pressure.

A gut-punch of force blasted from its tail as it roared by, growling low and violent from the east, tearing straight into Do Sang.

Whatever fight the Taliban had left, it was about to be shattered.

"Any station, this is Bearshark Two," Kinkade hesitated into the radio. "We've got two KIA, one MIA."

"Bounty Hunter en route to your position," the snipers rogered up first. Defying direct orders to stay in place, they were already running and gunning, charging down through the mountains. First to reinforce, they showed no hesitation.

"This is CAAT Black; we're inbound to you," Lieutenant Chris Brock squelched in over the radio net. His Marines had inserted us just hours earlier—three of them wounded in the blast that nearly cost us our lives. Two of the wounded loaded back up, their heads undoubtedly throbbing as much as mine. Their platoon roared south from their blocking position, tearing through Bar Now Zad, hammering Taliban positions with heavy machine guns and clearing a path to reach Matt's team.

Overhead, Scarface circled low, their rotors tracing the jagged spine of the valley. Hueys and Cobras strafed the mountainsides, engaging the fleeing Taliban and scanning desperately for the missing men.

Marines were in trouble, and they were coming.

In front of my team, the Marines we were covering were in contact. I shoved thoughts of Matt to the back of my mind. I had a team to lead and a mission to finish. My emotions would have to wait.

Without hesitation, we rushed down from the mountain to support them. For the next three hours, we fought through the small village—shoulders slamming and boots splintering through the brittle doors of mud huts—as we cleared and secured sections along the southwestern edge of town. The Taliban had pulled back—whether by design or pressure, we didn't know. We pressed on, meeting only small pockets of fleeting resistance.

With our mission in Bar Now Zad complete, we patrolled in broad daylight with the rifle platoon toward Do Sang, where the rest of the company was still locked in the fight.

My mind raced—fragments of what I'd witnessed looped over and over. Hazy as a dream. Every call and every shouted transmission replayed in my head. I could still hear his voice, frantic over the net, desperate for help.

Scarface circled above, and scattered reports trickled in—pieces of a nightmare we couldn't escape.

For hours, we walked—rifles slung, heads low, the enormous weight of loss pressing down.

An estimated twenty-five to forty Taliban fighters had overrun the split five-man recon element after air support checked off station.

Two KIAs and one MIA became three confirmed dead.

The sniper section eventually found the missing Marine. Scarface touched down at the base of the hill where the same snipers we'd bonded with—over frozen nights on opposite hilltops above the valley—linked up with the remaining members of Bearshark Two. Together, they loaded the bodies of our honored dead into the spinning helicopters.

By nightfall, the company had secured a compound west of Do Sang. The infantry platoon let us stay with them for the night.

Three of our brothers were gone. We just didn't know which ones.

But deep down, in the pit of my stomach, I already knew.

## The Names

12 January 0130 - Do Sang, Afghanistan

"This is Bearshark One, over." With our arms around each other's shoulders, I knelt between my ATL, Sergeant Joe Gillooly, and my Platoon Sergeant, Gunnery Sergeant Efrain Martinez. The makeshift company operations center sat in a large mud-brick courtyard. Stables, small rooms, and the smell of livestock. It would suffice for the night. The infantry Marines showed us compassion, trying to share the weight of the loss—yet no one would meet our gaze.

"Go ahead, Bearshark One," the watch officer at FOB Cafferata responded.

"I'm requesting the line numbers for Bearshark's KIAs." Line numbers served for roster identification and medical evacuation. Matt and I always joked that he was born to be a Marine—his last four digits were 0311, the military code for Marine infantry.

"Roger, standby." The voice hesitated. The three of us shared a somber glance.

"Hey, Bearshark, standby. First line number is India zero-three—"

I heard nothing else.

My ears rang.

My stomach twisted.

My head throbbed and spun—I choked.

My closest friend. My fiercest rival. My greatest mentor.

His name, his life, his entire existence reduced to a string of numbers over the radio.

Not him. Not Matt.

He was too smart. Too damn good. He was the one who always had the answer when no one else did.

The one we all looked to.

I dropped to my knees, gasping. The dirt, and dust, and pain swallowed my breath.

And for the first time in years, I begged a God I'd long forgotten.

This wasn't fair. This wasn't right.

I would've traded anything—anything—to have won that fucking coin flip instead of him.

It was the truth that broke me. He was better than me in every way.

"I'm sorry," the voice trailed off.

We turned toward my waiting team. Most of them were on their first deployment. They had never encountered the cold indifference and shocking finality of death. Standing in a semicircle in the middle of the courtyard, my team hung their heads, their icy breaths fading into the midnight sky above—waiting for me to speak the names.

I swallowed hard as tears streaked down my worn, grease-painted face.

"Hey, boys," I sniffled, shaking my head in a futile attempt to hold it together. "Team Two is safe back at Cafferata, but we lost—" My voice caught. I forced myself to push through.

"We lost Jamie, Nick, and Matt."

The words fractured in my mouth, and then—silence.

Corporal Jamie Lowe was an upbeat, kind-hearted Marine from Johnsonville, Illinois. He was eager and driven—the kind of Marine you wanted at your side. Matt took a liking to him right away, drawn to his unmatched work ethic as he mentored him and trained him to be his radio operator.

Nicholas Uzenski was a die-hard Yankees fan from Franklin, New York. He had just turned twenty-one and was a devoted family man with unwavering loyalty to his sisters. There was a purity about him, untouched by the world in a way that felt almost impossible out here. He had never touched a drink—not once. Even I teased him about it, but deep down, we all respected him for it.

And then there was Matt—a rambunctious kid from Altoona, PA. His summers were spent at the lakes or tearing through the countryside on his motorcycle, pestering the local Amish communities just for the hell of it. He joined the Marines at the same time I did, marrying his high school sweetheart, Yasmin, along the way.

Hard-shelled and quick-witted, Matt was a caring man once he let you in. He was always the first with a joke, reminding us that sometimes the best way to solve a problem was to go straight through it. I admired him for that.

I couldn't begin to comprehend Matt's final moments—a desperate attempt to control a rapidly deteriorating situation. The thoughts that must have raced through his mind haunted me. The chaos. The choices. The impossible odds. The carnage.

Matt had always done everything right. He was stronger, faster, smarter, and better than me in every way. He set the standard—the Marine I measured myself against. The one we all did. And yet, despite everything, despite his skill, his instincts, his relentless tenacity, he had ended up in an unwinnable fight.

And still, he gave everything—his last full measure—for his teammates.

No one on my team knew what to say.

They looked at me, unsure of what to do next. I understood my new role as their leader. I taught them how to grieve. How to share, how to laugh, how to joke, how to cry, and how to carry the weight together because none of us could bear it alone.

We spoke their names. We told their stories. And we wept—the kind of cry only a broken soul could understand. A guttural, visceral pain that tore from deep inside.

"For the honor of the fallen, for the glory of the dead," I said.

An epitaph written for Marines in World War I who struggled with the same reality nearly one hundred years before. The same impossible burden. It felt fitting.

And under the pitch-black sky, wrapped in the stillness of the Afghan desert, three stars in a line flickered above me.

I could feel their presence.

I couldn't bring myself to look up.

# 15

------

# ANGELA'S LETTER

February 2010 - Helmand Province, Afghanistan

*To whomever gets this letter:*

*Hi, my name is Angela. I'm 14 years old and live in Sunnyvale, California—that's the Bay Area (a lot of people don't know that). I'm writing this letter to you at exactly 10:48 p.m. because I found myself lying in bed, remembering what my teacher had told me the day before.*

Often, elementary and high school students across the country would write letters to deployed service members—short notes filled with gratitude, encouragement, and the kind of innocent hope only kids could offer. Some drew American flags or stick-figure soldiers in uniform. Others simply wrote, "Thank you for keeping us safe."

They didn't know our names, and we didn't know theirs. But the USPS bundled these messages—hundreds at a time—into care packages called "Any Marine Boxes" and shipped them to the front lines, trusting they'd find someone who needed them.

At Camp Leatherneck, near the dusty entrance to our recon company's barracks, a worn cardboard box in a corner overflowed with letters. Marines would often pass by, grab one at random, and slip it into a pocket. Later, maybe between patrols or before racking out, we'd steal a quiet moment to read.

Amid the uncertainty of war, those letters became a small taste of home—grounding us and reminding us why we fought. A bridge between two worlds: one at war, and one worth protecting.

"One minute!" the crew chief shouted through the pitch-black troop compartment.

Frigid night air whipped through the Osprey's door gun windows, mixing with the warm breath of Marines and the constant metallic scent of leaking hydraulic fluid. The only light came from the faint green glow of our night vision goggles, reflecting off our tense faces. Bearshark was fully operational again. Our three new combat replacements echoed the call down the line.

We were inbound to Marjah during a rare winter offensive in a country where fighting typically occurred after the spring thaw. A force of 15,000 troops from Afghanistan, the United States, Britain, Canada, Denmark, and Estonia had surrounded the Taliban-held city days earlier to strike when the enemy least expected. As the last major Taliban stronghold in the region, Marjah was already being whispered as Afghanistan's Fallujah.

Third Recon—call sign Task Force Raider—was tasked with sealing the breach between two infantry units. In the early hours of the battle, the infantry had punched into the city, but a gap opened in their line, allowing Taliban fighters and supplies to flood in unchecked. Our job was to slam the door shut.

Six Ospreys tore through the night, racing toward the objective under the cover of darkness. Enemy tracers lit the sky in erratic green bursts as the aircraft transitioned from flight mode to hover. The shudder of the rotors pulsed through the frozen air, a mechanical heartbeat pounding against the muddy fields below.

*You see, our class made a poster for the troops—especially for this guy who graduated from my high school. We wrote things like "thanks" and "good job."*

*Yesterday my teacher told us that a Fremont High School graduate—that's my school, Fremont High—had lost his best friend in the war.*

*But what she told us next really hit home for me. She told us how much joy this poster brought to the troops.*

*She told us that every morning, his friend would just look at the poster, and the poster would bring a smile to his face. It turns out he did this right up until the day he died. That is when I started crying. I never realized how powerful the words of a freshman in high school could be. So, I decided to get up and write this letter to you while my thoughts were fresh in my mind.*

*Now, I know this isn't some fantastic poster, but the intent is the same. After hearing what my teacher told me, I hoped I could touch some of the troops or at least brighten their day. That is what I aim to do in this letter, and I hope you hear these two words I'm about to say a lot: "Thank you."*

*Thank you for being so brave that you can stand up and fight for our country. Thank you for being so brave and selfless that you left your lives and loved ones to fight for people you don't even know. The bottom line is thank you for all that you do because every time you have to do something like stay up all night and look out or witness death and destruction you are protecting and saving me.*

"Thirty seconds!"

The high-pitched whine of hydraulics cut through the roar of the engines as the clamshell rear doors creaked open and the ramp dropped, revealing the sleepy Afghan countryside below. Frozen wind blasted into the troop compartment, carrying the sharp scent of mud and farmland. Dark irrigation canals cut through the flooded fields like black veins, glinting faintly in the moonlight.

The Ospreys banked hard, low and fast, descending the last hundred feet like a falling elevator. This was going to be a quick offload. I moved to the back of the ramp, gripping a wall strap for stability while scanning the landing zone as we barreled in.

The wheels kissed the soggy ground. Careful not to sink, the pilots held the engines at a 45-degree angle, throttles humming, ready to claw back into the sky.

"Let's go!" I shouted, stepping forward.

Bearing down on the flooded field, I leapt first into the darkness—*I wish Matt was here.*

My first boot hit the swampy ground, followed instantly by my point man, Corporal Jacobs. We cleared the ramp, only to be snatched by the Osprey's hurricane-force rotor wash. Weightless and flailing, we were tossed like rag dolls across the mud.

Small pockets of fire crackled in the distance—the city beyond was waking up. We needed to get out of this field.

For the next forty-five minutes, a hundred Recon Marines sloshed, waded, crawled, and even rolled through the flooded terrain. Two to three feet of freezing water in every direction. Every step a struggle. Rifles jammed with sludge, optics fogged, gear soaked. Some Marines—out of options and with limited water—had to piss on their rifles to break the mud loose.

Exhausted and soaked to the bone, we pushed into the outskirts, clearing the first few houses to set up a command center.

Two hours later, the sun would rise.

And the Taliban would wake up with 120 Reconnaissance Marines in their backyard.

*Well, it's 11:07 now, and I'm still not tired. If my parents knew I was still up they'd be really mad at me! But I am sure you know how that is! I don't really know what I want to say. It is hard for me to remember all my thoughts and then put them down on paper in an orderly fashion. My teacher said that troops loved to hear about current events, and that they may even like to know a bit about me. But I guess I will start with the first one. Unfortunately I'm only fourteen so I don't know too much. But I do know that there was a 7.0 earthquake that struck Haiti in early January (I believe Haiti*

> *is an island in the Caribbean). I know that many were injured and killed and some are still trapped under the rubble or waiting to hear if family members are alive. I know this isn't the happiest subject, but it's things like this that put your life into perspective, you know? In a totally different random note, the cellular phone companies AT&T and Verizon Wireless are battling it out. Those commercials just get funnier and funnier.*

*Brap. Brap. Brap.*

"Contact left!" someone yelled from the front of the patrol.

Three short bursts from a PKM shredded the narrow alleyway ahead, chewing mud and debris from the thick walls. A Taliban machine-gun team had split our platoon in half.

Still shaking off the adrenaline from our aerial insert, we realized the enemy had already scrambled at dawn to find us. They pushed forward fast, using ratlines and wadis from the tree lines bordering the flooded fields, sending patrols from the mud huts to probe our lines and try to box us in.

We'd spread our five platoons across the sector, headquarters holding the center.

"Let's go—get that gun in position!" Sergeant Gillooly yelled. Once we'd rejoined 3rd Recon at Camp Leatherneck, our mission shifted. We broke into three teams to spread experience throughout the platoon. Gillooly had been promoted to lead Team Three.

*Zzzt. Zzzt.*

A second surprise burst of machine-gun fire snapped down the alley, cutting off Team Two from the rest of us. The Taliban were pressing. We had seconds to counter the coming assault.

*Thunk. Thunk.*

Smoke grenades launched from our M203s, hissing down the alley to blind the PKM team. We followed with volleys of machine-gun fire of our own, trying to suppress, and to buy time. It wasn't enough. The Taliban pressed their advantage against our exposed flank, and Team Two was still pinned.

Desperate to fend off the onslaught from the isolated team, Gillooly and I jumped out from behind our compound wall. I broke right, sprinting into the alley under fire, drawing the machine gunner's attention away from their primary target. The hesitation worked—just enough. Team Two scrambled across the pockmarked dirt road, diving back into cover and reestablishing our base of fire.

"Rocket!" Gunny Martinez shouted.

Captain Kinkade checked his backblast and fired. The M72 Light Anti-tank Weapon screamed down the alley and obliterated the machine-gun position in a crescendo of smoke, dust, and noise.

The fight stalled for a moment, but the cat-and-mouse game persisted.

This wasn't a "normal" fight. It was Taliban versus Recon. Both sides hunted each other across a battlefield stretched between flooded fields and thick tree lines—a no-man's land with no clear front. The Taliban moved like ghosts. They knew the terrain and how to vanish into it.

But they had no refuge.

We had eyes in the sky.

Predator drones operated by specially trained Marines who coordinated attacks from above. The extended loiter time enabled our ground controllers to integrate the digital feeds into wrist-mounted video screens, tracking ahead of our patrols and analyzing the battlefield before we stepped into it.

By then, the US had fully committed to integrating air and ground. Joint Terminal Attack Controllers—JTACs—coordinated the chaos. Layers of death orbited overhead. NATO jets, helicopter gunships, and drones were all waiting on the call.

At the center of it all was Gunnery Sergeant Blaine Jones.

A firestorm in human form.

A wrestler from Indiana, his cauliflower ears and gravel-throated voice revealed everything you needed to know. This man brought the fight. The Recon boys loved him. He was one of us—meaner than a rabid animal, tougher than woodpecker lips, and smart enough to unleash hell on the Taliban before they ever saw us coming.

Jones didn't sleep. He existed on nicotine, caffeine, and sheer willpower, running on the fumes of stolen energy drinks and Marlboro Lights. Raining down the haunting shriek of GPS guided missiles—Jones was death on call.

He threaded firepower through the sky like a surgeon when it was time to strike. In Marjah, he killed countless Taliban—Hellfires screamed down from Predators, Apaches swooped low and raked tree lines with 30mm chain guns.

Blaine Jones didn't just win fights.

He saved lives—dozens of them.

Including mine.

> *Ooooh and I don't know if you're into animated science fiction fantasy movies, but there is this new movie* Avatar *that came out and it's like all the rage. All the shows were still sold out a month after it came out—which I think is pretty impressive! So much for important events. I guess trying to remember better ones, but it's a bit late, so my brain is like shutting down. Now I guess I could tell you a bit about me, though I don't even know if you'd be interested (hopefully you'll find this interesting—I find I amuse people with my life story). Although I am 14, I still sleep with stuffed animals and a night-light. I love the Backstreet Boys and Jesse McCartney, and I stand by my decision to like them even though I get so much ridicule. I impress people with my ability to speak Spanish almost fluently and precisely, even though I am from England and am tall with blond hair and blue eyes. Sometimes I even convince people I am Mexican. I just love that language!*

"Two men moving in from the tree line! Pasciuti, do you have a shot?"

Kinkade's voice echoed off the packed mud wall as Jacobs and I sprinted to the far side of our freshly cleared compound. My Eberlestock day pack bounced against my back, the built-in scabbard keeping my sniper rifle tucked and protected. We slid into position behind a crumbling mound of rubble. Jacobs yanked out his Leica rangefinder—the same model that had made sniper school a nightmare for me.

Chest heaving, I dropped to my back and tore off the makeshift rocket tube I'd rigged to disguise the rifle's profile. With the tube gone, I slid the rifle from its scabbard, screwed on my Surefire suppressor, and snapped the bipods into place.

*Click. Click.* Good to go.

I unstrapped my helmet and low-crawled forward, easing the rifle into position with only the scope and barrel exposed between the rocks.

The two men had crept in from the tree line—1,200 meters to our north—moving slow, eyes scanning, peering around corners as they approached the nearest building. They were careful. They knew we were nearby—just not where. One of them split off, cutting along a perpendicular wall from right to left.

"Distance?" I asked.

"I've got 990 meters. Wind at five miles per hour, gusting left to right," Jacobs replied. I had trained him well. "2nd Platoon's off to our right."

"Breathe," I reminded myself.

I inhaled the choking smoke from nearby burning buildings. My veins surged with adrenaline. The man moved with purpose, head on a swivel—ten meters from the wall's edge. I held my crosshairs there, timing the shot to hit him as he crossed.

*Exhale.* I flicked the safety off, finger sliding onto the sloped trigger. My grip tightened.

Seven meters.

*Inhale.* My mind cleared. Crosshairs blurred. At 1,000 meters, my bullet could hit anywhere inside a ten-inch circle, with a two-second time of flight. My calculations needed to be perfect. I waited for my math problem to come to its conclusion.

Four meters.

*Exhale.*

*Slow. Steady. Squeeze.* Four pounds of pressure.

The rifle *hissed*—the suppressed shot whispered against the chaotic fight beyond. The recoil rocked me back as my boots dug into the earth to keep me on target. My flight time provided just enough of a window to catch sight of my own vapor trail—a rare phenomenon in which a bullet's arc becomes momentarily visible as it cuts through moisture in the air.

The world slowed. From the top right of my scope, I watched the faint V-shaped trail streak toward the target.

One meter.

The round skimmed under his chin and slammed into the wall behind him. A cloud of dried mud exploded in his face. He stumbled, dazed—but alive.

I missed.

"Shit." I clenched my jaw. "Keep eyes on him."

Jacobs and I scanned the shadowed alleys beyond.

"Hey, P," Jacobs whispered. "He's coming back."

We stared in disbelief. Three more men rounded the corner, joining the first. Confused, he had returned to the fresh hole in the wall, pointing at the impact. They circled the mark, gesturing, analyzing, and focused on 2nd Platoon's position to our right—completely unaware we were there.

I settled my crosshairs at the center of the group.

*Exhale.*

Four pounds of pressure.

*I am very athletic, and my main two sports are basketball and soccer. I discovered four sports I absolutely can't play: softball, baseball, tennis, and water polo. What is weird about me is that with my athleticism comes major klutziness. People know to stay five feet away at all times, which is ridiculous because I don't trip that much, just about 100 times a day.*

*I am a pretty good student. I have like all A's and one B (darn math). I always say I love the rain until I'm in it, and I've never had a boyfriend. And I love reading but my optometrist says it makes my eyesight worse, which is ~~wierd~~, ~~wired~~, weird (ugh I couldn't spell that word!) because reading is supposed to be beneficial!*

*I love my friends, family, and my four cats (yes four!) too! I think I will leave it at that because my goal wasn't to make this letter about me.*

*Zzzt, snap*—two rounds cracked between Jacobs and me. Our platoon's position was compromised. The Taliban were on the move, maneuvering closer. Radio traffic spiked, and explosions echoed to our right. 2nd Platoon was engaged. The fight was on.

Our platoon rushed to the compound walls, opening fire into the tree line, tracking the silhouettes and bobbing heads shifting through the brush.

"Gunny, we've got chatter!" our Afghan interpreter shouted—listening to the Taliban's radio frequency. "They've got a recoilless rifle—they're moving it now!"

*Boom.*

*Boom.*

Enemy mortars crunched in the field ahead, walking their way toward us.

"Time to move," Gunny Martinez keyed over the net. "We're taking the next building." He paused. "P, have your team cover us as we bound."

"Copy. When it's clear, we'll head over," I replied, already packing up gear with Jacobs.

Back on the narrow-canalized street, the platoon pressed forward—crashing through rusted gates, clearing abandoned mud-brick houses as gunfire echoed in bursts across the company's front. The fight had spread, and it wasn't letting up.

Our team held the rear, the last line of defense against Taliban flanking maneuvers. Small two-man teams harassed our larger patrols from multiple angles to confuse our fire and limit our concentration of munitions. Smart, aggressive, and relentless. They'd earned my respect.

*Crunch—Boom. Crunch—Boom.* Two more mortars landed, closer now.

I turned to brief my team when an unholy scream tore through the air. My gut twisted. I knew that sound. That wasn't human.

*"INCOMING!"* I grabbed Jacobs by his vest, yanking him off the wall and throwing us both toward the nearest cover—a mud hut barely strong enough to hold itself up, let alone withstand what was about to hit.

The world detonated.

The ground convulsed as a shock wave slammed into my back, hurling fire and splintered debris through the air. I braced over Jacobs as the wall in front of me disappeared in a spray of heat and flailing mud. My ears pulsed while my body vibrated from the blast.

Dust, hay, and dried manure caked my face. I shook my head and grabbed Jacobs by the collar.

"Jacobs, you good?" He blinked through the dirt, wiping a trembling hand across his sweat-soaked brow. This was the second time we'd been blown up together.

His bloodshot eyes flickered toward me, unfocused. "Yeah . . . I think so."

"Good. Let's go—*now!*" I didn't let him finish. Gunfire rattled through the alleyways; sporadic bursts mixed with the screams of the dying.

My team regrouped near the battered metal door, barely hanging by a hinge, still swaying from the blast. I edged forward, rifle first, scanning outside.

A crater smoked in the street. Scattered around it were pieces—what was left of two Taliban fighters. They'd crept along the outside wall, waiting to shoot us in the back while we fought their main force. But they had waited too long.

The rest ran, disappearing into the narrow alleys. Useless. They knew what was coming next—death from above.

We regrouped with the platoon as the low thump of rotor blades echoed above us. A matte gray HH-60 Pave Hawk cut low through the smoke, its sleek fuselage caked in black exhaust and dirt. USAF marked its tail.

My stomach dropped.

*"Pedro" was inbound.*

Air Force Pararescue—PJs. Literal angels on our shoulders. Every Marine knew what it meant when they showed up. They didn't come for the living. They came for the dying.

Their motto: "These things we do, that others may live."

They flew into hell itself to pull a Marine out of it. If a man had even a flicker of life left, the PJs would fight to keep it from fading. The word *hero* wasn't enough.

Green and yellow smoke drifted over 2nd Platoon's compound as the streaking helicopter banked in, tail swinging hard to thread into the tight courtyard. The downwash whipped the smoke into an apocalyptic storm—dust, smoke, and desperation swirling in the rotor wash.

Seconds later, they lifted off again—one Marine fading in the back as green tracers and RPGs chased the bird into the sky.

Corporal Greg Stultz, from Brazil, Indiana. Caught low by a Taliban sniper—just under the plate. The PJs fought to keep him alive, hands slick with blood, performing surgery mid-flight.

His fight was over. Ours raged on.

Gunny Jones didn't waste a breath. With Pedro racing away, the airstrikes continued. Holding a radio in one hand and a map in the other, he unleashed the kind of hell that shattered men's wills. F/A-18s sliced through the cloud cover, releasing their payloads in pairs.

Five-hundred-pound bombs, tiny black specks, screamed through the air before smashing into the soft mud, splintering trees, and sending geysers of dirt and souls into the sky.

Scarface's spitting Cobras and Hueys raked the fading Taliban positions, unleashing volleys of Hydra rocket fire and 20mm fury from their chin-mounted cannon. They walked rounds through bunkers before chewing through alleyways, turning any escape into a dead end.

The battlefield shifted.

The tide had turned.

For now.

*So now I have to ask you a favor. If this letter touched you or brightened your day by any amount, please show this to as many others as possible. I hope that you, along with all your comrades, can come find this letter and read it in lonely times, and find comfort in the words that I have written. And I again want to say thank you for everything you do.*

*You guys are definitely my heroes!*

*Love always,*
*Angela*

The pilot's voice crackled over the radio frequency, hollow and tinny against the backdrop of the spinning engine's whine. "Urgent Surgical is now Routine . . . I'm sorry. We did everything we could."

There was guilt in the pilot's tone, but none of us blamed them.

The PJs weren't miracle workers—they were angels who fought death with their bare hands.

This time, death won.

Corporal Greg Stultz died on the way back to Leatherneck. He was twenty-two years old.

# 16

------

# A LACK OF A DECISION IS STILL A DECISION

## Ocean Spray

26 April 2012 - Undisclosed location
Northern Red Sea

Dawn broke over the hazy pink horizon as cold blasts of ocean misted over the bow of the USS *New York* as we cut through the Red Sea. The night before, we had slipped through the narrow fortified passage of the Suez Canal under the cover of darkness, emerging at daybreak into open waters. Now, leaning against the forward railing, I watched as bottlenose and spinner dolphins raced along the bow stem, their sleek bodies twisting and leaping in the churning, frothy wake.

Every morning, after a quick breakfast, my team and I headed topside to take a moment to breathe. We carefully maneuvered around the two large anchor chains on the narrow deck to feel the sun's warmth on our faces before the day's work began. We had trained too long and too hard to take anything for granted. So, we made time for fleeting moments of calm to break the monotony—a small indulgence—before we stepped back into the present.

## MIDDLE EAST AND NORTH AFRICA

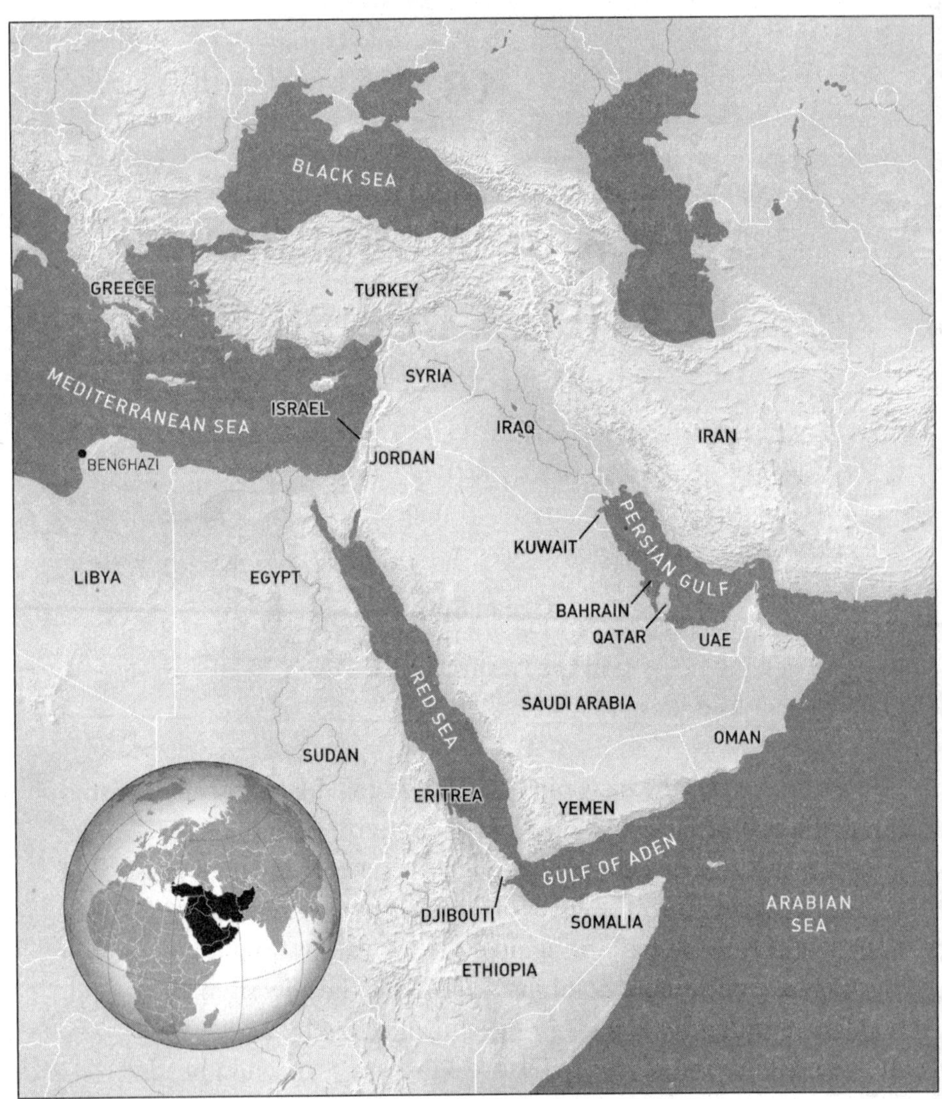

I was a Team Leader with Second Force Reconnaissance Company based at Camp Lejeune, North Carolina. Our twenty-four Marine Force Recon Platoon deployed with the 24th Marine Expeditionary Unit. Much smaller than a Carrier Strike Group, the three-ship armada transported 2,000 Marines, each one a crucial component in a system designed for rapid dominance. Fighter jets, attack and transport helicopters, tanks, artillery, and 1,200 infantry Marines and special operations capable Marines onboard at all times. The Marine Expeditionary Unit (MEU) was combat in a box—an instrument of American foreign policy capable of imposing order or destruction wherever the moment demanded. Our platoon lived at the razor's edge.

Born on the beaches of the Pacific Islands during World War II, Reconnaissance Marines built their reputation through grit, sweat, and sacrifice, becoming one of the best-trained and most highly equipped combat forces in the US military. Their mission has always been, and will continue to be, to live, eat, sleep, breathe, and, if necessary, die to give young infantry Marines the best chance of survival.

Accepting dangerous missions behind enemy lines just for the chance to tip the scales in another Marine's favor. Recon Marines never saw themselves as superior to the riflemen they served. The frontline Marines weren't our *risk*; they were our *reason*.

Unlike other special operations forces, Marine Recon was deliberately kept outside the US Special Operations Command (SOCOM) to ensure Marine Commanders always had direct access to "snake eaters" that could deliver when failure wasn't an option.

Typically, Reconnaissance Battalions operated under each Marine Division, supporting infantry battalions fighting within that division's area of operations. But some of us went further.

After time in Battalion Recon, some earned the title of Force Recon Marine. Assigned to the Marine Expeditionary Force (MEF), we operated as personal platoons under the direct command of some of the highest-ranking leaders in the Corps. That distinction came with harder training and higher stakes—combat diving, free-fall parachuting for deep insertion, long-range patrols well beyond the battle area, and close-quarters battle for raids and embassy reinforcement. The world was shifting, and our missions shifted with it.

Adept commanders saw Force Reconnaissance Marines as the fiercest, most capable warfighters in the infantry arsenal. At times, our role extended to supporting other special operations units—SEALs and Green Berets—who knew that when it mattered most, we were the ones to call.

For eighteen months before our deployment, we honed our capabilities along the eastern seaboard, redefining reconnaissance for the twenty-first century. Our mission was ambitious—to become one of America's best forward-deployed emergency response forces.

At the heart of this evolution stood the MEU Commander—a former Force Recon Officer, one of the OGs from Detachment-1 (DET-1), now a full-bird Colonel. He could smell bullshit from a mile away. His standards weren't just high; they were a wall of expectations. You either climbed or got crushed beneath them—especially if you were a Force Recon Marine.

His decades of experience, spanning both conventional and special operations, formed the bedrock of his presence. He didn't need to act in charge—he simply was. He didn't waste words or fill space with unnecessary noise. When he listened, he truly listened. His light blue eyes honed in like a raptor, weighing every detail of your assessment. A slight wince or grin was his only betrayal of emotion. With a high salt-and-pepper fade and immaculate demeanor, he was professionalism personified. Yet there was more to him than the rigid exterior of a senior officer.

He was calculated when necessary and deliberate in his decisions, yet approachable in a way few at his level were. Rank meant nothing to him when it came to interaction. Though he was the senior man in the region, he spoke to the lowest Private with the same respect he afforded a fellow commander—no condescension, no pretense, just genuine care. He didn't need the theatrics of "leaders eat last." His actions made it clear where he stood. I found that rare. More than that, I found it inspiring.

The new concept was the Maritime Raid Force, a purpose-built intelligence and assault unit capable of inserting deep behind enemy lines, gathering its own actionable information, and, if needed, hitting any target. Six Force Reconnaissance Marines formed the core of this self-sufficient force, reinforced with counterintelligence operatives, Explosive Ordnance Disposal techs, signals intelligence specialists, and naval gunfire liaisons. Each twelve-man team carried the full weight of the Marine Air-Ground Task Force at its fingertips.

As we trained, integration became second nature. Layered skill sets, uncompromising rehearsals, and increasingly complex missions forced us to rely on one another entirely. The MEU's true strength—its ability to project combat power anywhere in the world—did not reside in any single unit. It was in the team.

I led Honeybadger One. Most senior officers assumed our call sign was a nod to the dusty contingency plan buried in the wreckage of Operation Eagle Claw—the infamous 1980 failure to rescue American hostages. Others were convinced we'd pulled it straight from the viral YouTube video of a honey badger tearing through cobras, shaking off venom, and fighting for its place in the food chain like it didn't give a damn. We never corrected either group. Both versions had their charm and, honestly, both fit us just fine.

The name Honeybadger was better than Bearshark, but not much. Yet, as in Bearshark, our ethos was the same: No one was more important than the other. Each of us had a role, and every role had to be executed flawlessly.

We inserted under cover of darkness from 15,000 feet, high-altitude, high-opening parachutes slicing through the night. Twenty kilometers of silent flight beneath our canopies, night vision goggles locking onto the dim glow of our teammates—twelve ghosts drifting back to earth, staked twenty-five meters apart. The only sounds were the whisper of the flapping nylon and the occasional radio crackle. We touched down without a trace on an undisclosed Army drop zone, gathering quickly to begin an eleven-day reconnaissance patrol—observing the Army's elite Green Berets during their infamous "Q Course" selection.

The only problem was that the Army did not know we were coming. Compromise wasn't just failure—it had consequences.

For five relentless days and nights, we patrolled North Carolina's oppressive summer heat, covering eighty kilometers of unforgiving swamps and mosquito-infested thickets of poison ivy. We moved under the cover of darkness, navigating dense forests filled with vines and choking humidity, sweat soaking through our gear. Supplies were scarce, and water was even scarcer. We took what we couldn't find—pilfering from fields, paying wary farmers, sneaking into base housing under cover of night, and stealing water from the base General's garden spigot without a trace.

From the concealment of our hide sites, we observed unseen for four more days. We cataloged every movement, interaction, and nuance of the selection course and relayed it to our higher command. We mapped hierarchies, tracked routines, and noted weaknesses. They never saw us because they never knew we were there.

After we had mastered the foundations of long-range reconnaissance patrols, we transitioned to a triad of complex mission sets: maritime interdiction (pirate hunting), long-range limited-scale raids, and embassy evacuations. At the core of it all was a close-quarters battle. Unlike Fallujah, where the objective was brute force against an entrenched enemy, these operations required overwhelming smaller targets with speed, surprise, and precision. Whether patrolling on foot, inserting from the sky, or sliding down the rope of a spinning helicopter, we had to be surgical in our approach.

Close-quarters battle had evolved—every lesson written in blood. As a smaller force, we couldn't absorb casualties like a conventional infantry platoon could. With six to twelve men, we had no buffer. Our tactics became a balance of speed and tempo, a dance between aggression and patience. Traditional formations relied on sheer violence, while we required cunning. But if the moment called for it, we could instantly ignite the fuse of carnage.

We fired hundreds of thousands of rounds for months from every weapon system we carried. Accuracy was nonnegotiable, and rank meant nothing. The standard was the standard. You weren't on the mission if you couldn't place two rounds in a target's forehead at fifty meters in under 1.5 seconds or conduct a failure drill while transitioning between weapon systems on the move. The stakes were too high.

Flash-bangs and burnt carbon swirled in the fragmented air as we transitioned from the flat bays to the shoot houses. Instructors diligently paced the custom-built catwalks above, configuring bullet-absorbing walls into different room patterns while observing the unfolding scenarios. Drill after drill, we refined our flow, moving through rooms like water spreading across a floor. We funneled enemies into a final holdout, setting the tempo before unleashing our speed. A door creaked open, rifles ready, flash-bang thrown—1.5-second fuse—riding the bang into the room and flooding it with firepower. No one went in alone.

Then came maritime interdiction—Visit, Board, Search, and Seizure—an intricate symphony of timing and resources to reclaim pirated ships of all sizes. Spinning helicopters circled above, carrying aerial snipers who scanned the ship's exterior, waiting for any ill-tempered pirate eager to make a name for himself.

Rigid-hulled speedboats slammed into the hull below, grappling hooks snaking over the rails as my team climbed the fifty-foot hanging ladders to seize a foothold from the bottom up. Simultaneously, two other teams dangled from SH-60 Sea Hawks overhead, ropes unfurling beneath them as they fast-roped onto the deck from the top down. Twenty-four men appeared in thirty seconds—fifty more followed in the second wave.

Once aboard, we split into three teams, each with a single objective—take the bridge, secure engineering, and seize aft steering. My team fought to the bridge, eliminating everything in our path. Every round counted, and every squeeze of the trigger was deliberate. One stray shot could kill everyone on board. The words of my sniper instructors echoed in my mind, just as they had years earlier: You own every bullet you fire.

But most critically, we had prepared for the one mission we all hoped to avoid—embassy reinforcement. Fresh off the heels of the Arab Spring and navigating the chaos that rippled through the region, the need to safeguard our national assets abroad was not just a possibility—it became a probability. When diplomacy failed and chaos ensued, we were the last line of defense. The Maritime Raid Force would insert fast and hard, secure a foothold, neutralize any threats, and protect embassy personnel while preparing for a follow-on landing force. Classified doctrine outlined the playbook. We would come in hot, armed to the teeth, clawing our way inside while striking at anything in our path. This was why the MEU existed—America's 911 force. If we were called, every other option had already failed.

All of this specialized training brought us now to the USS *New York*, standing on the bow of America's newest warship as we sailed into the Red Sea. The Middle East was boiling, and we were headed straight for the fire.

## USS *New York*

In the aftermath of the 9/11 attacks, 7.5 tons of steel were salvaged from the twisted remains of the Twin Towers at Ground Zero. That steel was sent to Avondale, Louisiana, to Northrop Grumman's shipyard, where, in September 2004, three years to the day after the attacks, it was melted down and poured into the bow stem of a new warship. The USS *New York* was born—forever linking her to the memory of the victims and the resilience of the people of New York.

On March 1, 2008, the ship was christened at a ceremony attended by the families of 9/11 victims. A year later, on November 7, 2009, she arrived at New York Harbor for an official commemoration. Families walked her decks, seeing the tributes etched into her bones. Her inner corridors bore the names of New York's streets—Broadway, Wall Street,

Madison Avenue—and murals honored the FDNY and NYPD, the first responders who had charged into the flames.

In New York Harbor, the families of 9/11 victims had their first real glimpse of the USS *New York*'s impressive capabilities. Designed like a waterborne Trojan Horse, she was built to carry war to foreign shores—or provide relief to those in need. Her massive hull housed AAVs, MRAPs, and Landing Craft Air Cushions (LCACs)—hovercraft capable of surging troops and vehicles ashore.

Her flight deck accommodated MV-22 Ospreys and CH-53 helicopters, as well as a variety of Cobras and Hueys. Below deck, cabins and bunks were designed to support up to 800 combat Marines and their equipment.

More than just a transport, the USS *New York* was built for command and control. She could launch an amphibious assault under fire just as easily as she could function as a humanitarian lifeline in disaster zones. In 2010, she proved it, deploying to Haiti to assist survivors of a devastating earthquake.

Two years later, in 2012, she sailed with the 24th MEU to patrol the unstable Middle East. Her very existence served as a testament to the resilience of the American spirit. In a way, both our stories rose from the ashes of September 11th.

America's fight didn't end in the rubble of the World Trade Center—it began there.

### Family Meeting

`15 May 2012 - 1648 - Aqaba, Jordan`

"Hey, AJ, can we talk?" My Assistant Team Leader Staff Sergeant Aaron Titus, knelt beside my bug net on the hot sand. I was passing the time reading a dusty secondhand copy of a book from the Commandant of the Marine Corps' recommended reading list, *Ender's Game*, before evening chow at the expeditionary mess hall near the Jordanian port city of Aqaba. We were prepping for a two-week vehicle desert patrol training mission near the ancient city of Petra and planned to insert in a few days.

"Yeah, sure," I replied, catching the shift in his voice. "What's up? Everything okay?"

"Uh, yeah. Well . . ." He rubbed the back of his neck.

Aaron Titus—his name belonged to a Roman emperor deified for his combat prowess and love of his people. Titus lived up to that legacy. Five-foot-eight and thick-thighed, built like a battering ram, his physical strength was matched only by his intellect and task-driven focus. He was my backup, my balance, the guy who carried the weight when I couldn't and spoke the truth when others wouldn't. We had strong communication, but even in the best organizations, barriers like rank, experience, and pride could cloud the air. Titus had the courage to clear it.

"The team has a few things they wanted to share with you," he said carefully. "They asked that we have a family meeting." His polite Boise twang lifted at the end, trying to soften the blow.

A family meeting was our way of hashing out tough issues—a Knights of the Round Table discussion where honesty and accountability ruled. I had always preached "speed of truth," urging my men to speak up when something wasn't right. What I hadn't seen was that I had been sending mixed messages. Aaron wasn't just walking me into a team meeting. He was walking me into an intervention.

I found them already seated in a semicircle in the rocky sand. "Hey guys, what's up? Everything okay?" I asked, lowering myself cross-legged into the dirt. A few exchanged glances.

Aaron cleared his throat. "AJ, we love you, man. You're one of the most capable and proficient leaders we've ever had, and we'd follow you anywhere." He hesitated. "That's why we wanted to talk."

He paused, then cut to the chase. "I'll put it bluntly—you've gotta let us fly, dude. Everyone here came to this team with years of experience. But it feels like you're constantly micromanaging us. We trust you, but we don't feel like you trust us. We're not living up to our potential."

I found myself face-to-face with men who equaled or surpassed me in every way. They were the pinnacle of performance and intellect—the kind of warriors that movies tried to portray but never truly captured. Even the junior Marine on my Force Recon team had more time under NVGs than some Team Leaders I'd known in previous battalions. My heavy-handed leadership style—hardened in the infantry, reinforced as a sniper instructor, perfected in combat—wasn't just outdated. It was a liability.

Their words hurt, but they weren't wrong.

The truth was—I had changed.

Ever since Matt's death, I tried to hold on to every detail and every decision, as if my grip alone could prevent the worst from happening again. I convinced myself that control equated to safety—that if I managed every variable, I could outmaneuver chance.

My grip tightened, not from distrust, but from fear. I couldn't lose another friend like that—not again. I believed I was protecting them. But in reality, I was smothering the very things that made us strong: trust, autonomy, and initiative. I wasn't leading; I was holding on to a ghost.

The last eighteen months had taken their toll. And now, my team needed space to breathe.

For the next hour, I listened as each man described a moment when my sharp tongue or snap judgment had undermined them. Hearing the family I had built tell me about my flaws was surreal. I fidgeted with my dusty bootlaces, staring at the beige dirt as the sun sank behind them, casting vague silhouettes in the cool desert evening around us. I didn't defend. I didn't argue. I just listened—and took notes.

Finally, I exhaled. "I owe all of you an apology. I'm sorry. I didn't know, and I have no excuse. I can do better."

I stood. The team rose with me. I demanded loyalty to one another and accountability just the same. I said trust was everything, and I hadn't given them mine. They saw it. Worse, they said it out loud. If I couldn't trust them, I didn't deserve to lead them, and they knew it. If I didn't hold up my end, there would be nothing to belong to.

They recognized their words had stung, but they hadn't come from resentment; they came from love. They stemmed from a belief in me that I had lost. I needed to be stronger for them, and strength didn't come from control; it came from letting go.

"Aaron, you've got the team for the next few days. I need to get my head right."

They circled around me—hugs, handshakes, shoulder bumps. I wasn't their enemy. I was still their leader. But I had to *earn* that role again.

Failure is never easy. But sometimes, it's the most important thing we do.

## The Mission, the Men, and Me

Undisclosed time - Undisclosed date
Aboard the USS *Iwo Jima* - Undisclosed location

"Copy, two tangos down."

The scratchy voice broke through our speakers inside the USS *Iwo Jima*'s operations center.

We were the designated quick reaction force for National Mission Force raids, standing by in full kit. The hushed tension hummed as steady as the massive ship's engines. From inside our steel command center, we monitored the circling drone feeds in real time—hot white silhouettes moving across rooftops and alleyways. Radios spit static and half-sentences, each one layered over the next, fractured by gunfire and adrenaline.

Outside, our gear waited beside the spinning helicopters. We were the safety net—if things went sideways, we'd be in the air in under three minutes.

Over the past few months, the Maritime Raid Force had bounced across the Arabian Peninsula and East Africa—from the King of Jordan's Special Operations competition to long-range desert patrols through Petra's sandstone canyons, and the muggy ports of the Seychelles. After more than a hundred days at sea, we were always experimenting—refining our process, challenging old ways of thinking. Nothing was off-limits.

Everyone recognized that swift, decisive leadership was vital when circumstances demanded urgency. But, when we had the luxury of time, I looked to my team. We stopped pretending one-size-fits-all leadership worked. What we built was our own system. Fluid, grounded in respect, shared ownership, and adaptability. This wasn't about hierarchy for its own sake; instead, it was about knowing when thorough deliberation was helpful and when it could be a hindrance.

Leadership was a constant assessment of speed versus tempo. Knowing the difference was the job.

"Stand by, we've got conta—" *Boom. Boom.*

Explosions cut the net. "One friendly wounded."

Chaos erupted.

The team on the ground was engaged, and the Troop Commander was trying to orient—buried in darkness, surrounded by the fog of war, making real-time decisions with lives on the line. Across the command net, voices piled in—dozens of them—demanding updates, pushing information, grasping for control to help calm the storm from miles away.

The noise must've been unbearable.

Then—clarity.

"Break, break, break—clear the net," the element leader on the ground barked. "I'll assess the situation and update you in five minutes. Out."

We watched the drone feed as he calmly flicked off his radio. The flash of defiance silenced his superiors, reminding them that autonomy mattered—and he was capable. He was the man in the arena. Qualified and confident. He didn't need more voices. He needed space.

Within minutes, he came back on the net, organized and direct. His plan was straightforward, and his needs were specific. The joint staff recalibrated and snapped into support. The rest of the mission went off without a hitch.

They figured out what worked, and in learning from them, so did we.

We built a leadership culture grounded in mutual respect and a shared sense of responsibility—a social contract. Instead of viewing one another's weaknesses as faults to exploit, we treated them as gaps we worked to close together. Our success as a team was tied to one another.

Sure, we had our disagreements. In values-based decision-making these typically revolved around the methods rather than the underlying reasons. My team understood I trusted and appreciated them, and in return, they committed to the mission with the same sense of ownership. Like me, they just wanted to be heard and valued.

Still, when immersed in traditional leadership literature, I noticed a critical disconnect. Traditional leadership books often offered frameworks to maximize efficiency, productivity, or financial gain. The organization I served didn't define success in those terms. Our currency was sacrifice. Leading for profit and leading for values weren't just distinct skill sets; they were fundamentally different mindsets.

My struggles with academic theory stemmed from its consistent failure to hold up against real-world application. Scholars had long attempted to classify human behavior, attempting to fit it into data sets and predictable patterns. I saw that people were flawed and unpredictable, even tribal in their beliefs and worldview, and shaped by forces that no algorithm could fully encompass.

Often, the most effective way to understand how to lead someone was to ask them.

The academic and the practitioner often found themselves at odds, both wishing for the same thing: that the other could walk a mile in their shoes to better understand the intersection of theory and practice. So, I turned to those who had walked where I had, seeking the convergence of theory and reality. I read firsthand accounts of conflict, from Vietnam to Iraq, in search of patterns within the chaos. *We Were Soldiers Once…and Young* and *Black Hawk Down* illustrated the confusion and uncertainty that characterized most firefights, the relentless friction that turned every decision into a no-win scenario.

The book that resonated most with me was Pete Blaber's *The Mission, the Men, and Me*. Blaber's account as senior leader within one of the United States' premier special operations units was deeply personal and refreshingly honest. I appreciated that it captured leadership at the highest levels and the hard lessons he learned through struggle and self-discovery. His most poignant takeaway was to *trust the guy on the ground.*

He explained that rigid, top-down control stifled adaptability and undermined effectiveness—precisely what I had been doing. Years in the infantry had ingrained a heavy-handed approach, reinforced as a sniper instructor and then as a battalion Recon Team Leader, where preparing new Marines for immediate combat meant strict structure and absolute control.

After Matt died, I tried to control everything—every detail and decision. I told myself that I could keep my team alive if I could manage every variable. That control would keep the chaos at bay. But it wasn't leadership—it was fear masquerading as certainty. I was so afraid of losing another brother that I gripped the reins until my hands bled.

Blaber was right. Leadership wasn't about control; it was about trust. It meant providing intent-based guidance and empowering operators on the ground to act on firsthand observations rather than waiting for remote approvals. Unpredictable and rapidly evolving situations didn't allow for micromanagement. They demanded initiative, adaptability, and the confidence to make decisions when it mattered most.

As a leader, I had spent years enforcing discipline. Now, I needed to learn to let go.

It wasn't about compromising standards; it was about creating space.

My last stop was an old friend. During a rare visit to a neighboring ship, by pure coincidence—or maybe something more—I found an unexpected lifeline. Sergeant Major Rickey Jackson. He was now the senior enlisted Marine of the aviation squadron supporting our MEU. In a strange, full-circle moment, he had the chance to see what I had become—and, as always, he had more wisdom to share.

Somehow even bigger than I remembered, he stood with me along the swampy interior bulkhead of the hangar deck. Our ships cut lazy "gator squares" in the Arabian Sea as we caught up. I told him about my team, about our conversation months before, and how I had worked to adjust my leadership style.

He listened, quiet, nodding.

Then he grinned and hit me with the same blunt wisdom that had shaped me years earlier.

"Don't tell them you care—show them." He scoffed, almost annoyed at my overthinking and my air-quoted "research."

"I already told you—every man is in charge of his own destiny," he said, pressing his callused finger into my chest. "But he's also responsible for the success of others."

He leaned in, grinning now. "Make them better than you. That's the job."

He paused, then added with a wink, "Why do you think I took the time with you back then, Gunnery Sergeant P-Shoot? Someone did it for me."

## The Rise

Undisclosed time - Undisclosed date
Aboard the USS *New York* - Undisclosed location

"This is the TAO. Set General Quarters, set General Quarters!" The voice of the Tactical Action Officer blared over the ship's intercom as the sharp clang of alarm bells punctuated his transmission. *Ding ding ding ding ding.* "Up and forward on the starboard side, down and aft on the port side."

The USS *New York* came alive. Sailors scrambled through the narrow gray corridors; their voices sharp against the dull hum of diesel machinery. The deck beneath us lurched as she heeled to port, swinging us hard around. Something was wrong.

For two months we had prowled the waters off the coast of East Africa, hunting threats in the smuggler-choked arteries of the Arabian Sea. Black market shipping routes, Somali pirates, terrorist networks—this was their domain, and disrupting them was ours. Over the past two days, we had tracked a dhow and confirmed that the old trading vessel was secretly ferrying Iranian weapons to regional terror groups.

Our platoon would launch from the belly of the *New York*, speeding toward the diesel-powered relic in two rigid-hulled boats. Helicopters would cover our approach, buying us time to board, neutralize any resistance, and extract any intel we could from the vessel before sending it limping home or consigning it to King Neptune below.

We were six hours out.

The call for General Quarters had come too early.

Our leadership raced to the ship's command center. If answers were to be found, they were there. The cramped space buzzed with activity, lined with four long desks stacked with computers and monitors. Each station funneled intelligence into the nerve center, where tactical decisions unfolded in real time. This was the brain of the Marine Air-Ground Task Force—a force multiplier, giving us a competitive advantage in the chaos of modern warfare.

But the mission had changed. The *New York* had altered course, knifing north toward the heart of the Red Sea.

The simmering unrest that had emerged from the ashes of the Arab Spring had flared up again.

They needed the Marines.

## The Fall

11 September 2012 - Undisclosed time
Aboard the USS *New York* - Undisclosed location

"One minute!" The familiar call from the green-glowing crew chief caught my attention. I buckled my flight harness, checked my rifle, and attached my headset to communicate with the cockpit ahead. The Maritime Raid Force was loaded onto Heavy Lift CH-53 Super Stallions—commonly referred to as "shitters" because of the dark trail of exhaust the helicopter left in their turbulent wake. After final mission checks and quick confirmation briefs, we had boarded and prepared for our long flight.

The Arab Spring erupted in late 2010, starting in Tunisia and spreading across the Middle East and North Africa. Fueled by demands for democracy, justice, and economic reform, protests ignited in Egypt,

Syria, Libya, and Yemen, each unfolding with increasingly volatile outcomes.

In Egypt, the mass demonstrations in Tahrir Square forced the resignation of President Mubarak in February 2011. Syria's protests against Bashar al-Assad in March 2011 escalated into a brutal civil war, while in Libya, months of armed conflict culminated in the capture and unceremonious killing of Muammar Gaddafi in October 2011. The chaotic unraveling of the former regime left a complex web of militias fighting for power. The US State Department struggled to de-escalate the violence, its inefficiencies resulting in a delayed and ineffective response. Open protests surged in the streets, and by the summer of 2012, American personnel came under attack.

"Thirty seconds!"

The USS *New York* surged through the Red Sea, racing to position itself to support multiple diplomatic missions. Tasked with reinforcing vulnerable locations, we coordinated with adjacent and higher commands, crafting contingency plans for each embassy and outpost. The mission required meticulous assessments that balanced real-time intelligence with the need for immediate action.

Despite the daunting task of analyzing hundreds of classified documents and reconnaissance images, the platoon operated efficiently, leveraging its internal intelligence assets to assess each site's vulnerabilities and strengths. Our target was Benghazi, a diplomatic compound in northeastern Libya supporting anti-Gaddafi militants. It lacked the fortifications of a formal consulate or embassy, making it dangerously exposed to attack.

The whine of the Super Stallion's twin engines signaled power to the throttle as we wobbled up off the ship's deck. The wheels became light.

Armed with rifles, rockets, and shotguns, along with blueprints, breaching explosives, and diamond-tipped circular saw blades, we were prepared for anything. Local intelligence reports corroborated live footage of the area, indicating that mass protests near the US facilities had rapidly escalated, and the facility was under attack.

Our first step was to punch our way in. We'd fast-rope in, dropping supplies and equipment behind us. Next, we would destroy the aerial obstructions, clearing a path for the trailing landing force to touch down without interference. We designated two teams to secure the outstation and tasked my team with racing to the CIA Annex down the street. Uncertain if other Americans were nearby, we would be the first on the scene.

The birds hovered in place, rubber tires barely grazing the ship's deck. "What's going on?" I asked the pilot through my headset.

The drone of the engines nearly drowned out his voice as he responded.

"We're waiting on final approval; without the green light, we can't lift."

The Super Stallions touched back down, the hydraulic wheels bracing under the pressure as the engines waned only slightly.

Sixty agonizing seconds dragged by—my eyes scanned my team; blank, confused stares shot back as our minds raced.

Then five minutes. "Honeybadger, that's a negative. We don't have the go-ahead. Stand by." The engines shuddered to idle speed, conserving precious fuel for the long flight. Their hot exhaust poured in and mixed with the oppressive Arabian heat. We waited.

Thirty minutes passed. "That's a negative, Honeybadger. Still no word yet."

We passed around a small whiteboard, where I would scrawl messages to communicate any news to my team over the deafening whine of turbines.

At forty minutes, the birds powered down. The raid force disembarked, still wearing our combat equipment and armed to the teeth, and headed for the command center. Inside, we swarmed the room, caught between intelligence feeds and the droning cable news chatter on two small TVs mounted in the far corners of the room—frustration boiled with every tick of the clock.

By midnight, patience had turned to rage. "We'd have fucking been there by now!" snarled Titus. The platoon seethed. We weren't across the world, hours away, waiting for a diplomatic solution. We were here, geared up, armed, and ready. Did they understand we were here? Or worse, did they know and choose not to use us?

It wasn't the first time politics had stalled a fight, but that night felt different. Whether it was election-year restraint, bureaucracy, ego, or fear—whatever the reason—no call was made. An enemy force advanced toward vulnerable American citizens unchallenged while the US deliberated geopolitical implications.

The plan wasn't complex—it was violent and fast. It was what we did best. Yet, instead of moving, we became prisoners of hesitation, bound not by an enemy force but by the indecision of those too distant to comprehend the desperation.

We spent thousands of hours behind rifles and pistols, shooting until our fingers bled. We endured hundreds of backbreaking missions in every brutal environment the world could throw at us, spending dozens of months away from the families we left behind.

We rehearsed every scenario, drilled every contingency, and burned them into muscle memory.

We were built for this.

This was our moment.

I spent my entire career fighting for the right to be in these moments—to be on the line, to make a difference. But no training, no experience, and no amount of personal sacrifice could have prepared me for the agony of standing still.

Gunfire cracked through the television speakers as news reports flooded in. A second attack, security forces in full retreat—fighting in the street. Flames consumed the compound as silhouetted figures swarmed over walls.

A few of us pressed our heads against the cool metal of the ship's walls. Others slumped into weathered folding chairs, resting their heads in their hands, still in full combat load. Resigned to watching the nightmare unfold in real time. We knew the outcome but were powerless to stop it.

In a rare moment of compassion rather than division, the polished veneer of the cable news pundits cracked. Fear trembled in their voices as they pleaded, "Aren't there any Americans nearby who can help?!"

The platoon erupted in a single, furious roar, "We're right here!"

On that day, four Americans—including the US Ambassador to Libya—were left without desperately needed assistance. Our nation's leaders had callously abandoned them, sending them to their deaths through deliberate inaction.

In one ill-fated move on the global chessboard, the United States chose to do nothing.

Sacrificing a rook for no reason.

# 17

# UP AND OUT

### Reconnaissance Team Leader Course

October 2013, Recon Training Company,
School of Infantry, Camp Pendleton, CA

I first met Tommy Hartrick in 2013 when I arrived at the Reconnaissance Training Company aboard Camp Pendleton, CA. The company ran a series of advanced courses—Basic Recon Course, Marine Free-Fall, and the crown jewel, the Reconnaissance Team Leader Course (RTLC).

RTLC was born from the lessons learned over a decade at war and was designed to sharpen the art of leadership in the most unforgiving environments. Reconnaissance missions depended on Team Leaders, men who had to make life-or-death decisions with limited information and no margin for error. While some schools awarded badges, RTLC refined the intangible: command presence, decision-making under pressure, and the ability to lead the most dynamic and complex warfighters in the Department of Defense.

Gunnery Sergeant Tommy Hartrick was a walking contradiction. Tall, corn-fed, and direct—you always knew where you stood with

Tommy. Yet beneath his rugged exterior was a kindness few could match. His infectious smile disarmed even the toughest Marines, and his time as a Mormon missionary in Mexico City taught him patience in the face of adversity—even when targeted for his faith.

But kindness never dulled his edge. Tommy was one of the finest Reconnaissance Marines of our generation, a legend within the community. In August 2008, during an eight-hour battle in the city of Shewan, Afghanistan, he and his platoon stood firm against hundreds of determined Taliban fighters—killing over one hundred of them. His heroism earned him a Bronze Star; his large stature—making him a prime target for Taliban fighters—earned him the Purple Heart.

In 2010, when Somali pirates seized the German-flagged *Magellan Star* and took eleven hostages, Tommy led one of the assault teams. His twenty-four-man platoon secured the ship, working to rescue every hostage, and, with remarkable restraint, captured all nine pirates without a single loss of life. His reputation was the stuff of legends.

In 2012, First Force Reconnaissance Company named him Team Leader of the Year, and I selected him as my second-in-command to overhaul the critical Reconnaissance Team Leader Course. We set out to redefine what it meant to lead in the reconnaissance community.

## Hallowed Ground

4 May 2014 - Recon Training Company,
School of Infantry, Camp Pendleton, CA

"Hey, AJ, why don't you take a seat?" A calm voice summoned me.

The conference room at the Reconnaissance Training Company was unlike any I had ever experienced. A long, oblong walnut table stretched through the cramped space, surrounded by mismatched black cloth office chairs—worn from years of heated discussions. On the walls, a testament to our past; hundreds of black-framed photographs, the images of young Americans in their prime. Camouflage fatigues, rifles, and smiles frozen in time. Below each picture, two words and two dates: *Insert. Extract.*

Each frame held more than just a face. It carried a name, a story, and a sacrifice. These weren't just images; they were reminders of the price we paid for freedom—the cost of wearing the insignia on our chests. The brotherhood of Recon Marines had always been forged in blood and sweat, but it was held together by something stronger—the restrained tears shed for those who never came home.

We kept their names alive, not just as a reminder of the price we paid, but for the reasons we did. Our responsibility to one another. Every decision made in that room was under the watchful eyes of generations who accepted the same title but didn't live to carry it on. Could we quit, surrender, give up, looking into the eyes of men who didn't? It wasn't just about the future, but also the past. I stepped from the doorway into the small conference room where three men sat waiting—two of whom I respected more than almost anyone I had ever met.

Master Sergeant Mariota "Moe" Pa'u, a giant Samoan, embodied the warrior heritage of his ancestors in every aspect of leadership. For decades, he bled the recon colors of black and gold and managed our organization like his *uso*—his brothers. Next to him sat Master Gunnery Sergeant John "Big Daddy" Croft, a soft-spoken, barrel-chested force of nature with hands that resembled giant meat paws. He had been one of my closest mentors, providing a steadying presence in my career, especially after the loss of Matt.

At the far end of the table sat Tommy.

## Sometimes Life Presents the Same Lesson

Tommy Hartrick and I had spent the last seven months building something we both believed in. Together, we helped refine and relaunch the Reconnaissance Team Leader Course (RTLC). Guided by former course directors and an eclectic mix of some of the most proficient leaders in the reconnaissance community, we built a program to shape future Reconnaissance Team Leaders through education and adversity.

He came in with unmatched operational experience, a reputation for grit, and a no-nonsense style that commanded the attention of junior Marines when he entered a room. I brought a focus on planning, instruction, and big-picture design. On paper, we appeared to balance each other perfectly. In practice, our differences didn't just clash; they collided.

We were two type-A Marines, hard-wired for control, driven by intensity, and shaped by vastly different paths. We shared the same mission—but we didn't always agree on how to get there.

At first, we pushed through it. The mission came first. Between endless planning sessions, evolutions in the field, and long hours spent refining the course, we told ourselves we were just figuring it out. But the truth was, we were wearing each other thin. The tension bled into the cadre. Our disagreements weren't private anymore.

And eventually, someone had to say it out loud.

Croft leaned forward. "Okay, guys, we've got a problem." His voice bore the weight of someone who had seen this before.

"You two aren't communicating, and it's affecting the cadre."

Tommy and I were both well-intentioned and committed to the mission, but we couldn't seem to get past our differences. He was one of the best Reconnaissance Marines I had ever worked with—and perhaps the most stubborn man on the planet, second only to myself.

"You guys are two of our best," Moe added. "But if you don't work together, none of it matters." He exhaled, glancing at Tommy. "Let's hash this shit out before it festers. Tommy, why don't you start?"

Tommy drew a long and tempered breath.

"AJ, man, I love you, dude—you gotta know that," Tommy said, spitting tobacco into a small water bottle. "I respect the shit out of you. But some of the things you say cut me off at the knees."

I sat in silence. This meeting was becoming one of the most uncomfortable moments of my career.

"You've said—publicly—that you're the brains and I'm the brawn of RTLC—you've even compared me to an ogre when briefing." He shook his head, his voice tightening. "When you say that, it cuts, man. It takes away who I am, what I've done, and what I bring to this course."

His hands clenched around the bottle, knuckles turned white. "I get it—you're a smart dude. But you keep cutting me down."

Tommy Hartrick, a man capable of tearing me limb from limb, sat across from me, his eyes glassy with rage and pain as he fought to be a better man.

"I'm sorry," I said, my throat tightened. "I had no idea—I thought I was being funny."

I spent my childhood on the receiving end of ridicule, picked on for things I couldn't control. My intelligence became my shield—then my weapon. And now, without realizing it, I had become the very thing I hated most—a bully.

Moe broke the silence. "You two represent both sides of the reconnaissance community. You're both incredibly smart, with experience beyond most. But you need to understand—it's not about you."

He pointed to the frames on the wall. The words NEVER ABOVE YOU, NEVER BELOW YOU, ALWAYS BESIDE YOU hung above them. My eyes landed on Matt's picture. I thought of him and his devotion to his team. Beyond ego, vanity, and fame, he chose his men.

"It's about them," Moe finished.

Tommy and I grew up worlds apart, shaped by different beliefs and experiences that led us to view the world differently. In another place, in another life, those differences might have completely divided us. For a time, they nearly did. We allowed our focus to settle too much on where we disagreed—on the opinions we inherited, the ideas we carried from the worlds we came from. That narrow view bled into the team, making us weaker when we could least afford it. The stakes were too high for pride or ideology to obstruct our path. If we wanted to build a team that would empower others—and win—we had to view our differences not as threats but as tools. Strengths. A broader perspective to tackle the challenges ahead. Once we embraced that idea and trusted that our partnership could be built on respect rather than agreement, we became a true team—better than either of us could have built alone.

The idea that Reconnaissance Marines—or Marines in general—were unthinking, unfeeling, monolithic killers wasn't just wrong, it was damaging.

We pushed each other, made each other better, and somewhere along the way, we became friends. Between detailed planning sessions, long drives to training areas, and countless hours spent observing students, Tommy and I grew closer. We debated politics, religion, and the reasons behind our wars. We talked about training, leadership, and the weight of responsibility. Although Tommy and I came from different worlds, our shared sense of service to our country drew us together.

True to form, that didn't stop Tommy, or "Roach," as he was known, from messing with me. He took particular joy in playing tricks on my "city-slicker ass"—convincing me to mix Levi Garrett chewing tobacco with Big League Chew bubble gum or daring me to join him in eating handfuls of dried crickets from gas station rest stops. His rowdy laugh erupted as I gagged, cricket legs still stuck between his teeth.

Armed with decades of collective wisdom and an unmatched bias for action, our small cadre built something much larger than ourselves. Twenty-four Reconnaissance Marines from across the globe arrived to test their mettle, each one hungry to learn to lead the elite.

The Reconnaissance Team Leader's Course was not for the weak or faint-hearted. Purpose-built to break the unprepared, we led them through brutal, changing environments to build their resolve and force them to adapt, think, and learn. Hardship was the point. Because at the heart of it, what set Recon Marines apart wasn't just skill or intellect; it was the one thing our creed refused to let us do: quit.

Our cadre of battle-hardened instructors acted as consummate professionals. Their goal was to guide students through the curriculum while giving them room to experiment and grow under expert counseling. From in-depth classroom discussions at Camp Pendleton—where we dissected the intricacies of long-range reconnaissance and mission planning—to advanced communications drills and integrated operations with supporting units, every evolution had a purpose. Our mission was to forge battlefield architects. Team leaders capable of operating in both conventional and unconventional environments. Leaders who could think beyond the fight in front of them—and shape the one still to come.

In a reconnaissance mission, the Team Leader's role wasn't just to lead from the front—it was to think *up* and *out*. Their focus extended beyond the immediate engagement to encompass the larger operational picture. They needed to understand the context, inform higher command, empower their team members, and leverage external resources to shape the battle before it even began. Meanwhile, the Assistant Team Leader worked *down* and *in*, ensuring the team executed the mission while remaining positioned to make the greatest impact on the battlefield. It was a delicate balance—one foot in the present fight and the other shaping the future one.

After we had established their foundations, we took the Marines to Yuma, Arizona, into the sweltering badlands that blurred the line between training and survival. Yuma's magic was its austerity—because sometimes, being tough was just as important as being smart.

Nestled along the southern border, the expansive Barry Goldwater Range complex offered the perfect mix of Iraq's relentless deserts and Afghanistan's jagged, unforgiving terrain. It was the kind of place where you slipped live rounds to students—not for training, but as a contingency against rabid four-legged coyotes or the two-legged, rifle-carrying kind.

Here, we coordinated with Marine aviation units for long-range helicopter inserts and worked to pluck circling F-18s or F-35s out of the sky for aerial reconnaissance or simulated ordnance delivery. Yuma provided something rare—a safe environment where pilots and reconnaissance teams could train together, make mistakes, and learn the realities of each other's roles before combat forced them to.

Since the dawn of Marine Corps aviation, pilots had been the lifeline of ground forces, but pre-deployment training often forced everyone into silos. The first time many truly understood each other's worlds was when it mattered most—under fire. Yuma changed that. It provided a space for them to work through the friction, to fail without consequence, and to build trust.

The budding Team Leader's last stop was in the frigid waters of Coronado. The same waters where they had been baptized as Reconnaissance students years before was now their final test. A long-range amphibious insertion into a hostile beach, culminating in a limited-scale raid. Months of instruction, weeks of rehearsals, and hundreds of hours of planning had led to this moment.

### Final Mission

`12 August 2014 - 2230`
`Naval Amphibious Base, Coronado, CA`

Four black rubber boats skimmed across the glassy surface of San Diego Bay, moonlight tracing silver streaks along their V-shaped wakes. Their engines hummed in unison, a low, insect-like drone against the vast expanse. San Diego flickered in the distance—a world away from the shadowy figures crouched low against the gunnels. Four Marines pressed close, two lying against each tube, their knees brushing the waterline. Two more knelt at the rear—one scanning the darkness, the other focused on the faint glow of a nautical compass, guiding them not by sight but by heading.

Five miles offshore, their waiting transport floated—a pair of Navy Air Cushion Landing Crafts (LCACs), massive metal beasts hovering through the swells like giant manta rays. As the small boats approached, the sailors guided them up the LCAC's ramp. Then, with a rumble, the hovercraft came to life, forcing air beneath their hulls and lifting them above the ocean's surface like jets on a runway. The wind howled as they surged forward, racing out to sea.

At the insertion point, the Marines returned to their rubber raiding crafts to start the next leg of their journey as the LCACs faded into the horizon.

Miles later, staying true to their reconnaissance heritage, they silenced their engines and paddled toward the shore. The rhythmic slap of churning water and the crashing waves ahead were the only sounds. Scout swimmers slipped into the water first, finning ahead to secure the landing.

Once the signal was given, the teams paddled the final stretch, rode the crashing waves, and pulled their raiding crafts onto the sand before burying them beneath the dunes. The city loomed in front of them, its glow stretching across the horizon—unaware of the silent figures moving inland.

Under the cover of darkness, they infiltrated the base, navigating alleyways and dead spaces while closing in on their designated target. Inside, they cleared the objective of hostiles and uncovered the intelligence we had planted—puzzle pieces connecting back to earlier missions, decisions, and failures, culminating in the final revelations of their three-month scenario.

Every step of this mission drew from months of instruction. Planning, coordination, and creativity had to converge here. It wasn't just about completing the mission; it was about proving to themselves that they had evolved from Marines into leaders, capable of thinking, fighting, and enduring as Reconnaissance Team Leaders.

With the objective secured, they retraced their steps, slipping back through the base undetected and evading roving role players and military police as if the mission had never happened. The sun hinted at the horizon as they uncovered their boats and paddled through the surf, disappearing once more back into the sea, leaving only fading footprints in the sand.

## The Gunner

30 January 2017 - 0800
The Basic School, Quantico, VA

After fifteen years as an enlisted Marine, seasoned through numerous combat deployments and very comfortable in the mud—I found myself on unfamiliar ground. I traded my enlisted stripes and rockers for officer bars, leaving behind the close-knit camaraderie for the solitary path of officership. As a "Mustang," an officer risen from the enlisted ranks, I navigated both worlds, respected yet scrutinized by enlisted personnel and officers alike. I became a Chief Warrant Officer Two, Infantry Weapons Officer—better known as a Marine Gunner.

The Marine Gunner rank was an enigma, even within the Marine Corps. Marines revered it, but it remained virtually unknown outside the service. Signified by a single bursting bomb on our collar, Gunners held a near-mythical aura. At any given moment, there are over 30,000 infantry Marines; but only one hundred Gunners.

Marine Gunners traced their lineage to World War I, born from a need for seasoned battlefield leaders skilled in employing and instructing infantry battalion weaponry. The first Marine Gunners set the standard. Among them was Gunner Henry Hulbert, a legendary Marine who fought in some of the Corps' most storied battles: the Second Samoan Civil War, for which he earned the Medal of Honor, and later in World War I at Belleau Wood and Soissons, France, where he was killed in action at Blanc Mont Ridge, earning a Navy Cross and eternal respect.

Stepping into the Gunner role was a weight unlike anything I had ever experienced. I no longer simply carried out orders from above; now, I was expected to shape, mentor, and advise the next generation of Marine leaders at every level. My responsibilities shifted from operational execution to advising infantry commanders, ranging from Lieutenants to Generals, while carefully evaluating tactical proficiency and mentoring both Marines and young officers alike.

It wasn't just about knowing weapons and gear; it was about translating experience into knowledge and doctrine into reality. Gunners lived in an unusual space within the Marine Corps hierarchy. Although technically officers, we retained a gritty, enlisted pragmatism and were encouraged to speak truth to power, even when uncomfortable. Not from ego, but from a sense of responsibility to the men and women we served.

The journey from enlisted Marine to Marine Gunner wasn't about trading our rifles for rank. It was about elevating the entire Corps, passing on decades of earned wisdom, and ensuring the warriors who followed would uphold the tradition of excellence that defined our shared legacy.

## The Basic School

```
16 February 2017 - 2200
Range 3, Weapons Training Battalion,
Quantico, Virginia
```

Cold wind stung my face as I sat cross-legged, my rifle balanced on my lap. We were in our second week of training in the Quantico Forest. The Basic School (TBS) was the cauldron where raw potential met the callous demands of combat leadership. This was where Marine officers weren't born—but forged.

For many young men and women, stepping onto that frost-covered grass, speckled with goose droppings, was more than just a military rite of passage; it marked the first chapter in a narrative of responsibility that would define their identities for the rest of their lives.

TBS stood at the crossroads of theory and practice—where the study of history, conflict, and maneuver warfare textbooks collided with swampy fields and muddy trails. Each squad bay echoed with the energetic banter of young friendships among Second Lieutenants—most fresh from college—and the uneasy confessions of those soon responsible for the lives of enlisted Marines. This was no ordinary schoolhouse; it was a proving ground for those who had taken an oath to lead the finest fighting force in the world.

Amid the long lectures and seemingly endless hours in the classroom, these officers learned that rank alone meant little without the trust and respect of those they led. Leadership didn't come from a title but from how they acted. Their confidence had to be earned, step-by-step, order by order, and sometimes mistake by humbling mistake. The whirlwind of constant evaluations and field exercises wasn't meant to break them—it was designed to instill a sense of purpose and illuminate the harsh truth that leadership is often a solitary burden.

It was in this crucible of stress and doubt that they transformed. Like steel shaped in blistering heat, they absorbed not only the knowledge of centuries of conflict, but also the intangible lessons of humility, perseverance, and empathy. By the time they emerged from Virginia's frozen woods and swampy fields, they were no longer the fresh-faced college students who had arrived months before.

They were Marine Officers. Ready—though untested—to leave their mark on the Corps.

The green glow of my night vision goggles illuminated our makeshift range through the brooding winter flurry. I was on the seventh relay and waiting my turn, watching the second group of Warrant Officers try to align their infrared lasers on flapping paper targets fifty meters away. I was going to be there for a while.

I reflected on my frustration with the quality of the officer training—it was nothing like my own as a young enlisted Marine. I had been taught practice, not theory—what I saw as trained but not educated. Long lectures focused on the how but rarely explained the why behind our decisions. I hadn't formally studied our most fundamental doctrinal publication, *Marine Corps Doctrinal Publication 1*, until I was a Gunnery Sergeant fifteen years in. Every Second Lieutenant was issued it on day one.

*We weren't even speaking the same language*. I realized.

A sharp wrap to the back jolted me to my feet. "Hey, Warrant Officer—get on your feet!"

I stood and turned until our noses nearly touched. "You must have me mistaken for someone else, young man," I said.

"There's no sitting on the range, Warrant Officer," the frocked Captain shouted. Frocking was a military tradition that allowed an officer or NCO to wear a rank before their official promotion. This was his first class as an instructor, and he was already known for flexing his newfound "authority" that was well beyond his experience.

"Where I come from, we do things differently," I said, showing my irritation.

"What'd you say, Warrant Officer?" he barked. He couldn't see my face, only the glow of my night vision goggles.

"Captain," I replied, ignoring the taboo of not calling him "Sir." "I'm no Warrant Officer—never was. You can call me Chief Warrant Officer, or Gunner, or even AJ."

Due to the lengthy time-in-service requirements and the years of experience expected, Gunners bypassed the rank of Warrant Officer and were promoted directly to Chief Warrant Officer 2. The frocked Captain, still inexperienced, failed to grasp the nuance.

I'd just come from Training Command. We'd served under the same General, and I knew the rules as well as he did. I turned to the Captain and said, "But don't ever fucking kick a student again."

Other Captains rushed in, yanking the young officer back while publicly disciplining me for my insubordination and correcting him privately. Neither of us was right.

It was the second week of a four-month course, and I had already made a name for myself.

I had two major critiques of TBS. First, they operated within the confines of their own echo chamber, dismissing perspectives that didn't align with the traditional officer caste. Their inability—or unwillingness—to grasp the full spectrum of Marine Corps culture beyond their insulated ranks gave them a distorted sense of reality, often clashing with the complexities of the force they were meant to lead. The second was night land navigation.

While instrumental in instilling foundational values and core lessons in entry-level officers, our single Warrant Officer class experienced no curriculum modifications and, worse, no changes in our treatment. I felt it was an abdication of responsibility not to recognize the tremendous learning potential available by tapping into the collective experience instead of simply applying a superficial layer over it.

The twelve Gunners and 400 Warrant Officers in our class represented the very best that the Marine Corps offered. Top experts in their fields each came from the places that made the Marine Corps work.

Rather than embracing the opportunity, some young officers seemed to resent the Warrant Officers' expertise, viewing it as a threat to their own. That wasn't how Warrant Officers operated. We knew the rules—we weren't in charge, but we had the answers. Decades of real-world experience provided us with an unimaginable wealth of knowledge, and our sole job was to pass it on. While Warrant Officers were often a giant pain in the ass—to the right commander—we were never a threat; we were an asset.

Endless lectures in sloped auditoriums echoed the monotony I had endured years earlier. The young cadre feigned an understanding of a Socratic method of instruction, where we spent our nights reading thick stacks of doctrine, only to face tests on those lessons every morning. Our instructors sidestepped class engagement by throwing open-ended questions back at us to mask their lack of context. Used to instructing young Second Lieutenants with little real-world experience, they pushed us through concepts they barely understood, unaware of the depth we could provide.

I spent months unable to see beyond my resentment of the curriculum, and at times, I became disrespectful and downright toxic. My frustrations may have been justified, but my actions were not. Through my own irresponsibility, I alienated more senior officers than I won over, creating enemies where I should have built alliances.

I focused more on being right than seeking understanding.

When presenting a leadership scenario for discussion, a junior Captain quipped that a group of any rank would inevitably behave as irresponsibly as Lance Corporals. Marine Gunners were not typically known for a quiet disposition, and I was no exception.

I raised my hand in frustration and blurted, "Am I allowed to say dumb Lieutenant?"

The group laughed, but I had no real question—I was just irritated by the notion that young Marines were collectively stupid.

"Is there a problem, Gunner?" the Captain asked.

"Well, yeah, sir," I stood up and replied, "I just take issue with the idea that we're conditioning our officers to see enlisted Marines as liabilities."

"We're not doing that," snapped the Captain.

"Of course you are, not intentionally—well, I hope not intentionally—but you're doing it. Look at what we've called our enemies—Kraut, Jap, Charlie, Haji," I continued as he shifted uncomfortably—"we did that to dehumanize them—so we could kill them. You're doing the same here.

Lance Corporals aren't stupid; they're untrained." I was objectively correct—but still wrong. I'd lost an opportunity to make an ally.

### Land Navigation

"Chief Warrant Officer, Paskew... Pashat... Paskweti." The same Captain I'd snapped at weeks before about Lance Corporals stumbled over my name.

"There must be some mistake!" I yelled from the sizable crowd, half-joking to hide my shame. I had failed night land navigation—twice. Not only had I lost any shot at honor grad, but I was also on the verge of outright failure—all because of land navigation.

"Come grab your things before you head back out," the Captain said dismissively, without looking up.

"Sir, can we talk for a second?" I asked, trying to pull him aside from the hundreds other students who'd failed.

His eyes narrowed as he recognized me immediately.

"I know this sounds like an excuse, but I'd like to discuss this test," I said. His eyes glazed over as he raised an impatient eyebrow. "Sir," I sighed, knowing how it would sound, "I've navigated under canopy from thousands of feet in the air and underwater at night with only a chem light and a compass. I've taught at sniper school and been a recon instructor—ironically teaching land nav. With all due respect, I can navigate. I think this test is flaw—"

He cut me off. "Well, apparently you can't."

I deserved that.

I gritted my teeth and looked at the floor, trying to compose myself. "Yes, sir, I did fail. But this test doesn't match the actual skill set." TBS's night land navigation course was a strict dead-reckoning exercise. Land navigation involved a tangled mix of complex techniques, but dead reckoning was meant to be straightforward: Follow a heading for a specific pace count in a general direction. Typically used to locate hilltops and prominent terrain features, here it was simplified to searching for four-foot poles in the dark.

The course covered a 1,000-by-1,000-meter area. On one side, a long road acted as a catching feature. Along it were twenty small ammo boxes, numbered one to twenty, each secured to a four-foot metal stake and spaced exactly fifty meters apart. Another 1,000 meters to the northeast, twenty matching boxes were labeled A through T.

Each student received a random card starting from one of the numbered boxes, along with an azimuth and distance, to reach an unknown lettered box on the far side. After marking down the letter, we followed a predetermined azimuth and distance back, zigzagging through a series of points. In the end, our answers were checked against a key.

The system had three critical flaws. First, doctrinal publications warned that dead reckoning beyond 400 meters on rough terrain was, at best, unreliable. We traversed cliffs, dense underbrush, and a surging winter creek—maintaining a perfect heading was impossible. Second, our compasses had a built-in error margin of about three degrees. Over 1,000 meters, that alone could place us between two rusted boxes spaced fifty meters apart. If the card directed us from box one to box T, we'd end up traveling well over 1,400 meters. Third, any early miscalculation led to a cascading effect, throwing off every subsequent leg.

You could do everything right and still fail. This wasn't land navigation—it was an educated guess. Staring down the barrel of a third attempt, I saw no reason to keep trying the same thing and expecting a different result. I knew the boxes along the road were exactly fifty meters apart. If I marked their precise locations on my map, I could plot each one, calculate the azimuth and distance, convert from magnetic to grid, and identify the corresponding box on the far side. The goal wasn't just to wander the woods—it was to demonstrate mastery of navigation. My approach still met the intent. The rest of the sheet would just be a math problem.

"You're back quick, Gunner," the waiting officer quipped, snapping my answer sheet out of my hand.

He glared at me. "You passed," he hissed.

"Looks like I'm getting the hang of it," I shot back as I trotted away.

## Gunner School

24 May 2017 - The Basic School, Quantico, VA

"The most important tool a Gunner has is his voice," our final instructor, CWO4 Ray Browne, warned. The CWO4 Gunner opened his first class with the twelve remaining Chief Warrant Officers. We had graduated TBS, and while the rest of our 400 peers scattered back across the Corps, the twelve Gunners stayed behind.

Ray sat on an old white desk at the front of the class, his bald head gleaming under the fluorescent lights of our cramped corner classroom—the kind of head that suggested his brain was constantly running hot. Razor-smart and radiating intensity, he carried himself with a confidence born from years of hard-earned experience. His sharp eyes, set beneath a prominent brow, seemed capable of reading minds—or at least intentions. Browne's intensity hinted at a subtle chip on his shoulder, reminiscent of the one I carried. He was both mentor and challenger, deeply respected yet never above delivering blunt truth.

Gunner Browne was hand-selected within our community to represent and cultivate our lineage at The Basic School. His primary job mirrored a Gunner's typical role, shaping young Lieutenants during their crucial first months in the Corps. His secondary, perhaps tougher, role involved molding our diverse group through an intense five-month curriculum following our initial Warrant Officer course. It wasn't easy. We were a pack of near degenerates, frustrated after herding cats through TBS for the last four months. Gathered from every dark corner of the Marine Corps: stoic snipers, chain-smoking missile men, and salty rifle Platoon Sergeants who had "eaten" one too many close encounters with IEDs. Between us, we held enough medals for valor, heroism, and professionalism to wallpaper a small VFW hall.

Ray's job wasn't just to ensure we mastered tactical and technical skills; he also had to teach us how to communicate our knowledge and expertise. He continued, "The two fastest ways to lose that voice: First, be wrong. Second, be right, but act like an asshole doing it." He paused, almost locking eyes with each one of us.

"You can't just yell that you're right all the time—no one will listen. I get it. You guys are smart and experienced, probably smarter and with more experience than most in any room you step into. But you can't bully people into agreeing with you.

"You can't dictate your environment; you have to learn how to respond to it. You may have a good commander, you may have a bad commander, but regardless, they're going to be your commander. Whether or not you agree with him is irrelevant; your job is to be there for the Marines as a whole. I'm not telling you to kowtow or be a yes-man, but you need to know when to influence rather than argue. It's not how you feel, but how you respond that is important. Remember, commanders don't have to listen to you. The worst kind of Gunner is the one who's lost his voice."

With that, we launched into five intense months of dissecting the intricate mechanics of warfighting within the Marine Corps. We studied every tool available to an infantry commander, from the flight trajectory and penetration capabilities of a 7.62mm armor-piercing round to the blast radius of a HIMARS rocket—and everything in between.

Mastering the equipment was only the beginning. The second half of our course pulled us from theory into live-fire execution. First, we took a punishing two-week rifle and pistol course under the same instructors who trained Special Operations Forces (SOF). Then, we shifted to understanding the enemy—weapon and armor identification, weak points, manufacturing flaws, and the physics of destruction.

Finally, the culminating phase involved designing and executing a full-scale training scenario for over a thousand infantry Marines, each with varying skill sets and levels of experience. Every Marine had a role, and our job was to ensure they were positioned and prepared to deliver their full potential.

Like conductors in a symphony, we refined our sense of timing, rhythm, and force, ensuring that every instrument in our arsenal played in concert. Understanding weapons in isolation wasn't enough; we had to orchestrate them into a seamless, overwhelming crescendo.

At first, I was skeptical about transitioning from Marine to mentor. I knew I was a capable leader and educator, but I struggled to see how my skills could extend beyond direct combat. But as the months went by, my perspective shifted—my role wasn't shrinking; it was evolving. I came to understand that leaders' responsibilities evolve as their roles expand and their spheres of influence grow.

As a Marine Gunner, I was no longer the one pulling the trigger or maneuvering through the fight—I was shaping those who would.

"Hey, AJ, we've got a change of plans." Ray's voice cut in the second I picked up. A week had passed since I'd graduated, and I was somewhere in the middle of nowhere, driving my truck back to California.

"What's up, man? Everything okay?" I asked, sensing something was off.

"Your orders changed. A Gunner just got fired. The unit deploys in three weeks."

"What?" I shot back. I was supposed to be linking up with a battalion at the start of their training cycle—a good way to get my feet wet as a Gunner. Time to grow with the unit, learn their dynamics, and build a relationship with the Battalion Commander.

"We need you to take his spot."

I gripped the wheel a bit tighter. "Uh . . . yeah. Okay. Sure." As if I had a choice.

Ray exhaled, and I could hear the hesitation before he spoke again.

"There's one more thing." A pause. "It's not a good command climate." Another pause. "It's actually pretty toxic."

# 18

------

# MUTUAL RESPECT

**Trinity**

9 October 2017 - 1630
Honolulu International Airport, Oahu, HI

Stepping onto the hot tarmac at Honolulu Airport, the sharp, pungent sting of jet fuel battled for my senses with the soft, sweet scent of tropical plumeria (*melia*) and gardenia (*kiele*) flowers. A short drive along the iconic H3 highway snaked through the emerald mountains as rippled valleys cascaded toward the dense jungle below, pulling me deeper into the belly of the Koolau mountain range. Bright tropical sunlight pierced through the misty tunnel, momentarily blinding me as I drove onto the island's windward side. My mouth dropped in awe as an expansive blue ocean stretched beneath an impressionist sky with fluffy white clouds hovering close above waterfalled ridges. Turtle-green foliage collided with turquoise waters down the valley where the small Mokapu Peninsula, surrounded by soft, nearly white sandy beaches, came into view. Palm trees swayed lazily under skies so blue that they looked as though they were painted by an artist's fanned brush.

Arriving at the Marine Corps Base in Kaneohe felt like stepping into history. The Mokapu Peninsula has long been a fixture of military presence under the gray shadow of American expansionism in the Hawaiian Islands chain. Established as an Army base in 1918, it quickly became a strategic launching point for American operations across the Pacific. Before World War II, the Navy took control of the modest base and repurposed it as a seaplane airport and runway. On December 7, 1941, just minutes before the infamous attack on Pearl Harbor, the Japanese also targeted Kaneohe. The tranquility of its shallow bay waters and gently flowing grass was shattered by enemy fire. Today, despite its turbulent history, with scars long healed and bullet holes in hangars still visible, the base stands as one of Oahu's most breathtaking locations.

3rd Battalion, 3rd Marines (3/3), was first activated during World War II. Originating in North Carolina, it came of age in the fierce battles of the Pacific. Known as "America's Battalion," it carried a proud legacy forged through bravery and guts, often competing fiercely with an East Coast rival for the esteemed nickname. Three/three fought valiantly across the Pacific, enduring the unimaginable devastation of battles at Bougainville, the Northern Solomons, and Guam.

In Vietnam, 3/3 fought in the mud, starting with Operation Starlight in 1965, which marked the beginning of major American combat operations and continued through Khe Sanh, Quảng Trị Province, and the Tet Offensive. Throughout the Cold War, 3/3 remained ready across the Pacific, later deploying to Saudi Arabia and Kuwait during Operations Desert Shield and Desert Storm. The battalion carried its tenacious legacy into the War on Terror, deploying three times to Iraq and twice to Afghanistan, upholding the legacy of its predecessors. Since their formation in World War II, 3/3 had given over 1,000 American sons and daughters to foreign soil.

### The Meeting

11 October 2017 - 0800
Marine Corps Base, Kaneohe Bay, Oahu, HI

I met my new Battalion Commander with a handshake as fragile as an apology and an atmosphere that stank of insignificance. Short and gray-haired, his posture lacked the vigor I expected from someone of his rank.

Our first interaction quickly soured. Inside his expansive office, centered in a building with decades of history hanging from its walls, I glanced at his gear tree—barely used and showing no sign of wear and tear from field experience.

"Now, I know you recon guys do things differently," he began, his voice dripping with condescension, "but what this unit needs is discipline. Part of that discipline is adhering strictly to our gear SOP. You might hear some grumbling about it, and maybe Recon was more lax, but here in the infantry, we have rules." He paused, looking at me as if expecting agreement, while I ignored his comment. "And we follow them. Strict adherence—that's what keeps units tight and effective."

Inside, I seethed. His words and demeanor were a contradiction I had seen too often. Throughout my career, it was always those who projected authority the loudest, clinging obsessively to rules and regulations, who often hid their own inadequacies behind rigid facades. His hollow speech told me everything I needed to know about him, although I hoped my instincts were wrong.

His last combat experience dated back to 2003—a lifetime ago. Since Vietnam, our adversarial mindset had largely focused on Soviet-bloc countries, training for conflicts across the flat plains of Eastern Europe. This preparation paid off during the initial invasion of Iraq, when Marines fought a war on our terms with speed and violence of action, seizing resources and crippling the enemy's ability to fight.

But the War on Terror changed everything. Clear battle lines vanished, enemies no longer wore uniforms, and civilian casualties became tragically commonplace. My commander was trained, molded, and trapped in the mindset of a war that had already been fought and won, refusing to adapt to the complex, hazy conflicts we now faced.

Rigid conformity served its purpose when conscripted men waged wars of attrition, but these current Marines were different. They were born into a generation with the world at their fingertips, and they were smarter and quicker to adapt. They deserved leadership designed for the war they were actually fighting.

"Give me two weeks," I said. He looked at me and said nothing. "I'll take two weeks and be your directed telescope," I continued. "I'll work through every sector of the battalion and report back to you on where we stand, what we're doing well, and where we can improve." I stood up, shook his hand, thanked him for the meeting, and left him alone in his office, overshadowed by his large leather chair.

## The Marines

From administrator to logistician, from frontline infantry Marine to food service specialist or ammunition technician, I spoke with every Marine I could find. I wanted to understand not just their capabilities, but who they were. What made them tick? What drove them to show up every morning, lace their boots, and serve?

I met men and women from every corner of the country and every rank of our battalion. A Georgia Dawg with a twang as sweet as tea, proud of his roots. A machine gunner—the leanest, meanest I'd ever met—twice promoted and twice demoted. He chuckled, flashing a wide, goofy grin. "Nowhere to go but up!"

A sharp Punjabi Lance Corporal with a knack for business and a nose for numbers. His family emigrated to the United States from an upper-middle-class caste in India. He had no financial reason to serve the United States. Yet, he looked at me, almost in shock, and said, "Why wouldn't I? It's my family's home."

The NCOs and Staff NCOs, our enlisted leaders, and the backbone of the battalion shared their frustrations. If they wore black chevrons, they had an open forum with me. I met with the Lieutenants, young men and women eager for guidance, most of whom were experiencing their first deployment. They balanced a tightrope between loyalty to their Marines and obedience to the chain of command. They were the last line of command responsible for translating intent into action. As I spoke with them, I realized my worst fears had already taken root; uncertainty spread among their ranks. Nothing they'd learned at TBS or the Infantry Officer Course had equipped them for facing a toxic leader.

Finally, I sat with the Company Commanders. They endured the brunt of the *Little King's* wrath, suffering constant public ridicule for even minor deviations or missteps made by their junior Marines—errors he viewed as direct reflections of their leadership. Although I wasn't particularly close to them, I sympathized with their impossible situation. Bound by a system meant for their success, they were instead trapped in a cycle of failure and humiliation. Sadly, they chose submission, bowing to every unreasonable demand, never finding the courage or support to take flight and rise above the fray.

I discovered a battalion of highly competent Marines, filled with innovation, creativity, and a genuine desire to make a difference in the world, who were suffocated by their own leadership. They resented the heavy-handed disciplinary model that stripped them of their authority. When every decision was second-guessed by a higher command, why decide anything at all?

Before we even deployed, frustration was brewing. Their voices didn't matter. They weren't serving the Corps. They weren't serving each other. They were serving one man.

### The Note

Two weeks later, I returned with my report. Inspired by Dale Carnegie's *How to Win Friends and Influence People*, I prepared four pages of handwritten notes to add a touch of authenticity. I included constructive feedback from conversations throughout the battalion, highlighting clear opportunities for improvement and how I could assist. Unfortunately, the main frustration that emerged centered on our gear SOP.

Knowing the sensitivity of the subject, I tread cautiously. I agreed that having a standard operating procedure to outline essential equipment for specific missions made sense. However, I argued against this one-size-fits-all approach, referencing our manuals on a soldier's load and jungle warfare. I cautioned we were clinging to outdated presumptions of combat, insisting that every Marine's gear needed to be identical, down to the exact inch. These rigid guidelines often made little sense at ground level, causing understandable frustration among the younger Marines who sought the flexibility to personalize their gear, making it functional and intuitive for their specific roles. I hadn't encountered such top-down leadership since 2003.

Hundreds of Marines confided in me across the battalion. Their frustration wasn't simply about gear placement—it was about trust. If a Marine couldn't be trusted to make minor adjustments to their own lifesaving equipment, how could they be trusted to make any decisions at all? To them, it conveyed that Marines were seen as tools rather than people. The SOP represented total control over the unit, its functions, and even its thoughts. Every subordinate leader felt paralyzed by their inability to adapt. Any objection or even suggestion to modify the SOP was immediately crushed as an act of defiance.

I considered my role as more than tactical. It was to capture the pulse of the battalion, having once stood in their shoes myself. The report was not good. Morale was low, trust was eroding throughout the chain of command, and it seemed that each entity was doing just enough to avoid being fired. Our conversation led to little change. He dismissed my insights into his Marines' operational and emotional states.

His answer was brief. Scanning the report with less interest than a dinner menu, he slapped it into his palm, handed it back, and said, "Thank you, Gunner," abruptly ending our meeting. My relationship with him had been set.

## Smile in the Face of Adversity

```
10 December 2017 - 2200
Kadena Air Base, Okinawa, Japan
```

After a seven-hour flight, my fellow Marines and I landed in Okinawa, Japan. Since World War II, the islands of Okinawa had hosted Marine battalions on rotational deployments, providing stability in the South Pacific and acting as a powerful deterrent to potential adversaries seeking to make a move.

From there, our battalion took part in a series of training and partnership exercises across the South Pacific. These exercises cultivated relationships while sharing tactics, techniques, and procedures with partner nations, empowering them to defend themselves and democracy. Through it all, our operational culture remained compromised. Fear permeated our ranks—from fear of leadership to fear of delivering bad news. "No bad news to the boss," was murmured frequently during meetings.

This fear bred dishonesty, forcing commanders to make decisions based on false information. Lies could never help a commander see the environment clearly; without the facts, any decision would inevitably harm the Marines.

I sat conflicted in meetings, knowing the reality but watching the lies. I had to choose between my personal disdain for the man I was obligated to obey and my duty to the young Marines I served. I chose not to engage in the cycle of deceit because it ultimately endangered our Marines.

Many around me misunderstood power, thinking proximity to the commander translated to influence. Ambitious staff, eager for recognition, always contested the seats next to him. I believed true power stemmed from trust and honesty. So I deliberately chose my seat, positioned directly across from him down the long table, always within his view. I became his silent truth-teller. Through subtle gestures—a slight raise of an eyebrow or a cautious glance—I signaled to the commander when he needed to dig deeper.

I've never admired young Marines more than the ones I served with at that time. We continued across the Pacific, training with key regional partners. From Thailand's stifling heat during jungle exercises to the rugged, frigid mountain patrols near the Korean DMZ. Men and women came together to keep the battalion afloat, consistently rising to meet challenges head-on.

Our success would also be his. But our loyalty wasn't to him—it was to the Marines.

## A Minor Infraction

17 February 2018
Ban Chan Khrem, Chanthaburi, Thailand

Thailand's thick, humid summer clung to our skin as the jungle canopy fractured sunlight into beams of gold that shot across the leaf-covered mud. Hot red blood splattered from decapitated pythons onto the ground while I watched our young Marines learn survival from men who had long mastered this impatient environment.

Over four weeks, we trained with partner nations to hone our skills. We traded techniques on joint sniper ranges, patrolled jungle trails where the threat of tigers was more than just a myth, and learned to navigate the dense undergrowth with a predator's patience. The concussive roars of F-16 gun runs and artillery barrages shook the ground beneath us, merging our firepower with that of our allies in a display meant to bridge the divides of both language and culture while furthering our long history of fighting and training alongside Thai soldiers.

One afternoon, the heat hung heavy in a blanket of carbon and dust. A squad had just fought its way through a live-fire course dense with barbed wire, simulated enemy resistance, and pop-up targets that transformed the jungle into a living, shifting battlefield. Their leader, a large Sergeant from the Dakotas—and the best we had—knelt in the dirt, breathing hard, his rifle resting across his chest. Sweat traced clear lines down his pale face, darkened by smears of dust.

With a piece of bamboo, he scratched the layout of the fight into the mud, debriefing his Marines with a clarity beyond his years. He addressed each movement, highlighting what worked and where they had lagged behind. He didn't just critique—he guided, asking questions of the young Marines' thought processes when making a specific decision, shaping his men into something better than they had been just ten minutes before. When he finished, he looked up, meeting my stare and then that of the Battalion Commander. "Anything to add, gentlemen?" the Sergeant asked.

I clapped a hand on his salt-streaked cotton uniform shoulder and stood beside him to address his squad. "That was amazing, gentlemen; you reacted to the scenario well. We've got a few kinks to work out, but you addressed them in your debrief. *Get out, get on-line, and make a decision.* You pushed them hard, Sergeant, and your Marines performed. Great job."

"Well, there, Sergeant, I think everything was fine." The commander's words slithered between us. "But I have a real issue with your lack of discipline." My stomach turned, and I dropped my head. The Sergeant's head hitched, his eyes flicking across his men, searching for what he'd missed. His gear was squared away, his men had executed, and yet he had failed somehow.

"How can I trust you to do the big things right if you can't do the little things right?" The Colonel asked rhetorical questions with no answer, beginning to anger himself. "That's a lack of leadership." The Sergeant's fingers curled tighter around the bamboo. His back straightened. He was still searching himself, trying to find the mistake.

Then realization dawned. He had rolled his sweat-soaked sleeves twice—not to standard. He sucked in a breath, forcing himself to remain still. "I'm sorry, sir," he said. "It was just real hot." The Lieutenant Colonel pounced. A storm of beratement rained down, an assault that had nothing to do with the fight they had just won and everything to do with control. The words stripped away the Sergeant's leadership moment, reducing him to a man being scolded in front of his subordinates.

This commander couldn't lead or inspire, so the only things that gave him legitimacy was the tin on his collar and that trivial gear SOP. He held on to those values the way a zealot clutches sacred texts without bothering to look for truth outside their own experience. Satisfied with the damage, the Lieutenant Colonel turned and stalked off, muttering. The squad hesitated and followed, leaving the Sergeant standing in the jungle.

I stepped closer. He stood stiff, with blank eyes, his rifle across his chest, fists clenched below his half-unrolled sleeves. Near shaking, his gaze found mine—rage and shame swirling across his pupils. Through gritted teeth, he spat. Then he whispered, "I love the Marine Corps, sir. But I hate 3/3."

## Broken Note

10 April 2018
Susong-Ri Range, Pohang, South Korea

I kicked at the frozen dirt, rocks grinding beneath my boot as I stood with the senior enlisted infantry Marine in the battalion, watching one of our final company attacks unfold. The frigid, mountainous Korean morning air stung my throat while each exhaled breath curled up into the frigid atmosphere like wisps of smoke. Our position was just behind the main effort, and we walked the line as the Marines made their final assault on an enemy trench; their advance synchronized with the full weight of our supporting arms.

The range stretched like a long natural amphitheater carved into the mountains, its sloped terrain forming a vast corridor nearly 2,000 meters long. At its farthest end was the objective—a series of machine-gun bunkers and a simulated enemy trench. The infantry would fight into this canalized terrain, forced to adjust their fires in real time. The Master Gunnery Sergeant and I took up positions at the point of friction, where the wide base of fire would narrow into a tight funnel, allowing only a few Marines to advance at once.

The battle opened as planned, with its signature notes. An M1A1's main gun cracked, shattering the heavy fog as its round streaked into the distance; a second tank followed, its cannon barking in tandem. Steel and heat echoed down the long corridor into the hillside, tearing into the entrenched defenses at the far end of the range.

Then came the mortars. The dull thump of 81mm and 60mm tubes sent rounds arcing skyward, their descent a thunderous rainfall of destruction crunching into the frozen earth. Fire-for-effect missions strafed across the enemy position—some rounds punching deep into the ground, others air-bursting just feet above the trench line, annihilating anything that dared to rise above cover.

Fifty-caliber machine guns and TOW missiles followed, launching from anti-armor platoons as their Humvees raced along the range, each crew engaging designated targets. The percussion of M240s and M2s rolled like drums in a war march, their fire-red tracers streaking through the thick morning gloom. The infantry surged forward, pressing against the cold with the heat of their own supporting fire over both shoulders.

Now the battle belonged to them. Three platoons collapsed into two, then into a single tightening line along the trench. The assault force scrambled uphill; their fields of fire constricted by the narrowing corridor. The Master Gunnery Sergeant and I watched as two young Marines, fresh on their first deployment, found themselves at a decision point. Their movement funneled them together—one weapon would have to go silent to allow the other to fire. They had a decision to make.

We held our breath. The Marines halted, dropping low, indicating a lull in the pressure. They both rose to a knee, searching not for the enemy but for guidance. They locked eyes, then turned to find their Corporal behind them. The Corporal hesitated, turned behind him, and searched for his Sergeant. The crescendo of battle—an entire symphony of destruction—stalled on a single, broken note.

The attack's momentum shattered in an instant. A hesitation, a moment of fear—every Marine suddenly too afraid to make the wrong choice. And in that frozen second, the United States war machine choked on itself. The Master Gunnery Sergeant and I stood still, saying nothing. We already knew the truth. This wasn't a tactical failure. It was cultural.

That night at chow, the Battalion Commander arrived in pristine cammies, his boots unmuddied and his gear squared away. He made a show of it, waiting until the end to ensure every Marine saw he was the last to eat.

### New Commander

2 July 2018 - 0800
Marine Corps Base, Kaneohe Bay, Oahu, HI

Our unit returned home to Hawaii, ushering in a fresh changing of the guard. Most senior enlisted personnel and officers moved on, replaced by a new group of junior Lieutenants and commanders up the chain, including a new Battalion Commander.

Tall and borderline malnourished, the man carried himself with intention. His intelligence was undeniable, and his thoughts often ran so deep that he appeared to lose himself in them. He had a nervous tic—picking at the edges of his fingernails—that betrayed his constant contemplation. Unlike previous commanders, he wasn't imposing or overbearing; instead, he was methodical and quiet. My first meeting with him would set the tone for the next eighteen months.

He was kind and approachable. We swapped stories about our shared histories and laughed at the mistakes we had made along the way. He picked at the edges of his fingers and listened more than he spoke. My presence didn't threaten him; he understood my job was to ensure the battalion's success and recognized that success meant building a team.

His leadership style marked a shift from the heavy-handed, centralized authority I had grown accustomed to. During our initial conversation, I laid out the nuances of the battalion—who the young officers were, which Staff NCOs influenced them, and, most importantly, what drove the NCO corps.

"The Marines want to believe in you," I told him. "They also want a commander who believes in them. You have an incredible opportunity to seize this battalion by letting them show you how good they can be." He nodded, lowering his hands from the pyramid he had formed with his fingers against the top of his nose, his thumbs resting on his chin. He understood the dual loyalties I carried—one side of my collar still flat black like my enlisted rank, the other gold, marking my place among the officer corps.

"Anyone can have an opinion, but it takes experience to make an assessment," he said. "That's why I need you." Our first meeting was a success. He listened to my ideas, engaged in discussion, and encouraged debate. Before I left, we shook hands. As I turned to step through the red-trimmed threshold, I paused.

"Oh, there's one more thing. I'd like to talk about this gear SOP."

"Sure thing, Gunner," he said. "I look forward to hearing your thoughts."

This commander was different. He was an avid reader who urged his Lieutenants to read as well. He wanted them to study historical battles, analyze philosophical works, and immerse themselves in leadership journals. His goal wasn't just to tell them what to think, but to teach them how to think. He cared for his officers and challenged them, and in return, they began to grow. Freed from the chains of fear-driven discipline, our unit transformed. We traveled to Hawaii's Big Island, where the Marines moved through the razor-sharp ancient lava fields of Pohakuloa, a training area nestled between Hawaii's two largest volcanoes.

In one of those crossroads where past and present collide—reminding us how deep the roots of our profession run—I teamed up with the man who once guided me through the streets of Fallujah—my former sniper Team Leader. Now, Captain Blake Cole flew the AH-1 Super Cobra for the legendary Scarface, the same Marine aviation unit that had been the backbone of our support in Afghanistan. Heroes in the air and in my life carried us once again, this time shaping the next generation.

Our battalion hammered out its new identity through calculated, progressive training—developing and reinforcing skills through collective action. The goal wasn't just proficiency in fundamentals or combat power at the squad and platoon levels, but confidence—giving Marines the trust to make independent decisions and act without waiting for orders.

From there, our battalion boarded military airliners and flew to the Marine Corps' premier training facility—Twentynine Palms, California. The barren high desert, east of California's fertile valleys and just shy of Death Valley, had long served as a crucible for warriors. Originally an Army aviation center during World War II, it transitioned to the Navy before the war's end and eventually to the Marine Corps during the Korean War.

Generations of Marines had been forged there, mastering every weapon system in the arsenal. The jagged rock formations and arid landscape offered the perfect proving ground for maneuver warfare. Twentynine Palms humbled even the most seasoned units.

Here we faced the ultimate test—a service-level training exercise. A meticulously orchestrated sequence designed to push a unit to its limits. Joint fires integration ensured aviation and ground elements moved as one. It was a trial by fire, and we rose to meet it under our new commander's leadership. He didn't lead with volume or bravado, but with clarity, trust, and consistency. His style created space for each Marine to reach their full potential. In return, the Marines worked for one another, rather than personal gain. The mission became the Marine to our left and right. That sense of mutual purpose ran through everything we did, turning a group of individuals into something close to unstoppable.

## The Lieutenant

Months passed as yet another series of spending cuts, budget freezes, and political grandstanding bogged us down. Our deployment hung in limbo, caught in the crossfire of politicians more concerned with airtime than the future of our country's safety. Despite the uncertainty surrounding the battalion's deployment, they sent a Lieutenant and me ahead as the advance party to Okinawa, Japan.

In Okinawa, rumors resurfaced—an unused operational budget designated for an infantry battalion to train in Australia. Whispers had circulated for months, but now, with boots on the ground, we could go straight to the source. We approached our supporting regiment for guidance. The Lieutenant Colonel we spoke with confirmed it: Funds were available for training in Australia for four months. The only catch—we had to figure out everything else: training areas, ammunition, lodging, food, and flights.

One quick phone call back to my Battalion Commander stateside, and I laid it out: "Sir, let me take the Lieutenant down to Australia and see if we can set up a landing party." No hesitation. "Go for it, Gunner. Let's see what you can shake up."

Lieutenant Austin Duke was a rarity. Tall, fit, and dark-haired, he resembled our most famous Marine, John Basilone—he even shared his character.

We crossed paths at the Marine Corps Ball in Honolulu after our last deployment. Dressed in blues, I made my usual rounds, shaking hands and thanking Marines and their spouses. I spotted Duke at a table in the corner. He stood up as I approached. That's when I noticed it—this Second Lieutenant had more ribbons than I did.

"Who the hell are you?" I chuckled.

Duke smirked, glancing at his wife. "I'm your S4 Alpha."

"My S4, what?" I asked, narrowing my eyes.

"Your S4 Alpha—assistant logistics officer," he replied with a grin.

"No. I know what an S4 Alpha is," I shot back. "What are you doing as the S4 Alpha?"

"Well... it's a long story," he laughed. I bought him a few cocktails, ordered myself a Roy Rogers, and we talked. He had one hell of a journey. He'd started as an infantry Marine at the same time I did. In Fallujah, he led a squad and earned a Bronze Star for valor. He fought, bled, and then took the leap—applying for a commissioning and education program.

Graduating from TBS at the top of his class, he had his pick of career fields. He chose infantry. He'd already been a Squad Leader instructor at the School of Infantry before commissioning and had attended the coveted Infantry Officer Course as a Staff Sergeant.

Then the Marine Corps did what the Marine Corps sometimes does. Bureaucracy declared his previous course completion invalid because he hadn't attended as an *officer*.

Faced with the absurdity of retaking a course for a skill set he had already mastered, he pivoted. He opted for his second choice—logistics—a field that would benefit him and enable his dynamic skill set to assist Marines on the ground. One organization's loss was another's gain. I had the privilege of traveling the globe and working with one of our generation's finest infantry Marines.

And there we were: two infantry Marines, each with decades of experience, finding ourselves in new roles. *Logistics drive operations, and operations drive logistics.* With big ideas but no clear way how to execute them, we arrived in Darwin, Australia—hat in hand.

## Crescendo

23 May 2019 - 1836
Darwin, Northern Territory, Australia

As humid as Hawaii and as hot as the devil's armpit, the Australian Outback was as rugged as it was remote. Life here was raw, untamed, and unforgiving, producing soldiers who could endure the fires of hell itself. The Marines shared strong ties with Australian troops and frequently trained and fought together since World War II. The 1st Marine Division's own battle song, "Waltzing Matilda," was born in the Australian Outback, and the same southern constellation that arched across Australia's night sky was forever imprinted on the division's emblem.

Expansive, bright blue skies blanketed the dusty beige landscape that seemed to stretch forever. Flat, red earth punctuated by gigantic termite mounds, gnarled scrub, and crawling with creatures that seemed plucked from mythology. Wallabies and kangaroos darted through the brush—nearly missing my truck's bumper, while monstrous dinosaur-like beasts lurked in muddy rivers.

The real shock came from the fire hawks—birds so creative they'd snatch burning sticks from wildfires and drop them in dry brush, igniting new fires just to flush out their prey. An ironic lesson in tactical innovation, courtesy of Mother Nature herself. This was the Outback—brutal, beautiful, and absolutely unforgettable.

Joining forces with a rotational infantry battalion from California already in place—another seasoned Gunner was on deck. A fitness fanatic with a sharp mind and an even sharper tongue, Tyrell Shots didn't just do physical training—he lived it. He was a force of nature: bald-headed, quick-witted, and flashing a veneered grin earned from mouthing off in the wrong place. His smile matched my own crooked nose, evidence of our mutual dedication to learning lessons the hard way.

We became a powerhouse. With his ingenuity, my persistence, and our combined work ethic, we partnered with a planning team that was relentless in its bias for action. Thanks to the tireless dedication of American and Australian forces stationed across the Pacific, we developed a comprehensive logistics and training plan in just three weeks. Twelve hundred Marines would lift off from Okinawa and land in Australia, ready to push themselves through the most punishing and realistic training we could design.

We began with the basics, teaching the first steps—stripping everything down to fundamental infantry skills at the individual level. Then came the partners; four-person fire teams navigated live-fire ranges, with each scenario choreographed to reflect patterns seen in combat.

Next, we introduced the beat. Squads of fifteen took turns weaving through increasingly complex scenarios, sharpening their movements and syncing their rhythms.

With each evolution, the tempo increased, and the intensity rose. Timing, endurance, and cohesion created rhythm as the training rose toward its peak. Then came the symphony—a full-scale, company-sized heliborne assault into a heavily fortified enemy position. One final, demanding performance would test every step, note, and nuance.

## The Triad

31 August 2019 - 0729
Mount Bundy Training Area,
Northern Territory, Australia

I leaned forward, bracing in the dry seasonal creek bed as rotor wash kicked up dust and debris around me. I stood in the landing zone, waiting alongside our battalion's second-in-command and senior enlisted. Together we formed a triad that influenced every level of the battalion.

The infantry Executive Officer—known as the XO—was the battalion's second-in-command, but his role went far beyond just being next in line. If the Commanding Officer was the brain and vision of the unit, the XO was the circulatory system—keeping every element in sync. He was also the commander's sounding board and pressure valve. When tough calls had to be made—tightening timelines, reallocating resources, holding a company to the standard—the XO took that weight, allowing the CO to preserve focus and momentum. He carried the burden of making the machine efficient without letting it become rigid. The best XOs didn't chase credit. They chased continuity. Though their impact was rarely loud, it was always felt.

Major Nate Rollins was everything an infantry officer should have been—calculated, bold, and teachable. He performed at levels two ranks above his own simply because he refused to do less. Before the Marine Corps, Nate paid his way through college by dodging hooves and horns as a rodeo clown and cattle roper in Huntsville, Texas. His subdued demeanor masked a toughness that never needed to announce itself.

A slight scar on his bottom lip told one of a hundred stories—this one about the day a wild bull sent a horn straight through his mouth. But you'd never hear him tell it. No bravado, no embellishment. Just a nod, a half-smile, and a "Yeah, that one stung a bit." He was polite, professional, and as steady as they came—a true Texan.

The Operations Chief was the senior enlisted within the operations section. While others drafted plans or led missions, it was the ops chief who made sure everything in between got done. He was the pulse of the battalion's daily operations. He tasked companies, coordinated training, managed rehearsals, and kept every moving part—ammo, transport, timelines, comms—in check. When the battalion shifted from training to combat, the ops chief was one of the first to the command post and one of the last to leave. He influenced the plan, briefed the team, and tracked every unit in the field, often on little to no sleep.

Master Gunnery Sergeant Pete O'Brien was the most Boston man I'd ever met—loud, funny, and constantly chewing bubble gum like it fueled his next joke. His two favorite baseball teams were the Boston Red Sox and whoever was playing the Yankees. He came from a long line of O'Briens who did two things: be Irish and join the Marines.

If Nate was the quiet, steady hand of Texas grit, Pete was the rowdy, fast-talking Northeasterner who filled every room with energy. He never walked—he strode. A hip-hop fan like me, we'd blast Outkast and Wu-Tang while bouncing through the Outback in my diesel Ford Ranger, the CB radio squawking as we dodged kangaroos behind a "roo guard" that had already seen its fair share of impacts.

But for all his bravado, Pete was my rock. A kind man with an incredible heart. He loved his Marines as fiercely as his own children—though, like my father, he bore the guilt of loving them from afar. Pete never talked about himself. He only cared about one thing: "Giving these Marines a better chance than I had." And I respected the hell out of him for it. He wasn't just a mentor to the enlisted Marines—he was a mentor to me.

### Turn It Up to 11

`31 August 2019 - 0731`
`Mount Bundy Training Area,`
`Northern Territory, Australia`

The first Osprey touched down in a red cloud of dust and rotor wash. A swirling wall of sand and noise transformed the already thick, humid air, stinging my face and filling my lungs with the memorable taste of jet exhaust and earth. The V-22's engines whined as the rear ramp dropped, spilling out the first wave of Marines from Captain Mike Davidson's Lima Company. Overhead, Cobras and Hueys prowled in slow, menacing loops.

First off the bird, Mike approached my position. We stood at the edge of the large field, watching his Marines shake off the landing and form up in platoons, moving forward with the kind of efficiency that only comes from doing it a hundred times before.

Mike and I walked similar paths. Both Mustangs—first enlisted, then officers—but our journeys to this moment had split somewhere along the way. He had been an infantry Marine and fought the same battles I did, but he stepped away for college, earned his commission, and returned to lead years later. He was on his final deployment, fulfilling what he saw as his highest honor: commanding a Marine rifle company.

Our relationship had always been built on mutual respect. I designed the fight and shaped the chaos his Marines would step into. His job was to lead them through it. We understood each other. The night before, we sat up swapping stories, laughing at the absurdity of where life had taken us—two Sergeants who had chewed the same dirt, grew up, and now stood on opposite sides of a war game, each enabling the other in different ways.

As the last Marines poured from the Ospreys, the Cobras broke off, banking toward their holding pattern. The first artillery barrage rolled in, deep-throated booms pounding the earth from dozens of kilometers away. Our snipers and forward observers, already in position, coordinated helicopter gun and rocket runs between artillery and mortar fire volleys, softening the zone before the infantry pushed forward.

Mike stood, squared his shoulders, and locked eyes with his Marines as they fanned out and began their advance. I followed close behind. My job was to be at the point of friction where the fight was thickest, ensuring the mission's success. And like any good commander, Mike did the same.

The infantry surged forward through the jagged maze of checkered underbrush—pawns in the opening gambit, pressing the attack. Overhead, mortars arched like knights leaping over walls before descending, causing chaos and devastating the enemy's will. Missiles streaked horizontally across the sky before smashing into burning targets, sending towering bursts of flame and debris into the air.

Machine guns rattled in synchronized rhythms, cutting diagonally across the enemy's front at right angles. Rockets launched their final assault, a queen delivering decisive blows that punched through the defenses and carved open corridors for the advancing infantry. The pressure from the two rockets still reverberated through the heavy clouds of carbon-soaked air.

No longer a mass, the Marines broke into tactical teams, waves surging against the enemy's shores. Rifled grenades slammed into their targets, peppering defensive strongholds. Balancing speed with tempo, fire, and maneuver, each calculated step was a deliberate move in an unforgiving game.

A hail of gunfire erupted across the front of the enemy trench. Two Marines rushed forward to make entry. One dug into his grenade pouch, hands shaking from adrenaline and pressure, while the other laid down suppressing fire. The Marine's eyes widened as he turned the grenade in his palm.

*Thumb Clip*—His thumb swept the metallic safety off the grenade spoon.

*Pull Pin*—His sweat-soaked glove twisted and yanked the second safety away.

*Prepare to Throw*—"Frag Out!" the young Marine shouted, cocking back, the entire squad hinging on this moment.

*Throw*—The dark green ball flew from his hand across the pale blue sky. The third safety was released, and the weapon was alive. The same sound heard by generations of young Americans on foreign shores—a conductor's subtle tap to begin the final act.

Pawns poised for promotion.

*Ting.*

# 19

# THE FUTURE FIGHT

## The Case for Change

*The United States Marine Corps I lead in 2020 finds itself, like the rest of the US defense establishment, at a crossroads. The passing of our nation's "unipolar moment" and the emergence of revisionist great power competitors in China and Russia, coinciding with a sea change in the character of warfare driven by social and technological change, demand that we move rapidly to adapt to the circumstances of a new era. This article lays out the case, as I see it, for the sweeping changes the Marine Corps needs to make to meet the principal challenges facing the institution: effectively playing our role as the nation's naval expeditionary force in readiness while simultaneously modernizing the force to play its necessary roles in the operating environment described in the National Defense Strategy (NDS)—and doing both within the fiscal resources we are provided. Deep institutional change is inevitable when confronting modernization on this scale, and that type of change is hard. The urgency of change and the institutional reform and innovation necessary to achieve it have not diminished in the two years that have passed since the publication of the NDS. The ideas expressed below are not unique or original to me—forward thinkers across the defense establishment, academia, and industry have given voice to them for years. But the time to act is now... The NDS offers clear guidance at the strategic level as to the general nature of the change required; at my level, as a service chief, appear the institutional challenges and trade-offs of recruiting, training, educating, and equipping Marines to give the combatant commanders the tools they need to execute the strategy... Even Marine infantry battalions, the capability perhaps most central to my service's historical record and self-image, will become fewer and perhaps smaller, a move that is fully justifiable in a force that will no longer be sized for large-scale sustained ground combat. Changes in these key units will be informed by the recent experiences of highly distributable ground units operating within adversary weapons engagements zones, including those of our own special operations forces.*

*—General David H. Berger,*
*Thirty-Eighth Commandant of the Marine Corps*

## Sunset

28 January 2020 - 0730
School of Infantry, Camp Pendleton, CA

The scent of coastal sagebrush and dog fennel swirled through the morning calm—a lifetime of memories stirred as I absorbed the landscape. Yellow-hued wildflowers and blazing-orange California poppies speckled the rain-soaked green hillsides. Low scrub clung to the rocky slopes, shaped by ocean winds heavy with salt and rain. The rocky trails, worn smooth by decades of Marines pounding through them, twisted through dry creek beds and climbed brutal inclines, showing little mercy to those who underestimated them.

In 2002, fresh off the yellow footprints in San Diego, I was a wide-eyed grunt racing through lessons on live fire and forced marches. By 2005, sniper school drilled the discipline that defined my craft and my life. In 2007, I returned as a sniper instructor, shaping the next generation of precision thinkers. A year later, those same hills transformed me into a Reconnaissance Marine, teaching me to navigate both the complexities of combat and the unique terrain of the human condition. By 2014, I was back again, this time teaching Recon Marines—sharpening their skills as we patrolled the same ridgelines and valleys that had once molded me.

My journey had come full circle. I had one final tour left and it brought me back to where it all began—the School of Infantry.

I stood at the threshold of my final chapter, closing the book on a career defined by people, sacrifice, and the drive to shape those who would follow. This time, I wasn't just passing through—I was here to build something that would last.

I entered the service as a scrawny kid full of ambition and little direction. Over time, I attended thirty formal schools with every branch of the US military, graduating either as an honor grad or in the top 5 percent of each course.

But I didn't get there alone. Through it all, it was the men and women within those educational frameworks—often working against the system—who ensured I had every opportunity to succeed. Their mentorship, patience, and belief in my potential shaped my entire life.

Now, it was my turn to give back. I set out to reform infantry Marine education at its most basic level—the social contract. I knew these would be the most challenging years of my career because the battlefield ahead wasn't combat, but honoring a service I loved by confronting its flaws, owning its failures, and pushing it forward for the next generation.

## Babbo

27 February 2020 - 0930
School of Infantry, Camp Pendleton, CA

Within weeks of arriving at Pendleton, armed with the Commandant's intent for wholesale reform and a bias for action, my office buzzed with life.

Crazy plans, half-baked ideas, and a flood of "in my experience" comments flashed across my cramped, cold workspace.

My phone buzzed in my chest pocket, pulling my attention away from the heated conversation around me. The screen showed my father's name *Giuseppe*. Not unusual this early in the morning—but still a little odd.

Since he'd gotten sick, he'd lost most of his ability to speak. He would call sometimes, and all I'd hear was a faint groan in the background. It was his way of reaching out, letting me know he was there, thinking of me.

I'd usually keep the line open, toss the phone back in my pocket, and go about my day, keeping him close while I worked.

"Hey, Dad—you good?" I asked, half-knowing he couldn't answer.

"Angelo, it's Gail." My stepmother's voice trembled.

Her words broke apart in a near-whimper. "Your father's gone."

A hollow ringing swelled in my ears—the familiar pang of a mortar blast echoing in my head.

"I'm sorry, sweetie," she whispered.

I turned to the Marines standing in front of me.

"My dad just died," I said, the words feeling strange in my mouth.

"I'm sorry," one replied, a voice without a face.

Everything blurred. My feet moved, but I barely registered it. I walked to my Colonel's office, muttered something, and left. Thirty minutes later, I was on the highway, chasing the long spine of California north. The Five Freeway stretched ahead, a river of green valleys swallowed by towering golden-brown foothills, the world passing without sound. I drove with the radio off. I didn't cry. Instead, I screamed. A raw, terrified bawl of someone who'd entered another life. A life without a dad.

My father had been dying for years. Parkinson's, but not the kind most people know. His hands didn't shake. The disease ravaged his mind.

I watched the man who had once been larger-than-life fade for years. The one who planted grapes from the old country in his backyard, hoping someday to make wine. The man who could tie a hundred knots from his days climbing trees when he first arrived in America. Who, in his own gentle, funny way, taught me how to be American.

That man was already gone.

A shell remained—the frail body of a beautiful soul whose mind and heart had shaped my own. But his stare remained. His gaze was as bright as a constellation, and he had the unmistakable look of a father watching his son, his eyes filled with the purest pride.

Though my father couldn't speak much toward the end, his eyes were enough.

He died one week before the pandemic changed the world.

He never had a funeral.

A week later, I loaded what was left of him into the passenger seat—a box of old cowboy boots, dog-eared photos, and memories—and drove south. Leaving felt wrong, but I didn't know what else to do. My heart hurt in a way I couldn't explain, and I searched for anything to make sense of it. The only thing I could do was look to the future. The work was important, and it was waiting. I knew he would've wanted me to get back to it.

### *The Sassy Six*

The next Monday came, whether I was ready or not. The weight of everything I had left behind felt suffocating, but years of training kicked in. I boxed up the grief, set it aside, and turned toward what lay ahead. The mission hadn't changed—build the team, change the infantry.

The first step in building something new was assembling the right team. While many had experience, I needed a ragtag collection of infantry Marines who met the only two requirements I truly cared about: They had open minds, and they gave a shit.

Dave DeLong was the first to join. A young Captain from upstate New York—lean, wiry, and probably too smart for his own good. A mechanical engineer by trade, he had a rare ability to break down complex problems with *clinical* precision. He also had an uncanny ability to frustrate me more than most, which is a pretty high bar to clear if you ask anyone who's worked with me. Dave was the brains of the operation, but I never let him know it.

Dave was old enough to have the weight of several deployments showing in his eyes, yet still young in ways that mattered. He believed that hard work alone would push him forward, and he hadn't been worn down by the realization that advancement in a large organization wasn't always about competence. It was about alignment. About playing the part, adopting the right tone, and quoting the right doctrine. The system didn't survive by promoting outliers—it absorbed them, reshaped them, or spat them out. DeLong hadn't learned that yet, which is why he was perfect.

Then there was Gunnery Sergeant Blake Burkhart—a seasoned warfighter straight out of a movie set. Salty as the ocean and about as forgiving. Beneath his stern veneer was a closet computer engineer and avid gamer. He was the kind of guy who could rewire a radio or rewrite an entire operating system if he got bored enough. His out-of-regulation, slicked-back hair matched his slick Scottish sense of humor—dark and just inappropriate enough to make senior officers nervous. He kept us honest, kept us grounded, and made sure no one got too high on their own bullshit—especially me.

Then came the Sergeants—Jude Stewart and Danny O'Day—*Ace* and *Gary*. The inseparable duo never quite understood the generational joke and uncanny resemblance behind their nicknames. These two overachievers had made a fateful mistake weeks earlier: They walked into my office late one afternoon and told me they were bored, asking if I had any projects for them. Gunny and I glanced up from a nosebleed-inducing PowerPoint slide and chuckled.

"How would you like to change the Marine Corps?" I asked. They laughed, not realizing how serious I was. They were young, eager, and hadn't seen combat, which they saw as a weakness. Gunny and I saw it as an advantage. "Listen, guys," I told them, "Some of the worst Marines I know have a Combat Action Ribbon, and some of the best I know don't. It's all a matter of chance. Frankly, I don't give a shit, and neither should you."

"You have no bad habits," Gunny chimed in. "We're building the Marine of the future—you're going to help us do it, and we'll need your imagination."

Having just been in the fleet, they were our fact-checkers. We had to run every crazy idea by them first. After all, I was on my way out. *We* were on our way out. Whatever we built, they were the ones who'd have to live with it.

"If someone gives you shit," I told them, "Tell 'em to run their gun, not their mouth. You two are the future." I leaned forward. "A lot of experienced dudes refuse to adapt, clinging to past successes. You're gonna have to hold your own." I smirked. "Just remember—don't be wrong."

The last to join was a young Lieutenant with subtle frat-boy vibes. Mark O'Connell was highly educated, highly adaptive, and—shocking no one—an engineer. Clearly, I had a type.

Born into a long lineage of military officers known for their trailblazing spirit, Mark's mother was one of the first women allowed to fly in the US Air Force. One of his grandfathers fought as a grunt in World War II, and his other grandfather fought with Recon in Korea before becoming a pilot in Vietnam, eventually rising to become a Deputy Commandant of the Marine Corps. Mark possessed an unparalleled understanding of military culture at all levels and had a talent for weaving historical references with modern problems, which made the rest of us reevaluate our intelligence.

And then there was me—the loud, stubborn, soon-to-be-retired leader with a night school diploma, put in charge of this little band of misfits, armed with a rank that forced people to pay attention. The six of us, backed by local commanders who were either visionaries or had simply *run out of fucks to give*, set out to change the Marine Corps.

Above my office door, I hung our guiding principle: *No Approved Solutions*—a reminder that the problems we faced wouldn't be solved by following someone else's playbook. Our team devoured literature to shape our collective mindset. From the aggressive accounts of how a maverick Air Force pilot named John Boyd transformed a generation of strategic thinkers to the war epics chronicling the leadership of Alexander of Macedon. Our thought leadership reading list also grew to include less conventional works, from the sci-fi visions of educating young warriors in *Starship Troopers* and *Ender's Game* to the long-view leadership philosophy presented by Simon Sinek's *The Infinite Game* and John Maxwell's *The Five Levels of Leadership*.

With the Commandant's intent and backing of foundational documents, we felt prepared with a solid framework to tackle the challenges ahead. There were no sacred cows; any Marine caught saying, "*This is how we've always done it*," had to pay in push-ups.

We started calling ourselves the *Fab Five* until the addition of the Lieutenant forced a name change. Gunny, in his infinite Highlander wisdom, pointed out that *Pasciuti's Cuties*—a tragic autocorrect from a group text—was infinitely funnier.

Eventually, we landed on *The Sassy Six*.

If we were going to change the Marine Corps, we would at least have some fun doing it.

## The Last One Hundred Yards

Our Commandant advocated for sweeping changes to adapt to an evolving world where dogmas, traditions, and outdated assumptions about young Marines' capabilities acted as obstacles. A significant part of creating a lasting path forward with this transition involved reevaluating our entire training continuum.

Like any ideological shift, stalwarts clung to the past, convinced that *maneuver warfare* would remain unchanged—just as the *attritionists* before them had believed. *Attritionists* relied on numbers. *Maneuverists* depended on speed. Yet, a dangerous new reality existed from the advancements in enemy surveillance and weapons systems.

Detection by these cutting-edge enemy technologies all but guaranteed the destruction of unprotected infantry forces. The future of warfare demanded a different approach. Success would hinge on thinking Marines, capable of operating in highly decentralized environments spread across hundreds of miles, often without traditional support hierarchies. Mass formations launched from naval fleets or supported by towering stockpiles of munitions mattered little in an era where survival required stealth, endurance, and the ability to thrive in violence. Our Commandant called for small teams of thoughtful, adaptive men and women—Marines who could analyze the shifting battlefield and act decisively within their commander's intent. In the wars on terror, we faced enemies whose actions were only limited by their resources and imagination. Marines of the future would have to do the same.

Every conflict shaped and reshaped our legacy—from the wooden masts of colonial ships to the trenches in France, the coral beaches of the Pacific, the frozen mountains of Korea, the jungles of Vietnam, and the bloody streets of the War on Terror. At the heart of it all, victory always came down to one thing: a Marine and a rifle.

Our mission was to give that Marine the best chance of success.

## Defining the Problem

In the early months of 2020, intent on action and operating without orders, an ambitious team at the School of Infantry sprang into action. Twenty Marines and civilian curriculum designers sat salivating and crowded around an old conference room table.

As with any well-conceived plan, our initial meetings were chaos. Loose concepts and strong opinions ricocheted around the room, dominating the atmosphere with shouting matches, chest-thumping, and *rank*-measuring contests. We were getting nowhere. Trapped in a cycle of reasoning based on decades of small-unit success, we tried to force a nebulous future construct into outdated frameworks. We were trying to solve an equation without understanding the problem.

"This is ridiculous. We don't need to be doing this," an old Master Sergeant spat.

"We've never lost a war. If it ain't broke, don't fix it," another voice interjected, drawing confused looks from the group.

"We need more guidance from the top—what does the Commandant want this Marine to do?" someone shouted.

"All I need a grunt to do is walk a long distance with a pack," came another response from a senior officer.

I had enough. "Stop!" I shouted. "This is madness. We've got to do this differently." I glanced at Gunner Mic Skinta—a legend. Sniper extraordinaire. Bald, stocky, and perpetually pissed off. He was always the most experienced person in the room, which made him the least impressed by grandstanding and long-winded theatrics.

Originally from Pennsylvania, he did a stint as a Gunner in a reconnaissance unit in San Antonio, Texas, returning as if he had just come off a cattle drive. When not in cammies, he wore square-toed ropers and sported a Stetson hat big enough to pick up satellite signals. Having developed a newfound appreciation for calling people "Hoss," it seemed Texas had left its brand.

"Gunner Pasciuti is right," he said, spitting wintergreen Copenhagen chewing tobacco into an old Sprite bottle. "If we keep going down this path, we're either going to end up with a grunt trained for the war we just fought, or just spin our wheels until we tire ourselves out." The room went silent as his twang lingered in the air.

"Okay, here's what we do." I scanned the surrounding faces. "This room has hundreds of years of infantry experience, but we're getting nowhere by yelling over each other. The Commandant gave us mission-type orders—frameworks, end states, and the *why* behind them. He left it to us to determine the *how*."

"He's provided us with three documents to use as a reference," an eager Captain DeLong interjected.

"Exactly." I pointed. "We need to start with a shared understanding." Two days later, we regrouped. Our discussion focused on three key documents: the unclassified National Defense Strategy, the Commandant's article "The Case for Change," and the Commandant's Planning Guidance—identifying sweeping changes across the Corps.

Every Tuesday and Thursday during the following months, we held an open forum for any infantry Marine on base. From machine gunners to snipers, demolition experts to mortars—and everything in between—the only requirements were to read the three documents and check your rank at the door. While the rest of the country grappled with the horrors of the pandemic, our team of Marines concentrated on tackling a different problem.

We started with the end in mind. Setting aside the unknowns of naval shipping, ship-to-shore connectivity, or logistical support, we determined that the most dangerous—and most likely—scenario would involve future Marines trudging across an exposed shoreline under enemy fire, fighting through an entrenched defense network and surviving hidden ashore with minimal support for an undetermined amount of time.

An honest analysis of current and future threat environments across the twenty-first-century battlefield introduced the concept of multi-domain conflict, in which war is fought not only on land, at sea, and in the air but also in space and cyberspace. This shift placed young Marines, often nineteen to twenty-one years old, in a far more complex battlefield. Threats were no longer two-dimensional, and outdated doctrine pushed primitive tools—and by extension, primitive thinking—into environments where old rules could not survive.

This newer, more adaptive, and faster form of combat required a corresponding change in education and training. Previous models conditioned young Marines to recognize a situation and respond with a templated solution: A stimulus produced a rehearsed response. Rapid technological advances and the spread of new weapons, optics, and tactics meant that training Marines to react with canned solutions made little sense when we had no idea what they would actually face in combat. We started calling it the "sharks with lasers" problem because, at some point, you just expect the next war to appear with something as ridiculous and unpredictable.

From that vision, the Marine Corps Training and Education Command deliberately identified the skills essential for future warfare against a peer adversary. Hours of phone calls, detailed video conferences, and countless PowerPoint presentations culminated in identifying thirty-nine critical infantry behaviors—a blend of traditional warfighting fundamentals and future combat requirements.

Some behaviors preserved continuity: mastering the service rifle, patrolling, and land navigation. Others indicated a cultural shift, highlighting the importance of embodying our warfighting philosophy, where success relied on decentralized decision-making, technical proficiency, and the ability to out-think and outmaneuver the enemy.

To make this overhaul effective at the entry level, we narrowed it down to twenty priority behaviors—the nonnegotiables. These became the cornerstone of the course, developed through a process that incorporated feedback from all four Marine Divisions.

The easy part was over. We had defined the end state. We needed to work backward to determine how to bring this Marine to life.

## That Which Gets Measured Gets Improved

`17 September 2020 - 1630`
`Training and Education Command, Quantico, VA`

Frustrated voices erupted across the swampy auditorium in Quantico. I was back again, attending another mind-numbing conference devolving into bickering for the hundredth time. This session convened to gather input on developing performance evaluations within the scope of our evolving curriculum.

"You guys already have buckets," a frustrated Marine Forces Special Operations Command (MARSOC) Colonel snapped, standing as the room quieted. His usually reserved voice carried substantial weight.

By the mid-2000s, Marine units had settled into a predictable rhythm before deploying to combat zones, following a checklist that every unit diligently completed. Commanders marked off tasks, demonstrating readiness and proficiency. While this system was undeniably necessary, it only tracked completion and often overlooked quality. How well Marines performed often went unrecorded, lost in an extensive binary system focused solely on "mastery" or "non-mastery."

The unintended consequence became deeply embedded in our institutional fabric. Since education started shifting toward passing tests, Marines naturally focused their efforts on meeting the minimum standard. Well-intentioned instructors began dropping hints or giving *foot stomps*—just enough to ensure the Marine who struggled could pass, while those who excelled were given no opportunity to grow further.

Assessing a Marine's capability required more than a checkmark—it needed nuance. Something had to change.

"What do you call them—behaviors? Fine. *Behaviors*." The MARSOC Colonel grabbed a stubby blue dry-erase marker from the conference table and strode toward the whiteboard at the side of the room.

Outcome-based learning recognized that achieving the bare minimum did not equate to true mastery. The binary assessment system left too much room for interpretation. How could a commander distinguish between a skilled Combat Marksmanship Coach and a Marine who barely qualified on the range? Technically speaking, both had passed the tests, but they were not operating at the same level.

"You've got to separate them to provide a clearer picture." His faded woodland camo sleeve brushed against the board as he sketched a spiderweb. Eight sharp lines shot out from the center. "These are your behaviors."

Then he drew expanding rings around the center point. "Each circle represents a level—one through five—indicating how proficient a Marine is at that behavior."

"When we pull back and assess these Marines, we can finally see the bigger picture." He smiled, tapping the board. "Our *objective* informs our *subjective*."

The alternative approach provided a far more accurate assessment of a Marine's ability to perform individual and collective skills in realistic and dynamic environments.

"These Marines are mountains, and this is the map," he proclaimed as he capped his pen with a loud snap.

## Nerd Alert

I burst into the conference room on my first day back with *The Sassy Six*, excited by a fresh problem to solve. If we were going to create a revolutionary course, we would need a revolutionary way of evaluating. As any self-respecting group of nerds would, we drew inspiration from video games, particularly sci-fi and fantasy. Gamers choose characters based on clearly defined attributes, strengths, and weaknesses. For example, archers excel in range and precision, thieves rely on cunning and stealth, and knights depend on strength and endurance for close combat.

So why couldn't we apply that same clarity to assigning roles in the infantry Marines?

If done right, commanders could assign Marines roles aligned with their natural aptitude. Snipers, for instance, often tended to be leaner and more methodical, while machine gunners were usually louder and bigger, with egos to match. Neither needed to resemble the other—each was unique and equally vital.

Outcome-based learning provided the framework. We would evaluate each Marine's quantitative and qualitative skills in specific behaviors using five clearly defined levels: Novice, Advanced Beginner, Competent, Proficient, and Expert. Detailed grading rubrics and descriptive "word pictures" helped evaluators determine where a Marine ranked on the scale.

As Marines progressed through the tiers, they gained the ability to perform tasks with less supervision, operate in more dynamic environments, and eventually teach those skills to others. To graduate from the course, each student had to meet the minimum requirements for all twenty infantry behaviors while also being encouraged to excel at all of them.

Unlike the old program, in which Marines had three chances to pass a task and were never evaluated again, the new curriculum employed continuous assessment. Students received regular counseling and feedback through behavior-based report cards, which identified their strengths, weaknesses, and opportunities for growth. At graduation, these report cards acted as warm handoffs to gaining units, providing squad and platoon leaders a comprehensive overview of each Marine's abilities.

Our ideas gained traction when the Corps released its latest doctrine, MCDP 7: Learning. Then–Brigadier General Lorna M. Mahlock captured what we had been chasing:

"As a lifetime serial learner, I have found that ordinary people can do the extraordinary if they are committed to experiential learning, are intellectually curious, and possess an unquenchable desire to acquire new knowledge... this may be our only advantage in the future fight."

From thinkers in Washington, DC, to doers in the field, the time had come to align our efforts, unify our vision, and fundamentally reshape how we trained and educated Marines. We had figured out what we needed to do—and we were ready to measure it. Now, the biggest step left was figuring out how to teach it.

## The Fight

Over the next year, the Schools of Infantry—East and West—collaborated on opposite ends of the country through a pandemic as best we could. We talked, we shared ideas, and we argued. We fought over everything that mattered—and plenty that didn't. At one point, our relationship was so tense that we could've disagreed about the time of day. We both wanted the same thing: a better-prepared, more capable young infantry Marine. The challenge was agreeing on how to get there—and what, exactly, that Marine should look like.

Nasty emails, yelling matches over the phone, and near-brawls when we physically faced each other—our relationship was fractured at best. Each team retreated into our silos, planning what we believed would be the best version of success. Not only did we disregard the other side's input, but at times, we outright defied it.

Fortunately for us, our commanders—blessed with a healthy distance from the day-to-day fight—maintained a stoic temperament and did their best to remain objective during the deliberation process. After a series of agonizing sessions in humid, stagnant conference rooms across the country, we presented our plans to our commanding Generals. To no one's surprise, the Generals often gave the same directive: compromise.

"I understand each of you is passionate and has your own way of doing this," one said. "But you're going to have to work together—because the answer can't be no."

Through gritted teeth and tough conversations, we found compromise—almost everywhere. Over time, we even came to respect each other's positions. Each ideology became a necessary counterweight to the other. Progressive ideas helped us navigate the future, while conservative values ensured we didn't lose our souls on the way there. Neither side was entirely right—or entirely wrong.

What began as an adversarial relationship slowly shifted into mutual understanding. We realized that if neither side were willing to give ground, we would hurt the very Marines we were trying to help.

We weren't two sides of the same coin. We were two halves of a whole.

## From Instructor to Coach

Outcome-based learning and our reimagined approach to student evaluation provided us with a strong foundation—a solid starting point for rethinking how we did business. We knew we had to go deeper if we were serious about developing more capable, more lethal, and ultimately more thoughtful entry-level infantry Marines. The training model wasn't the only thing that needed reform. We also had to look hard at the culture and method of instruction itself.

Our approach to entry-level training had grown stale. Over decades without reform, it became anchored in a mindset that assumed every student was actively trying to fail. Instead, we founded the course on a core belief that every Marine had limitless potential.

It wasn't just a slogan. It had to be our operating principle.

We combined Maslow's traditional hierarchy of needs with modern educational design principles. In our model, students were no longer expected to claw their way to the top—they became the center of our universe. For too long, attrition-based warfare concepts had shaped industrial instruction models. Education had become more about throughput than transformation, pushing large numbers of students through rigid, checklist-driven curriculum designed for speed and scale.

That approach had its place in the past. It made sense in moments of national mobilization, where numbers mattered more than ability. But we were no longer preparing Marines for a war of that generation. We were preparing them for a war of evolving complexity.

Military historians and strategists have long examined the generations of warfare through the lens of evolutionary change. Shifts in tactics, formations, and the incorporation of new technologies characterize each generation. Specific dates didn't define transition points; collisions did. When one force adapted and the other didn't.

Warfare's generational shifts reflect a long arc of hard-learned lessons. First-generation warfare—line and column tactics, massed formations, and attrition-based thinking—was ingrained in us at boot camp, a ceremonial holdover from centuries past. That model shattered with the onset of World War I, as second-generation warfare and the machine gun erased any illusion of honor in massed frontal assaults. Thousands were cut down, formation after formation, running into walls of bullets with the desperate hope that the machine guns would eventually grow tired.

In response, third-generation warfare emerged. It emphasized speed, surprise, and attacking the enemy's capacity to wage war—through logistics, communication, and command. Blitzkrieg, maneuver warfare, and combined arms became our tradecraft. Victory wasn't about ground; it was about disruption.

But then a timeworn tactic resurfaced—a generation of warfare interwoven in our own colonial roots—an ideological insurgency. In Vietnam and again in the War on Terror, the enemy refused to fight on our terms. And why would they? No earthly power would directly engage a Marine Air/Ground Task Force. So, they chose asymmetry. They blended into the population, struck at random, and waged a war not just on the ground—but in the public's minds. Uniforms vanished. Front lines dissolved. It was never about defeating us. It was about outlasting us and breaking our national will. The Marine Corps stood on the edge of yet another generational shift.

Russia's unprovoked annexation of Crimea offered a shot across our bow, a glimpse into the future—a conflict that fused all past generations of warfare into one. But this time, it included an additional dimension: persistent precision. Drones and remote systems turned tanks into targets. Mass formations of humans, gathered as they had been for millennia, were erased with a keystroke. Not by a soldier, not even by a sniper, but by a machine, executing with icy indifference.

Marines had always been at the forefront of adaptation—it was in our blood. Historically underfunded and often overlooked, we had to move faster, innovate constantly, and outwork everyone. We weren't gritty by choice; we were gritty because we had to be—and we made it our virtue. America didn't want a Marine Corps. She needed one—the ones you called when something had to be destroyed overnight. To snatch victory from the jaws of defeat.

In traditional warfare, defenders choose the location, while attackers choose the time. But in the wars we anticipated, that formula was breaking down. No matter where we went, we'd meet an enemy already there—waiting, prepared, and equipped with the same technologies we once relied on to preserve our strategic advantage.

This was the future, and it was already here. The next fight wasn't just about the constant of Marines and their rifles but also their minds. And that meant the student had to be the number one priority.

Our first step was to rethink the instructor-student relationship from the ground up. For decades, we relied on a fear-driven, authoritative model—in which students quickly learned to stay quiet, stay low, and, above all else, avoid mistakes. Fear didn't build initiative. It didn't teach judgment under pressure. It didn't breed confidence. And I'd seen firsthand what that looked like in combat—Marines more afraid of doing the wrong thing than stepping up to do the right one.

We inherited classrooms built for efficiency, not effectiveness. Three hundred Marines crammed into an uncomfortable orange amphitheater with a lone instructor pacing in front of a glowing PowerPoint projection, droning through a lesson as Marines drifted in and out of consciousness. At some point, those semiconscious students stopped being the reason we wanted to become instructors. Instead, they became the obstacles that kept instructors from getting home to their families sooner.

No matter how much a young instructor wanted to help, they often lacked the bandwidth—or the support—to provide meaningful guidance. The system reduced their role to that of an evaluator, not a teacher. It reinforced a transactional relationship that mirrored the sacred cow of Marine Corps training: Do what you're told or suffer the consequence.

So, we moved toward a different kind of leadership.

We built a model rooted in presence, mentorship, and professional care—not coddling, but coaching. We laid the foundation for that vision in an old classroom we named the *Hasbrouck House*—after the famous site where General Washington once commanded the Continental Army. We hand-selected instructors for their tactical experience, emotional intelligence, and willingness to grow alongside their Marines. By socially engineering the traits we wanted to see in future leaders, we could plant the seeds for long-term change. The instructors would shape the students, and the students would eventually become instructors. Over time, the culture itself would evolve.

These weren't recruits anymore. These were Marines—men and women who had already earned the title, had stepped up to serve, and deserved to be treated like the infantry Marines they were training to become.

To support this shift, we restructured the course at its core. We assigned each squad of students to a single Sergeant Instructor—one leader responsible for their Marines' entire educational experience. In return, the students became a direct reflection of that leadership.

As training intensified, the Squad Leader's role evolved from teacher to tactical leader. They managed their Marines through increasingly complex challenges, including patrols, supported live-fire attacks, urban combat scenarios, and force-on-force exercises.

We built a social contract. The student's success became the instructor's success and the instructor's development became part of the student's growth. This continuous, close relationship between them fostered a positive feedback loop and created something rare in entry-level training: trust.

The symbiotic relationship would allow Marines to deepen their understanding of their training, receive immediate, constructive feedback and apply it in real-time. Instructors would no longer be distant evaluators—they would be present, invested, and accountable for their squad's development.

A sense of ownership, emotional investment, and trust between the instructor and the Marine were not byproducts; they were the root cause of a healthy and effective training culture.

With this new culture of shared success established, instructors and students never lost sight of why they were both there.

The School of Infantry, where my journey as a student began, was preparing to launch its most significant ideological shift in generations to determine if we had replaced fear with trust in cultivating a more effective next generation of Infantry Marines.

On January 20, 2021, the first Infantry Marine Course began. No ceremony. No fanfare. Just a handful of instructors and wide-eyed Marines sitting in the same balmy classroom I had occupied twenty years earlier—only now, they were about to experience a fundamentally different course. A program built from thousands of hours of argument, failure, and stubborn collaboration—a collective effort by hundreds of Marines and civilians across the institution who recognized that the future demanded something different. What emerged wasn't perfect, but it was authentic. It carried the fingerprints of every Marine who had ever said, "We're here to make them better," and finally had the space to prove it. We weren't just designing a course—we were laying the foundation of a new era. One that viewed the Marine not as a product of tradition, but as the living manifestation of adaptation.

# 20

------

# DAWN

## Ender's Game

23 April 2021 - 0930
School of Infantry, Camp Pendleton, CA

"Excuse me, Gunner, sir," a young Marine stood and raised his hand. We were days before the final mission week, taking an operational pause and briefing the Marines before their last push. The entire class rested on large outdoor bleachers. The lone Marine's voice trembled, carrying a soft Spanish accent.

"What's up, stud?" I said, shooting a glare at a few Marines who were snickering. I'd spent my life watching people judge my father's thick immigrant accent and wasn't going to let that happen here.

One of our cultural shifts was in how we addressed students. While officially prohibited by the Marine Corps, derogatory or insulting slang had long been socially accepted—a misguided rite of passage. It harkened back to darker lessons, where dissociative language was used to divide and diminish people, so we could do unspeakable things to them. Under our new model, instructors had three options: address students by their last name, by their rank, or simply as "stud"—short for student—a title we used as a badge of respect, rather than disdain. Any infraction was met with immediate removal from the situation and dismissal from the Instructor cadre. There were no second chances for disrespect.

I paced in front of the restless crowd, mingling and shooting jokes back and forth—the kind of environment where Marines could speak their minds—professionally, of course.

"It's just Gunner or sir, Marine," I said with a chuckle. "What's up?" One hundred fifty-one pairs of eyes locked onto him. His olive cheeks flushed.

"Gunner—S—" he stammered through nervous laughter from the crowd. "Gunner, I . . . I hear you're good at chess."

I was not good at chess.

Originating in sixth-century India and passing through the Persian Empire into the hands of European aristocracy, both slaves and kings played chess for generations. Chess was more than a game; it was an intellectual exercise that sharpened critical thinking, built adaptability under pressure, and enhanced tactical thinking because it required constant decision-making. All of those skills contributed to military strategy, which is why historically, chess was often taught to future officers as part of their training.

We had introduced chess on the first day to entry-level students at the School of Infantry. This had not been done before, but we regarded chess as a fundamental catalyst for enhancing overall student thinking. The thousands of subtle decisions the game required shifted a student's mindset from fear to action. Chess taught our infantry Marines not only what to think but also how to think.

"Who told you that?" I smirked.

"I dunno, sir. That's what the other guys are saying."

"Was there a question in there, young man?" I deflected.

Sure, I may have forced chess into the curriculum—but that didn't mean I was any good at it. We conceived it during one of *The Sassy Six*'s fried-brain Friday huddles—what we unapologetically called the *Imaginarium*: part venting session, part brainstorming. One of our marksmanship instructors had joined us and mentioned that his recon platoon had been using chess to enhance decision-making during close-quarter battles and live-fire training, with incredible results.

It was a spark.

In dynamic environments, chess served as the perfect mirror for the fog of war. So we brought the chess board to life. We layered the game across our real-life tactical framework: Pawns became light infantry—numerous, exposed, always moving first. Knights moved like drones and indirect fire—unpredictable, three-dimensional threats. Rooks mirrored missiles—arching over terrain to strike deep into an enemy's safe space. Bishops were machine guns—lethal from angles, shaping the fight. Queens represented dynamic, limited but devastating tools—rockets and grenades—that punched the enemy in the teeth. And the king? The king was the commander. Essential to the mission—but useless without the team.

Once the Marines grasped the basics, we introduced stress. Fire teams squared off with ten seconds for each move. Every lost piece resulted in five push-ups for each team member. As fatigue set in, so did mistakes. Mistakes compounded until something broke. Instructors enjoyed surprising engaged students by quickly rotating the game board and forcing the attacker to defend their own plan. The victors would advance while the losers sulked away to regroup.

Chess spread like wildfire. When they ran out of push-ups, they kept playing for bragging rights. Those games sparked conversations, rivalry, mutual understanding, and adaptability. It was our *Ender's Game*.

Back at the bleachers, the Marine squared his shoulders. His teammates shrugged him forward.

"Gunner," he said, finding his footing. "I'd like to challenge you to a game of chess." The bleachers erupted—roars, laughter, and the energy of young twenty-somethings seeing a shot at history.

"That right?" I pulled off my dusty eight-point cover and wiped my brow. "Alright. Let's make it interesting."

"You win, I do a hundred burpees. I win, you ALL do a hundred burpees."

Chaos. Screaming. The gauntlet was down. Their collective fate was sealed.

And there he stood—this quiet, unsure Marine, from a story not so different from my own, interwoven into the beauty belonging to the American tradition. A young man, uncertain and searching for his place in the world, now sat across from me as an equal.

"You're on!" he grinned, then added, "Sir," correcting himself.

## The Pool Deck

25 April 2021 - 0530
School of Infantry, Camp Pendleton, CA

I paced the side of the pool deck beside them like an anxious father. A soft white mist rose from the frothing blue pool and drifted into the cold black morning. The sky still clung to the night as the first squad of Marines slipped into the water.

This was the start of their final mission. A simulated amphibious insertion into unfamiliar terrain, where they would patrol, hunt, and fight their way across Camp Pendleton. We designed a week of the most challenging days possible, each crafted to reflect the realities of modern conflicts and the uncertainties of future ones. Each student would navigate through purpose-driven events to assess individual skills and their performance as a team. Combat was a collective effort, and everyone had to do their part. We provided them with the tools and established a framework to evaluate endurance, decision-making under pressure, adaptability, and resilience. They didn't know what was coming; it wasn't just their validation. It was also ours.

The swim qualification they completed at boot camp wasn't enough. We saw it in their movements, the hesitation in their eyes, and the data. So, we held the line. They deserved better. The memory of the 2020 tragedy—when we lost eight Marines and a sailor off the California coast—hovered as heavy as the fog.

That weight shaped our determination. If we were going to send these Marines to the fleet, they wouldn't just survive in the water—they'd dominate it. We didn't check boxes; we built swimmers. The cost in time was steep, but it was worth every second. No Marine would sink in frigid waters, wishing they'd been taught how to survive. We owed it to them. The standard was the standard. If they didn't meet it, they didn't pass. Anything less was an abdication of our duty to the fleet. Lower it once, even slightly, and you poison the whole system, passing a liability to some unsuspecting commander down the line.

Steam rose in gentle wisps from the surface—formless, slow-moving, and catching the glow of the pool lights—as it curled into the dawning coastal air. Their breath fused in unison, rising in clouds with each exhale. They moved through the water in tight teams, green fatigues clinging to their shivering lean frames. Nothing else moved—no birds, no breeze—just breath. The only sound was the slap of tired limbs laboring through the pool, rifles balanced on their waterproofed rucks pushed ahead of them.

Squad by squad, they completed their swim, gathered their gear, changed into dry boots, and disappeared into the brush.

## Layer Cake

Three squads formed a platoon as they moved toward their next objective. The days of long, exposed movements down dusty trails were gone. Instead, they rotated squads in and out of overwatch in satellite patrols to cover every movement. No one moved without someone else watching.

Over the next forty-eight hours of their final mission, they would be locked in a nonstop churn: patrolling against one another, launching hasty attacks, setting ambushes, and slipping through the sagebrush in the dark on endless night patrols.

These Marines spent the past four months training to think independently and adapt to a constantly changing environment. While rank and experience were necessary, a functional team culture required information to flow up and down the chain of command. Our combat instructors laid the groundwork, then stepped back—creating space for experimentation and iteration within defined boundaries.

Drawing on my experiences attending formal military schools around the world, I understood that classroom instruction had its place, but real learning occurred in the field. We committed to keeping Marines in the field more than anywhere else. Being a grunt wasn't about being comfortable; that was a lesson best learned early.

At the heart of our approach was problem-based learning and steady, deliberate coaching—not yelling—purpose-driven instruction. We didn't coddle them—we challenged them. Our rifle marksmanship program became the vehicle. We partnered with professional shooters, clinical psychologists, and Federal Air Marshals to create a range environment that encouraged decisions rather than reactions. Every repetition became a chance at judgment, stress management, and a bias for action.

We relied on adult learning theory because the missions awaiting these Marines would not be simple. Each skill was carefully layered on top of the previous one—reinforced with intention and directly connected to their future roles. We provided them with the "why" and the space to take ownership of the "how."

We stripped away outdated elements like forced marches, rigid formations, and exposed pack staging. Those tools had their place—but the Marine School of Infantry wasn't one of them. Discipline wasn't determined by how straight a line looked or how a Marine marched, but by how they mastered their environment.

Lessons occurred in squad bays or deep in the field—never in sterile classrooms. Once a skill was taught, it was put into practice. Students trained with rifles, mortars, missiles, machine guns, and grenades under the same conditions they would use them in. Marines patrolled to the range the night before, slept in the field, and executed live fire at first light. Patrolling wasn't just a block of instruction. It was how we moved.

Land navigation evolved from the simple act of "finding a stick in the mud" into a tactical mission. Marines navigated alone, built field-expedient radios, and contacted our command center for their next grid. Five points by day, five by night. Each leg tested their field craft, terrain association, and situational awareness.

Instead of complaining about recruitment numbers or unnecessarily criticizing a new generation, we redefined our value proposition.

We clarified how their actions as individuals shaped and impacted the collective and that they were responsible for one another as much as themselves.

We believed previous new Marines made questionable decisions because we failed them. They weren't given the space or expectation to think. For decades, an industrial-age model conditioned entry-level Marines to regurgitate answers on command without regard for context. Their training focused on specific solutions to specific problems—not on assessing a situation and devising a solution. And at times, that created learned helplessness. Even when options existed, they hesitated, not out of incompetence but from fear—or simply a lack of training. We trained this group of Marines to break that cycle.

We understood future battlefields would demand speed, adaptability, and initiative. A thinking Marine—confident, capable, and decisive—would always be a force multiplier. We reinforced key truths through tactical decision games and guided discussions: rushing did not create tempo. What created tempo was the cascading effects of accelerating decision-making through trust and preparation.

Initiative wasn't optional, and their decisions in training weren't random. They were grounded in a clear commander's intent that was introduced early and echoed often. With that clarity and confidence in their judgment, they didn't wait for permission. They created momentum. And with it, incredible combat power.

### The Range

Two days later, a cloud of thick brown dust billowed up from the boot-worn path as the first platoon of Marines trotted toward the firing line for their individual marksmanship evaluations. Dirt-caked, soaked in sweat, and running on little more than pure stubbornness, the battered young Marines formed a loose semicircle, waiting for the range brief.

For the last few days, sleep came in stolen moments, snatched under a bush, on a bed of leaves, and once even halfway through a Meal, Ready-to-Eat. Hunger gnawed at them.

It was their first pause in over seventy-two hours. Sunken eyes and uniforms crusted with salt and dirt cut like contour lines on a map. And yet, there they stood—every last one of them.

Behind the firing line, a team of medical professionals assessed them as they waited. Clinicians, physical therapists, and chiropractors worked in sync under the watchful eyes of two sports scientists who had designed the entire physical program.

My guidance to them mirrored the guidance I had once received. Build a program that prepared Marines to win the collective future fight.

Their job wasn't to count reps or chase gym numbers. The lifts, runs, and rucks were just data points. What mattered was whether a Marine could move under stress, absorb hardship, and still accomplish the mission. Over time, we gave our scientists the space to shape best practices and training regimens that built strength and staying power.

The bench presses and squats still had their place—but only if they translated to performance. A dead lift score meant nothing if a Marine couldn't endure.

The shift from traditional gym sessions to a hybrid of strength and functional fitness was a battle of its own. There were a few racks, no mirrors—just movement, under load, over time. It took some convincing, but the instructors won that fight too.

One Marine, wheezing, raised a shaky arm and pointed at a group of unfamiliar men standing behind the line—heavily armed, geared differently, and far too clean. "Uh, sir... who are they?"

I glanced over my shoulder. "That's our control group," I said, dry as the dirt under my boots. "Don't worry about them."

He blinked. "Copy."

Side by side, from 500 meters to bad breath distance, our class of Marines and the control group ran through every range. Each stage simulated a phase of combat—long-range engagements, maneuvers under fire, and the snap decisions and split-second violence of close-quarters battle. The assessment was purpose-built by a cadre of Marines and expert shooters across the Corps. It tested every facet of combat performance under stress. We had no interest in how they shot a rifle when they were well-rested. We wanted performance on demand.

We digitally fed each Marine's score into the instructors' tablets, providing instant feedback and objective data. This was only the second time our Marines had seen this range. The test they conducted that day would follow them to the fleet, where it would evaluate the next generation of infantry.

An hour later, the dust settled. The results were in. I promised a specific Reconnaissance Battalion on the West Coast—one known for its unmatched level of training—that I would never share the outcome, and I never did.

## Speed *and* Tempo

28 April 2021 - 1430
School of Infantry, Camp Pendleton, CA

"Thirty seconds," the Sergeant Squad Leader muttered, flicking his watch.

Kneeling together in a damp ditch tangled with reeds and bamboo, the young Marines of 2nd Squad looked up at him. Shadows stretched across their tired green faces, highlighted by the reflections of generations of Marines who had knelt in the same soil. The weight of lineage hung as heavy as their armor.

Squads rotated through their culminating attack, a purpose-built range designed to reflect a future fight's size, scale, and potential realities. Pneumatic machine-gun bunkers blasted heat and sound. Stationary pop-up silhouettes marked a shallow trench line.

But the real surprise—the trick up our sleeve—was the robots.

Armored, maneuverable, and reactive, they moved through the range like a thinking enemy. A controller accompanied each squad, initiating unique scenarios: an entrenched defense, a panicked retreat, and reinforcements arriving over the hill. No two runs looked the same. Each Marine had to navigate the unknown.

*Pomp. Pomp. Pomp.* Mortar thumps punched skyward over their left shoulders. 1st Squad launched the attack.

My eyes scanned the squad and caught on a young Marine—Private Johnson. A kid from Louisiana, raised hard, with no father in the picture. His basketball coach told him he'd never amount to anything. He reminded me of a man I once knew. Now he knelt in the mud with us, running on fumes, pushing harder than he ever imagined, held together only by adrenaline. He kept his eyes locked on his Squad Leader.

This was his shot.

I knew that look. Tight jaw and hunter-focused stare. Fear overcome by purpose. I'd worn it once myself.

*Rip, rip, rip.* 3rd Squad's 240Bs erupted to the right, strafing the exposed trench line with angry red tracers. Dirt and dust exploded in geysers, rising like ghosts toward the bunkers ahead as the machine guns cut into the bobbing targets.

"Now. Let's go," the Squad Leader barked, waving them forward.

The squad surged from the ditch. Hunched low, rushing into their last covered position before the assault. They held, waiting and letting the storm ahead break the simulated enemy's will.

"Go!" the Squad Leader yelled.

The squad split—two elements peeling off like halves of a pincer. The right flank dug in and opened fire, laying down a curtain of rounds to buy the left flank time to maneuver. Scoped rifles picked off targets while grenades arched from launchers, peppering the enemy's obscured front.

Low and fast, the left flank broke off, sprinting across the dry creek bed. They advanced under the cover of terrain, billowing green smoke and the steady hammer of machine-gun fire.

Wide-eyed and panting, they dropped flat onto the reverse slope. Chemicals pulsed through their tired limbs, and hitched breaths labored as they sipped water, waiting for the call. They had seconds to find their courage.

"Contact front!"

The weary Marines pushed themselves to their feet and surged over the final hill. A cascade of fire and fury erupted—rifles, machine guns, grenades. Every weapon they had trained with roared to life.

Each shooter had a suitable target, and each trigger pull represented a decision.

Their last hundred yards.

A Private Team Leader sprinted between Marines, yelling orders, checking ammo, and shouting casualty reports while keeping his eyes forward, tracking the effects of his team's fire.

"You two! Eleven o'clock—150 meters, movement! Hit 'em with a 203!" the young Marine snapped. "You—cover him!" He dropped low and slid back down the hill, scanning—not for orders, but for the signal. Across the creek, his Squad Leader was already looking for him. Once the left flank was in place, the Squad Leader would push with his assault element on the right, rushing the trench line under a volley of covering fire.

Sensing the moment and knowing he had only seconds to maintain his tempo, the Squad Leader broke from his position and sprinted down the hill toward the Marine across the creek. "Good?" he shouted.

The Marine caught his eye—thumbs up, sharp nod—then turned and hauled back to his team.

*Cue the Queen.*

"Rocket!" Hot tracers erupted from the left hill as explosions rocketed the enemy's front—direct hits carving space as automatic rifles shredded gaps just wide enough for the right flank to push through and drive the assault.

I followed close behind. Precision shooters shed their distance and turned primal, pressing within fifty meters of the final objective and bounding forward with speed and violence.

*Thumb. Clip. Pull pin. Throw.* Two grenades arced forward. A hail of gunfire followed.

A young Private bounded forward—eyes locked behind his rifle's scope.

*Bang. Bang-bang.* He glanced left. His team was with him. Two robot targets burst out of the smoke, charging the team's exposed right flank.

"Contact right!" he screamed, swinging his rifle on instinct, unleashing a tight cone of fire. Two down. His teammates surged, screaming through the smoke, rifles up, firing on the move—closing the last gap, crashing the line like a storm. The Marines took the hill. And for a moment—the chaos quieted.

Smoke hung low as brass casings shimmered gold across the cratered earth. A small fire flickered in one bunker; thick black smoke wafted from the melting plastic. From twenty feet away, I watched. Steam arced off the Marine's shoulders, mixing with sweat and the morning dew pooling along the rim of his helmet. His chest heaved as he worked to slow his breath, while scanning for his team, already preparing for the next phase. Then—he paused.

Almost instinctively, he turned, eyes connected with mine—Private Johnson—my stud from Louisiana.

## One Last Test

29 April 2021 - 1922
School of Infantry, Camp Pendleton, CA

The sky above burned pink and orange, a dying fire behind rolling hilltops as the sun fought its inevitable descent. A heavy fog crept across the dimming landscape, swallowing the last of the day's dying light. As the fog thickened, the colors faded into gray, muting the world into an eerie silence.

Our team had inserted kilometers away and patrolled up the shadowed spine of a ridgeline overlooking the cold valley below. Slick with sweat and cami paint, we moved low through cascading terrain that dropped into a wide valley of rolling hills—the ground our prey now moved through.

It was the last night of their culminating event. Three platoons, each running on fumes, had spent the previous five days in constant contact—fighting the scenario, fighting each other, and now, without knowing it, being hunted by us.

They had pushed nearly ninety kilometers through rocky trails, dry creek beds, poison-oak-choked draws, and sunbaked ridgelines. Every movement was dictated by fragmentary orders and evolving scenarios that forced them to think, adapt, and lead without rest. They stalked, ambushed, maneuvered, assaulted, and evaded—constantly shifting and never comfortable.

In nine hours, someone would jolt these Marines awake with gunfire and simulated artillery to begin a twenty-kilometer contact patrol, dragging them up a 1,700-foot climb through the coastal foothills before they fought their way to friendly lines—and one final surprise—a warrior's breakfast of boxed eggs, rubberized bacon, bear hugs, and handshakes.

When they finally completed this training, representatives from their gaining squads and platoons would be waiting, ready to welcome them to the fleet and their new families. Tired, fed, and finished, we would hold loose formations and distribute awards and diplomas as they joined the long lineage of heroes who had fought in every clime and place all over the world for the way of life they held dear.

But first, they had to make it through the night. They were cold. Wet. Filthy. Blisters on blisters. MREs gone. Socks soggy. Minds fried. Exactly where we wanted them.

This concerned neither comfort nor victory. This was about breaking through—pushing them far enough that they couldn't fake it. Far enough that character, not ego, would decide what came next. They had passed every test. They had risen above anything we expected. But I still wasn't convinced.

## Sunrise

`30 April 2021 - 0123`
`School of Infantry, Camp Pendleton, CA`

To keep it fair, our small hunter-killer team received only a rough grid—no precise coordinates. No advantage. Just the gift of the chase. Coastal sagebrush tore at our sleeves as our small patrol snaked through mist-soaked cactus, inching down the ridgeline in a slow, deliberate line, moving only when the wind masked our steps.

The heavy, frigid night air transformed the world into spectral shadows and silhouettes.

Camp Pendleton was quiet. It took me back. Images hit like waves—spilling, plunging, surging into one another—a carousel of memories spinning too fast to hold. Faces. Voices. Names I hadn't said in years. Memories etched in dirt and blood and time.

I thought of the teachers and recruiters who pulled me from obscurity and pointed me toward purpose. I thought of the Marines of 3/5—the brotherhood that baptized me. I remembered Corporal Olsen and the fire and smoke from spitting helicopters. He never left me behind. He took me under his wing when all I had was panic.

I remembered Gunny Jackson, steady, and kind, who pushed me to follow my dreams, defining the entire trajectory of my life. I remembered the bravery of Greg Rund, Shane Kielion, J. P. Blecksmith, Ross Smith, and Ray Plouhar—who met death with fire in their eyes. I remembered Blake Cole and Jimmy Proudman, who taught me the weight of leadership—and what it took to carry it well.

Then came sniper school—my own hell week. Without food, warmth, or sleep, there was only pain, misery, and suffering. I remembered Corporal Payne and Staff Sergeant Slafsky, men who recognized something in me I hadn't yet earned. They broke me down and built me back up. They taught me how to believe in myself.

I remembered Afghanistan. The cold. The calm. The heartbeat before the blast. I remembered the ones who saved my life—not once, but twice. The Chris O'Connors. The Blaine Joneses.

Then I heard Matt's voice. The last time. Panic on the radio. Static. I would've given anything for one more shot at that coin flip.

I saw my team's lost, angry faces aboard the USS *New York*, crying tears of rage we couldn't explain, locked out of a fight we knew we could have won.

I saw the young Recon Marines I had helped shape, standing tall under rubber boats, bearing the weight of the mission before they fully understood what it meant. I saw the Marines with whom I served across the Pacific—who taught me more about leadership and empathy than any classroom ever could.

All of it hit at once. I wasn't here because of me. It was because of them.

I crested the ridge in one fluid motion, my body slipping into the rhythm that years had carved into instinct. Behind my thermals, I scanned the far ridgeline—right to left, slow and steady—searching for the faint glow that would betray their presence.

Three stars flickered above—my old friend Orion. The hunter in the sky. My reminder of home and all the cold nights spent away.

White danced across the black-and-white screen—faint heat signatures on the next ridge. It was hard to tell through the fog. Movement. A small element peeled off; their white silhouettes were unmistakable. I tracked them as they slipped behind a hill and disappeared into a narrow draw. We would ambush them there.

We slid down the forward slope, feet first on our backs. Low cactus and hanging branches brushed past us. These were the same paths I had walked in Recon School with Matt. Two knights, fates bound together—one taken off the board too soon.

I rechecked the ridgeline, clearing our route. A glint caught my eye. I focused the lens. Gone. "Probably just the fog," I whispered.

We never saw the next generation for their differences; we saw them for their potential. They learned differently, spoke in different terms, and were driven by different things. That didn't make them less. Just different.

It was on us to adapt. Change the method, not the mission. Meet them where they were—and pull them forward.

We moved in close. I felt it in my chest—the charge, the energy, the tension, the subtle shift in the air.

I crept along the slope, one foot silent after the other. The earth gave slightly under my weight. Sweat traced down my grease-painted brow, beading on the tip of my nose before falling to the dirt.

I felt them before I saw them. My wide, panicked eyes glowed green under my night vision goggles. To my left—a rustle in the brush.

*Snap.* I twisted toward the sound. They weren't supposed to be there. We had been countered. Instinct took over. I raised my rifle. The familiar cold stock settled against my cheek. My team coiled behind me—pieces aligning behind the move. I stood to launch the assault. Took one step.

Twelve infrared lasers lit up my chest. I was no longer the predator. I had become the prey.

I smiled—*checkmate.*

# EPILOGUE

**August 30, 2021**—The United States concluded the Global War on Terror, marking the end of a chapter shaped by two decades of persistent conflict that transformed the military, redefined modern warfare, and altered the global landscape. The ripple effects of the war extended far beyond the battlefield, destabilizing regions, reshaping alliances, and influencing international relations, while leaving a legacy of sacrifice, uncertainty, and unanswered questions about the costs of war.

**October 1, 2023**—Chief Warrant Officer 3 (Gunner) AJ Pasciuti retired after twenty-one years of service.

**December 15, 2023**—In a shocking move, the Marine Corps disbanded the Scout Sniper Program, making it the only US military branch without snipers, dismantling a specialized and necessary capability that had been refined over 105 years. This decision, motivated by a cost-benefit analysis favoring generalized marksmanship and autonomous aerial systems as more economical options, erased a century of proven human capability, ingenuity, and combat effectiveness. The ultimate cost will be paid in the lives of service members in the next conflict.

**October 6, 2024**—The National Museum of the Marine Corps in Quantico, Virginia, opened its newest wing dedicated to the wars in Iraq and Afghanistan. Among the artifacts is Corporal Tommy Parker's recovered M40A1 sniper rifle. No longer a weapon of war, it stands as a symbol of sacrifice, brotherhood, and the bond that brought it home.

**June 1, 2025**—The Infantry Marine Course was officially rescinded, marking the end of a student-centered, outcomes-based program designed to produce adaptable and cognitively agile warfighters. In its place, the Marine Corps reinstated a pre-9/11 training model, citing personnel shortages and resource constraints. The revised approach de-emphasized critical thinking, cohesion, and individual development in favor of rote memorization, repetition, and mass throughput.

# LETTER TO THE LEADER

To the Leader,

A leader's only true obligation is to hold the hope that tomorrow will be better than today, and to share it with those they serve.

That hope isn't born from blind optimism. It's earned—shaped by discipline and rooted in dignity, accountability, and personal responsibility. It demands openness, a teachable spirit, and a mind that remains curious rather than cynical about the future.

Cynicism often masquerades as wisdom. Don't be fooled. It's merely fear of failure wearing a mask of caution. The opposite of cynicism isn't naive optimism—it's trust. By trusting no one, the cynical leader may not lose, but they will also never win.

Trust in ourselves and in one another builds something greater than any single individual. It allows us to demand more—from those above us, those beside us, and those we lead. A leader doesn't trade in insults or manufacture division for personal gain. Instead, we forge communities—lifting groups of people toward a shared vision of something bigger than themselves.

Leaders do not convince people they are sick and then present themselves as the cure. That's not leadership. That's manipulation. It's beneath us.

Leadership is a gift. It's the sacred opportunity to place the needs of others above our own. It's the belief that people can rise above anything when united by purpose. They can adapt, overcome, and choose faith in one another over the fear of the unknown. It begins with believing in ourselves.

Hope is not a reflection of poor judgment; it is a powerful force that sees the same world the cynic does but imagines a different outcome. That's a path worth walking.

To you, the leader who will dedicate your life to the betterment of others and our world: Wherever you are, whatever your challenge, no matter the odds—ignore the cynics. They've forfeited their hope. You have not.

I will forever remain,

Never above you, never below you, always beside you.

Amatangelo Pasciuti

# ACKNOWLEDGMENTS


Writing a first book feels a lot like stepping into a dark forest. There are no trail markers, no map, no stars to illuminate the path; just the weight of your idea and the sound of your doubts keeping pace behind you.

The idea lingered for years like a faint melody, flickering in and out of reach. Some days, I could hear it clearly. Other days, it was drowned by the rustle of self-doubt: Who am I to tell my story? What have I done that others haven't done better? Why me?

I knew men who were stronger, smarter, and braver. Some were still out there doing the work, while others never made it home. Yet the idea lingered. Was it ego? Was I chasing my own reflection in print? Or was it something deeper, an obligation to a generation born of war? Because if we didn't tell our story, who would?

The first spark came from Ryan Fugit, who lit the match and gave me permission to try. His encouragement pushed me past my fear and into the first words. Next came Daniel Ketchell and Sarge, who didn't just believe in the story, but breathed life into it. They opened doors, made introductions, and reminded me that *Darkhorse* was worth telling.

At UTA, Byrd Leavell created a space where purpose and authenticity mattered. I was a stranger in a strange land, and he helped me navigate it with dignity. Alongside him, Matt Baugher, Tim Burgard, and the HarperCollins Leadership team took a chance, stoked the flame, and helped transform the dream into something tangible, step by step, and page by page.

The Council included some of the brightest minds and most deeply patriotic Americans I've known: Beth Axelrod, Erwin Hosono, and Greg Hosono, who opened not only their home but also their hearts, along with Taylor Hebble, Jeff Phaneuf, and Lam Nguyen. They dedicated their time, shared their candor, and had the courage to tell me the hard truths. They kept me honest. They anchored the voice of *Darkhorse* in values bigger than ourselves.

Dr. Kelly Bare at the University of San Francisco didn't just read the manuscript; she studied it. With the heart of a true educator, she immersed herself in its pages, offering critique, encouragement, and belief in a story that wasn't hers to bear. She reminded me that the best teachers don't just instruct; they *invest*.

Then came the mentors—wisdom drawn from decades of thoughtful reflection: Jill and Tim Dunkin, whose conversations wove through theology, politics, the Constitution, and the cosmos. They taught me that leadership isn't just a title but a practice and a lifelong journey. Their worldview, both pragmatic and deeply hopeful, helped shape my own. I still believe, because of them, that we can make the world a better place—one kind gesture at a time.

And Neil, who shared the weight and the journey. From beachside campfires to endless phone calls where we cowrote from different coasts, just listening to each other breathe. You were my guide, my sounding board, the one who listened patiently through every half-baked idea and every ideological rant. You gave me tools and helped me remain true to the voice that mattered.

And then there was Sarah.

My teammate. My North Star. The one who held me as I wept for the friends I'd buried deep in memory. The one who urged me forward when fear whispered I wasn't enough. Your love didn't just support me; it believed in me. Through every edit, every conference call, every late-night breakdown, you stood beside me. Never behind. You placed my dreams, our dreams, above your own. "Thank you" will never be enough.

To the men and women I served alongside, who made *Darkhorse* possible: the story may bear my name, but the journey was never mine alone.

Thank you for walking beside me.

—AJ

# GLOSSARY

**AAV** – *Assault Amphibious Vehicle*. An armored, tracked vehicle used by the US Marine Corps to transport Marines and equipment from ship to shore, especially during amphibious assaults and beach landings. Commonly referred to by Marines as a "track" or "Amtrack," it carries up to twenty-one combat-loaded Marines and is operated by a crew of three.

**AT-4** – A single-use 84mm anti-tank rocket designed for use against armored vehicles and fortified positions.

**ATL** – *Assistant Team Leader*. The second-in-command behind the Team Leader (TL) in small units, typically within reconnaissance elements or sniper teams.

**Black Hawk Helicopter** – The UH-60 Black Hawk is a utility helicopter primarily used by the US Army. Variants are used across other branches under different names: the MH-60 Seahawk in the US Navy, primarily for maritime operations, and the HH-60 Pave Hawk in the US Air Force, used for combat search and rescue missions. While names and mission sets vary, all are built on the same core airframe and serve as essential workhorses for troop transport, MEDEVAC, and tactical support.

**CS Gas** – *Ortho-chlorobenzylidene malononitrile*. commonly known as tear gas, is a riot control agent used to incapacitate individuals through irritation of the eyes, nose, throat, and lungs. Despite the name, CS is not a true gas but a fine particulate that becomes airborne when dispersed. In Marine Corps boot camp, recruits are exposed to CS gas in a controlled environment known as the "gas chamber" to simulate chemical attack conditions and build trust in their protective equipment and training.

**DAGR** – *Defense Advanced GPS Receiver*. A small, handheld GPS device used by Marines and other US military personnel for land navigation, target location, route planning, and coordination in both training and combat environments.

The DAGR provides highly accurate positioning data—latitude, longitude, and elevation—and features military-grade encrypted access, protecting it against jamming and spoofing by enemy forces.

**DET-1** – *Detachment One*. USMC DET-1 was a small, specialized Marine Corps unit established in 2003 as a proof-of-concept to assess the viability of integrating Marines into US Special Operations Command (USSOCOM). Comprised of Force Recon Marines, intelligence specialists, and support personnel, DET-1 operated alongside Navy SEALs under Naval Special Warfare Group One. Its success in combat deployments—particularly in Iraq—directly influenced the formation of MARSOC (Marine Forces Special Operations Command) in 2006, making DET-1 the acknowledged precursor to MARSOC and the Marine Corps' formal entry into SOCOM.

**DOPE** – *Data on Previous Engagements*. The recorded ballistic information a sniper uses to accurately engage targets across varying distances and environmental conditions. DOPE includes scope adjustments (typically in MOA or mils) based on factors such as range, wind speed and direction, temperature, humidity, and altitude. This data allows snipers to make precise, repeatable shots by referencing how their rifle and ammunition performed in similar conditions.

**EOD** – *Explosive Ordnance Disposal*. Specialized military personnel trained to identify, disarm, and dispose of explosive threats such as IEDs, unexploded ordnance, and booby traps. EOD teams played a critical role in Iraq and Afghanistan, often operating under extreme pressure to protect troops and civilians from hidden or complex explosives.

**FOB** – *Forward Operating Base*. A secured military installation used to support tactical operations, typically located in hostile or semi-permissive environments. FOBs were common throughout Iraq and Afghanistan, serving as launch points for patrols, staging areas for logistics, and hubs for intelligence and command operations. Many Marines and soldiers lived and fought from FOBs during their deployments.

**HALO/HAHO** – *High Altitude, Low Opening* and *High Altitude, High Opening* are advanced parachute insertion techniques taught in Marine Recon training. Both involve jumping from high altitudes—often above 10,000 feet—to clandestinely insert Marines behind enemy lines. In HALO, the parachute is deployed at a low altitude to minimize time under canopy and reduce detection. In HAHO, the chute is deployed shortly after exit, allowing for long-distance gliding to the target area. Both methods are used for stealth operations requiring precision and minimal visibility.

**HOG** – *Hunter of Gunmen.* A HOG is a fully qualified Marine Scout Sniper who has completed the demanding Scout Sniper School. The title represents more than expert marksmanship—it reflects tactical skill, fieldcraft, mental resilience, and the ability to operate in small teams or alone deep behind enemy lines. Within the sniper and broader Marine community, earning the HOG title is a respected milestone. Knowledge and respect are passed down from HOGs to PIGs (*Professionally Instructed Gunmen*), a term referring to snipers still in training.

**HOG's tooth** – Upon graduation, new HOGs receive a symbolic 7.62mm round known as the HOG's tooth, representing the bullet meant to kill them. Tradition holds that as long as a sniper carries their HOG's tooth, they cannot be killed by enemy fire.

**Humvee (HMMWV)** – *High Mobility Multipurpose Wheeled Vehicle.* A light tactical vehicle widely used by US forces for transport, patrols, and support roles in both Iraq and Afghanistan. Known for its versatility and off-road capability, the Humvee served as a workhorse for military operations—though it later drew criticism for its vulnerability to IEDs in sustained combat zones.

**IED** – *Improvised Explosive Device.* A homemade bomb constructed and deployed by enemy forces, often hidden along roadsides, buried in the ground, or disguised as everyday objects. IEDs were a primary threat to coalition forces in both Iraq and Afghanistan, responsible for a significant percentage of casualties during the conflicts.

**INDOC** – *Indoctrination.* In Scout Sniper training, INDOC refers to the initial screening and evaluation phase that Marines must pass before being accepted into a Scout Sniper Platoon or considered for the Scout Sniper Course. The Sniper INDOC tests physical fitness (e.g., hikes with heavy packs, obstacle courses), marksmanship, land navigation, fieldcraft, and observation skills. It is designed to assess mental toughness and discipline under stress, identifying Marines with the endurance and aptitude to become Scout Snipers. Passing INDOC does not guarantee entry into sniper school, but it is a critical prerequisite for selection and further training.

**LAR** – *Light Armored Reconnaissance.* Refers to specialized Marine Corps units equipped with light armored vehicles to conduct reconnaissance, security, and economy-of-force operations. LAR units are designed to move quickly, provide early warning, and gather battlefield intelligence while maintaining a balance of mobility and firepower.

**LAV-25** – *Light Armored Vehicle.* An eight-wheeled, highly mobile armored reconnaissance vehicle used by LAR units. Armed with a 25mm M242 Bushmaster chain gun, the LAV-25 is employed for scouting, screening, and limited offensive operations. It carries a crew of three and can transport up to six additional scouts.

**LCAC** – *Landing Craft Air Cushion.* A high-speed hovercraft used by the US Navy and Marine Corps to transport troops, vehicles, and equipment from ship to shore. Unlike conventional landing craft, the LCAC rides on a cushion of air, allowing it to traverse both water and land—including beaches, mudflats, and rough terrain—making it ideal for rapid amphibious assaults and logistical support in areas with limited infrastructure.

**LPD** – *Landing Platform Dock.* A large US Navy amphibious warfare ship designed to transport and land Marines, vehicles, and equipment during amphibious operations. LPDs carry a mix of amphibious vehicles (such as AAVs or ACVs), landing craft, and aircraft—including helicopters and MV-22 Ospreys. These ships play a key role in supporting Marine Expeditionary Units (MEUs), enabling both beach landings and inland insertions. Ships like the USS *New York* feature a well deck for launching landing craft and a flight deck for rotary and tiltrotor aircraft operations.

**M1014 (Benelli M4)** – A semiautomatic 12-gauge shotgun used by the Marine Corps for close-quarters combat and breaching operations. Known for its reliability and versatility, the M1014 is well-suited for urban warfare and room-clearing missions.

**M107 (Barrett .50 cal)** – A semiautomatic anti-materiel rifle chambered in .50 BMG, used to disable equipment, light vehicles, and engage long-range targets. Also referred to by Marines as the *SASR* (*Special Applications Scoped Rifle*), it provides unmatched standoff power and penetration.

**M16A2** – Adopted by the US Marine Corps in 1986, the M16A2 was the standard-issue 5.56mm service rifle throughout the late Cold War and into the early phases of the Iraq and Afghanistan conflicts.

**M16A4** – The M16A4 is a modernized variant of the M16A2 and became standard issue for Marine Corps infantry units starting in 2004. While still chambered in 5.56mm, the A4 introduced a removable carrying handle and a flat-top Picatinny rail system, allowing for the mounting of advanced optics and accessories. Though still in use today, the M16A4 is now primarily issued to non-combat units, as newer platforms like the M4 have largely replaced it.

**M18A1 Claymore** – A directional anti-personnel mine that projects steel fragments in a 60-degree arc when detonated. It can be triggered by tripwire or command detonation and is used for ambushes, perimeter defense, and force protection.

**M1A1 Abrams** – A main battle tank used extensively in large-scale combat operations, particularly in Iraq. Equipped with a 120mm main gun and advanced armor systems, the M1A1 offers superior firepower, protection, and maneuverability on the battlefield.

**M2 Browning (.50 cal)** – A heavy machine gun chambered in .50 BMG, used for vehicle-mounted and fixed defensive positions. The "Ma Deuce" has been in service since World War II and remains a cornerstone of heavy weapons employment for its range, power, and reliability.

**M203/M320** – A single-shot 40mm grenade launcher traditionally mounted under the barrel of service rifles (*M203*) or used as a standalone weapon (*M320*). It provides infantry units with indirect fire capabilities for engaging targets behind cover or in defilade.

**M240B/G** – A belt-fed medium machine gun chambered in 7.62mm. The *M240B* is commonly used in fire support roles by dismounted infantry, while the *M240G* is adapted for vehicle mounts and general-purpose applications. Weighing roughly 25.6 pounds, it offers range, power, and reliability in sustained firefights.

**M249 SAW** – *Squad Automatic Weapon.* A belt-fed 5.56mm light machine gun used for suppressive fire in infantry squads. It provides a high rate of fire but is heavier and less accurate than the M27 in sustained engagements.

**M27 IAR** – *Infantry Automatic Rifle.* Originally introduced to replace many *M249 SAWs* in infantry fire teams, the *M27* is now the standard battle rifle for all infantry Marines. Chambered in 5.56mm, it offers a blend of precision and sustained fire, combining the accuracy of a rifle with the suppressive capabilities of an automatic weapon.

**M4 Carbine** – Developed in the 1980s, the *M4* is a compact, lightweight version of the M16A2 designed for versatility and close-quarters combat. It fires 5.56mm rounds and features a shorter barrel and collapsible stock. First adopted by US special operations units in 1994, the M4 quickly proved its value in a variety of mission sets.

**M40A1/A3/A5** – A bolt-action 7.62mm sniper rifle used by Marine Scout Snipers for precision engagements since Vietnam. Each iteration (A1, A3, A5) reflects upgrades in optics, modularity, and durability. Known for reliability and long-range accuracy, the M40 series was a mainstay in the sniper community for decades.

**M67 Grenade** – The standard-issue fragmentation hand grenade used by US forces. Designed to produce lethal fragments in a radius of up to five meters, the M67 is employed for clearing enemy positions, bunkers, or confined spaces.

**MARSOC** – *Marine Forces Special Operations Command.* The Marine Corps component of US Special Operations Command (USSOCOM), established in 2006. MARSOC conducts direct action, special reconnaissance, and foreign internal defense missions worldwide.

**MEF** – *Marine Expeditionary Force.* The largest Marine air-ground task force (MAGTF), consisting of a command element, ground combat element, aviation combat element, and logistics combat element. A MEF is capable of sustained operations in major conflicts.

**MEU** – *Marine Expeditionary Unit.* Often referred to as "combat in a box," a MEU is a self-contained, forward-deployed force capable of rapid response to a wide range of missions including combat, humanitarian aid, and crisis response.

**MK19** – A fully automatic 40mm grenade launcher typically mounted on vehicles or tripods. It delivers sustained, high-volume indirect fire and is used to suppress enemy forces, destroy light cover, and engage soft-skinned vehicles.

**MOS** – *Military Occupational Specialty.* A numerical designation used by the Marine Corps to identify a Marine's specific job or combat role.

**MRE** – *Meals, Ready-to-Eat.* Pre-packaged, shelf-stable rations used by service members in the field when regular food services are unavailable.

**MRAP** – *Mine-Resistant Ambush Protected Vehicle.* A heavily armored vehicle developed in response to widespread IED threats during the Iraq and Afghanistan conflicts. Its V-shaped hull is designed to deflect blast energy away from the vehicle and its occupants.

**NDS** – *National Defense Strategy.* A high-level strategic document released by the Department of Defense outlining the US military's objectives, priorities, and force posture in relation to emerging global threats.

**Osprey (MV-22)** – A unique tiltrotor aircraft used by the US Marine Corps that combines the vertical takeoff and landing capabilities of a helicopter with the speed and range of a fixed-wing airplane. The *MV-22 Osprey* was adopted for its ability to transport troops and equipment farther and faster than traditional helicopters. It is frequently used to rapidly insert and extract reconnaissance teams and infantry units in both combat and training environments.

**PFT** – *Physical Fitness Test.* A standardized annual test used by the US Marine Corps to measure physical readiness. It includes three events:

- Pull-ups or push-ups (upper body strength)

- Plank hold (core strength; replaced crunches in 2020)
- Three-mile run (cardiovascular endurance)

Each event is worth up to 100 points, for a total possible score of 300. Minimum standards vary by age and gender, and all events must be passed to meet the minimum standard.

**PIG** – *Professionally Instructed Gunman.* A term used for Marine sniper trainees who have not yet completed Scout Sniper School and earned the title of HOG (*Hunter of Gunmen*). PIGs are attached to Sniper Platoons, learning under the guidance of experienced snipers. The transition from PIG to HOG is a significant rite of passage in Marine sniper culture.

**PKM** – *Pulemyot Kalashnikova* – A general-purpose, belt-fed machine gun developed by the former Soviet Union and still widely used around the world. It fires 7.62×54mm rounds at a rate of approximately 700 rounds per minute. When mounted on a tripod with optics, the PKM has an effective range of 1,000 meters or more, making it a reliable weapon for sustained medium- to long-range fire.

**PVS-14** – A more modern, versatile night vision monocular used by US military forces. Also employing Generation III technology, the *PVS-14* can be helmet-mounted, handheld, or weapon-mounted, offering improved clarity, durability, and flexibility over previous models like the PVS-7B. It remains widely used across all branches for its effectiveness in both combat and reconnaissance operations.

**PVS-7B** – A model of US military-grade night vision goggles (NVGs) that use Generation III image intensifier technology. Worn as a head-mounted monocular unit, the *PVS-7B* was standard issue for US forces—including the Marine Corps—throughout the 1990s and early 2000s. Though bulky by modern standards, it provided reliable night vision capability in low-light and no-light environments.

**RAP Round** – *Rocket-Assisted Projectile.* An artillery or tank round equipped with a small rocket motor to extend its range beyond that of a standard shell. RAP rounds are primarily used in indirect fire systems like howitzers to reach distant targets with greater accuracy and effectiveness.

**Raufoss Round** – Refers to the *Raufoss Mk 211*, a .50 caliber (12.7×99mm NATO) multipurpose armor-piercing incendiary (API) round. Developed by Norwegian company Nammo Raufoss, this round is designed to penetrate armor and detonate on impact, delivering both kinetic and explosive effects. It is widely used by NATO forces for anti-materiel roles.

**RTLC** – *Reconnaissance Team Leader Course.* An advanced-level, joint-service training course designed to qualify experienced Recon Marines to lead reconnaissance teams in combat. RTLC is intended for graduates of the *Basic Reconnaissance Course* (*BRC*) who are on a leadership track within recon units. RTLC is regarded as one of the most demanding and comprehensive leadership courses in the Department of Defense.

**SMAW** – *Shoulder-Launched Multipurpose Assault Weapon.* A reusable, shoulder-fired rocket launcher used by the US Marine Corps, designed for destroying bunkers, fortified positions, and light armored vehicles. It fires a variety of rounds, including high-explosive dual-purpose (HEDP) and anti-armor rockets, making it a versatile tool for urban and close-combat operations. Later replaced by the MAAWS—*Multi-role Anti-Armor Anti-Personnel Weapon System.*

**Super Stallion (CH-53E)** – A heavy-lift helicopter used by the US Marine Corps, designed to transport large payloads, including vehicles, artillery, and troops—even in austere or contested environments. The *CH-53E Super Stallion* is the Marine Corps' primary heavy-lift platform, equipped with three engines and seven rotor blades, enabling it to carry substantial loads over long distances. It is commonly used for logistical resupply, troop movement, and combat support operations.

**SVD Dragunov** – A semiautomatic designated marksman rifle (DMR) developed by the former Soviet Union, designed to engage targets at medium to long ranges with greater accuracy than standard infantry rifles. While capable of a theoretical cyclic rate of up to 750 rounds per minute, it is intended for precision fire rather than sustained automatic use. The Dragunov remains in use by many military forces and irregular units around the world.

## Marine Corps Operating Forces Breakdown

**FMF** – *Fleet Marine Force.* The Marine Corps' operational component, assigned to the US Navy's fleets. It includes the Marine Expeditionary Forces (MEFs), which serve as the principal warfighting commands.

**MEF** – *Marine Expeditionary Force.* The largest warfighting unit in the Marine Corps, capable of sustained operations across the full spectrum of conflict. Commanded by a Lieutenant General (Three Star), each MEF is composed of:

- **Marine Division (MARDIV)** – Ground Combat Element
- **Marine Aircraft Wing (MAW)** – Air Combat Element
- **Marine Logistics Group (MLG)** – Logistics Combat Element

- **Command Element** – Headquarters and command support

There are three active ME-Fs:

- **I MEF** – Based in California
- **II MEF** – Based in North Carolina
- **III MEF** – Forward-deployed in Japan

**Marine Division (MARDIV)** – The ground combat element of a MEF. Includes multiple infantry regiments, supported by artillery, armor, reconnaissance, and engineer units. Commanded by a Major General (Two Star).

**Marine Regiment** – Typically consists of three infantry battalions and a Headquarters Company. Commanded by a Colonel.

**Marine Battalion** – Comprised of 800–1,200 Marines. Organized into:

- Three Rifle Companies
- Weapons Company
- Headquarters and Service (H&S) Company. Commanded by a Lieutenant Colonel.

**Company** – Approximately 150–200 Marines. Composed of:

- 3 Rifle Platoons
- One Weapons Platoon (in rifle companies)
- Headquarters Element. Commanded by a Captain.

**Platoon** – Around 40–45 Marines. Comprised of:

- 3 Rifle Squads
- Platoon Commander (Second Lieutenant or First Lieutenant)
- Platoon Sergeant (Staff Sergeant)

**Squad & Fire Team**

- **Marine Rifle Squad** – Led by a Sergeant, includes:

  Three Fire Teams of Four Marines each

- **Fire Team Composition:**

  Team Leader (Corporal)
  Automatic Rifleman
  Rifleman
  Assistant Automatic Rifleman / Grenadier

### Marine Combat Unit Hierarchy Overview

- **Fire Team** – Smallest tactical unit (four Marines)
- **Squad** – Three Fire Teams + Squad Leader (thirteen Marines)
- **Platoon** – Three Squads + Leadership and Support
- **Company** – Three Platoons + HQ Element
- **Battalion** – Several Companies (800–1,200 Marines)
- **Regiment** – Several Battalions

### MOS - Common Troop Roles

- **0302 - Infantry Officer.** Leads infantry units; responsible for planning and executing ground combat operations.
- **0306 - Infantry Weapons Officer (Marine Gunner).** A Chief Warrant Officer specializing in infantry weapons and tactics; senior technical advisor to commanders.
- **0311 - Rifleman.** Core infantry role. Trained in direct combat, fire team tactics, and close-quarters engagement.
- **0313 - Light Armored Vehicle Crewman.** Operates and maintains Light Armored Vehicles (LAVs) in reconnaissance and mechanized infantry roles.
- **0317 - Scout Sniper.** Precision marksman skilled in long-range target engagement and tactical reconnaissance. Requires completion of Scout Sniper School (formerly 8541).
- **0321 - Reconnaissance Marine.** Specially trained to conduct deep reconnaissance, surveillance, and amphibious operations. Assigned to Force or Division recon units.
- **0331 - Machine Gunner.** Operates crew-served machine guns such as the M240, M2 .50 cal, or Mk19 grenade machine gun. Provides suppressive fire support.
- **0341 - Mortarman.** Employs 60mm or 81mm mortars to deliver indirect fire support for infantry operations.
- **0351 - Infantry Assaultman (phased out).** Specialized in demolitions and shoulder-fired rocket systems (e.g., SMAW). Merged into 0352 in recent restructuring.
- **0352 - Anti-Tank Missileman.** Operates anti-armor missile systems like the Javelin. Trained to engage and destroy enemy armor and fortified positions.

- **0365 - Infantry Squad Leader.** Leads a rifle squad of approximately thirteen Marines. Responsible for tactical employment and welfare of the squad.
- **0372 - Critical Skills Operator (CSO).** Special Operations–qualified Marine serving in MARSOC (Marine Raiders). Trained in unconventional warfare, direct action, and foreign internal defense.
- **0621 - Field Radio Operator.** Handles tactical communications, including radio setup, encryption, and coordination of air and artillery support.

## ABOUT THE AUTHORS

AJ PASCIUTI grew up in a vibrant, blended family in Sunnyvale, California, surrounded by artists, working professionals, and blue-collar small business owners. As the son of Italian and Argentine immigrants, he was raised to see America through a lens of gratitude and possibility: to dream big, serve others, and measure success not by status but by impact. In his final year of high school, AJ watched in horror as the United States was mercilessly attacked on September 11. Just three weeks later, driven by a deep sense of duty to protect the country and values that shaped him, he enlisted in the United States Marine Corps.

AJ began his military career as a Rifleman and Team Leader with the renowned 3rd Battalion, 5th Marines, 1st Marine Division, deploying three times in support of Operation Iraqi Freedom. During one of these deployments, he played a key role in a historic sniper vs. sniper mission—tracking down and eliminating a notorious enemy sniper known as "Juba" while recovering a stolen Marine sniper rifle. This marked the first mission of its kind by an American service member since the Vietnam War.

AJ continued his service as a Recon Team Leader and Platoon Sergeant with 3rd Reconnaissance Battalion, deploying to Helmand Province, Afghanistan, from 2009 to 2010 in support of Operation Enduring Freedom. From 2010 to 2013, he served with 2nd Force Reconnaissance Company, deploying with the 24th Marine Expeditionary Unit as a Force Recon Team Leader.

Committed to mentoring the next generation of Marines, AJ returned to instructor duty with the Reconnaissance Training Company from 2013 to 2017. During this time, he was selected for the highly competitive Infantry Weapons Officer program, marking his transition from enlisted to officer, and deployed twice to support global response operations in the Indo-Pacific region.

In January 2020, AJ's career came full circle when he transitioned to the School of Infantry–West Infantry Training Battalion. There, he led the development of the Infantry Marine Course, a groundbreaking initiative that modernized the foundational training for enlisted Marines, better preparing them for the complexities of modern warfare.

It is his fundamental belief that service beyond ourselves is the hallmark of what it means to be American, and that values, rather than politics, are what tie people together.

AJ holds a master of business for veterans from the University of Southern California, a master of public leadership from the University of San Francisco, and is currently pursuing a PhD in leadership studies at the University of San Diego.

NEIL MCGINNESS is a *New York Times* bestselling content creator and writer. In 2021, McGinness partnered with the world's #1 bestselling author, James Patterson, to develop the *New York Times* bestselling series The Shadow Thrillers (Little Brown). McGinness's most recent nonfiction book, on the origins of superheroes, *Pulp Power* (Abrams, 2022), was a bestselling new release in graphic novel/comic book criticism and adopted for an American Literature course curriculum by a major university.